D1590165

Insanity
on Trial

Perspectives in
Law & Psychology

Sponsored by the American Psychology–Law Society/Division 41 of the American Psychological Association

Series Editor: **BRUCE DENNIS SALES,** *University of Arizona, Tucson, Arizona*

Insanity on Trial

Norman J. Finkel
Georgetown University
Washington, D.C.

Plenum Press • New York and London

Library of Congress Cataloging in Publication Data

Finkel, Norman J.
  Insanity on trial.

  (Perspectives in law & psychology; v. 8)
  Bibliography: p.
  Includes index.
  1. Insanity—Jurisprudence—United States. 2. Criminal liability—United States. 3. Insanity—Jurisprudence—Great Britain. 4. Criminal liability—Great Britain. I. Title. II. Series: Perspectives in law and psychology; v. 8.
  K5077.F56 1988   345.41′04   88-19701
  ISBN 0-306-42899-7   344.1054

© 1988 Plenum Press, New York
A Division of Plenum Publishing Corporation
233 Spring Street, New York, N.Y. 10013

Printed in the United States of America

To my wife, Marilyn Jean Zalcman

Acknowledgments

The following publishers and authors have granted permission to quote from previously published works:

Edinburgh University Press, for Smith, R. (1981). *Trial by medicine: Insanity and responsibility in Victorian trials;* and for Walker, N. (1968). *Crime and insanity in England, Vol. I: The historical perspective.*

Little, Brown & Co., for Kalven, H., Jr., & Zeisel, H. (1971). *The American jury.* Phoenix edition.

The Free Press, a Division of Macmillan, Inc. for *Knowing right from wrong: The insanity defense of Daniel McNaughton* by Richard Moran. Copyright 1981 by The Free Press.

Cambridge University Press, for Moore, M. S. (1984). *Law and psychiatry: Rethinking the relationship.*

The Society for the Study of Social Problems, (c) 1959, for James, R. M., Jurors' assessment of criminal responsibility. Reprinted from *Social Problems, 7, 1,* Summer 1959, pp. 58–69, by permission.

W. H. Freeman for *Left brain, right brain* by Sally P. Springer and Georg Deutsch. Copyright 1981, 1985. Reprinted by permission.

Oxford University Press, for Hart, H. L. A. (1968). *Punishment and responsibility: Essays in the philosophy of law,* and for Robinson, D. N. (1980). *Psychology and law: Can justice survive the social sciences?*

Washington Post Writers Group, for Krauthammer, C. (1987, May 8). Let Hinckley go. *The Washington Post,* A23. Reprinted by permission.

Unwin Hyman LTD, for Wootton, B. (1959). *Social science and social pathology.* London: George Allen & Unwin LTD.

University of Chicago, Office of The Law Review, for Wasserstrom, R. A. (1967). H. L. A. Hart and the doctrines of *mens rea* and criminal responsibility. *The University of Chicago Law Review, 35,* 92–126.

Northwestern University, School of Law, 62, *Journal of Criminal Law and Criminology, 313,* (1971), for Dix, G. E. Psychological abnormality as a factor in grading criminal liability: Diminished capacity, diminished responsibility, and the like.

Alan A. Stone, for Stone, A. A. (1984). *Law, psychiatry, and morality: Essays and analysis.* Washington, DC: American Psychiatric Press, Inc.

Pantheon Books, a Division of Random House, Inc., for Foucault, M. (1973). *Madness and civilization: A history of insanity in the age of reason.* Translated by Richard Howard.

Routledge and Kegan LTD, for Fingarette, H. (1974). Self-deception and the "splitting of the ego." In R. Wollheim (Ed.), *Freud: A collection of critical essays.* The article was taken from *Self-Deception.*

From Hermann, D. H. J. (1983). *The insanity defense: Philosophical, historical and legal perspectives.* Courtesy of Charles C Thomas, publisher, Springfield, Illinois.

Richard Restak, for Restak, R. (1987, May 17). The fiction of the 'Reasonable Man.' *The Washington Post,* C3.

The Johns Hopkins University Press, for Kittrie, N. N. (1971). *The right to be different: Deviance and enforced therapy.* Baltimore, MD.

Yale University Press, for Goldstein, A. S. (1967). *The insanity defense.* New Haven, CT.

University of Illinois Press, for Roesch, R., & Golding, S. L. (1977). *A systems analysis of competency to stand trial procedures: Implications for forensic services in North Carolina.* Urbana, IL.

Arenella, P. (1977). The diminished capacity and diminished responsibility defenses: Two children of a doomed marriage. Copyright 1977 by the Directors of the Columbia Law Review Association, Inc. This article originally appeared in *77 Col. L. Rev. 827.* Quoted by permission.

Philosophical Library, for Jean-Paul Sartre's *Being and nothingness.* Translated by Hazel Barnes. Copyrights by Philosophical Library, 1956, 1984.

For Kirschner, B. (1978). Constitutional standards for release of the civilly committed and not guilty by reason of insanity: A strict scrutiny analysis. *20 Ariz. L. Rev. 233.* Copyright 1978 by the Arizona Board of Regents. Reprinted by permission.

Associated Faculty Press, for Gerber, R. J. (1984). *The insanity defense.*

University of California Press, for Fingarette, H. (1972). *The meaning of criminal insanity.* Berkeley, CA. © 1972 The Reagents of the University of California; and for Fingarette, H., & Hasse, A. (1979). *Mental disabilities and criminal responsibility.* © 1979 The Regents of the University of California.

For Finkel, N. J. (1984). Psychology and the courts. In R. J. Corsini (Ed.), *Encyclopedia of psychology,* Vol. III. New York: John Wiley, 122–124. Copyright 1984 John Wiley & Sons. Reprinted by permission.

The American Psychiatric Association, for *Statement on the insanity defense.* (1982, December). Washington, DC; and for *Diagnostic and statistical manual of mental disorders (Third Edition—DSM-III).* (1980). Reprinted by permission.

Plenum Publishing Corporation, for J. Monahan & H. J. Steadman (Eds.), *Mentally disordered offenders: Perspectives from law and social sciences.* New York. Articles by Steadman & Hartstone, and Winick; for Gazzaniga, M. S., & Le Doux, J. E. (1978). *The integrated mind;* and for Finkel, N. J., & Sabat, S. R. (1985). Split-brain madness: An insanity defense waiting to happen. *Law and Human Behavior, 8,* 225–252.

Preface

The insanity defense debate has come full circle, again. The current round began when John Hinckley opened fire; in 1843, it was Daniel M'Naghten who pulled the trigger; the "acts" of both would-be "insanity acquittees" provoked the press, the populace, a President, and a Queen to expressions of outrage, and triggered Congress, the House of Lords, judges, jurists, psychologists, and psychiatrists to debate this most maddening matter. "Insanity"—which has historically been surrounded by defenses, defenders, and detractors—found itself once again under siege, on trial, and undergoing rigorous cross-examination. Treatises were written on the subject, testimony was taken, and new rules and laws were adopted. The dust has settled, but it has not cleared. What is clear to me is that we have got it wrong, once again.

The "full circle" analogy and historical parallel to *M'Naghten* (1843) warrant some elaboration. Hinckley's firing at the President, captured by television and rerun again and again, rekindled an old debate regarding the allegedly insane and punishment (Caplan, 1984; Maeder, 1985; Szasz, 1987), a debate in which the "insanity defense" is centrally situated. The smolderings ignited anew when the *Hinckley* (1981) jury brought in its verdict—"not guilty by reason of insanity" (NGRI).

The popular press fanned those sparks, to some degree, telling us that ordinary citizens were inflamed and embittered over the *Hinckley* decision—a decision reached by 12 ordinary citizens. The sentiments of the press following *Hinckley* were reminiscent of those surrounding history's most celebrated insanity case, that of Daniel M'Naghten. When M'Naghten was acquitted on grounds of insanity (he allegedly attempted to assassinate the Prime Minister, Sir Robert Peel, but killed Peel's secretary, Edward Drummond, instead), the press reacted (Moran, 1981, p. 13). The *Illustrated London News* noted that "within the previous three years there had been five assassination attempts, three against the sovereign, and not a single criminal had been duly punished." The paper decried "the natural tendency of society to refuse to contemplate them (assassins) in any other light than as acts of madness." *The Times* hoped that the "soft headed" would not "twist and torture" minor incidents of peculiar behavior in the accused's background into "symptoms of insanity." Both papers feared that the law's deterrent effect and society's need for retributive justice were being thwarted. The *Standard*, among other papers, published the following barb as a reflection of the public outrage:

> CONGRATULATIONS ON A LATE ACQUITTAL
> Ye people of England: exult and be glad
> For ye're now at the will of the merciless mad.
> Why say ye that but three authorities reign—
> Crown, Commons, and Lords!—You omit the insane!
> They're a privilg'd class, whom no statute controls,
> And their murderous charter exists in their souls.
> Do they wish to spill blood—they have only to play
> A few pranks—get asylum'd a month and a day—
> Then heigh! to escape from the mad-doctor's keys,
> And to pistol or stab whomsoever they please.
> No the dog has a human-like wit—in creation
> He resembles most nearly our own generation:
> Then if madness for murder escape with impunity,
> Why deny a poor dog the same noble immunity?
> So if dog or man bit you, beware being nettled,
> For crime is no crime—when the mind is unsettled.

"Unsettled" aptly describes where the insanity issue stands today, much as it did in 1843. President Reagan, not only unsettled but wounded by one of Hinckley's shots, voiced his own complaint with the insanity defense following the *Hinckley* decision; Queen Victoria, who was herself attacked on seven different occasions by alleged madmen (Walker, 1968), vented her ire following the *M'Naghten* decision. The Queen, acting through the House of Lords, took the unusual step of summoning the 15 Justices before the House to answer questions aimed at clarifying the insanity issue. The President, acting through Attorney General Smith, went before the Judiciary Committee of the United States Senate (1982, p. 26) to propose new legislation to reform the insanity defense and "restore the balance between the forces of law and the forces of lawlessness."

Senate and House of Representatives' Subcommittees held hearings, took testimony from experts, and even invited *Hinckley* jurors to testify to explain their decision. At one point, there were 18 separate bills on insanity in the House, and 8 in the Senate (Arenella, 1983). Scholars joined the debate, by speaking out at professional meetings, public forums, and before Congress, and by writing tomes, commentaries, and exegeses on the topic. The American Bar Association, the American Psychiatric Association, the National Mental Health Association, the Association for the Advancement of Psychology and the American Psychological Association, the American Civil Liberties Union, and the American Medical Association issued position statements and recommendations on the matter; they all differed, with the variance ranging from slight to diametric. State legislatures were also busy enacting new laws that ran the gamut from abolishing the insanity defense to resurrecting *M'Naghten* to creating what Robinson (1982b) labeled the oxymoronic "guilty but insane" verdict. Most unsettling.

In England, following M'Naghten's trial, the matter of insanity was apparently "settled" when the Justices answered the queries posed by the House of Lords. Their answers came to be known as the M'Naghten Rules. Even though the Justices hedged and begged certain questions (e.g., the question of expert testimony—how far can experts go in answering the "ultimate" question of responsibility and are they usurping the jury's prerogative?), the Lords seemed satisfied. Congratulations circulated the upper chamber (Moran, 1981, p. 13), and none of the Lords "was tactless enough to point out that if the judges' answers represented the law M'Naghten should have been convicted."

The Lords may have been tactful, but the alienists, the forerunners of our modern-day forensic psychiatrists and psychologists, were far less charitable. The alienists believed that the M'Naghten Rules were already fatally flawed, based as they were on an outmoded psychology: the portrait of "Moral–Legal Man" embedded in the M'Naghten Rules did not fit with the then current portrait of "Psychological Man," which the alienists derived from natural law. To the alienists, the Law had forsaken "reality" in favor of fiction, an act that was itself symptomatic of insanity.

In the United States, the matter of insanity in federal jurisdictions was apparently "settled" when Congress passed and the President signed into law the "Insanity Defense Reform Act of 1984." This is a remarkably unremarkable piece of legislation for a number of reasons. By lopping off "the volitional test" (i.e., the so-called "irresistible impulse" test or the second prong of the ALI test), it leaves us with the first prong of ALI, which is itself a semantic and cosmetic version of *M'Naghten*. This test was supposed to leave us and the jury with a clearer picture of insanity; it was hoped that by using this test psychological experts would be able to provide the jury with a reliable diagnosis of the defendant; but in the *Hinckley* case, 13 different diagnoses of the defendant were offered by the experts (Stone, 1984), along with sharp disagreement as to whether Hinckley was responsible or not. In short, if we would have applied this new test to *Hinckley*, the jury's picture of both Hinckley and insanity would still be chaotic and contradictory.

It seems as if, in our full circle repetition, we have reinvented the M'Naghten wheel—a wheel that had been emended, elasticized, and distorted for one hundred years of precarious functioning before it finally broke. In 1953, 110 years after *M'Naghten*, the late Justice Felix Frankfurter gave testimony before the Royal Commission on Capital Punishment (*United States v. Currens*, 1961); Frankfurter minced no words when he said, "I think the M'Naghten Rules are in large measure shams." Like the alienists a century earlier, Frankfurter recognized that psychological knowledge had advanced beyond what was known in M'Naghten's time, and he failed to see "why the rules of law should be arrested at the state of psychological knowledge of a time when they were formulated." Why is it, then, with all our advantages of hindsight and history, Congress chooses as its new direction an old dead end?

David Wexler (1985), writing about the "many proposed and enacted insanity defense reforms" that "were triggered or shaped by the furor caused by the *Hinckley* verdict," stated that "legal reform efforts conceived in such an atmosphere are rarely satisfactory. Often, so-called solutions fail because the underlying problem itself has not been adequately and properly defined." (p. 537) I quite agree.

In my view, Congress (and various state legislatures as well) opted for the "quick fix," which fixes almost nothing and finesses just about all of the fundamental issues. In returning to a M'Naghten type cognitive test without empirical support (Rogers, 1987a) for its efficacy, coupled with placing the burden of proof on the defendant without a sound, conceptual reason for doing so, the Insanity Defense Reform Act supporters appear to have made an expedient, pragmatic response to public fears about how easy it is for a defendant to plead insanity and escape punishment. The problem, however, is that those fears are based on popular, *but erroneous*, beliefs.

Beyond what the Insanity Defense Reform Act does is what it fails to do—it fails to address many of the fundamental, central concerns related to insanity: the role of the expert witness and the place of social science in the courtroom; the gray area of "partial insanity"; the principal reasons we punish and excuse; the hopes and faded dreams of rehabilitation, what therapy and treatment can and cannot do; the consequence of an insanity acquittal; and more. After so much debate and testimony, I believe this new law recapitulates old errors, fails to address, let alone rectify, old mistakes, and makes some new mistakes to boot. More importantly, and sadly, it leaves us no closer to either understanding insanity and the tough issues that it raises or effecting a conceptually sound schema for dealing with the problem.

"Insanity"—this most unsettled problem—is the central focus of Insanity on Trial. It is this author's opinion that in order to achieve the greatest clarity we must widen the field of focus. There is much more to the topic of insanity than particular legal tests and instructions to the jury; there are consequences and implications for the defendant, society, the victim (and the victim's family), the courts, and the mental health professionals. Our beliefs about punishment, treatment, and mental illness are involved. Fundamental questions concerning the proper relationship of law and psychology—between morality and medicine (science)—are in need of answers. And to even ask the right questions, an appreciation of the historical developments in Anglo-American law with respect to insanity is essential.

The book is divided into four main parts, the first of which presents the historical development of Anglo-American insanity perspectives. I believe that this historical context is crucial for understanding the fundamental issues that have animated the insanity debate. In presenting the historical context, I will do more than just recount the famous cases that inspired changes in the law: I will focus on the questions that were raised and the answers given, and will suggest where Anglo-American law may have taken a wrong turn.

The first two chapters tell the tale. It is a story with a fascinating cast of characters: the *dramatis personae* include a King or two, a Queen, a President, and a Prime Minister; Bishops, Lords, and Ladies; judges, jurists, and jurors; doctors, alienists, psychiatrists, and psychologists; the press and the populace; the bewitched, bothered, and bewildered; and there is even a wild beast. These two chapters are chronologically divided: the first, from King Æthelred to Queen Victoria, takes us from the tenth-century Saxon law through the M'Naghten trial in 1843; the second, from M'Naghten to Hinckley, brings us to the present. We begin by seeing how the secular Saxon law, with its focus on the overt, visible act, comes to be modified and overshadowed by ecclesiastical law, where "inner facts"—intent, the will, *mens rea*—become central and determinative of culpability. As "inner facts" (e.g., the mind, the psyche) loom larger, we see a problem growing: where do we draw the line between sane and insane? By reviewing the various lines that were drawn (i.e., the insanity defense tests from 1723 to the present) and why they failed to hold, we meet the compounding problems of temporary insanity, partial insanity, and automatism that cast a gray shadow over the shifting, widening, and dimming line.

In Chapter 3, "The Courtship of Law and Psychology," I review psychology and psychiatry's growing involvement with the law and the reasons for it. Recognizing that most courtships are two-way streets, this chapter will also cover the court's turn toward psychological answers—to treatment as opposed to punishment—and the consequences that have followed. As the "therapeutic state" grew, so did contention. We will see how it came to pass that these two disciplines of Law and Psychology came to woo and woe and wonder about what went wrong. As in most marriages, there were hopes for mutually supportive arrangements, unspoken promises, and hidden agendas. And there was, like in many marriages, "the morning after." Where are these disciplines now, and the issues that unite and divide them? Are they still married, divorced, separated, or seeking reconciliation? And most important, what is the proper relationship between law and psychology?

The second major division deals with background issues—basic concepts, false hopes, and erroneous beliefs. No discussion of "insanity" would be complete or intelligible without thoroughgoing consideration of "mental illness"; this concept is the subject matter of Chapter 4. When psychological experts take the witness stand and tell us and the jury that the defendant is mentally ill, what do they mean, what does it tell us, and what does it imply? What is "mental illness," how is it defined, and what kind of concept is it (i.e., medical, scientific, moral, metaphoric)? These are the starting questions. From there, we go on to consider how "mental illness" relates to those key psychological, philosophical, and legal concepts of "personhood," "responsibility," "mens rea," "diminished capacity," and "insanity." I put forth and defend the thesis that psychological experts, with their concept of "mental disease" and their theories of psychic life, have not unraveled, nor can they ever alone unravel, the Gordian knot of insanity.

Chapter 5 deals with therapy (treatment), its theoretical underpinnings, its modes, and its morals. There is an assumption that is often made by the courts that therapists can treat and rehabilitate the insane, and there are proposals being put forth to rectify "the insanity mess" that would place greater emphasis on therapeutic treatment than on considerations of responsibility, culpability, and punishment. As therapist and therapy surround the issue of insanity while the therapeutic perspective is poised to engulf it, there is a need to examine the nature of therapy, to understand it as an ethical–moral undertaking, and to note its successes, failures, and, most of all, its limitations.

Chapter 6, the last of the background issues chapters, takes up the topic of punishment and the insane. The old Roman adage that "madness is punishment enough" clearly implies that we should not punish the mad, and ecclesiastical law, which is now our law, states that we cannot impose punishment where we cannot find blame; yet we hear today the claim that the insane escape punishment, which implies that they are blameworthy. What are the facts, and what are the principles that ought to guide us? This chapter begins with popular, but erroneous, beliefs about the insane and punishment in order to get at the facts. Then we move on to principles and a consideration of two crucial questions: When may we punish? And why do we punish? By understanding the "when" and the "why," we will also come to understand the principled basis for continuing to exculpate the insane defendant, and why this continues to engender confusion and conflict. This chapter closes with a preview of future directions and dead ends, and some recommendations for a sound and sane course.

With historical and background issues developed, Part III, *Prevailing Currents, Unsettling Consequences,* looks at insanity from three different perspectives: that of the lay person (the juror's perspective), that of the neuropsychologist, and that of the defendant-turned-patient. Chapter 7 deals with the ordinary citizen who sits on a jury and must decide whether the defendant is sane or insane. Using recent empirical work that shows that whichever test of insanity the jurors use, the particular test *does not* seem to matter, this chapter explores the lay person's intuitive understanding of insanity. Do jurors "twist and torture minor incidents of peculiar behavior in the accused's background into symptoms of insanity" (as *The Times* of London editorialist feared), or what? The premise of this chapter is twofold: (1) that the juror's perspective matters and needs to be uncovered, and (2) that for a future test of insanity "to sit well," it must not only harmonize with our notions of "Legal–Moral Man" and "Psychological Man," but it must make sense to, and square with, our common-sense notions of insanity.

Chapter 8 uses a very unusual case—a case of split-brain madness—as a vehicle for exploring the neuropsychological perspective. This perspective is important because current advances in neuropsychology, about the relationship between brain and mind and between behavior and our hemispheres, threatens to topple some of our most sacred assumptions about personhood, responsibility, and insanity. Have we arrived at that point where science is set to replace the Law, having demonstrated that the latter is based on mythic, and empty, concepts?

Chapter 9 looks at insanity from the patient's perspective. We start with a defendant who may never get to trial (i.e., because he or she is found "incompetent to stand trial") and end up with a defendant (found "not guilty by reason of insanity") who then, typically, becomes an involuntary patient. In this chapter, the legal, moral, and ethical questions that arise across this dispositive journey from defendant-to-patient are herein explored, along with the inconsistencies between civil and criminal pathways.

The fourth and last part of this work presents future directions and recommendations. In Chapter 10, the essence of insanity is the topic. We begin with a defense of an insanity defense and go on to show how the insanity defense is different from other excusing conditions and why, on principled grounds, shifting the burden of proof to the defense is conceptually sound. Then, the essence of insanity is developed, rooted not in *mens rea*, but in *mens*. The need for a unifying doctrine is proposed, and I critically review various proposals (e.g., abolishing the insanity defense, *mens rea* proposals, H. L. A. Hart's proposal, Lady Wootton's proposal, fine-tuning the NGRI approaches, diminished responsibility and capacity to doctrines, and GBMI—"guilty but mentally ill") to show why they fail to promote and achieve coherence.

In Chapter 11, a new test for insanity is put forth. I defend the thesis that the long-standing *actus reus—mens rea* division contributes to our problems and creates loopholes, and I propose a simple corrective. Furthermore, I identify a short-sightedness in our view of culpability and propose a revision of Fingarette and Hasse's (1979) "Disability of Mind" Doctrine to take into account culpability for bringing about one's disability of mind. Trial procedures and test instructions to the jury are developed, along with the consequences for each verdict.

In the concluding chapter, the courtship of law and psychology is reconsidered. The role of the psychological expert before, during, and after the trial is examined, and recommendations are made. The major emphasis of this chapter is the current and future state of the courtship, which is paradoxically withering and widening, marked by a passionate ambivalence, and mired by veiled values and value conflicts. I will show that the apparent conflicts—science vs. morality, free will vs. determinism, and paternalism vs. autonomy—turn out to be simplistic, confused, and either not the point or beside the point. My concluding tenet is that Justice can survive the social sciences, but, moreover, that each can enhance the other; it requires both sides to see their blindness, limits, and limitations, and to face squarely our moral questions, ethical obligations, and the shortcomings of our knowledge and wisdom.

ACKNOWLEDGMENTS

Putting together a book of this scope requires help in a variety of forms. I've gotten it, and for that, I am both grateful and appreciative. To my editor at Plenum, Eliot Werner, my thanks for your encouragement and timely advice; to Bruce Sales, editor of the Perspectives in Law and Psychology series, for your support, and for directing me toward sources and reviewers that enriched this work, my graditude. To those who reviewed the manuscript, David Wexler, Stephen Morse, and Murray Levine, your suggestions, questions, and well-wishes were apt, on the mark, and welcomed. For updating me as to their latest work, my thanks to John Monahan and Hank Steadman.

To my colleagues here at Georgetown University, to Dan Robinson, Jim Lamiell, Steve Sabat, Pete Wales, Warren Reich, and Tom Beauchamp, for your own works, comments, and suggestions, from all of which I have benefited, my thanks; to my students, graduate and undergraduate, Tony Pinizzotto, Margery Miller, Tory Starbuck, and Sharon Handel, for your own efforts that brought sources and findings to my attention, my thanks; and to Georgetown University, for a summer grant that came at a needed time, my appreciation.

For a psychologist to navigate through legal waters, good counsel is a necessity; this I've had over the years, and I render my thanks to Paul Friedman, Nick Kittrie, Ed Modell, Gary Fields, Debbie Fields, and Bill Long. To Jeanne-Marie Peterson and Rachel Freed, for typing the manuscript, and to Ken Wallgren, whose computer wizardry saved me time and headaches, my gratitude. And to my wife, Marilyn, for your professional acumen and personal support, for wise and warm words that sustained this writer and enhanced his work, a thanks that words inadequately convey.

Norman J. Finkel

Contents

IV. Future Directions and Recommendations

I

Historical Development of Anglo-American Insanity Perspectives

1

An Historical Look at Insanity Defenses

FROM KING AETHELRED TO QUEEN VICTORIA

The Anglo-American benchmark case commonly cited as the historical beginning of the insanity defense is *Rex. v. Arnold* (1723). At the close of the case, Judge Tracy, addressing the jury, articulated what came to be known as the "wild beast" test of insanity. Contrary to this foreshortened view of the insanity defense's genesis, this case was neither a landmark nor the beginning of the story: for by the time the wild beast reared his head and roared in the Arnold case, he had already become a familiar, domesticated by centuries of jurists' papers. Long before the wild beast test became the law of the land, ideas regarding insanity were discussed, questions regarding its nature were debated, and legal approaches that were to have lasting consequences were formulated. Thus, the beast's roar in *Rex v. Arnold* was, by then, mere paper tiger purring. It is to the history that preceded the beast that we now turn.

SECULAR SHORTCOMINGS AND ECCLESIASTICAL ENTWININGS

In pre-Norman England, the secular code, which might loosely be called "civil law," was based on principles of compensation and retaliation

(Walker, 1968). For example, if a man committed a wrong, such as by destroying another's property, he was held responsible and expected to compensate the victim. Compensation for the injury or liability was paid under the threat of feud. This operative, Saxon system was summed up in the phrase "buy off the spear or bear it."

The first point I wish to make regarding this system, and one that quickly became difficult, is that it was based on "strict liability" (Hart, 1968). In strict liability, or the so-called objective theory of liability as developed later by Justice Oliver Wendell Holmes, Jr., only the outer conduct of the accused is relevant; "inner facts," such as thoughts, intentions, and motivations, are not considered necessary for conviction. In current times, there are still a few strict liability offenses on the books in some jurisdictions, and Hart (p. 20) gives as examples selling liquor to an intoxicated person, possessing an altered passport, and selling adulterated milk. Hart believes that most people reject strict liability offenses as not fitting with our common-sense notions of what is blameworthy. We do see distinctions between premeditated murder and death caused by accident or between tax fraud and an arithmetic error on our tax returns, and we expect our laws and punishments to reflect these moral distinctions. Under a strict liability system, such moral distinctions vanish.

The Saxon system of compensation was strict, since the amount of compensation due was not determined "by the extent to which the offender was to blame." Whether the accused premeditated, acted recklessly, negligently, or by accident did not matter; rather, the amount of compensation due was determined "by the status of the victim and the seriousness of harm" (Walker, 1968, p. 15).

A second difficulty of this system is that there are certain crimes that were *botless*, where compensation could not wipe out the crime. For example, if a man breaks into another man's house, steals the victim's valuables, rapes his wife, murders his son, and burns the house down, the victim could, theoretically, break into the perpetrator's home (if he had one), steal commensurate valuables (if there were such), rape his wife (if he had one), murder his son (if he had one), and burn his house to the ground. While some form of retaliation could be taken, the losses and harms suffered were not, in many cases, compensable. Beyond mere pragmatic difficulties, such a system appears too barbaric and immoral: it requires the victim to act just as wrongly as the perpetrator. What emerged by the eleventh century to deal with botless crimes and such inequities was a crude but discernible criminal law.

What had been an offense between victim and perpetrator, and which often then pitted their respective families against one another in a feud, soon became the State v. the perpetrator. It was not, for example, Ronald Reagan v. John Hinckley, but the *United States v. Hinckley*. And Lord Onslow, who "Mad Ned Arnold" shot and wounded, and who would have been, under the Saxon system, the major claimant in the case, now has to take a back seat at the trial of *Rex. v. Arnold*. It is now the King, the State, or the Government against the offending party. Two questions are now raised: Why did this change come about? And what consequences followed?

It was claimed that the perpetrator not only offended the victim, but breached the King's Peace. There was an injury of the public order, and this breach served as the rationale for the State's intrusion into what had been a private, personal dispute. The State not only intruded, but quickly eclipsed the victim as central claimant. The perpetrator had to pay a *wite* to the King for the breach (Hermann, 1983). If he could not pay, or if no monetary payment could compensate for the offense (i.e., in botless crimes), then punishments such as forfeiture of property, imprisonment, or death could be imposed.

One consequence of criminalizing these personal, tort disputes such that the State becomes *the other party* is that the victim gets left out. This result, even today, does not sit well with either victims or juries (Sales, Rich, & Reich, 1987). For victims and the families of victims, and here I cite drunk driving cases that result in death or serious injury as one example, the criminal law's focus and punishments are perceived by many as misplaced and unfair: the victim's injuries and the family's losses and anguish appear to be secondary concerns at best or disregarded entirely.

As for ordinary citizens who sit on juries, Kalven and Zeisel (1971) note, in their classic study *The American Jury,*

> "it bears repeating that it took centuries for the law to come to the position that the state is the other party in a criminal case, a view which, as we have seen, the jury does not entirely embrace." (p. 257)

Jurors, as the researchers show, still tend to view such matters as torts and personal disputes and, taking such a perspective, may weigh certain factors that the law considers "extralegal" (Visher, 1987) or irrelevant, yet, to the jury, these factors do seem morally and legally relevant. While these consequences will be more fully addressed in subsequent chapters, the point for now is that both strict liability and the criminalization of personal disputes tended to create breaches between the moral position as embodied in the Law and the common-sense, moral position of its citizens.

The secular law, with its inherent difficulties of strict liability and botless crimes, was modified primarily by two major influences: the Church and the insane. Ecclesiastical law, a system that existed alongside the secular (Walker, 1968), "was concerned not with liability for restitution but with culpability for sin" (p. 15). "Culpability" was hinged to "intent" and those *inner facts* that, in the Church's view, needed to be considered and weighed before moral guilt could be established. *Mens rea*, the term that denotes evil mind or wickedness of intent, was thus an ecclesiastical insertion into secular law that modified and compromised the strict liability model.

We see the influence of the Church's position in the tenth-century laws of King Æthelred, which were reportedly drafted by Archbishop Wulfstan (Walker, 1968):

> And if it happens that a man commits a misdeed involuntarily, or unintentionally, the case is different from that of one who offends of his own free will, voluntarily and intentionally. (P. 16)

The case becomes different in at least two ways, as the example of the insane offender will illustrate. First, as to the matter of guilt, or more particularly, moral guilt, insane offenders present us with unsettling questions regarding their intentionality. If their will wasn't free, if their intention wasn't voluntary, or if their actions were involuntary, then shouldn't we judge them less accountable, less guilty, or perhaps not guilty at all? And the second difference that results from the ecclesiastical insertion deals with punishment: for if the insane offenders' actions need to be judged differently from the voluntary and intended deeds of ordinary citizens, then punishment should be modified rather than strictly and universally applied. Æthrelred's laws (Walker, 1968) go on to state that,

> . . . likewise he who is an involuntary agent of his misdeeds should always be entitled to clemency and better terms owing to the fact that he acted as an involuntary agent.
>
> Careful discrimination shall be made in judging every deed, and the judgement shall be ordered with justice, according to the nature of the deed . . . in affairs both religious and secular; and, through the fear of God, mercy and leniency and some measure of forbearance shall be shown towards those who have need of them. For all of us have need that our Lord grant us his mercy frequently and often. Amen. (p. 16)

The mercy was the "King's mercy." The King was the one person who could properly interfere with the legal process of strict liability that would otherwise carry a case to its punishing and grim conclusion, even if the harm was unintentional or the product of an insane rather than an evil mind.

It is clear that the tenth- and eleventh-century laws were coming to grips with the sick, insane offender. The laws of Cnut, Æthreled's successor, go even further (Walker, 1968):

> . . . we must make due allowance and carefully distinguish between age and youth, wealth and poverty, freemen and slaves, the sound and the sick. . .
>
> Likewise, in many cases of evil doing, when a man is an involuntary agent, he is more entitled to clemency because he acted as he did from compulsion.
>
> And if anyone does anything unintentionally, the case is entirely different from that of one who acts deliberately. (p. 17)

Embedded in these laws are notions that are with us today. We see an analogy being drawn between youth and sickness (an analogy that runs through the history of the insanity defense); we see the notion being proposed that insane individuals act out of compulsion (i.e., that they could not control their impulses); and we see signs of punishment being replaced by pity, mercy, and leniency and from there, to clemency and exculpation.

There were other notions, already developed by the twelfth century, that have direct bearing on the insane and what should happen to them. First is the notion that an obligation exists between the insane individual and his or her family and kinsmen: the obligation, stated in the following quote from Saxon law, obliges the kinsmen to both compensate the victim and protect the insane from retribution (Walker, 1968).

> If a man fall out of his senses or wits, and it come to pass that he kill someone, let his kinsmen pay for the victim, and preserve the slayer against aught else of that kind. (p. 15)

We see much the same Saxon notion expressed in the Norman laws of Henry the First (Walker, 1968):

> A person be deaf and dumb, so that he cannot put or answer questions, let his father pay his forfeitures. (p. 17)

The first notion establishes a family obligation to pay compensation; the second holds the family responsible for deterring the insane individual; and the third notion reminds the family that insane individuals should be treated leniently. The idea of leniency in dealing with the insane derived from Roman law, but intention or its absence was not the concern: the Roman recommendation for leniency was based on the idea that madness itself was punishment enough. If one's *illness was one's retribution*, then it follows that any further punishment would be inhumane.

To summarize the evolution and entwinings of secular and ecclesiastical notions to this point, we see a movement away from civil law and compensation to criminal law and punishment. We also see, particularly when the accused is insane, how the ecclesiastical notion of *mens rea* and the secular concept of strict liability collide. One result of the former's modifying influences on the latter was to bring "inner facts" forward; and it was just those "inner facts" that significantly altered how insane individuals were both judged and punished. We also see in place the "King's mercy" (the mechanism by which punishment is mitigated or precluded) and obligations incurred by the family to (1) compensate, (2) protect, and (3) deter. As to insane individuals, who were likened to a child, we must make due allowance; and because they are already adequately punished, we may do no more, save restrain them. As victims of their own punishing affliction, our attitude and actions, like that of Lord's, must be merciful and lenient. Amen.

PARTIAL INSANTIY—THE EMERGING GRAY AREA

So far I have been using the words "insanity" and "madness" without differentiating types and shadings. In Chapter 4, "The Concept of Mental Illness (Disease)," the current variety of disorders that appear in the psychiatric literature will be detailed. For now, it is enough to simply note that types, shadings, and classifications of disorders have appeared in the "psychiatric" literature for centuries, as far back as the Hellenic age. In resuming this chronological tale with a consideration of the laws of thirteenth-century England, we begin to see that certain differentiations of "insanity" were fast becoming problematic.

One such distinction was between "idiocy" and "madness": "idiocy" was regarded as a permanent condition, typically existing from birth, and a condition that can be likened to what the present century calls "subnormal intelligence" or "mental retardation"; "madness," on the other hand, was regarded as a temporary, sometimes reversible condition. This distinction, which appeared in the Statute on the King's Prerogative, affected the King's proprietary interest in the person and property of the insane. By this time, the wardship of lunatics and their lands had passed out of the hands of their parents, then out of the hands of the feudal lord, and were now in the hands of the King. These holdings could be profitable. For the permanent condition of idiocy, the King was expected to provide the idiot with maintenance for necessities but was entitled to the profits. But for the madman, the King's hold on the estate was temporary: thus, if the madman recovered his senses, he was entitled to recover his lands and any profit that resulted while he was "temporarily out of his mind."

Bracton, the leading jurist of the thirteenth century, whose words would later appear in Judge Tracy's "wild beast" instructions, made additional distinctions. In his treatise *On the Laws and Customs of England* (1915), Bracton wrote (Walker, 1968):

> . . . for a crime is not committed unless the will to harm be present. . . And then there is what can be said about the child and the madman, for the one is protected by his innocence of design, the other by the misfortune of his deed. In misdeeds we look to the will and not the outcome. . . . (p. 26)

Bracton, who was certainly familiar with Roman law's position on children and insanity, reasoned that a person who was *non compos mentis* (no power or possession of mind) or *furiosus* (a raving, raging beast), was totally lacking in discretion (Robinson, 1980). Bracton goes on to say, in reference to madness, that they

> are not very different from animals who lack understanding (*ratio*), and no transaction is valid that is entered into with them while their madness lasts. For some of them sometimes enjoy lucid intervals, others suffer from continuous madness. . . (Walker, 1968 p. 28)

The implication is clear: the idiot's contracts are never valid, but for the madman, his contracts would be valid if they were enacted during lucid intervals, when understanding and discretion were assumed present. To be precise about what Bracton and others of that age meant by "discretion" and "understanding," I quote from Walker's (1968) commentary on the above passage:

> In the psychology of Bracton's day *"ratio"* could signify either understanding of the nature of one's act or knowledge of its wrongness, and it was recognized that madmen might lack either. In the passage quoted, however, Bracton was talking about madmen's contracts, not their crimes, and almost certainly had in mind their understanding of the nature of their acts. Almost certainly, too, this is what "discretion" meant. For if a child committed a felony the question was whether he had reached the age of discretion, which in the thirteenth century was not seven (the crucial age in Roman law when it was assumed that the child could tell good from evil) but twelve. . . In Bracton's day discretion seems to have meant "Knowing what was what," and it was this sort of common sense that was lacking in both children and the insane. (p. 28)

Here again, with Bracton as with Roman law, we have the linking of madness, childishness, and the brutishness of the "dumb animal"—creatures all lacking rationality. But the madman was different from the beast and child: he could "snap back in," so to speak, being furious at one time, in right mind at another; and it was this lack of constancy, this temporal fickleness, that led to legal headaches in matters of wardship, contracts, and crimes.

The four centuries that begin with Bracton and end with Sir Matthew Hale (who died in 1676), the author of "the clearest statement of the law and its procedures at any single time in this period" (Walker, 1968, p. 35), has been described as "a period of clarification rather than progress." Clarifications and distinctions appear in the writings of Sir Edward Coke (1552–1634), who has often been described (Robinson, 1980) as the "greatest common lawyer in the history of English jurisprudence" (p. 37). Coke distinguished two types of "idiocy" on the basis of severity: *fatuitas* was analogous to "severe" or "profound" retardation, whereas *stultitia* was a less severe but still subnormal intelligence. As regarding crimes and culpability, however, this distinction would not lead to differing verdicts, since Coke includes within the *stultitia* diagnosis someone who "knows not good from evil"; thus this less severe condition was severe enough to excuse.

Coke, Like Bracton before him and Hale who followed, made the distinction between permanent dementia and temporary lunacy. Naturally, it was temporary insanity that created the greater difficulties, but on this point Coke was unequivocal: For the lunatic to be excused on the grounds of insanity, he must prove that at the time of the act he was *furiosus*—totally insane. Hale would subsequently add that the lunatic may be lucid at the time of the trial, and while this did not bar him from pleading insanity as his defense (Walker, 1968), the onus was clearly "on him to show that his crime had not been committed in a lucid interval" (p. 38).

When we examine the writings of Sir Matthew Hale, Lord Chief Justice of England, we see that he devoted an entire chapter in the *History of the Pleas of the Crown* (1736) to "the defects of idiocy, madness and lunacy in reference to criminal offences and punishments." His thinking was far from superficial: he was not only versed in "the psychological theories of his day," but had also written a book called *The Primitive Origination of Mankind, Considered and Examined According to the Light of Nature,* in which he discussed the psychological and physiological differences between man and animals. Hale's view on "partial" insanity, the subject of this subsection, follows (Walker, 1968):

> There is a partial insanity of mind . . . ; some persons that have a competent use of reason in respect of some subjects, are yet under a particular dementia in respect of some particular discourses, subjects or applications; or else it is partial in respect of degrees; and this is the condition of very many, especially melancholy persons, who for the most part discover their defect in excessive fears or griefs, and yet are not wholly destitute of the use of reason; and this partial insanity seems not to excuse them in the committing of any offence for its matter capital; for doubtless most persons, that are felons of themselves, and others are under a degree of partial insanity when they commit these offences. . . . The best measure that I can think of is this; such a person as labouring under melancholy tempers hath yet ordinarily as great an understanding, as ordinarily a child of fourteen hath, is such a person as may be guilty of treason or felony. . . . (p. 38)

Hale recognized that there are certain conditions where the reason is not totally, but only partially, impaired. A rough and modern translation of those conditions would include delusions, depression, and criminality itself. If the partially insane individual had enough understanding (equivalent to the child at the discretionary age of 12 or 14), then he was guilty. So while Hale recognized the condition of partial insanity, he would not excuse it.

But cracks in Hale's position were already developing. He went on to distinguish the disorder *dementia affectata,* or "induced witlessness," brought on by drink or drugs, and comparable to what is now called "substance abuse" disorders. Hale added a rider that

> if heavy drinking had caused "an habitual or fixed phrenzy" he should be treated by the law as if it were involuntarily contracted—a principle that was to save several Victorian alcoholics from the gallows". (Walker, 1968, p. 39)

What hath Hale wrought? In *dementia affectata,* we have a condition that is self-induced: certainly, at the beginning of this disorder, there was intent to drink; but what was first a voluntary and intended action, we are now to regard as habitual and uncontrollable—and to be treated as if it were a disease involuntarily contracted. Whereas in mere drunkenness we attribute *mens rea* regarding any criminal actions that follow, not so for the alcoholic. Hale's sobering, if not disquieting rider, "introduced a seam, if not a crack, in that wall of reasoning that was built in ancient Rome and maintained largely without breach throughout the seventeenth century" (Robinson, 1980 p. 39).

The seam cracked wide open in Scotland, where Sir George Mackenzie of Rosenhaugh (1636–69), known more commonly as "the Bluidy Mackenzie," shattered the existing wall of reasoning between total and partial insanity. As a result, Scottish law broke out of the confines that would constrain if not straitjacket Anglo-American law for the next three centuries. Yet, at the time of their inception and in the years that immediately followed, Mackenzie's notions were either ignored or dismissed as applicable perhaps to Scotland but certainly unworkable elsewhere. His idea, however, did not lie at the bottom of some Scottish firth. Like a message in a bottle cast upon the tides, it eventually washed ashore in England, as the 1957 passage of the Homicide Act reveals, and, in the same decade, it landed in California, of all places, where the plea of "diminished capacity" reintroduced Mackenzie's idea on this side of the Atlantic.

Mackenzie, who had studied in Holland, was influenced by the Dutch legal writer Matthaeus. Matthaeus's ideas (1644) were translated into Mackenzie's words (1678):

> . . . once a man has been furious, or is furious at intervals, we shall presume that his crime is more likely to have been committed in his fury, . . . since fury is a sticking disease (*morbus durabilis*)". (Walker, 1968, p. 139)

This idea proposed that certain fluctuating and cycling diseases, such as melancholia (depression) and anxiety states, were really durable, persistent, and continuous diseases; thus, even in the individual's lucid moments, we should infer a disease process operating. While Hale and others saw in the lucid intervals the absence of both disease and the grounds for exculpation, Mackenzie inferred that beneath the pattern of lucid–fury intervals lay disease. By implication, then, cases of temporary insanity were not just alternations between totally insane and totally lucid intervals; rather, the lucid interval itself was tainted and affected by the underlying disease. Hence, the individual's reason during a lucid interval could not be equated with the normal reasoning of a person not afflicted by such a sticking disease. In these cases, temporary insanity leads to a partial impairment (i.e., partial insanity), and both temporary and partial insanity move a wee bit closer toward "total" insanity in that some degree of mitigation appears warranted. Here are Mackenzie's words (Walker, 1968):

> Possibly that judge would not be much mistaken who would remit something of the ordinary punishment in all crimes committed, even where the lucid

intervals are clearly proved: for where madness has once disordered the judge-
ment, and more where it recurs often, it cannot but leave some weakness, and
make a man an unfit judge of what he ought to do. . . It may be argued that
since the law grants a total impunity to such as are absolutely furious therefore it
should by the rule of proportions lessen and moderate the punishments of such,
as though they are not absolutely mad yet are Hypochondrick and Melancholy
to such a degree, that it clouds their reason. . . . (p. 139)

"Diminished responsibility" offered an option to the partially insane
defendant and his lawyer that the Anglo-American system lacked. In the
latter system, the law offered only two choices—guilty or innocent by
reason of insanity: you were either responsible, culpable, guilty, and subject to punishment or you were totally insane, lacking all *mens rea,* and
were therefore excusable. In the Anglo-American system, it was either/or,
with no in between. In Scotland, Mackenzie carved out an in between, a
reason for it, and a response to it—mitigation.

The Act of Union with England came a generation after Mackenzie
(Walker, 1968), and "the ways in which the Scots legal system diverged
from that of England were glossed over and reduced" (p. 140). Mackenzie's ideas and their implications resurface in the post-*Hinckley* wake,
and they will surface again in subsequent chapters; but for now, we return
to England and to an encounter with the "wild beast."

BEYOND THE BEAST

In *Rex v. Arnold* the jury did not take very long to find "Mad Ned
Arnold" guilty of shooting and wounding Lord Onslow, even though
Arnold's brother, other family members, and members of the local community gave evidence attesting to his insanity. A servant testified that Arnold
frequently complained that Lord Onslow was bewitching him with devils
and imps. All of this testimony pointed to insanity. He was not an idiot
from birth, but a lunatic who "hath his intervals." The prosecution maintained that Arnold's buying of the powder and the shot revealed that he
was functioning in a lucid interval, that he had intent, and thus had *mens
rea.* The jury agreed.

It was not so much the facts as the judge's summary that marked this
case as historically significant. Mr. Justice Tracy said (Walker, 1968):

If he was under the visitation of God, and could not distinguish between
good and evil, and did not know what he did, though he committed the greatest
offence yet he could not be guilty of any offence against any law whatsoever: for
guilt arises from the mind, and the wicked will and intention of the man. If a
man be deprived of his reason, and consequently of his intention, he cannot be
guilty: and if that be the case, though he had actually killed Lord Onslow, he is
exempted from punishment: punishment is intended for example, and to deter
other persons from wicked designs; but the punishment of a madman, a person

that hath no design, can have no example. This is on one side. On the other side we must be very cautious; it is not every frantic and idle humour of a man that will exempt him from justice, and the punishment of the law. When a man is guilty of a great offence it must be very plain and clear before a man is allowed such an exemption; therefore it is not every kind of frantic humour, or something unaccountable in a man's actions, that points him out to be much a madman as is to be exempted from punishment: it must be a man that is totally deprived of his understanding and memory, and doth not know what he is doing, no more than an infant, than a brute or a wild beast, such a one is never the object of punishment. . . . (p. 56)

Judge Tracy's summation, however, broke no new ground: far from introducing major innovations, the speech merely repeated centuries-old thinking. The Ecclesiastical notion of guilt arising from the mind and the intention is evident. The Roman notions regarding the child, knowing good from evil, and of madness being punishment enough are apparent. Bracton's ideas of discretion, of knowing "what from what," along with the term "brute," are incorporated. And Coke and Hale's position regarding total insanity is upheld.

So what is noteworthy in this summation? Not all that much. Tracy deleted the term *brutus,* which meant "animal" as opposed to "human," and replaced it with "brute or wild beast"; while this may connote in the jurors' minds more raving and roaring, it is not the stuff that earmarks a landmark. On a smaller scale, something within the trial itself was noteworthy, more for the fact that it would open a future psychiatric door than for what happened then: that "something" was a prosecution objection to evidence of behavior subsequent to the crime being heard, which was overruled by Judge Tracy. This ruling paved the way for medical witnesses to enter the courtroom and give testimony based on examinations performed after the crime. In Arnold's case, however, the defense called no such witnesses.

In the 1760 case of *R. v. Ferrers* (1760), the Earl Ferrers called on his behalf Dr. John Monro, Physician Superintendent of Bethlem, who had examined not Ferrers but Ferrers' uncle, who was regarded as a lunatic and had died at Bethlem. Monro was the second of four Monros who superintended Bethlem for over a century, and the fourth Monro, Dr. Edward Thomas Monro, was the major medical witness called by the defense in the case of Daniel M'Naghten. This Monro's testimony, which was no doubt weaker for the fact that he had not examined Ferrers himself, did not weigh heavily; the House of Lords unanimously pronounced Ferrers guilty, and included among the 117 peers finding for guilt was

. . . the earl who had acted as his legal advisor. At his hanging the newly devised mechanics of the drop failed to work properly, and the executioner had to resort to the old practice of jumping on the back of the slowly strangling man." (Walker, 1968, p. 63)

Ferrers eventually expired. And while the wild beast continued to reign, the beast's days were already numbered. The legal stalking of the beast continued, and, as we will see with the case of James Hadfield, the beast was about to receive a near-fatal wound.

HADFIELD FIRES, BUT ERSKINE HITS THE MARK

Although James Hadfield (*Hadfield*, 1800) fired his pistol at King George III and missed, his legal counsel, Erskine, hit the mark—calling the notion of total insanity an illusion, and argued that a person could be "absolutely mad for a day." Hadfield was acquitted, and the "wild beast" staggered (Finkel, 1980).

There are similarities and differences between Hadfield's madness and that of Arnold's, but when both are weighed, it appears that Arnold was the madder of the two; yet it was Hadfield who was acquitted while Arnold was found guilty. Why was this so? The explanation, it seems, lies not in the facts. Both Hadfield and Arnold bought pistols. Hadfield headed for Drury Lane Theatre with the intent to fire on the King as he entered the royal box. Hadfield made no attempt to evade capture, and when he was taken to the musician's anteroom and interrogated by the Duke of York, the King's brother, he seemed quite rational; far more rational than Arnold appeared when he was caught.

Worse, or so it would appear to all but Erskine, Hadfield knew what he was doing, planned it, understood the nature and quality of the act, and knew that murder and treason were wrong. Furthermore, it was clear that Hadfield was no idiot. So how did the brilliant Erskine, who had formerly defended Tom Paine but was now playing an apparently weak hand with Hadfield, trump the very able prosecution led by Mr. Abbott (who would soon be appointed Lord Chief Justice) and triumph over the beast? The reasons, I believe, were fourfold: the intended victim, George III, played a part; so too, did Hadfield's particular symptoms; and of course, there was Erskine's strategy; and finally, but often overlooked, was the jurors' perspective.

King George III, whose own "insanity" was well known, offered Erskine a wonderful foil for his client. The King clearly had "his moments," his depressive bouts and his episodes of rage, such that the once clear distinction between sane and insane had now become royally shrouded. When played against such a regal backdrop, Hadfield's lucid and delusive moments might be viewed sympathetically by jurors whose views on insanity were no doubt tutored by their Windsor King's reigning bouts.

Chief among Hadfield's symptoms was his delusion. Hadfield believed that the Savior's second coming was imminent, but that Christ would be outraged not only by the worldly state to which the faithful had fallen, but by the monarch's sunken state as well. As Christ had his John the Baptist to pave the way the first time, so should it be for his second sojourn. Hadfield's mission was clear to him—"to rid the world of said monarch so that a more wholesome climate might greet the Redeemer" (Robinson, 1980, p. 41). And what is more, Hadfield wanted to be executed for his treason.

While Hadfield's delusion provided the jury with evidence for insanity of a kind, Erskine used another of Hadfield's symptoms for some spectacular legal grandstanding. As Walker (1968) writes,

> His client had obvious and disfiguring wounds in the head, acquired in action against the French six years before. One of these had penetrated the skull, so that Erskine was able to invite the jury to inspect the membrane of the brain itself. An officer of his former regiment testified that before Hadfield had been wounded he had been an excellent soldier, but afterwards had been incoherent, with "manifest symptoms of derangement." The regimental surgeon recalled how he had been compelled to have Hadfield tied to a bed for a fortnight. Erskine then called Dr. Creighton from Bethlem to the stand who testified that in his medical opinion Hadfield's madness was probably the result of his wounds, and although in law it did not matter what the cause was . . . we can guess that this must have made a favourable impression on a war-time jury. (p. 76)

Erskine's strategy was not to show that Hadfield met the "wild beast" standards; he couldn't, since his client knew right from wrong, and his desire to be executed revealed that he must have known that his intended act was unlawful. What Erskine did, and did skillfully, was attack the very credibility and basis of the "wild beast" test itself. "He made great play with Coke's requirement that 'there must be a total deprivation of memory and understanding.' " (Walker, 1968, p. 77)

"If a TOTAL *deprivation of memory* was intended by these great lawyers to be taken in the literal sense of the words:—if it was meant, that, to protect a man from punishment, he must be in such a state of prostrated intellect, as not to know his name, nor his condition, nor his relation towards others—that if a husband, he should not know he was married; or, if a father, could not remember that he had children; nor know the road to his house, nor his property in it—then no such madness ever existed in the world." (Robinson, 1980, p. 42).

Erskine went on to lay out the real essence of madness. In madness, "reason is not driven from her seat, but distraction sits down upon it along with her, holds her, trembling upon it, and frightens her from her propriety." The madman is deluded, he reasons from false premises, "because a delusive image, the unseparable companion of real insanity, is thrust upon the subjugated understanding, incapable of resistance because unconscious of attack" (Walker, 1968, p. 77).

It is hard to say how aware even Erskine was of the implications of his masterly rhetoric. He had redefined the essence of insanity, removing it from its centuries-old conception of total baseness and centered it upon delusion; he replaced the mythical "lunar" theory of madness with "medical model" notions of a diseased brain; and he spoke of "motives irresistible," which we cannot control because we are unconscious of the fact that *they* are in control.

Erskine's brilliant summation would have fallen on deaf ears if the jurors' views of insanity had been consistent with the "wild beast" test; fortunately for Hadfield, they were not. Erskine's description of insanity must have fit more closely with the jurors' intuitive ideas about what is and is not insane than the "wild beast" test did. An independent jury, who rejected both the prosecution's case and the judge's instructions, ultimately decided the wild beast's fate in a practical way; to the jury, the beast was passe, an image and legal test that had been transformed by their verdict into fiction and history. The law, however, would still cling to the "wild beast" test for another 43 years, until *M'Naghten* (1843) legally delivered the death blow.

Not everyone was satisfied with the verdict, or with the prospect of Hadfield walking or stalking the streets. Judge Kenyon feared for the safety of "every man of every station, from the king upon the throne to the beggar at the gate" (Walker, 1968, p. 78) if Hadfield was released. The dispositive issue had to be addressed. Parliament hastily drafted the *Insane Offenders Bill* (1800) to take into strict custody those who were acquitted "on grounds of insanity," until "His Majesty's pleasure to be known"; retrospective phrasing in the Bill's language made it applicable to Hadfield, who was eventually committed to Bethlem. So Hadfield was acquitted, yet confined. A verdict of "innocent by reason of insanity" would now trigger a different dispositive course than the typical "not guilty" in other trials: in the latter case, defendants walked from the courtroom free, whereas in the former cases, acquittal and liberty would now part company. And while the beast took a beating, it nonetheless survived, though staggering badly. We now turn to its demise, and to the case of Daniel M'Naghten.

M'NAGHTEN

It was 1800 when Hadfield fired his pistol at George III and missed. In 1786 and 1790, George III was also the target of two other attacks, the first by Margaret Nicholson, who "made an incompetent thrust with a penknife" (Walker, 1968, p. 74), and the second by John Frith (R. v. Frith, 1790), who threw a stone. In 1812, Bellingham shot the Prime Minister, Spencer Perceval. In 1840, Oxford fired at Queen Victoria and missed. On five other occasions pistols were fired at Victoria, and on another occasion "she was struck on the head with a brass-knobbed cane" by an "insane officer in her army" (Walker, 1968, p. 186). Monarchs and ministers, so it appears, were the favorite targets of madmen.

On Friday, January 20, 1843 (Moran, 1981, p. 40), in broad daylight, Daniel M'Naghten, who was following an unsuspecting gentleman, walked up behind him, put the muzzle of his pistol into the victim's back, and fired. He was about to fire a second pistol when a policeman, who had seen the act, seized him. At 9:15 the next morning, Inspector John Massie Turney asked M'Naghten in an off-handed way, "I suppose you are aware who the gentleman is you shot at?" The Inspector reported that M'Naghten's reply was, "It is Sir Robert Peel, is it not?"

It was not. M'Naghten's shot, which had reputedly been intended for the Prime Minister, had in fact hit Peel's secretary, Edward Drummond. As it turned out, the shot proved to be the death blow for both Drummond and the "wild beast."

When M'Naghten's reply was reported in the papers, his remark was taken as a self-indictment: he had to be insane. Except for the inconsistencies. During his interrogation, his

> manner was polite and self-possessed, his intelligence and learning above the ordinary. . . A *Times* reporter present at the questioning observed: "His demeanour throughout was cool and collected." Commenting on the question that filled every one's mind. . . , the reporter wrote: "There did not appear any evidence of insanity." (Moran, 1981, p. 9)

Another inconsistency, and one that was never cleared up, was how it came to pass that this woodturner had in his pocket a deposit receipt on the Glasgow and Ship Bank for 750 pounds, a remarkable sum given M'Naughten's circumstances. M'Naghten's one and only public statement of his motives was the following (Moran, 1981):

> The Tories in my native city have compelled me to do this. They follow, persecute me wherever I go, and have entirely destroyed my peace of mind. They followed me to France, into Scotland, and all over England. In fact, they follow me wherever I go. I cannot sleep nor get no rest from them in consequence of the course they pursue towards me. I believe they have driven me into a consumption. I am sure I shall never be the man I was. I used to have good health and strength but I have not now. They have accused me of crimes of which I am not guilty, they do everything in their power to harass and persecute me; in fact, they wish to murder me. It can be proved by evidence. That's all I have to say. (p. 10)

This statement has been generally regarded as evidence of M'Naghten's delusions. However, Moran brings to light some interesting facts that raise an altogether different possibility and motive—that M'Naghten may have been speaking the truth—and that the murder was a political act taken in self-defense, rather than an insane, deluded, assassination attempt. In Moran's (1981) words, "It may well be that the only real delusion M'Naghten ever suffered from was the delusion that he had shot the prime minister" (p. 40).

To backtrack, the climate of the time was stormy. The Chartist movement was gaining strength and was particularly strong in M'Naghten's Glasgow. Chartist riots had occurred. The Anti-Corn Law League had formed and focused its ire, which included assassination plans, on the Tories. Peel had in place his newly created and much dreaded Metropolitan Police Force, as well as Tory spies and agents throughout England and Scotland. One such agent, Robert Lamond, was M'Naghten's alleged persecutor. M'Naghten had a shop on 79 Stockwell Street in Glasgow, paying 9 pounds for rent. But the right to vote was reserved for the "10-pounders." When his rent was raised to 12 pounds, he was eligible, but Lamond's harassing tactics, such as increasing the poor rate assessments and challenging the voting roles, made it difficult for M'Naghten to exercise his right. The Tories also practiced bribery, "cooping" (abducting an opponent's supporters until after the election), and hiring "bullies" to harass and assault voters. M'Naghten, an orator and Chartist sympathizer, was a target.

In light of these facts, M'Naghten's own statement does not appear as delusional as it may have sounded at first. Perhaps he was striking back, defending himself against a series of escalating harassments that might, if unstopped, lead to his own murder? Was it an act of self-defense? A much-provoked reaction? Or was the unexplained 750 pound note a payment for a political assassination that simply did in the wrong man?

These other possible motives were largely ignored by both the prosecution and defense. For the prosecution to prove that a political assassination had occurred would have required Peel and the Tories to reveal and summon their spies and agents to the stand. M'Naghten's attorney was Alexander Cockburn, whose strategy was "insanity," and who called nine medical experts to the stand. No, this was to be history's most famous insanity case; all else was moot.

The solicitor general, Sir William Follett, presented the prosecution's case. He offered no motive for M'Naghten's act and conceded, perhaps too quickly, that the defendant was mentally ill. His strategy was to fall back to Hale's distinction between partial and total insanity, which he quoted, and to recite Justice Tracy's "wild beast" criterion. His argument, in short, was that M'Naghten was not totally insane, could distinguish between right and wrong, and was thus subject to punishment.

M'Naghten mounted one of the best financed defenses of any insanity case to that time. The court made the 750 pounds available to M'Naghten, and he was defended most ably by Cockburn and three other barristers.

> What Cockburn did argue was that the prisoner's insanity "takes away from him all power of self-control." Like Erskine, therefore, he had to persuade the judges to accept a test of insanity that was not really recognized by the criminal law without allowing them to realize what they were doing. And, like Erskine, he managed it. At the end of his speech, when every one's attention must have been flagging more than a little, he came as near as he dared to a summary of his argument:

> "I trust that I have satisfied you by these authorities that the disease of partial insanity can exist—that it can lead to a partial or total aberration of the moral sense and affections, which may render the wretched patient incapable of resisting the delusion, and lead him to commit crimes for which morally he cannot be held responsible. . ."
>
> The reference to "aberration of the moral senses and affections" was an attempt to smuggle the new notion past their lordships under the disguise of inability to tell right from wrong. (Walker, 1968, p. 94)

The authorities that Cockburn drew on were nine medical experts. Dr. Edward Thomas Monro, the last of the four generations of Monros to occupy the chief medical position at Bethlem, testified for the defense.

> The act with which he (M'Naghten) is charged, coupled with the history of his past life, leaves not the remotest doubt on my mind of the presence of insanity sufficient to deprive the prisoner of all self-control. I consider the act of the prisoner in killing Mr. Drummond to have been committed whilst under a delusion: the act itself I look upon as the crowning act of the whole matter—as the climax—as a carrying out of the pre-existing idea which had haunted him for years." (Moran, 1981, p. 105)

Of note here is the fact that the prosecution failed to object to the doctor overstepping a boundary between medical "facts" and legal conclusions: instead of restricting his testimony to the defendant's mental impairment, this expert witness was allowed to testify as to whether the defendant could conform his behavior to the law—i.e., whether he was legally insane. Follett didn't object, and Judge Tindal permitted it, not only for Monro, but for all medical experts. This permissiveness disturbed many, who saw medical experts usurping "the power of the jury by acting as the judges of facts" (Moran, 1981, p. 104).

Justice Tindal's latitude went even further: the last two medical witnesses to be called by the defense had not even examined M'Naghten; they had merely sat in court throughout the trial and observed the defendant's behavior, yet they were allowed to testify. Forbes Winslow, the author of *The Plea of Insanity in Criminal Cases* (1843/1983), was one of two, and he did not have "the slightest hesitation" in pronouncing Daniel M'Naghten insane.

In addition to actual witnesses, Cockburn was allowed to quote extensively from other sources, one of which was the work of the noted American expert on medical jurisprudence, Dr. Isaac Ray. Ray had written *A Treatise on the Medical Jurisprudence of Insanity* (1838/1983) and held a position, strongly influenced by French psychiatry and law, that gave a wide exemption for insane offenders. Ray's position was that tests such as knowing right from wrong, knowing the nature of the act, or even delusion, were all too narrow. Ray's own view was that if the mental unsoundness "embraced the criminal act within its sphere of influence," then the defendant was exempt from punishment; the "mental unsoundness" he had in mind was severe degrees of disorder. This test became the law of

New Hampshire, and nearly one hundred years later, it was adopted by the District of Columbia in the Durham Rule.

What Cockburn did was to use one of Ray's most penetrating observations to undermine the prosecution's reliance on Hale. Ray (1838/1983) noted that in Hale's day,

> ". . . insanity was a much less frequent disease than it is now, and the popular notions concerning it were derived from the observation of those wretched inmates of the mad-houses whom chains and stripes, cold and filth, had reduced to the stupidity of the idiot, or exasperated to the fury of a demon. Those nice shades of the disease in which the mind, without being wholly driven from its propriety, pertinaciously clings to some absurd delusion, were either regarded as something very different from real madness, or were too far removed from the common gaze, and too soon converted by bad management into the more active forms of the disease, to enter much into the general idea entertained by madness. Could Lord Hale have contemplated the scenes presented by the lunatic asylums of our own times, we should undoubtedly have received from him a very different doctrine for the regulation of the decisions of after generations." (p. 16)

Cockburn went on to embrace the definition of insanity put forth by Lord Erskine in his defense of Hadfield. Like Hadfield, M'Naghten showed a kind of insanity "where imagination . . . still holds the most uncontrollable dominion over reality and fact" (Moran, 1981). M'Naghten reasons "with subtlety" from faulty premises. Cockburn cited modern medical science, whose views were that the mind was divided into two separate parts: one part contained the intellect, the other part contained the moral faculties, and included sentiments, affections, propensities, and passions. Medicine, he claimed, has shown us that one part may be diseased while the other remains sound. But disease in one part can make a person "the slave of uncontrollable impulses," or what Erskine called "motives irresistible." Cockburn cited the great Scottish legal scholar Baron Hume, who said that when such a delusion is present, when

> he is possessed with the vain conceit that . . . (someone has) come there to destroy him, or that he has already done him the most cruel injuries, and that all about him are engaged in one foul conspiracy to abuse him, as well might be but utterly ignorant of the quality of murder. Proceeding as it does on a false case of conjuration of his own fancy, his judgment of right and wrong, as to any responsibility that should attend it, is truly the same as none at all." (Moran, 1981, pp. 95–96)

After the last medical witness testified, Justice Tindal stopped the trial. He asked Follett if he planned to counter the medical testimony offered by the defense, and Follett answered in the negative. Follett withdrew the Crown's case against M'Naghten, uttering "I cannot press for a verdict against the prisoner." Tindal reminded the jury that "the whole of the medical evidence (was) on one side." As Moran (1981) stated, after asking the jury if they required further instruction, Justice Tindal virtually gave them a directed verdict. "If you find the prisoner not guilty . . . on the ground of insanity . . . . proper care will be taken of him." Daniel M'Naghten, like Hadfield, was acquitted on grounds of insanity and sent to Bethlem. The verdict sent Queen Victoria, the House of Lords, and much of the press and populace, into "fits." (p. 108)

In an unusual step, the House of Lords summoned all 15 Justices and demanded clarifications. Questions were posed, and three months later the justices returned to the upper chamber with their answers. Their answers, save for Mr. Justice Maule, reduced to the following two rules:

> [1] To establish a defense on the ground of insanity it must be clearly proved that, at the time of committing the act, the party accused was laboring under such a defect of reason, from disease of the mind, as not to know the nature and quality of the act he was doing, or he did know it, that he did not know he was doing what was wrong.

This rule was amplified with the comment that the knowledge of right and wrong refers to "the very act charged" rather than to "knowledge" in the abstract.

> [2] Where a person labors under partial delusions only and is not in other respects insane," and commits an offense in consequence thereof, "he must be considered in the same situation as to responsibility as if the facts with respect to which the delusion exists were real." (*United States v. Currens*, 1961, note 5)

The last question asked by the House related to medical testimony; the question stemmed from the testimony of Winslow and Phillips, the two medical experts who had not interviewed M'Naghten but based their remarks solely on courtroom observation.

> The question lastly proposed by your Lordships is: "Can a medical man, conversant with the disease of insanity, who never saw the prisoner previously to trial, but who was present during the whole trial and the examination of all the witnesses be asked his opinion as to the state of the prisoner's mind at the time of the commission of the alleged crime, or his opinion whether the prisoner was conscious at the time of doing the act that he was acting contrary to law, or whether he was labouring under any and what delusion at the time?" In answer thereto, we state to your Lordships, that we think the medical man, under the circumstances supposed, cannot in strictness be asked his opinion in the terms above stated, because each of those questions involves the determination of the truth of the facts deposed to, which it is for the jury to decide, and the questions are not mere questions upon a matter of science, in which case such evidence is admissable. But, where the facts are admitted, or not disputed, and the question becomes substantially one of science only, it may be convenient to allow the question to be put in that general form, though the same cannot be insisted on as a matter of right. (Moran, 1981, pp. 173–174).

This last answer both hedges and begs the question. It says, on the one hand, that the medical expert should not be asked his *opinions* on the facts, for that is for the jury to decide, but then the answer offers a loophole—"where the facts are admitted, or not disputed"—which allows a judge who is so inclined to permit the defense wide latitude. What is more, and here is where the answer begs the question, that part of question regarding witnesses who never saw the prisoner prior to the trial is not addressed.

So much for the problems and the Justice's answers. The Lords seemed satisfied, and congratulations circulated the upper chamber. And none of the Lords "was tactless enough to point out that if the judges' answers represented the law M'Naghten should have been convicted" (Moran, 1981, p. 102).

2

From M'Naghten to Hinckley
YESTERDAY'S ANSWERS BREED TODAY'S QUESTIONS

M'Naghten, having been found innocent by reason of insanity, was led away to Bethlem; the Justices, having dealt with those thorny questions posed by the House of Lords, retired; and the Lords, satisfied with the Judge's rules, adjourned. The applause from the House of Lords had barely died down when the doubters and detractors took over. The M'Naghten Rules were quickly attacked on a variety of fronts, with the critical chorus containing a curious mix of bedfellows; ironically, the Rules were attacked by some for being too liberal and by others for being too conservative. What is today's discord over the insanity defense was yesterday's disarray.

THE RULES RUN AFOUL

The Rules appeared to be a significant and radical break with what had been. To those who held a dire view, it appeared as if the fabric of legal, psychological, and social entwinings that had been woven together for centuries was fast unraveling. Hadfield may have split a seam, but M'Naghten left a rent.

From the Queen to the commoner, from alienist to jurist to journalist, doubts were voiced. Queen Victoria, who was naturally concerned with future acts of treason, murder, and mayhem against the monarch and her ministers, worried that the Rules would undermine deterrence. She was by no means the only one to worry.

> The possible increase in acquittals owing to insanity, the possible role of the insanity plea in encouraging murder, and the effect of commuting capital cases because of insanity, were . . . topics for judicial and journalistic alarm. (Smith, 1981, p. 29)

Some believed that the Rules had widened the definitions of insanity too far, and they were fearful that many more individuals, particularly those with milder disorders, or worse—criminals without disorders but possessing better than average acting abilities—would seek and employ the insanity defense successfully.

Many alienists, on the other hand, reached the opposite conclusion, fearing that the courts would accept only what today we would label as "severe psychotic disturbances" as warranting exculpation. From their viewpoint, the Rules were too restrictively drawn, thereby eliminating the defense from those who should appropriately employ it. Many alienists prophetically envisioned the now defenselessly insane dangling at the gallows.

While the wild beast had indeed died, society was left in uproar. Would the M'Naghten Rules set loose the beasts within society? Or would society, with its hangman's noose ever ready, unleash its worst retributive instincts on those who were already punished enough by their madness? As for M'Naghten himself, he was installed in the criminal lunatic department of Bethlem Hospital. Whether M'Naghten attained peace of mind within that locked universe or was weighted down with woes, we do not know. We do know that outside the asylum peace was not to be found, for the fate of the M'Naghten rules had yet to be weighed.

THE DUST SETTLES, BUT DOES NOT CLEAR

Many of the fears and prophecies that were offered following the articulation of the Rules proved to be unfounded when the facts are examined. Walker's (1968, pp. 86–87) figures regarding murderers who were acquitted as insane reveal no change in the percentage in the 10-year period following M'Naghten from the 10-year period that preceded the Rules: in both periods, 7.5% of trials for murder resulted in acquittal on grounds of insanity. While the figures didn't change, "perceptions" had changed, and changed dramatically. In the eyes of many, "acquittal" and "innocent" still implied "freedom," even though Hadfield spent his last days in Bethlem and M'Naghten would spend his last days in Broadmoor hospital. A successful insanity defense more than likely led to incarceration for life, particularly when the defendant was perceived as dangerous; the public's perception, however, was slow to catch on to the fact that "insanity" had turned "acquittal" into a euphemism.

The insanity defense, which had for so long been a legal and psychological matter, had now become an emotional issue; as such, it became a *symbol* to those who opposed the Rules of society losing control. To the Rule's opponents, the insanity defense represented an escape from blame, punishment, retribution, and death.

The alienists, who organized as a group in 1841 as the Association of Medical Officers of Asylums and Hospitals for the Insane (which became the Medico-Psychological Association in 1865), were viewed in many quarters with great suspicion: not only did alienists help get insane defendants off through their testimony at trial, they helped the insane escape trial altogether by asserting that the insane were unfit to plead (Smith, 1981). As Walker (1968) notes, "the key to this escape route for the insane offender has been in the hands of the prison doctor ever since such an official came into existence" (p. 226).

Moreover, in the public's perception, alienists were frequently identified with the "abolitionists," those who wished to do away with capital punishment altogether. While most alienists were in fact not abolishionists, they were generally against hanging when insanity raised reasonable doubts about a defendant's responsibility and culpability. The alienists' support of the insanity plea was, after all, "a plea for the life of the prisoner" (Smith, 1981, p. 27), and if the plea was successful, the ritual of hanging and the public's thirst for retribution would be thwarted.

The alienists tried to counter this criticism. Forbes Winslow, for one, described confinement as punishment (Smith, 1981):

> To talk of a person escaping the extreme penalty of the law on the plea of Insanity, as one being subjected to no kind or degree of punishment, is a perfect mockery of truth and perversion of language. Suffer no punishment! He is exposed to the severest pain and torture of body and mind that can be inflicted upon a human creature short of being publicly strangled upon the gallows. If the fact be doubted, let a visit be paid to that dreadful den at Bethlehem Hospital . . . where the criminal portion of the establishment are confined like wild beasts in an iron cage. (p. 27)

The alienists' defense, like that of Winslow's, failed to silence the critics, some of whom marshaled their own evidence.

> "Dr. Hood gave critics of the insanity defence ammunition when he stated that, out of seventy-nine patients acquitted for murder and sent to Bethlem, between 1852 and 1858, "in several cases no symptom of insanity has been evinced during the period of residence in the asylum . . . the jury acted upon the evidence of the medical witnesses, who had formed erroneous opinions of the cases." (Smith, 1981, p. 30)

The alienists, jurists, and the public were also in conflict about the nature and extent of expert testimony in the wake of the Rules. Would the

Rules give additional impetus to the already frightening trend in medical expert testimony? Would we see a replica of M'Naghten's trial, where expert after expert, some who never examined the defendant, paraded confidently to the stand to testify? Would psychiatric opinion and jargon befuddle a jury and effectively usurp their function?

Taking the opposite opinion were the alienists, who feared that the Rules would restrict medical testimony; to back up their fearful prediction they cited signs of growing unfriendliness by the courts toward the scientific expert.

> "The most scientific witness may be cross-examined as if he were a fraudulent bankrupt, and every effort made to render his evidence unintelligible to the jury or unworthy of evidence." The degree to which practitioners felt themselves to be on trial is indicated by how many of them wrote on the subject." (Smith, 1981, p. 14)

The M'Naghten Rules have been the subject of critical review for over a century. Much of the criticism, both legal and psychological, has focused on the particular words and phrases, their meaning and implications. Over this period of time the fate of the Rules has varied: in some jurisdictions they stand; in others, they have been modified, replaced, or declared legally dead. Within our current climate of change following the *Hinckley* decision, the Rules have been receiving renewed attention. It is time to take a fresh, discerning look at the Rules and its criticisms to determine what is valid and not and to see if a resurrection is in order.

To Know the Nature and Quality of the Act

The particular words and phrases that constitute the M'Naghten Rules have provoked great psychological, legal, and semantic debate for over a century. At the center of much of the historical controversy is the phrase "to know the nature and quality of the act he was doing." The verb "to know" creates numerous difficulties. What does it mean when we say a defendant "knew" what he was doing? Surely M'Naghten and Hadfield knew what they were doing if we restrict the meaning of "to know" to mean merely sensory awareness of their movements during the crime: both defendants knew they had a gun in their hands and not a guava melon; surely both knew they were aiming a pistol and squeezing its trigger; and both knew that the target was a human being rather than a tree. No, neither Hadfield nor M'Naghten's perceptions of the weapon, their movements, or the target were that distorted. There may indeed be cases where hallucinations, delusions, or altered states of consciousness so distort perceptions that it can be said of such individuals that they do not know what they are doing in this restricted sense, but the actions of M'Naghten and Hadfield were not such instances.

What more, then, do we mean by the phrase "to know"? We can

expand our meaning to include an "emotional knowing," derived in part from our human ability to empathically stand in the shoes of the victim: we can infer the shock, horror, anguish, terror, pain, or even death of another human being. When we use the phrase "to know" in the M'Naghten Rules, do we mean to include an "emotional" realization? Keeping this question in mind, let us consider the following hypothetical case.

When a child of 6, well-schooled by violence on television and familiar with both toy and real guns at home, points a loaded pistol at a parent and fatally fires, can we say he "knew" what he was doing? We may feel that he knew what he was doing in the restricted, sensory sense, yet conclude that he lacked an emotional appreciation or fuller realization of his act. But what about the *Hadfield* and *M'Naghten* cases? In *Hadfield* and *M'Naghten*, both defendants knew that their acts infringed on another: they understood (knew) that the nature and quality of their act, if successful, meant the murder of a human being. And yet like the juries that found them innocent by reason of insanity, we may still feel that in some *crucial* sense they did not know.

Expanding the term "to know" even further, do we include within the meaning of "to know" the realization that the act is a crime? Or going still further, do we expect a person to know that it is morally wrong? Both Hadfield and M'Naghten knew that murder was a criminal act, that it was a violation of the law. And we can infer from their behavior both prior to and following their acts that they had a *moral sense;* indeed, they had a very strong sense of right and wrong; yet two juries found them innocent by reason of insanity.

The great American doctor, Isaac Ray, whose work *A Treatise on the Medical Jurisprudence of Insanity* (1838/1983) became one of the most influential works on the subject, highlighted what for him was the *crucial sense* in which insanity distorts knowing. Ray noted that in insanity, even when accompanied by delusions, the individual typically knows what is morally right and wrong *in the abstract* and indeed may abhor murder *in general.* However, the individual may fail to connect *his particular act* with the general moral position he espouses, and it is this *dissociation* of the general and the particular that, for Ray, reveals the "defect of reason" of insanity; and it is in this sense that we can say of a person that he *did not know* "the nature and quality of the act he was doing, or if he did know it, that he did not know he was doing what was wrong."

Ray's point goes beyond the question of mere knowing. Reading into Ray's remarks and translating them into twentieth-century terms, it may be said that "not knowing" can be regarded as a symptom of insanity, but not its *essence:* an insane individual may know, but may be insane nonetheless becuase of a defect of reason that keeps two ideas separate—when they *ought to be conjoined.*

Going beyond Ray, who stops short of the mark, we have in the cases of *Hadfield* and *M'Naghten* two deluded individuals. In Hadfield's belief system, his attempted act, killing the King, represents to him a higher moral good, for it paves the way for Christ's return. In M'Naghten's belief system, where he is hounded by enemies, chief of which is the Tory government headed by Peel, his act becomes something akin to self-defense. In both instances, Hadfield's and M'Naghten's, their particular criminal acts—when viewed from their *internal* frames of reference—are not instances of legal, moral wrongfulness, although we, who stand outside their peculiar reference frames, see them so. The point is that it is not just a case of two related ideas kept apart and dissociated. Hadfield's and M'Naghten's particular acts have been subjectively, distortedly, delusionally redefined, so even if they bring together in mind their particular act with the abstract moral and legal right from wrong, there is no contradiction!

The alienists and medical critics of the M'Naghten Rules, however, had not gone this far and in this direction in their analysis. When they questioned the meaning of "to know." they were taking exception to what they perceived to be the law's "cognitive," "intellectual," or narrow construction of the words. The alienists argued vigorously that the law was incompatible with naturalistic descriptions of insanity and disease—for "in Nature" there "were no sharp dividing lines between reason, emotion, and volition . . . yet the law was creating such 'artificial lines'" (Smith, 1981, p. 16). To back up their claims, alienists presented cases to show that insanity did not only, or even primarily, affect the intellectual faculties, but affected the emotions, will, or the "whole" of the personality. They argued that even in the most serious of disorders, what today we would classify as serious psychoses, the law's narrow type of knowledge could be found (Goldstein, 1967). This narrow, intellectual knowledge was absent only in the "totally deteriorated, drooling, hopeless psychotics of long-standing, and congenital idiots," according to Zilboorg (1943, p. 273).

This assertion—that the Rules were based on an already outdated psychology—has been made so often and so insistently by critics that it has been taken as a truism. The alienists' contention, which has remained "unchanged throughout the last hundred years" (Smith, 1981, p. 16), was repeated by Justice Frankfurter in his testimony before the Royal Commission 110 years after M'Naghten. Yet there are grounds upon which to challenge this belief.

Goldstein (1967) reviews the empirical evidence and finds "that very few appellate courts have imposed the restrictive interpretation. Indeed, most of the courts which have addressed themselves to the question have favored a rather broad construction" (p. 49). In a number of states

> the jury is told that an accused "knows" only if he "understands" enough to enable him to judge of "the nature, character and consequence of the act

charged against him" or if he has the "capacity to appreciate the character and to comprehend the probable or possible consequences of his act." (p. 49)

What we have here, is in part a false issue. The issue is not whether "to know" is narrowly or broadly construed; nor is the central issue whether the framers of the Rules were using an updated Psychology; the central issue, is whether the framers captured the essence of insanity—an essence that is in accord with our legal, psychological, and common-sense notions of what is and is not insane.

With the issue thus drawn, Herbert Fingarette's (1972) analysis of the Rules is a noteworthy exception, for he credits the framers and the phrase "defect of reason" with more wisdom than the critics have heretofore acknowledged (Fingarette & Hasse, 1979). Fingarette points out that the phrase "defect of reason" has been frequently omitted by judges in their instructions to the jury, while being regarded by many critics of the Rules as a mere redundancy—adding nothing to the subsequent phrases concerning knowledge of the nature, quality, and wrongness of the act. Fingarette finds within the connotations of this overlooked and under-valued phrase something very close to the essence of insanity, as he would define it. While his position will be developed more fully in later chapters, for now it is sufficient to challenge the truism that the Rules are both too narrowly construed and too cognitively tilted.

WRONG

The word "wrong" brings its own ambiguities, some of which we have already anticipated. Does "wrong" mean *legally* wrong? Or does it mean *morally* wrong? And if legal and moral are distinct, which takes precedence, and who decides? The case of Hadfield provides a clarifying illustration. Hadfield knew that killing George III was legally wrong, yet he acted on a "higher," albeit deluded, belief that eliminating the King was a moral necessity. But clearly, if we let personal standards rule, we are all in big trouble, particularly when an individual's belief, such as Hadfield's, is far out of tune with the rest of society's.

It has been argued that the moral position of a defendant must be the position that is supported by the majority of society. But even when there is concordance between the beliefs of the defendant and society, we are not necessarily out of the woods. Take, for example, cases such as mercy killing, suicide, and abortion, where a large segment of society may judge these acts to be morally just, yet according to the laws of some jurisdictions they remain legal wrongs. English courts have endeavored "to remove the ambiguity by holding that the accused must be aware that the act was legally wrong" (Goldstein, 1967, p. 52), whereas courts in the United States have split, with some holding that "wrong" is an act prohibited by law while others hold that "wrong" means moral wrong "according to generally accepted standards."

DISEASE OF MIND

The phrase "disease of mind" was left undefined by the framers of the Rules, and this almost complete absence of judicial definition of mental disease has continued to the present. Yet there has been an assumption, repeated so often in the literature that it is taken as yet another truism in some quarters, that the M'Naghten Rules restrict "disease of mind" to embrace "only a limited number of psychoses and the most extreme forms of mental defect" (Goldstein, 1967, p. 47). Factually, an examination of historical cases reveals that the truism simply isn't: cases involving infanticide, automatism, sleep walking, somnambulism, vigilambulism, fugue, amnesia, hypnomania, blackouts, epilepsy, posttraumatic stress, and drunkenness have successfully invoked the insanity defense. Thus, the range and variety of diseases of the mind that have been successfully allowed under M'Naghten have been far more generous than critics have acknowledged.

IRRESISTIBLE IMPULSES

The legal absence of a definition of "disease of mind" left unanswered questions, and in the last half of the nineteenth century, the most pressing question centered on what came to be known as "irresistible impulses." Alienists had recently described a disorder, "impulsive insanity," whose symptoms were emotional and volitional incapacity. This disease of mind often left reason (and the ability "to know") undisturbed, yet, to the alienists it represented an inability to control one's actions. The alienists concluded that individuals with such a disorder could not be held responsible, although the law held them so.

In France, at the beginnings of the nineteenth century, the great Pinel described a disease featuring emotional and volitional disorder (Smith, 1981):

> He observed that intellectual clarity persisted in the midst of paroxysms, even those leading to "automatic atrocity." He therefore described a disease called "manie sans delire" (lucid mania or mania without delusion). (p. 36)

> Prichtard coined the term "moral insanity" to describe what Pinel had labeled *manie sans delire*, and what others writers called "instinctive madness":

> "In this disorder, the will is occasionally under the influence of an impulse, which suddenly drives the person affected to the perpetration of acts of the most revolting kind, to the commission of which he has no motive. The impulse is accompanied by consciousness; but it is in some instances irresistible." And the

physiologist, W. B. Carpenter, noted that the basic element in insanity was a "deficiency of volitional control." (Smith, 1981, p. 39)

The position of the medical community was that the law ought to be consistent with accepted medical facts, but, when it came to the M'Naghten Rules, "legal law" was out of step with the "natural law"; the implication, of course, was that the Rules ought to be widened. The law, you may remember, had already been confronted by the problem of irresistible impulses in *Hadfield* (1800), when Hadfield's attorney Erskine talked of "motives irresistible." Hadfield, who was facing not the Rules but the even more restrictive "wild beast" test, was acquitted on grounds of insanity nevertheless, as the jury found Erskine's appeal persuasive. Whereas judges, jurists, and legislators make "official" law, it is the jury, composed of laymen, who applies, construes, misconstrues, or disregards the law, and, in a fashion, makes "unofficial" law. If the common-sense perspective of the ordinary citizen and juror embraces "irresistible impulses" as part and parcel of insanity, then pressure builds on the official lawmaking bodies to fall in step. In the case of "motives irresistible," jurors and alienists were reaching similar conclusions, though official law lagged behind.

The English jurist most responsible for pushing the law to embrace "irresistible impulses" was Fitzjames Stephen. Stephen's own thinking on this matter, however, reveals not only changes, but an almost complete reversal. The young Stephen was at first highly critical of the "irresistible impulse" notion. Writing in an 1855 paper, he noted that "there may have been many instances of irresistible impulse of this kind, although I fear there is a disposition to confound them with unresisted impulses" (Walker, 1968 p. 105). By 1862, Stephen, still considered the stout defender of the M'Naghten Rules, granted that if an impulse was irresistible, then the defendant was entitled to acquittal since "the act was not voluntary and was not properly his act" (Walker, 1968, p. 106). He still noted that if the impulse was resistible, "the fact that it proceeded from disease is no excuse at all." But by 1883, in his *History of the Criminal Law of England*, he argued that the Rules were incomplete:

> If it is not, it ought to be the Law of England that no act is a crime if the person who does it is at the time . . . prevented either by defective mental power or by any disease affecting his mind from controlling his own conduct, unless the absence of the power of control has been produced by his own default. (Walker, 1968, p. 106)

Although the law had not changed, Stephen was prepared to make English juries see it his way, and he took the opportunity in the trial of William Davis (*R. v. Davis*, 1881). Davis attempted to murder his sister-in-law because "the man in the moon told me to do it. I will have to commit murder, as I must be hanged" (Walker, 1968, p. 107). In Stephen's summary of the case for the jurors, he noted that "both the doctors agree that the prisoner was unable to control his conduct, and that nothing short of actual physical restraint would have deterred him." The jury acquitted Davis on grounds of insanity. Other judges, citing Stephen's lead, began to follow suit. While the law of England was still the M'Naghten Rules, an unofficial widening was occurring.

The official brakes were applied to this unofficial widening when, in 1922, the Court of Criminal Appeal had an opportunity to authoritatively ratify the irresistible impulse in reviewing *R. v. True*, but they did not do so. They commented

> that the judge had been too generous to True when he told the jury that irresist-
> ible impulse would have constituted criminal insanity. The M'Naghten Rule,
> which mentioned only knowledge of the nature and quality of the act or its
> wrongness, was "sufficient and salutary." (Walker, 1968, p. 108).

That was that. But not quite. The Home Secretary gave True a reprieve on the grounds of his mental condition. This reprieve produced an outcry and a lingering confusion between official and unofficial law regarding irresistible impulses.

On this side of the Atlantic, the "irresistible impulse" rule was added to M'Naghten in many states and in the federal system, with its lineage "at least as old as that of *M'Naghten*" (Goldstein, 1967, p. 67). In an Alabama case, *Parsons v. State* (1887), if a person lacked "freedom of will," his power *to choose* right from wrong would be subverted. The Parsons doctrine was incorporated in the federal rule in *Davis v. United States* (1897), when the court added the "irresistible impulse" notion onto M'Naghten: an accused would be classed as insane if

> though conscious of (the nature of the act) and able to distinguish between right
> and wrong . . . yet his will, by which I mean the governing power of his mind,
> has been otherwise than voluntarily so completely destroyed that his actions are
> not subject to it, but are beyond his control.

Goldstein (1967) notes that

> The "irresistible impulse" rule was widely heralded by many lawyers and psy-
> chiatrists as the way to remedy all that was wrong with *M'Naghten*. More re-
> cently, however, in a remarkable reversal of position, the rule has been dis-
> missed summarily by most commentators on the theory either that it adds little
> to *M'Naghten* ("merely a gloss"), or that is expands the insanity defense far too
> much, or that it is impossible to apply, or that it is without scientific basis. (p. 68)

In the recent *American Psychiatric Association Statement on the Insanity Defense* (1982, p. 11), the Association states that "the line between an irresistible impulse and an impulse not resisted is probably no sharper than that between twilight and dusk." Perhaps the older Fitzjames Stephen should have heeded his more youthful utterances; if he had, we might have avoided the twilight–dusk distinction, and the darkness that followed.

Another critic of this distinction is Lady Wootton (1960, 1963). Regarding this darkness,

> Lady Wootton says that a man's responsibility or capacity to resist temptation is something "buried in (his) consciousness, into which no human being can enter," known if at all only to him and to God: it is not something which other men may even know; and since "it is not possible to get inside another man's skin" it is not something of which they can ever form even a reasonable estimate as a matter of probability. (Hart, 1968 p. 203).

Chief Justice Brian, in 1477, put it this way: "the thought of man is not triable; the devil alone knoweth the thought of man" (Hart, 1968, p. 188). Whether it be the devil's realm or God's, psychiatry claimed it had the power to enlighten the courts as to the dark impulses of a defendant's soul. In believing it could discern resistible impulses from irresistible, the medico-psychological champions led the courts and the law further from the light of objective reality into the darkness of our subjective, psychic mystery. Why did the history of the insanity defense take this deepening plunge? Subsequent chapters will hopefully provide answers; for now, Daniel M'Naghten's cryptic words will suffice:

> When asked what had brought him where he was, he replied, "Fate." "And what is fate?" "The will of God—or perhaps," he added quickly, "of the devil—or it may be of both!" and he half-closed his eyes, and smiled (Moran, 1981, p. 119).

ISAAC RAY AND THE DURHAM RULE

As we have seen, the M'Naghten Rules created difficulties for alienists and others almost from the outset. The last subsection focused on one of *M'Naghten's* apparent shortcomings—that it did not take into account *will* or *volition;* this shortcoming prompted many alienists like Pritchard and jurists like Stephen to press for the addition of a "control test."

A more radical approach to the problems and limitations of the M'Naghten Rules was quick to germinate. This new direction was most clearly articulated by the American doctor, Isaac Ray. As Walker (1968, pp. 89–90) notes, Ray was strongly influenced by French psychiatrists and by French law. The Code of Napoleon of 1810 had included a wide exemption for insane offenders: *"Il n'y a ni crime ni delit, lorsque le prevenu etait en etat de demence au temps de l'action. . .* (article 10)," which translates: There is neither a crime nor an offense (misdemeanor) when the accused person was in the state of insanity (madness or lunacy) at the time of the action. Ray pointed out that New York State had enacted a similar principle, that "no

act done by a person in a state of insanity can be punished as an offense. . . ." Walker (1968) comments that

> in theory this was generous in the extreme. It called for no investigation into the
> relationship between the "state of insanity" and the act: all that had to be shown
> was that at the time of the act the offender was insane. . . .
>
> Ray did not go quite so far as to recommend this formula. What he sug-
> gested was that "if the mental unsoundness, necessary to exempt from punish-
> ment, were required by law *to have embraced the criminal act within its sphere of
> influence*, as much perhaps would then be accomplished as is practicable within a
> specific enactment." (p. 90)

It was Isaac Ray's personal influence on Judge Doe that led the latter to
inject this principle into the criminal law of New Hampshire.

> Doe's sympathy with Ray's views influenced Chief Justice Perley's opinion, in
> *State v. Pike* (1869), that if "the killing was the offspring or product of mental
> disease" the defendant should be acquitted and that the presence of disease was
> a fact to be determined. This expressed exactly what some alienists wanted: the
> law's recognition of a factual relationship between disease and deed which
> exonerated responsibility." (Smith, 1981, p. 18)

It was a more radical step than the "irresistible impulse" addition to
the Rules because it avoided the outdated psychology of a mind divided
into faculties such as reason, passion, and will; rather, it seemed to be an
expression of a more modern psychology that conceived of a person as an
integrated personality. Ray's radical formula etched its way into law in the
granite state of New Hampshire; and while no other state embraced Ray's
formula, it was an idea that would resurface time and again on both sides
of the Atlantic.

In England, Ray's position was much debated, but never adopted.
Following the Court of Criminal Appeal's unpopular decision in the True
case (1922), the government appointed a committee headed by Lord Atkin
to consider what changes, if any, should be made when the plea of insanity
was raised as a defense. The Atkin Committee heard from the Medico-
Psychological Association, which, in effect, proposed replacing the
M'Naghten Rules with Isaac Ray's formula. The British Medical Association, on the other hand, made the more conservative recommendation that
the irresistible impulse test be added to the Rules. The Atkin Committee
favored the latter, more conservative solution, but the Government
favored neither and made no moves to change the Rules.

After World War II, the Royal Commission on Capital Punishment
(1949–1953) took up the issue again. By this time, the Medico-Psychological Association, which now called itself the Royal Medico-Psychological
Association, reversed its position on the Ray formula: instead of favoring
abrogating the Rules for the Ray formula, the Association was content to
live with the Rules so long as they were interpreted "elastically." Other
members of the Commission were not content to rely on "interpretation"
as a solution and, instead, proposed two preferred alternatives: one was

the Ray formula, "to abrogate the Rules and to leave the jury to determine whether at the time of the act the accused was suffering from disease of mind (or mental deficiency) to such a degree that he ought not to be held responsible" (Gowers, 1953, p. 116); the other was the irresistible impulse addition.

The Ray proposal excited the most controversy. Its advocates doubted that further tinkering with the words of the Rules would yield a clearer dividing line for the jury. Lord Cooper, who was Lord Justice General for Scotland, told the Commission that whatever words judges gave to juries, "the latter simply retired and asked themselves 'Is this man mad or is he not?'" Since jurors were reputedly doing what the Ray formula suggests they do, why not place, as Hale (1736) had done, stout confidence in the English jury:

> Yet the law of England hath afforded the best method of trial that is possible of this and all other matters of fact, namely by a jury of twelve men all concurring in the same judgment. . . . (Walker, 1968, p. 110)

The critics of Ray's formula noted that the formula *was not a rule at all*, since it provided no standard of responsibility for the jury. The critics worried that in the absence of a standard, the juries were (1) more likely to be swayed by expert testimony, (2) more likely to reach inconsistent decisions, and (3) more likely to use their personal feelings about the defendant. As Goldstein (1967) remarked, "Whether the psyches of individual jurors are strong enough to make that decision, or whether the 'law' should put that obligation on them, is open to serious questions" (p. 82). The bottom line was that neither the Ray formula nor the irresistible impulse addition was adopted in England.

The Royal Commission report did have an effect on Judge Bazelon of the United States Court of Appeals for the District of Columbia. In writing the opinion in *Durham v. United States* (1954), Bazelon formulated what came to be known as the "product rule" test (which was Isaac Ray's formula and the law of New Hampshire since 1869):

> If you the jury believe beyond a reasonable doubt that the accused was not suffering from a diseased or defective mental condition at the time he committed the criminal act charged, you may find him guilty. If you believe he was suffering from a diseased or defective mental condition when he committed the act, but believe beyond a reasonable doubt that the act was not the product of such mental abnormality, you may find him guilty. Unless you believe beyond a reasonable doubt either that he was not suffering from a diseased or defective mental condition, or that the act was not the product of such abnormality, you must find the accused not guilty by reason of insanity. Thus your task would not be completed upon finding, if you did find, that the accused suffered from a mental disease or defect. He would still be responsible for his unlawful act if there was no causal connection between such abnormality and the act. These questions must be determined by you from the facts which you find to be fairly deducible from the testimony and the evidence in this case.

The case of Monte Durham is an interesting one. Monte Durham had a history of mental illness of an on-again, off-again nature: not only was he labeled with a variety of diagnoses, such as "unfit" and "psychotic," but at other times he was pronounced "fit" and "recovered." In May, 1951, he was discharged for the third time from St. Elizabeth's Hospital. On July 13, 1951, he broke into a house. Following his arrest and indictment, psychiatric examination in September, 1951, revealed that he suffered from hallucinations. However, at the trial, which was conducted under the M'Naghten Rules plus the irresistible impulse addition, the question of insanity concerned *the time of the act*. Durham, like most other defendants who plead insanity, was examined not at the time of the act but afterwards; in this case, it was two months after the act. The expert witness, Dr. Gilbert, was asked by the defense counsel, Mr. Ahern, if, in the former's opinion, Monte Durham's period of insanity "embraced" the date July 13, 1951. Dr. Gilbert answered "Yes." The original court in the case remained unimpressed, and stated:

> I don't think it has been established that the defendant was of unsound mind as of July 13, 1951, in the sense that he didn't know the difference between right and wrong or that even if he did, he was subject to an irresistible impulse by reason of the derangement of mind. . . . *There is no testimony concerning the mental state of the defendant as of July 13, 1951, and therefore the usual presumption of sanity governs* (Durham, pp. 865–866).

The Court of Appeals thought this presumption was an error requiring reversal. They voted that

> the inability of the expert to give categorical assurance that Durham was unable to distinguish between right and wrong did not destroy the effect of his previous testimony that the period of Durham's "insanity" embraced July 13, 1951". (Durham, p. 868).

This difference of opinion between the lower court and the Court of Appeals is reminiscent of the difference between Lord Hale and "the Bluidy MacKenzie"'s positions on temporary-to-partial insanity (see Chapter 1). When Hale regarded the lucid intervals, he did so with the presumption of sanity; MacKenzie, on the other hand, regarded diseases as more "sticking," and he would presume that the disease was still operating, effecting, and certainly embracing the time of the act. Whereas the seventeenth-century British jurist Lord Hale would favor the lower court's presumption in Durham, the seventeenth-century Scottish jurist MacKenzie would embrace Bazelon's opinion.

Judge Bazelon went on to replace the old test (M'Naghten plus irresistible impulse) with the "product rule," which held that "an accused is not criminally responsible if his unlawful act was the product of mental disease or mental defect" (Durham, pp. 874–875).

"The court was convinced not only that his rule was substantively sound but that it would usher in a new era of harmony between psychiatrists, and lawyers" (Goldstein, 1967, p. 83). Psychiatrists would be freer to fully inform the jury about the defendant's mental disease without confining their remarks to M'Naghten criteria. Lawyers could now ask their expert witnesses questions about the defendant's wide and varied symptoms, along with their psychiatric meaning and significance. Bazelon also believed that the Durham rule was premised upon the modern psychology of an "integrated personality." When enough time had elapsed for the effects of the Durham rule to be assessed, it became clear that "Durham did not produce the results that Bazelon wanted" (Smith, 1981, p. 19).

In many ways, the critics of *Durham* and of Ray's formula were right. In giving no definition or standards to the meaning of "mental disease," a "void for vagueness" was created, and, as a predictable result, psychiatrists stepped in even further to fill the void. In giving greater latitude to the expert witness, the psychiatrist was freer to jargonize. Psychiatric testimony became even more "technicalized," since the experts were now free to expound on "mental illness" and its broad ramifications, rather than being restricted to the issue of whether the defendant's mental illness weakened his responsibility and knowledge of right from wrong to the point of exculpation. This shift allowed the expert to move from the narrow and confining quarters of law and morality to the more comfortable, spacious, and familiar grounds of mental illness. (Leifer (1964) comments on one result:

> This "technicalization" of psychiatric testimony has resulted in the paradox that although one of the purposes of the Durham Decision is to insure that the moral decision is made by the jury rather than the expert, the facts on which the decision is to be based are so technical that the jury must hear the psychiatrist's conclusion as to whether the act was a product of mental disease or not, which is equivalent to an opinion about responsibility. Far from making their own decision, the jury can only agree or disagree with one of two psychiatrists, each of whom present technical language which the jury cannot understand. Thus, it tends to be the psychiatrists, rather than the facts, that influences the jury; the effect is that the moral decision is placed more firmly in the hands of the psychiatrist, although more subtly. (p. 828)

Beyond merely "technicalizing" their testimony, the Durham rule raised to a more heightened degree the "ultimate issue" problem. The "ultimate issue," as it has come to be called, is whether experts should be permitted to go beyond "the facts" and give their opinions regarding the defendant's responsibility. Should psychiatric experts be allowed to state whether, in their opinion, the defendant knew right from wrong, was responsible or not, or was criminally insane or not? Wasn't the "ultimate issue" supposed to be left for the jury to decide? "Technicalizing" their testimony runs the risk that it is incomprehensible to the lay juror; giving their conclusions as to the "ultimate issue" runs the even greater risk of usurping the juror's function altogether.

The "ultimate issue" is certainly not new, nor is it solely related to

Durham. The Justices who articulated the M'Naghten Rules were aware of the issue when they answered the Lords' fifth and last question: in their answer, the Justices tried to draw a line between matters of fact (science) and the determination of the truth of the facts ("which it is for the jury to decide"). However, their next sentence tended to obscure the very line they just drew:

> But, where the facts are admitted or not disputed, and the question becomes substantially one of science only, it may be convenient to allow the question to be put in that general form, though the same cannot be insisted on as a matter of right. (Walker, 1968, p. 102)

The "line" between fact and opinion became further obscured with the "irresistible impulse" addition, as psychiatric witnesses claimed to have the power and scientific expertise to discriminate twilight from dusk and motives irresistible from motives simply not resisted.

What *Durham* did, despite Bazelon's warning "against permitting the psychiatrist to usurp the jury's role" (Goldstein, 1967, p. 103), was to give greater latitude to lawyers to ask their witnesses about the mental life of their client. It should come as no great surprise that lawyers would want to bring out the strongest possible statements in favor of their client, be it the defendant or the state; and conclusions regarding the "ultimate issue" would certainly be more weighty than jargonized discourses on psychic life. While the "line" between "facts" and the "ultimate issue" had been growing more obscure for quite some time, the *impression*, following *Durham*, was that it had now all but vanished.

Impressions are important; but so are facts. While we will consider empirical evidence regarding the jurors' perspective in Chapter 7, for now let us simply note that there is evidence to challenge the notion of Leifer and others that the jury has become more dependent on psychiatric opinions such that "the moral decision" lies "more firmly in the hands of the psychiatrist."

On another point, as Leifer and others indicate, it seems clear that *Durham's* openness to expert testimony did increase the frequency of that sorry spectacle known as "the battle of experts": in this spectacle, both sides, prosecution and defense, call to the stand their own experts, all with impeccable credentials, all of whom attest with equal certainty and eloquence, that the accused is both sane (prosecution) and insane (defense). In the eyes of the public and press, the profession is in danger of being convicted for lunacy (Finkel, 1980).

Durham represents the furthest swing of the pendulum in the efforts to broaden and liberalize M'Naghten. It went further than the irresistible impulse addition, which merely added another criterion while retaining the remnants of the long-faded faculty psychology. But *Durham*, despite Bazelon's hopes and good intentions for premising the rule on the "new psychology," still speaks about conduct as a "product" of "mental disease." It has been said that the "product" requirement assumes a compartmentalized mind—a mind where "mental disease" causes some unlawful acts and not others. With "product" undefined in *Durham*, it is up to the expert and the juror to determine whether this particular act was or was not a product. The results have not been productive.

In 1962, the pendulum began to swing the other way, as the court in *McDonald v. United States* (1962) concluded

> that some effort should be made to explain what was meant by "mental diseases" as a guide to experts, lawyers, judges, and jurors. . . . In short, Durham had traveled a remarkably circuitous path toward the conclusion that the jury needed some guidance, that words like "mental disease" and "product" were inadequate, and that the standard would have to incorporate somehow a description of the sorts of effects of disease that were relevant to compliance with the criminal law. Those effects, inevitably, were very much like the ones which were central to the broadened *M'Naghten* and "control" tests. (Goldstein, 1967, p. 86)

THE ALI FALLBACK

The American Law Institute (ALI) made its recommendations for a new insanity test one year after *Durham*. In making its recommendation, ALI rejected the advice of its own psychiatric advisory committee, which favored *Durham*. What ALI proposed was similar to an alternative that the Royal Commission had considered; it included elements from M'Naghten and the "control test," but with new words and phrases for both parts (American Law Institute, 1962):

> (1) A person is not responsible for criminal conduct if at the time of such conduct as a result of mental disease or defect he lacks substantial capacity either to appreciate the criminality of his conduct or to conform his conduct to the requirements of law.
> (2) As used in this Article, the terms "mental disease or defect" do not include an abnormality manifested only by repeated criminal or otherwise antisocial conduct.

The term "appreciate," which implies emotional as well as intellectual understanding, has been substituted for the narrower and much criticized M'Naghten term "to know." The phrase "criminality of his conduct," clearly implies a breach of law, whereas M'Naghten's "wrong" was ambiguous as to whether it meant "legal" or "moral" wrong. With the phrase "he lacks substantial capacity," the ALI advocates sought to clarify what had been troubling to many long before M'Naghten: they hoped that references to "total insanity" (which still made their way into judges' instructions to the jury when the former occasionally made reference to "total" or "complete" destruction of capacity) would be eliminated.

When it came to the "control" test part, ALI substituted "to conform his conduct to the requirements of law" for "control" and avoided any reference to what Goldstein (1967) called the "misnamed 'irresistible impulse' rule" (p. 67). And last, in part (2), they attempt to bar the insanity defense from psychopaths and recidivists.

The ALI test can be seen as an attempt to swing the insanity pendulum back from the apogee of *Durham*. It more clearly differentiates mental disease from the question of criminal responsibility; it specifies criteria for relating the two; and it draws a boundary line that prohibits the extension of the concept of mental disease to embrace psychopathy. Politically and socially, ALI recognized that *Durham* had gone far beyond what legislators, judges, and the public would accept—turning the question of insanity over entirely to psychiatrists.

In swinging back, though, the ALI test runs into some old problems. "Appreciate" may be broader than "to know," but it is still vague and undefined; the same point can be made for "substantial." The test, as it is worded, assumes a compartmentalized mind, which was earlier criticized as being incompatible with the "new" psychology. In returning to a "control" test, even under the term "conform," it implicitly affirms the belief that psychiatrists can differentiate whether a defendant can't or simply won't conform, which is the old twilight–dusk dilemma. And finally, the concept of mental disease or defect remains undefined.

While the ALI test has been criticized, the preceding difficulties with *Durham* surely tempered the edge of many a critical thrust. The critics, too, have become more realistic, if not pessimistic, in realizing that a "perfect" definition of insanity may be an illusory and unobtainable dream; this increased capacity to appreciate the reality of insanity and the limitations of words may account for the fact that the ALI test was accepted in more states and federal circuits than *Durham*. It also turned out to be the test that John Hinckley was tried under.

DIMINISHED RESPONSIBILITY

The British considered versions of the Durham product rule and the ALI test in their Royal Commission hearings, yet adopted neither. What they formulated in the 1957 Homicide Act was "diminished responsibility," a concept that can be traced to Scotland and the notions of "the Bluidy Mackenzie." This concept, which was both older and more innovative than the American solution, was greeted with characteristic British conservatism. What was uncharacteristic of the British, though, was that when final adoption came, the English version was even more generous to the defendant than the Scottish version. In the words of Walker (1968) "the adopted child had outgrown its twin" (pp. 155–166).

How did it come to pass that the child was adopted? There was a confluence of factors. An early call for its consideration came from Fitz-james Stephen (1883), who favored the logic of the Scottish expedient (Walker, 1968).

> Whereas the English law allowed only two possibilities . . . the Scots allowed a third: that he was sufficiently disordered to deserve not complete exemption from the usual punishment but a mitigation of it. (p. 147)

Stephen, like other English lawyers, "chafed in the narrow harness of the M'Naghten Rules," and suggested that

> . . . the law ought . . . where madness is proved, to allow the jury to return any one of three verdicts: Guilty; Guilty, but his power of self-control was dimin-ished by insanity; Not Guilty on the grounds of insanity. (p. 147)

Another part of the confluence came from an unusual crime—infan-ticide (Hoffer & Hull, 1984). The last execution of a mother for murdering her baby occurred in 1849; after that time, the Home Office routinely com-muted the death penalty. The routine reprieve put judges in an awkward position: because the offense was murder, they had to pronounce the death penalty fully knowing that it would never be carried out. To avoid this hypocrisy, judges and other witnesses before the Capital Punishment Commission (1864–1866) recommended "some lesser category of crime into which such cases could be brought" (Walker, 1968, p. 128). Fitzjames Stephen expressed an opinion consistent with many contemporary alien-ists, that

> women in that condition do get the strongest symptoms of what amounts almost to temporary madness, and . . . often hardly know what they are about, and will do things which they have no settled or deliberate intention whatever of doing. . . .

As Walker comments, Stephen "was even bold enough to hint that less harm was done by such homicides than in other cases."

Over the next 50 years various bills were introduced to change the crime to manslaughter, though none were successful until 1922. The Infan-ticide Bill of 1922 created a new crime called "infanticide." The problem with this legislation was its language, which was overly generous: it al-lowed a judged to sentence a woman for this new crime as if she were guilty of manslaughter where only "the balance of her mind" was dis-turbed, "without requiring that it be so disturbed as to affect her 'self-control' or 'responsibility'" (Walker, 1968. p. 131). This bill went further than even *Durham* dared to go, since it equated a mental disorder with insanity without even requiring, as *Durham* did, that the act be a product of the disorder. The Infanticide Act of 1938 modified the 1922 law by making it clear that the act applied only if the child was under 12 months of age, but it too did not causatively link the disorder to traditional concepts of criminal insanity, responsibility, and control.

What the Infanticide Bills of 1922 and 1938 created was an intermediate verdict, as "diminished responsibility" would do in 1957; but by their liberal wording, they opened the law to a possibility they surely had not intended. Walker (1968) describes such a possibility when he writes:

> . . . her counsel could safely say to the court "she knew that she was killing the child, and that this was morally and legally wrong. She had not lost her self-control, and could have refrained if she had wanted to. Her temporary disorder was in fact quite unconnected with what she did. But you have had evidence that at the time the balance of her mind was disturbed by reason of her not having fully recovered from the effect of giving birth to the child, and so you must find her guilty not of murder but of infanticide." This was of course the last thing that the draftsmen had in mind. Implicit in their wording is the presumption that if at the time the balance of her mind was disturbed for the reasons given then there must have been sufficient causal connection between this disturbance and the act to reduce her responsibility for the act. This presumption is of course quite foreign to English law; in the case of both the defence of insanity and the defence of diminished responsibility the causal connection must be established and not presumed. (p. 135)

There was still another historical factor, that of "special verdicts," which contributed in an indirect way to the British receptivity to the Scot's "diminished capacity." "Special verdicts," as they were called, have been invoked historically for a number of crimes such as homicide by self-defense, sleepwalking, and insanity. Hadfield's case is illustrative in that following the verdict Parliament hastily passed the Act of 1800, which sanctioned a special verdict and a different treatment of a defendant found "not guilty."

The "special verdict" can be viewed as the creation of an option not currently available; the impetus for such "legal creativity" generally arises when society finds the classic choice of either guilty or innocent too limiting. In Hadfield's case, the available choices fit neither the crime nor the defendant: the jury could not find Hadfield guilty, yet the alternative, innocent, would set a dangerous individual loose. In creating a statutory special verdict (the Act of 1800), a compromise between the two traditional alternatives became available. "Not guilty by reason of insanity" purportedly was an acquittal, since it used the words "not guilty"; on the other hand, it functioned more like "guilty" than "acquittal" since it allowed judges to confine such defendants.

In 1882, Queen Victoria was urging another special verdict. She wrote, as quoted by Walker (1968):

> . . . if this was the necessary effect of the law, Her Majesty thinks it worth consideration whether the law should not be amended. . .
>
> Punishment deters not only sane men but also eccentric men, whose supposed involuntary acts are really produced by a diseased brain capable of being acted upon by external influence. A knowledge that they would be protected by an acquittal on the grounds of insanity will encourage these men to commit

desperate acts, while on the other hand certainty that they will not escape
punishment will terrify them into a peaceful attitude—towards others. (p. 189)

Queen Victoria wanted the special verdict to sound more like a finding
of guilty. A few months later, the Trial of Lunatics Bill passed, and the
"guilty but insane" option became available, but with it came some judicial
confusion. If it was a "guilty" verdict, then the defendant could appeal,
which was not the case with the euphemistic "acquittal"; if it was really an
acquittal, then the prosecution could not ask for a special verdict, "since
that would amount to asking for an acquittal" (Walker, 1968, p. 190). In
1914 the House of Lords decided that it was an acquittal and therefore
could not be subjected to appeal. Thus, while the Act changed the words,
in fact, it changed nothing.

Victorian lawyers were neither kind nor just in their assessment of
Queen Victoria's reasoning. Some, like Sir Herbert Stephen, son of Fitzjames Stephen, claimed that she did not understand the doctrine of *mens
rea*, and these unchivalrous critics alluded to "the fact that she belonged to
a sex which was supposed to be weaker in jurisprudence as well as in
other matters" (Walker, 1968, p. 190). Withstanding these slanders,

> The Queen seems to emerge from the affair with more credit than the lawyers.
> For her, the Act of 1883 was a harmless means to a reasonable end—the discour-
> agement of insane and unpredictable attacks by means of a nominal deterrent
> which made no difference to the actual fate of the attacker. It is a remarkable fact
> that up to the passing of the Act she suffered seven such attacks, but after it
> none, although she lived another eighteen years." (Walker, 1968, p. 192)

This "special verdict" episode represents a reaction to the constraints
of the traditional two choices. For all the debate and slander that surrounded the Act of 1883, it should be noted that the special verdict was
neither novel nor innovative: it turns out to be a nominal play on words,
substantively changing little; but in the developing historical context that
would eventually produce a third choice, it plays a germinal part.

That third choice, Scotland's "diminished responsibility," finally came
to fruition in England by way of the Homicide Bill of 1957. The Homicide
Bill contained a clause providing for the defense of diminished responsibility. That section of the bill was recommended by the Heald Committee and
endorsed by Lord Kilmuir, who was then Lord Chancellor.

> Where a person kills or is a party to the killing of another, he shall not be
> convicted of murder if he was suffering from such abnormality of mind (whether
> arising from a condition of arrested or retarded development of mind or any
> inherent causes or induced by disease or injury) as substantially impaired his
> mental responsibility for his acts or omissions in doing or being a party to the
> killing. (Walker, 1968, p. 150)

Further sections of the bill made it clear that (1) it was up to the
defense to raise the issue, and (2) if the defense was successful, the accused

would be convicted of manslaughter (in Scotland, the accused would be convicted of culpable homicide), and then (3) judges could decide among the choices of life imprisonment, imprisonment for a fixed period, a fine, probation, or absolute or conditional discharge, and (4) if medical evidence was presented at the sentencing stage, the judge could commit the defendant to a mental hospital.

The debate in Parliament largely centered on the term "abnormality of mind" and the words in parentheses that followed. "Abnormality" seemed to some to be wider than other phrases, such as "weakness of mind," "aberration of mind," "unsoundness of mind," "a state of mind bordering on, though not amounting to, insanity," "partial insanity," "great peculiarity of mind," and "infirmity or aberration of mind or impairment of intellect." The English draftsmen "chose the widest possible term, 'abnormality,' and then proceeded to qualify it by listing the way in which it might be caused" (Walker, 1968, p. 151). By qualifying the term, they hoped to limit the defense to states of mind that psychiatrists or neurologists recognized as pathological. Nevertheless, concerns were voiced "that the Homicide Act had flung wide the half-closed door by which the mentally abnormal could escape conviction for murder" (Walker, 1968, p. 158).

Surprisingly, in the 1958–1960 period following the passage of the Homicide Act, the "half-closed door" remained where it was. According to Walker (1968), there was a decline in the percentage of those found "insane on arraignment" and those found "guilty but insane," and this decline in both of those categories was "compensated by verdicts of 'diminished responsibility,' *but no more*" (p. 158). Of the first 100 cases that successfully employed the diminished responsibility defense, all but eight were sent to prison, and most of them received "life" or lengthy fixed terms of three years or longer. In point of fact, the new defense probably sent a number of murderers to prison who would formerly have been committed to mental hospitals.

But the "half-closed door" does begin to slowly widen with time. When the figures are examined for the years 1957 to 1962, two-thirds went to prison. However, in the 1964–1965 period, the percentage of those who went to prison drops to one-third. Without examining each case in detail, we have no way of knowing whether the particular dispositions made good sense or not. But before we judge a law based on how it is administered, it is wise to remember that how this law is applied is a separate question from whether the creation of this third option serves the public, professionals, courts, and defendants in a better way than the traditional two choices.

In the United States, a third option, "guilty but mentally ill" (GBMI), was proposed, and, in some states, adopted, despite a spate of criticism. The American Bar Association, the American Psychiatric Association, the

National Commission on the Insanity Defense, and representatives of the Association for the Advancement of Psychology and the American Psychological Association all rejected GBMI. As one critic (Slobogin, 1985) put it, the GBMI verdict is "an idea whose time should not have come." When the American Psychiatric Association issued its Statement on the Insanity Defense in December, 1982, nine states were experimenting with a "guilty but mentally ill" verdict or its equivalent. The American Psychiatric Association notes that "while some psychiatrists believe that the 'guilty but mentally ill' verdict has merit for dealing with problems posed by the insanity defense, the American Psychiatric Association is extremely skeptical of this approach" (pp. 9–10). Much of their skepticism involves administrative concerns, and those we will ignore for the present to focus on the more substantive issues. Regarding these, they say,

> "Guilty but mentally ill" offers a "compromise" for the jury. Persons who might otherwise have qualified for an insanity verdict may instead be siphoned into a category of guilty but mentally ill. Thus some defendants who might otherwise be found not guilty through an insanity defense will be found "guilty but mentally ill" instead.
> The "guilty but mentally ill" approach may become the "easy way out." Juries may avoid grappling with the difficult moral issue inherent in adjudicating guilt or innocence, jurors instead settling conveniently on "guilty but mentally ill." The deliberations of jurors in deciding cases are, however, vital to set societal standards and to give meaning to societal ideas about responsibility and nonresponsibility. An important symbolic function of the criminal law is lost through the "guilty but mentally ill" approach. (American Psychiatric Association, 1982)

Peter Arenella (1983) makes a similar point in his testimony before the Ninety-Seventh Congress. The House of Representatives' Subcommittee on Criminal Justice had a number of bills (e.g., H.R. 6702) containing provisions permitting the court or jury to return a "guilty but mentally ill" (GBMI) verdict in federal courts. Arenella stated the following:

> Finally, giving the jury the GBMI alternative raised the distinct possibility that juries will avoid confronting the difficult question of whether it is just to hold the offender criminally responsible by returning a "compromise" GBMI verdict. I suspect that the GBMI verdict proposal is actually designed to assuage the public's legitimate concern over the possibility that dangerous defendants who are acquitted will be released prematurely from mental hospitals. Concerns about social control may justify reforms which would rationalize post-acquittal procedures. They do not justify convicting persons who were not responsible for their acts and sentencing them to a term of punishment based on culpability that is not present. (p. 277)

It seems that some of the critics underestimate jurors, whereas empirical evidence suggests a more flattering portrayal of jury and juror decisions. Beyond that, some critics ignore the distinct possibility that having only two choices has forced jurors to acquit (e.g., on grounds of insanity) some defendants who they do find *culpable in part* and who, in their opinion, need treatment; again, some empirical work with mock jurors reveals that jurors do ask themselves that question, "What ought to be done for this person?" and when the answer seems to be "treatment," they may fashion the *only* verdict open to them, "not guilty by reason of insanity," even though they also believe the defendant to be responsible *in part* and culpable *in part*. And finally, both statements take an anachronistic position regarding responsibility and culpability: these positions maintain that a defendant is either responsible or not, or culpable or not, when for the last 140 years alienists, psychiatrists, and psychologists have been making the point that mental illness is *graded*—not dichotomous—and thus responsibility and culpability should be similarly graded. When we have similar gradations of culpability in the law (i.e., in the Model Penal Code, we have four forms of *mens rea*, or criminal intent: "intentionally," "knowingly," "recklessly," and "negligently" acting), why is it that insanity should remain ungraded?

The questions regarding those concepts of mental illness, responsibility and culpability, will be taken up in greater detail in subsequent chapters, as will the defense of "diminished responsibility." For now, it is enough to lay out the evolution, enactment, and contention that swirls about this defense, as it seems to around all such defenses. Yet before this chapter closes, some attention needs to be given to one more option—that of abolishing the insanity defense entirely.

ABOLISHING THE INSANITY DEFENSE

Two chapters on the history of the insanity defense, coupled with the current hue and cry from media and political figures, are enough to raise the question "Might we best extricate ourselves from this maddening labyrinth by abolishing the defense entirely?" Typically this question arises out of frustration and fades as the last disquieting trial ebbs into history. When Chief Justice Brian, in 1477, warned that "the thoughts of man are not triable," his warning failed to stop courts, professionals, and lay jurors from delving deeper and deeper into those thoughts that, in the good judge's opinion, "the devil alone knoweth." But something has changed today. Two states, Montana and Idaho, have abolished the defense, falling back on *mens rea* to "carry the freight" (Morris, 1982, p. 65). Other states may follow. The Supreme Court has already ruled in State v. Strasburg (1910) and Sinclair v. State (1931) that some form of an insanity defense seems constitutionally required (Gerber, 1984), but which form remains an open question.

The reaction to calls for abolishment from jurists and professional experts has generally been negative. Most often the defenders of the insanity defense cite our Anglo-American tradition, as the following quote

from the American Psychiatric Association's Statement on the Insanity
Defense (1982) reveals:

> The American Psychiatric Association. speaking as citizens as well as psy-
> chiatrists, believes that the insanity defense should be retained in some form.
> The insanity defense rests upon one of the fundamental premises of the criminal
> law, that punishment for wrongful deeds should be predicated upon moral
> culpability. However, within the framework of English and American law, de-
> fendants who lack the ability (the capacity) to rationally control their behavior do
> not possess free will. They cannot be said to have "chosen to do wrong."
> Therefore, they should not be punished or handled similarly to other criminal
> defendants. Retention of the insanity defense is essential to the moral integrity
> of the criminal law. (p. 9)

To the abolitionist, citing "tradition" seldom satisfies. As Morris (1982)
puts it, "operationally the defense of insanity is a tribute, it seems to me, to
our hypocrisy rather than to our morality" (p. 64). And if turnabout is fair
play, abolitionists can cite their own historical traditions, ancient and modern: the pre-Norman, Saxon law, based on "strict liability," and Holmes'
"objective theory of liability" both focus on outer conduct, excluding from
consideration those devilishly troubling "inner facts." "Why," entreat the
abolitionists, "can we not return to objective, observable, outer facts?"

They deserve an answer.

I will offer one, using an illustration that does not involve insanity to
make the point. In this example, a man has been killed by gunshot and the
assailant has been taken into custody. A crime has been committed, and
the prosecution must build a case and present a charge. But what charge?
A carefully premeditated murder? A murder hastily conceived and enacted
within moments? A reckless prank, intended to scare but not kill, that
fatally misfires? A negligent display of a pistol thought to be empty, but
was not? A provoked quarrel that escalated? Or an act of self-defense?

How is the prosecution to decide based on "outer facts" alone? Must
not the prosecution, as the jurors who will eventually hear the case, consider those "inner facts" that deal with intentions and those "triable
thoughts" of man? Even when insanity is not a consideration, objective
liability breaks down. We are, as a society, uncomfortable treating all the
above possibilities as the same, punishing them all equally. That "the
punishment fit the crime" is a principle we hold dearly and one that neces-
sitates an understanding of the crime beyond its observable facts. And we
have crimes in our statutes, such as recklessness, negligence, and gross
negligence that require of a jury to make fine discriminations based usually
upon inferred intentions.

If we abolish the insanity defense because we are uncomfortable with
"inner facts," more than just the insanity defense will topple. This, I believe, we are unprepared and unwilling *in principle* to do. If we try to retreat
to the *mens rea* formula, as former Attorney General William French Smith

proposed in his testimony before the Judiciary Committee of the United States Senate (1982), which would return us to the "wild beast" test, in effect, we still have the *Hadfield* problem.

If we cannot finesse the insanity issue, then we must return to the fray. This we will do in detail in Chapters 10 and 11. The purpose in tracing the historical roots, major evolutions, and running contentions surrounding the insanity defense is to leave us better prepared to find more workable options later, rather than blindly retracing many of history's dead ends without ever knowing it.

One final topic remains in this historical developments section: the courtship of law and psychology. The central question is how it came to pass that these two disciplines, law and psychology, came to woo and woe and wonder about what went wrong. And the point of such an inquiry is to educe the principal and pragmatic grounds for a proper relationship between two disciplines that do, and must, interact.

3

The Courtship of Law and Psychology

THE FIRST PROFESSION

In the beginning there was psychology, primitive yet powerful. So it appeared to the anthropologist, Sir James George Frazer, in his epic, *The Golden Bough* (1963, p. 52). In that work, Frazer takes us back to a time of savage societies, before communities and cultures evolved, when out of the undifferentiated group emerged the first profession. They came to be known as magicians, sorcerers, shamans, and wizards, and, as individuals, rose to "a position of much influence and repute," oftentimes acquiring "the rank and authority of a chief or King."

It is important to understand Psychology's early beginning and potency for two reasons. The first is to counteract the widespread but illusory notion that psychology, psychiatry, and psychotherapy are somehow new disciplines whose parentage began with Freud. It is clear from Freud's own writings (1963) on the topic that he shared no such illusion. "In the first place, let me remind you that psychotherapy is in no way a modern method of healing. On the contrary, it is the most ancient form of therapy in medicine."

The second reason is to bring to light the multiple roles the magician

49

played in those societies, for those roles created fissures, tensions, and a legacy that is still with us today. Frazer notes that before separate specialties evolved, the magician wore many hats: he or she was a healer, a herbalist, a priest, prophesier, politician, and establisher of societal rules and social mores. Shamans were not only powerful and paternal, they were preemptive. Mircea Eliade (1964) a noted authority on shamanism, writes that

> this small mystical elite not only directs the community's religious life but, as it were, guards its "soul." The shaman is the great specialist in the human soul; he alone "sees" it, for he knows its "form" and its destiny. (p. 8)

With a "job description" such as this, it should be no surprise that

> the profession accordingly draws into its ranks some of the ablest and most ambitious men of the tribe, because it holds out to them a prospect of honour, wealth, and power such as hardly any other career could offer.
> . . . The general result is that at this stage of serial evolution the supreme power tends to fall into the hands of men of the keenest intelligence and the most unscrupulous character. (Frazer, 1922, pp. 52–53).

The ancient therapist could be extraordinary and sagacious or a charlatan and trickster; the assessment of "the profession," therefore, was likely to be a mixture of veneration and suspicion. When the modern descendants (e.g., alienists, psychiatrists, and psychologists) enter the court, take the witness stand, and recite their credentials, the court and the community are apt to perceive not only the modern therapist, but the ghosts of his or her illustrious and nefarious forebears.

One tension that has produced contention involves the magicians' private and public sides: what they "know" about the soul and the dark interior of human emotions and motivations is shrouded in secrecy, oftentimes in a "private" language unintelligible to the public; yet in their public role, with its impact on the whole community, they must make themselves understood. When the modern healer and forensic expert enters the courtroom to offer testimony, he or she often speaks in a language and thinks in dynamics that are foreign to lawyers, judges, and jurors.

As the roles of the magician began to differentiate into separate specialties, a fissure grew between the medical, scientific side, and the psychological, spiritual perspective. Some healers would talk of souls, while others of the body: the latter spoke a language akin to physics; the former, to metaphysics. Between these two perspectives fundamental disagreements arose regarding mind and brain, their importance, and their relation. The medico-scientific perspective believed that mental abnormalities were ultimately to be explained in terms of lesions and brain chemistry; pitted against this view was a perspective that maintained that psychology was not reducible to mere physiology. All sides would have their say in the coming comingling and courtship with law; unfortunately, however, the speeches of the psychological experts were all too often metaphorically and contradictorily mixed, leaving their audiences with some reasonable doubts about the validity of this *new* science.

MEDICINE AND MORALITY

The beginning of the courtship, perhaps the very first date, occurred in the year 1656. The historian Michel Foucault explains the importance of the date and what followed in his work *Madness and Civilization: A History of Insanity in the Age of Reason* (1973). In that year, a decree was issued that founded the Hopital General in Paris. More than just an administrative reorganization that brought several existing establishments under a single administration, the decree established a "semijudicial structure" by which the King could confine individuals without trial or appeal simply by issuing *lettres de cachet*. Those hospitals, many of which were former leprosariums that had been emptied of that scourge and scapegoat, soon came to house a new collection of "social marginals": the poor, the mendicants, spendthrift fathers, prodigal sons, blasphemers, libertines, criminals, and, most of all, the insane. Within these walls, power and direction would fall to the physician.

Foucault (1973, p. 64) cites this landmark date as marking a distinct rift in the reason–madness nexus. In the Renaissance, reason and madness confronted one another and dialogued: in *King Lear* and *Don Quixote*, the mad "floundered about in broad daylight"; in Hieronymus Bosch's (Gibson, 1973) paintings, such as *The Cure of Madness* and *The Ship of Fools*, they were publicly portrayed; in Sebastian Brant's (Zeydel, 1944; Maher & Maher, 1982) *Das Narrenshchiff* (The Ship of Fools) and in Erasmus's (1735/1958) *Moriae Encomium* (The Praise of Folly), the discourse was poetic and spirited. But in the Age of Reason, which became the age of confinement, silence fell.

> In the serene world of mental illness, modern man no longer communicates with the madman . . . the man of reason delegates the physician to madness, thereby authorizing a relation only through the abstract universality of disease. . . The language of psychiatry, which is a monologue of reason *about* madness, has been established only on the basis of such a silence. (Foucault, 1973, pp. x–xi).

Physicians were no longer chieftains and kings, but within the hopitals, *Zuchthausern*, and houses of correction (Howard, 1784), they still ruled. The classical age of the seventeenth and eighteenth centuries was an age of the great physicians: Thomas Sydenham, who was called "the English Hippocrates" (Comrie, 1922), wrote the *Complet Method of Curing Almost All Diseases* (1695); Thomas Willis (1679) was credited with "liberating hysteria from the old myths"; and Robert Whytt (1767) was physician to King George III. If the King would place his health in the hands of such physicians, surely the confined insane were receiving just medicine.

As it turns out, physicians were prescribing a mix of medicine, morality, and metaphor. Take, for example, the theories and treatments of hysteria. The seventeenth-century physicians had finally discredited the Greek theory of hysteria: the womb, they discovered, did not dislodge, float, and somersault within the interior space of the woman. While that explanation was discarded, a theoretical vacuum was left. The theoretical vacuum and physical interior would quickly be filled by a host of theories. One theory proposed that the interior was filled with a humid heat, while another proposed a hot, dry effervescence. Yet another theory focused on the heaviness of blood, thick and stagnant, while still another saw the fluids as volatile and having excessive mobility. In the realm of chemical analogues, one view saw hysteria as a fermentation, alkaline in nature; another theory viewed it as a chain of acidic reactions.

There were moral and medical theories as well. The body's interior space, filled with humors and animal spirits seen only with the eyes of the mind, attacked and racked by disease, served as a ready Rorschach for mental–moral projections. Women, more so than men—because women were more delicate, less firm, and because they led a softer life—were the subject of much "medical" speculation. Their spatial density became a moral density, too yielding to disease because morally they were too lax. Without a proper moral and physical density, their frail fibers, like violin strings too taut, would resonate too strongly and carry the movements of their imagination and the heat of their passions too far.

> And as a result, one [a woman] was both more innocent and more guilty. More innocent, because one was swept by the total irritation of the nervous system into an unconsciousness great in proportion to one's disease. But more guilty, much more guilty, because everything to which one was attached in the world, the life one had led, the affections one had had, the passions and the imaginations one had cultivated too complacently—all combined in the irritation of the nerves, finding there both their natural effect and their moral punishment. (Foucault, 1973, p. 143).

PUNISHMENT, TREATMENT, AND THE PRESUMPTION OF EXPERTISE

"Punishment" and "treatment," concepts that seem antithetical, were confused, fused, and rolled into one. If "idleness" was both the cause and the sin of insanity, then work was its fitting remedy. Hoping to capitalize on the cheap labor of the inmates and turn a profit, a number of *Zuchthausern* actually specialized in a particular product: spinning in Bremen and Berlin, weaving in Hanover, wood shredding in Hamburg, polished optical glass in Nuremberg, and milling flour in Mainz. While the profit failed to materialize, the "therapy" of work remained firmly in place. A motto inscribed on a *Zuchthausern* in Mainz read "If wild beasts can be broken to the yoke, it must not be despaired of correcting the man who has strayed" (cited in Howard, 1784)

Here we see the "wild beast" imagery, along with a model of *domestication*. The "beast," like the child, needed to be tamed and yoked to the social, moral order. The physician would administer the hospital, tame the beast, and domesticate the child; and in these ways, the physician would serve all the functions Frazer ascribed to the ancient shaman: the physician would administer therapeutics and potions, serve as secular priest and surrogate parent, and would be the prescriber and preserver of a social, moral order. All of these functions, to repeat, were carried out independently of the courts.

From the vantage point of the physicians, alienists, and psychiatrists, the medico-psychological perspective assumed eminent domain over the insane. After all, they were the appropriate professionals in this jurisdiction, not the courts. Indeed, they had been functioning in a juridical as well as a therapeutic capacity since 1656. And their *parens patriae* power had been sanctioned by none other than the King. If a certain haughtiness was evident on the part of alienists when they took the stand in insanity cases, it perhaps becomes understandable when cast in this historical light. To the alienists, it was not they, but the courts, who were the interlopers.

MEDICINE'S INSECURITIES AND INROADS

The medical experts' "haughtiness" hid a hollowness that no amount of jargon and empirics could cover. Beneath their public utterances regarding natural law and the nature of disorder—which, for the most part, they delivered on the witness stand with all the airs of medical certainty—the medical profession and perspective were subject to suspicion and open to challenge. Within the helping profession, the greatest challenge was mounted by the "moral therapists," men such as Pinel in France and Tuke in England. Moral therapy, which has been called "the first mental health revolution" (Hobbs, 1964), viewed man and disorder in a much more "psychological," "emotional" way than the medical accent on bodily dysfunctions. What Thomas Szasz (1961) in the twentieth century would call "problems of living," the moral therapists would identify as stresses of life that were psychological in nature and that they referred to as *moral causes* (Bockoven, 1956).

In 1793, Pinel, who was physician and superintendent at the Bicetre hospital, pled for permission and authorization from the ruling Commune to remove the chains and fetters from the patients.

> It was no accident that the first mental health revolution occurred in France. . .
> The French Revolution had already provided the vocabulary: liberty, equality,
> and fraternity. But it was Phillipe Pinel who daringly asked that these rights be
> extended to include those hospitalized in mental institutions". (Finkel, 1976b, p.
> 19)

The Commune, whose president at the time was Cauthon, was suspicious, and the crippled Cauthon, carried on a litter, visited Bicetre. The inmates hurled epithets and feces at him, after which the following dialogue ensued (Zilboorg & Henry, 1941, p. 322):

> Cauthon: Well, citizen, are you mad yourself that you want to unchain these
> animals?
> Pinel: Citizen, it is my conviction that these mentally ill are intractable only
> because they are deprived of fresh air and of their liberty.
> Cauthon: You may do what you please, but I am afraid that you are the victim of
> your own presumptions.

Moral therapy spread to England where the philosophy was put into practice by William Tuke and his fellow Quakers at the Retreat near York. Similar reforms occurred in Italy, Germany, and America. The treatments at the new asylums related to the word "morale," and were designed to promote hope, zeal, spirit, and confidence. The cure and discharge rates (Tuke, 1813/1964), which were the highest for any period of psychiatric practice, prompted Bockoven (1956) to call moral treatment "psychiatry's forgotten success" (p. 177). Whereas Sydenham prescribed cathartics for the bowels and Willis prescribed emetics to induce vomiting, and numerous other physicians prescribed bleeding and sundry other physical remedies (Finkel, 1976a), the moral therapists reached a different conclusion. Samuel Tuke (1913/1964) wrote the following regarding the judgment of Dr. Thomas Fowler, the physician appointed to attend at the Quaker Retreat near York:

> But the sanguine expectations, which he successively formed of benefit to
> be derived from various pharmaceutic remedies, were, in great measure, as
> successively disappointed; and, although the proportion of cures, in the early
> part of the Institution, was respectable; yet the medical means were so imper-
> fectly connected with the progress of recovery, that he could not avoid suspect-
> ing them, to be rather concomitants than causes. Further experiments and obser-
> vations confirmed his suspicions; and led him to the painful conclusion, (painful
> alike to our pride and to our humanity), that medicine, as yet, possesses very
> inadequate means to relieve the most grievous of human diseases.
> Bleeding, blisters, seatons, evacuants, and many other prescriptions, which
> have been highly recommended by writers on insanity, received an ample trial;
> but they appeared to the physician too inefficacious to deserve the appellation of
> remedies. . . . (p. 111)

Dr. Fowler and the Quakers were in full accord with Dr. Pinel in France in their "comparative estimate of moral and medical means" (p. 132). In estimating moral means to be the superior medicine, they were implying a different view—a psychological view—of disorder. Medicine's "certainty" and "haughtiness" on the witness stand belied these fundamental disagreements within.

Insecurities and doubts neither daunted nor stayed the medico-psychological incursions into the legal realm of insanity. In fact, inroads had been made on a variety of fronts: the medico-psychological perspective remained dominant in the area of "involuntary commitment" of mental patients long before civil law statutes were codified and judicial review became commonplace; and medical experts were already dealing with questions of competency to manage money, property, write wills (testamentary capacity), and stand trial (insanity on arraignment). In addition, medico-psychological opinion frequently came into play after sentencing. In England, where the Home Secretary granted reprieves (i.e., continuing the practice of "the King's mercy"), it was not uncommon for the Home Secretary to cite medical opinion as the reason for commuting the sentence of an alleged insane offender who was found guilty at trial. If medical opinion did not sway the judge and jury during the trial, it still could carry the day at the review phase. And finally, as noted in the *Hadfield* case, where Parliament hastily drafted and enacted the Insane Offenders Act of 1800, the "acquitted" would now be turned over to the medical profession and their asylums for incarceration and treatment. If medico-psychological opinions and prescriptions were determinative before and after trial, then why not *during* the trial? And why not, then, in the writing of law?

To the medical establishment, these questions seemed so logical, whereas the legal "resistance" seemed fearfully irrational. From the medical point of view, physicians were not seeking some "new" inroad; rather, they were asking the courts and the community to sensibly (and medically) complete a circuit that had already been well paved.

DIVESTMENT

By this time, the reader may be questioning the metaphor of a courtship. If there is one, it seems to be entirely one-sided. And furthermore, the suitor, the medico-psychological discipline, seems more covetous than conciliatory. Is a covenant being sought, or is eminent domain the not-so-hidden end?

Actually, the courtship does go both ways. The other side of the courtship involves the process of *divestment*. Nicholas Kittrie (1971) gives the following meaning and examples of divestment:

> The criminal law in the United States has been undergoing a process of divestment—a relinquishing of its jurisdiction over many of its traditional subjects and areas. Many classes of criminal offenders are no longer subject to its sanctions: the mentally ill, the juvenile, and, at times, the alcoholic, the drug addict, and the psychopath. (p. 4)

When Kittrie looks at the best estimates for these divested groups and their sum, it leaves "only 46 out of every 100 Americans subject to the sanctions of the criminal process" (p. 5). He goes on to address both the motivation and implication of this process:

> This process of divestment has not been motivated, on the whole, by societal willingness to begin tolerating the conduct or condition previously designated as criminal. Instead, divestment has most frequently indicated a shift from criminal sanctions to a different system of social controls. Thus divestment, carried out in the name of the new social emphasis upon therapy, rehabilitation, and prevention—as contrasted with criminal law's emphasis upon retribution, incapacitation, and deterrence—has produced new types of borderline proceedings and sanctions, lodged between the civil and criminal law. (p. 5)

The impetus for divestment came from a change in the theory of criminology that occurred in the nineteenth century. Classical criminology, formulated in the eighteenth century's Age of Reason, was based largely on the ideas of Cesare di Beccaria (1880). His theory stressed the following points: criminals should be punished because they are individuals who have free will, which makes them responsible for their acts, and those criminal acts infringe upon the rights and liberties of others; "crime could best be prevented by punishing certain overt acts rather than by attempting to administer vague standards of moral virtue"; punishment should be proportionate to the crime and indifferent to individual differences, and the penalty is "measured by whether it suffices as a punishment, not by whether it succeeds at reformation"; punishment should serve as a future deterrent to the particular offender and to others as well; rules and procedures should be strict; innocence should be presumed; and punishment should be swift (Kittrie, 1971, p. 21).

Beccaria's ideas, along with John Howard's recommendation to establish a national penitentiary and Jeremy Betham's "pragmatic enlightenment," constituted the classical criminology. In the second half of the nineteenth century, the classical view, with its "free-will, egalitarian, yet mechanistic approach" (Kittrie, 1971, p. 24), came under sharp attack and rebuke from deterministic criminology. The challenge to the older view "stemmed from a growing scientific awareness of the multiplicity of the social causes of crime and the diversity of criminal types." This positivist orientation, which relied on experimental methods of analysis, combined social and constitutional determinism. In both types of determinism, psychology would play a dominant role.

Criminologists like Cesare Lombroso and Enrico Ferri were leading advocates of this new school of thought. This new approach fitted perfectly with psychiatric determinism, whose advocates, men such as Pritchard and Maudsley, viewed crime as moral insanity. When Ferri proposed abolishing criminal responsibility and moral guilt in favor of the idea that "punishment should fit the individual, not the offense," psychiatry and psychology smiled. This is just what the alienists had been arguing. When the new criminologists advocated humane measures to protect society and change the individual, rather than punishment fitting the crime, an open invitation was apparent to psychology, psychiatry, and the behavioral scientists; and the invitation was quickly accepted.

The causes of crime and their effective treatments seemed to fall squarely within the domain of the medico-psychological field. Heredity, constitutional factors, brain lesions, instincts, personality, unconscious drives, complexes, "the internal psychological makeup of the individual" (Kittrie, 1971, p. 29), became the central, relevant constructs. Almost overnight, when measured in "historical time," the concept of "punishment" had been replaced by the concept of "treatment." Less than one hundred years later, when the United States Supreme Court reviewed *Williams v. New York* (1949), Justice Hugo Black had this to say: "Retribution is no longer the dominant objective of criminal law. Reformation and rehabilitation of offenders have become the important goals of criminal jurisprudence." Divestment had moved swiftly (Kittrie, 1971, p. 33).

> At the end of the nineteenth century, juveniles were formally exempted from traditional criminal sanctions and proceedings. A special court was born on July 1, 1899, under an Illinois law that established a juvenile court in the City of Chicago. Through subsequent legislative and judicial actions, psychopaths (in the 1930s), drug addicts (in 1962), and alcoholics (in 1966) were similarly removed from the jurisdiction of the criminal law. (Kittrie, 1971)

The process of divestment implied a change in principles. A number of principles that had served as "sacred" pillars of insanity law were declared "profane" and knocked down. *Mens rea* ("evil mind" or the awareness of wrongdoing), which had been required for establishing moral guilt and necessary for administering punishment, was seen as less and less applicable to more and more offenders. A number of cases and courts took the position that the alcoholic and drug addict are devoid of *mens rea* when in the grip of their addiction. Without *mens rea*, criminal sanctions could not follow.

The principle of punishment was also taking a kick to the shins, being viewed as inappropriate or as "cruel and unusual," in violation of the Eighth Amendment to the United States Constitution. This line of attack was revealed in the *Robinson* (1962) case, which involved a drug addict.

> It is unlikely that any State at this moment in history would attempt to make it a criminal offense for a person to be mentally ill, or a leper, or to be afflicted with a venereal disease. . . Even one day in prison would be cruel and unusual punishment for the "crime" of having a common cold.

The Court not only invalidated punishment in this case, but supported the therapeutic approach (p. 660).

The principle of punishment fitting the crime seemed absurd when rehabilitation was the aim. A prison sentence of 10 years, or 20, or 30 was not logically sound when the goal was cure. "Time" needed to be *indeterminate*—however long it took to cure the sick person (e.g., the mentally ill, delinquent, sexual psychopath, addict, alcoholic). And the principle that punishment should come *after* the crime was viewed as an ineffective intervention point: "prevention" became a new guiding principle, and with it, a system of noncriminal procedures to control and treat *potential* offenders came into existence.

These emerging new principles and approaches, made possible by the union of a changing criminological theory coupled with a psychological endorsement, opened the door to what Kittrie called "The Therapeutic State." It is a state in which therapy replaces condemnation; where scientific considerations of social effectiveness outweigh religious, moral questions of right and wrong; and where a beneficent hand (*parens patriae*), based upon the curative power of science, is extended to the allegedly insane.

BLIND JUSTICE SEES A WOLF IN SHEEP'S CLOTHING

Not everyone was willing to take the beneficent hand of medicine, particularly when it was offered to the courts in insanity cases. One such resistant judge was Baron Bramwell. Judge Bramwell, whose most caustic comments were aimed at the alienists, was characterized by them as "prejudiced and vindictive" (Smith, 1981, p. 105). The alienists cited Bramwell's more outrageous utterances to back up their claim and discredit him. Bramwell had argued more than once that in cases where uncontrollable impulses were alleged "the need for punishment was even greater: the stronger the punishment the stronger the deterrence. 'I would control it by the fear of hanging, mad or not mad'" (Smith, p. 105).

Bramwell may have been the most vociferous opponent the alienists faced in the courtroom, but he was by no means a lone voice. The opposition to medicine, to its therapeutic orientation and its "medicalization" of morality, represented a significant and sizable faction of jurists. Prejudice, vindictiveness, and other unseemly motives may have been operating—on both sides. The alienists' dismissal of the opposition as merely irrational was itself a form of blindness.

The opponents of the medico-psychological perspective had a case. "Deterrence" was one issue that concerned and united the Queen, the commoner, and jurists such as Bramwell. Insanity was a judgment of nonresponsibility that voided culpability, and it left the "crime" unpunished. Moreover, it left fears that this escape route would foster more crimes, followed by more frequent pleas of insanity. The alienists' claims that the insane would not be deterred by punishment were rebutted by counterclaims that they could. Bramwell said (Smith, 1981) the unhappy madman is a person who requires the threat more than anybody else, because, from the condition of his mind, he is more likely to have some temptation to commit the offense, and less intelligence to deter him from doing it. (p. 74)

Another point the opposition made was that the intrusion of medical views would usurp the jury's function. Some alienists were bold enough to rejoin that that's how it should be—that it was a medical decision, requiring specialized knowledge beyond the ken of laymen and lawyers. Yet many alienists testified in common language, invoking commonly available criteria in making their diagnoses. Many laymen, along with judges like Bramwell, assumed that they could exercise the same critical common sense. For Bramwell (1874), laymen (and jurists) had an additional advantage: they kept "in mind the law's retributive and utilitarian functions," which alienists seemed all too willing to overlook.

More than usurping the jury's function, medicine threatened to usurp the court's function as well. Parallel and competing discourses were occurring: the law discoursed about guilt whereas medicine discoursed about disease; moreover, medicine claimed that the law's discourse was irrational and inappropriate. Here are Maudsley's (1876) words:

Thus then when we take the most decided forms of human wrong-doing, and examine the causes and nature of the moral degeneracy which they evince, we find that they are not merely subjects for the moral philosopher and the preacher, but they rightly come within the scope of positive scientific research. (p. 33)

"Positive scientific research," the flag and contention of medicine, was unfurled before a legal system that "epitomised social reaction and unreason" (Smith, 1981, p. 14). Science had come of age, presaging a new era, claimed the alienists. This is an era where responsibility gives way to disease, where theology and psychology yield to physiology, where conventional morality is superseded by natural law, and where the Law itself is replaced by Medicine.

Some alienists went even further: instead of contending that morality was being replaced by a "value-free" science, these alienists believed that medicine could bring about a new moral order. Their public utterances were often extravagant, if not alarming, like the following by Dr. Wigan: "I firmly believe that I have more than once changed the moral character of a boy by leeches to the inside of the nose" (Smith, 1981, p. 64). Perhaps the leading extremist among the alienists was Forbes Winslow (1854), who sincerely believed that medicine could bring about a new moral order. For Winslow, only in a state of health was the mind open to moral truths (Smith, 1981).

Thus he believed that the tyranny of a Nero or a Robespierre might be "undetected, unperceived, unrecognised mental disease, in all probability aris-

ing from cerebral irritation or physical ill-health." His logic implied the medi-
calisation of all crime and the elimination of all tyranny by a good system of
medical policing. This was extreme, but it indicated the direction in which the
insanity defence led. It proposed the creation of a society in which evil and
retribution had no meaning. Few Victorians were prepared for this. Even the
alienists, Winslow among them, were caught in the tension between morality
and management. But in their eyes, the scientific study of nature provided an
objectively valid way forward. (p. 33)

But the law did not yield. It was more than a matter of who had the
best arguments. In this arena, the law had history, tradition, and power on
its side; and what is more, it was in this arena—before a judge, bounded
by legal rules, netted in an adversary process, and decided by ordinary
citizens—that the alienist-gladiator had to enter to stake a claim. "The
law's lineage and power meant that it was medicine, rather than law,
which had to justify itself" (Smith, 1981, p. 67). More than one alienist
decried this "home field" advantage.

The extension of the Therapeutic State threatened more than the
court's hold over insanity cases. The views of Winslow and Maudsley were
applicable to all criminality, not just to insanity cases. Robbers, burglars,
pickpockets, or what have you, have their own nerve centers, heredity,
unconscious, and environment: their wiring and machinery, both endowed and conditioned, were programmed. The agent in the machine was a
myth. Determinism left no inner place for the language of "responsibility"
and "free will" to reside. Thus "responsibility" and "free will"—those
superstitious, archaic remnants, homeless in a hard-wired brain but given
sanctuary within the law—were threatened by the spectre of medicalization, which could only lead to their extinction.

From the law's viewpoint, this mechanistic view of all human behavior
"was a fatal flaw in the medical discourse" (Smith, 1981, p. 81), and they
homed in on it. Maudsley (1876) for one, invited this attention with
provocative statements like the following:

> It is certain, however, that lunatics and criminals are as much manufactured
> articles as are steam-engines and calico-printing machines, only the processes of
> the organic manufactory are so complex that we are not able to follow them.
> They are neither accidents nor anomalies in the universe, but come by law and
> testify to causality; and it is the business of science to find out what the causes
> are and by what laws they work. (p. 28)

As Smith (1981) remarked,

> If lunatics and criminals were "manufactured," the implication was that the law,
> being drama rather than technology, was superfluous. It was a small logical step
> to claim that not only legal judgment but also moral judgment was supersitition.
> Jurists therefore attacked the insanity defence as a slippery slope to moral and
> political anarchy. (p. 81)

Jurists opposed to medicalization got some unexpected help from within the ranks of the alienists themselves. Dr. Thomas Mayo, a leading expert on mental disease, and conservative in his views, became an anathema to the alienists. Mayo's views and cautions gave the legal opposition the expertise it lacked when it came to evaluating critically the nature of medical "facts." And from a scientific perspective, there was much that was suspect.

Many alienists, when they testified and wrote on the topic of insanity, confounded observation and interpretation, passing it all off as *fact*. Diagnosis, which is such an important ingredient in the weighing of insanity claims, oftentimes rested more on inference and interpretation than on direct observation. The disease wasn't seen, only inferred from the behavior. Yet, to the alienists, the inference was so self-evident that it was taken *as fact*. Let us use an illustration we are familiar with from a previous chapter (see Chapter 1). In the *Hadfield* case, the defense attorney Erskine rubbed Hadfield's head wound, presented evidence regarding the injury, and speculated that there was a connection between Hadfield's disfigured brain, his delusional ideas, and his attempted assassination of King George III. Let us grant the diagnosis, that Hadfield had an organic brain syndrome. But so did many returning from the war with head wounds. However, very few developed delusions regarding Christ's second coming, and none, save Hadfield, purchased a pistol to fire on the King. The *causal* relationship between the disease and the criminal act was still missing.

Alienists, in their courtroom diagnosing, got into more hot water by failing to recognize the circularity and fallacy of their diagnostic procedures. Many times they would infer a disordered mind because of the nature of the defendant's prior acts, and then because they inferred a diseased mind, they pronounced the criminal act "insane." Winslow didn't see this as circular: in defense of this practice he exclaimed, "The act itself bears insanity stamped on its very face!" (Smith, 1981, p. 59).

The so-called science of medicine was actually quite split. In theory, and particularly when alienists discoursed on the pathology of insanity, they wrote about physiology in physical–chemical terms. In this regard, they relied heavily upon neurological concepts. Maudsley (1863) noted that "the physician who studies insanity as a disease finds, then, that he has mainly to do with the reflex action of the spinal cord, and of the sensory ganglia, and of the ganglionic cells of the cerebral hemispheres" (p. 327). But in practice, particularly when it came to diagnosis, the language was psychological, and their testimony on the mind disordered seemed familiarly metaphysical.

In regard to this physical–metaphysical split and discrepancy, most alienists remained blind, save when they attacked Dr. Mayo and hurled the very same charge at his doorstep. The medical journal *The Lancet* (1855) had this to say:

> Dr. Thomas Mayo came forward to propound, not evidence, but metaphysical speculations; and to apply to a living fellow-creature his famous doctrines of abstract mental disease, of insane responsibility, and the propriety of making madmen the subjects of criminal punishment." (Smith, 1981, p. 138)

The Lancet, speaking for "the modern mental physiologist," "considered Mayo's statement that 'the immaterial element may be just as subject to its proper affectations as the material one' dangerous nonsense" (Smith, 1981, p. 119).

The alienists, fighting a two-front campaign against jurists like Bramwell and physicians like Mayo, were caught in still another dilemma: they could not connect their general theories with specific, individual diagnosis. Their general theories talked of brain lesions—impaired *structures*—but they were really dealing with impaired *functions.* Here again, they confused and fused the two. Alienists claimed in their own defense that postmortem examination would detect the lesion (which, more often than not, it did not); but in the present life of the defendant, at the moment of trial, alienists could not furnish *the facts* of structural damage and its causal link to behavior. Even the jurist Fitzjames Stephen, who was open-minded to medicine and studied the latest works on the topic of insanity and responsibility in preparing to draft a criminal code, found the connection between theory and fact to be too weak. Smith (1981) put it this way:

> Stephen's search for a usable medico-legal formula was frustrated. He hoped that medical men would supply him with scientific facts which could become legal facts. But alienists did not have this kind of knowledge.
> "If medical men could tell lawyers precisely how A's mind was affected in relation to a particular act by the mental disease under which A was labouring when he did that act, the lawyers could tell whether or not the act was a crime; but this is just what medical men cannot tell. Generally they can only say that A did in fact labour under a particular disease with the nature of which they are very imperfectly acquainted, but how that disease may have been related to any particular action of A's in most instances they cannot tell at all." (p. 58)

What we have at this juncture, beginning at the middle of the nineteenth century, is an ardent courtship that has turned into a heated struggle. The courts had practical and substantive problems to weigh regarding insanity and responsibility. Regarding the dark interior and mystery of the mind, jurists were blind. In turning to the medical profession, they sought light. But the lights of medicine were fed by a heroic optimism that neurophysiological concepts could solve the problem. The medico-psychological perspective, ardently represented in court by the alienists, believed that those concepts had solved the problem already. This was their blindness. In prematurely announcing that science had arrived and a new era had dawned, their contention became pretention. What had arrived were brain mythologies.

What is clear from the developing historical picture is that divestment continued and the Therapeutic State grew. But in the area of criminal insanity, medicine's progress was slowed, and, in some areas, stymied. What the medico-psychological perspective had on its side was time: time for new facts to accumulate, for their professional standing to rise, and for the developing portrait of Psychological Man to come into clearer focus. When (and if) they did, their opinions on matters of criminality and insanity would be persuasive, and their claims, undeniable. In the meantime, if the M'Naghten Rules were "elastic" enough, the alienists could stretch them; if they couldn't stretch enough, some new test would have to be found. And when, rather than if, such a new search began, medico-psychological influence would be ready.

The courtship, stormy as it was, would continue; it had to continue.

THE PSYCHOLOGICAL AGE

Between Wilhelm Wundt's establishment of the first experimental psychology laboratory at Leipzig in 1879 (Fancher, 1979) and the present, "psychology" in its widest sense truly came of age. Its nineteenth-century pioneers, the likes of Wundt, James, and Charcot, were succeeded by the likes of Pavlov, Watson, Binet, Freud, Jung, Piaget, and Skinner, to name but a significant few. In little more than a century, psychology and psychiatry moved from the fringes of philosophy and medicine "to chairs of eminence and couches of opulence in the finest universities and neighborhoods in the Western World" (London, 1964).

The impact, input, and infusion of psychological knowledge goes far beyond medicine and academia. Educational theory, practices, and testing bear the imprint of psychology. In areas such as business, organizational practices, advertising, politics, and diplomacy, psychological knowledge has been incorporated at an accelerating speed. The literature and schools of painting of the twentieth century have penned and painted psychological wisdom. And psychotherapy, once regarded disdainfully as a heresy within medicine, has become one of the twentieth century's established religions (Frank, 1961; Zilbergeld, 1983).

The prestige and acceptability that eluded the nineteenth-century alienists have now been acquired and accredited. In the terms and practices that relate most closely to insanity and the law, twentieth-century medico-psychological experts assume the witness stand with a far greater confidence than their forebears did: their descriptions of types of mental disorders are more detailed and discriminating; their diagnostic tools are more varied and validated; their knowledge regarding physical and psychological causation is grounded more solidly in empirics; and their treatments, be it physical, chemical, electrical, surgical, or psychological, are more potent.

Legal changes in insanity law in both England and in the United States did come about (see Chapter 2), with the medico-psychological perspective providing much of the impetus. In the United States, Isaac Ray's influence was a deciding factor in changing New Hampshire's law. In the States, as opposed to England, the irresistible impulse test was added in many jurisdictions. And the Durham Rule, by which Judge Bazelon hoped that psychiatrists could more fully inform the jurors as to the nature of a defendant's mental disease, became law in the District of Columbia, Maine, and the Virgin Islands. In England, the medico-psychological perspective was often deciding in bringing cases of automatism to a not guilty by reason of insanity verdict. The infanticide bills that were passed in England relied heavily upon what psychologists had to say regarding the physical and psychological effects of childbirth. "Diminished responsibility," which was imported from Scotland to England, recognized a different perspective of Psychological Man than had *M'Naghten*. And in both the United States and England, psychiatry continued to wield considerable influence, before and after trial, regarding who was judged to be insane on arraignment and who was judged insane enough to warrant the Home Secretary's mercy. Thus, significant, substantive changes in insanity law did result from medico-psychological input; and the law, to paraphrase Justice Frankfurter, was not arrested at the state of psychological knowledge when *M'Naghten* was formulated, but attempted to keep in step with medico-psychological advances.

A MEDICO-PSYCHOLOGICAL RETREAT

The question that the House of Lords put to the Justices following the M'Naghten verdict regarding how far medical experts could go in their testimony still remains. We have seen that the great majority of nineteenth-century alienists wanted to go all the way—answering not only the test question "Was the defendant, at the time of the act, aware that he or she was acting contrary to law?" but answering the ultimate question, "Was the defendant responsible?" In the twentieth century, we see evidence of a cautious, if not tactical, retreat on the part of the medical expert. Goldstein (1967) states that "there is widespread agreement that an expert witness may not be asked whether the defendant was "responsible." The reason for regarding this question as improper derives from a recognition, not evident to nineteenth-century alienists, that "the concept of responsibility is made up so inextricably of psychiatric, legal, and moral issues that it is regarded too complex to put to any individual" (p. 97).

But we still have the test question: May experts be asked their medical opinion as to whether the actual defendant, or a hypothetical, had knowledge of right and wrong? And *was this a medical* opinion? In the United States, the majority of courts took the position that it was a proper medical question. In the trial of Guiteau (*United States v. Guiteau*, 1882), the assassin of President Garfield, the court stated:

> If a witness is competent to give his opinion as to the mental condition of the accused, he is competent to state his opinion as to the degree of capacity, or of incapacity, by reason of disorder, and whether the disorder seemed to have reached such a degree as to deprive him of the knowledge of right and wrong. That capacity or incapacity is itself a question as to the extent of the disorder, if disorder exists, and is not a conclusion to be drawn from the existence of insanity. These witnesses were competent to speak to the question of sanity or insanity, and therefore, as to this question as to one of its degrees. (p. 546)

Curiously, and I think erroneously, the courts were going too far; certainly further than many psychiatrists felt comfortable going. Moreover, the courts seemed to be equating "insanity" with "mental disorder," thus overlooking the earlier distinction that the former was a legal concept whereas the latter was medical; in equating the two, and then asserting that "knowledge of right and wrong" is but an extension of the reach of a disorder rather than an inference, the courts seemed to be granting just what the nineteenth-century alienists had claimed.

But the voices of twentieth-century psychiatry were divided. Some, like Guttmacher and Weihofen (1952), maintained that it was "a fact question" (p. 294). On the other extreme was Zilboorg (1949), who stated that

> to force a psychiatrist to talk in terms of the ability to distinguish between right and wrong and of legal responsibility is—let us admit it openly and frankly—to force him to violate the Hippocratic oath, even to violate the oath he takes as a witness to tell the truth and nothing but the truth, to force him to perjure himself for the sake of justice. (p. 79)

The Group for the Advancement of Psychiatry (GAP, 1954) acknowledged that the issue of "knowledge" involved the nonmedical issue of legal responsibility, and by answering such a question, the psychiatrist was treading on "the juryman's function." Jerome Hall (1965) maintained that the disclaimers by psychiatry had gone too far: Hall recognized that morals and values were entwined with the question of knowledge, but he maintained that the psychiatrist, with his greater insight into the patient's value system, was in a better position than anyone else to answer such a question.

There were reasons for psychiatry to back away from the test and ultimate issue questions that they had fervently pursued a century ago. Perhaps they were more aware of their limitations, more conscious of the distinctions between legal and medical, factual and inferential matters. Antagonism to the Rules and the criminal procedures had built, as did the awareness that engaging in the process of determining criminal liability might undermine subsequent therapeutic effectiveness. Oaths and ethics, on the one hand, and trying to convey "psychiatric truths" while conforming to the Rules on the other, seemed to some to be incompatible.

Judge Bazelon, the author of the *Durham* rule, attempted to make it easier for psychiatrists to input in their own terms but without usurping the jury's role. To be relieved of responsibility under Durham, it must be proved beyond a reasonable doubt that the defendant was suffering from a diseased or defective mental condition and that the act was a *product* of the abnormality. What is called for is a causal connection between illness and act. But Leifer (1964) argues that the relationship is not a factual question but a definitional one. Leifer writes that "mental disease is not an independent variable which is inversely related to the dependent variable of free choice, but it is *by definition* inversely related to it" (p. 828). While I believe Leifer is wrong on that point, I do not doubt that some who testified committed the logical error of assuming that mental illness abrogates intention and responsibility. The trend under Durham's wider latitude, a trend that was pushed by lawyers wanting their expert witnesses to make the strongest case possible, led to the asking and answering of the test question. The lawyers asked, and the experts answered, but the answers didn't always agree. A battle between opposing experts was not what the nineteenth-century alienists had in mind.

Of late, the medical profession has retreated to more defensible ground. The recent American Psychiatric Association Statement on the Insanity Defense (1982) reflects this retreat.

> When, however, "ultimate issue" questions are formulated by the law and put to the expert witness who must then say "yea" or "nay," then the expert witness is required to make a leap in logic. He no longer addresses himself to medical concepts but instead must infer or intuit what is in fact unspeakable, namely, the *probable relationship* between medical concepts and legal or moral constructs such as free will. These impermissible leaps in logic made by expert witnesses confuse the jury. Juries thus find themselves listening to conclusory and seemingly contradictory psychiatric testimony that defendants are either "sane" or "insane" or that they do or do not meet the relevant legal test for insanity. This state of affairs does considerable injustice to psychiatry and, we believe, possibly to criminal defendants. These psychiatric disagreements about technical, legal, and/or moral matters cause less than fully understanding juries or the public to conclude that psychiatrists cannot agree. In fact, in many criminal insanity trials both prosecution and defense psychiatrists do agree about the nature and even the extent of medical disorder exhibited by the defendant at the time of the act.
>
> Psychiatrists, of course, must be permitted to testify fully about the defendant's psychiatric diagnosis, mental state and motivation (in clinical and commonsense terms) at the time of the alleged act so as to permit the jury or judge to reach the ultimate conclusion about which they, and only they, are expert. Determining whether a criminal defendant was legally insane is a matter for legal fact-finders, not for experts. (p. 14)

On other matters, such as where the burden of proof of insanity should rest—on the defendant or the prosecution—the American Psychiatric Association (1982) "is exceedingly reluctant to take a position" and leaves this matter "for legislative judgment" (pp. 12–13). Even on matters where traditionally they have had hegemony, as in involuntary treatment and release following insanity, the American Psychiatric Association now believes

> that the decision to release an insanity acquittee should not be made *solely* by psychiatrists or *solely* on the basis of psychiatric testimony about the patient's mental condition or predictions of future dangerousness. (p. 16)

To more fully understand this retreat, as well as to assess the current (and predict the future) state of the courtship, we must turn to a final subsection, where the Therapeutic State, along with its assumptions and adherents, finds itself back in court, albeit in a very different role.

HEALER HEAL THYSELF, OR ELSE. . .

> It is, unfortunately, an all too common sight today for patients to enter the courtroom seeking relief from their healers as well as from their disorders; and therapists, formerly the defenders of mental health, now have to defend themselves and their practices". (Finkel, 1980, p. ix)

It has been remarked on more than one occasion that we live in a litigious age. In recent times, therapeutic practices of both the voluntary and involuntary variety have been brought before the court with increasing frequency (Finkel, 1984a), and a whole area of "mental health law" has resulted. The most vociferous critic of modern therapeutic practices, the psychiatrist Thomas Szasz (1963, 1970a, 1970b, 1973, 1976, 1977, 1978), is no longer a lone voice, having been joined by a chorus of professional and legal opinion. What had been isolated and infrequent arias on maddening mental health practices has now become a crescendo.

One of the earliest critics of "madhouses" and "mad-doctors" was the English novelist and journalist Daniel Defoe (Szasz, 1973, pp. 7–8), who, in 1728 exclaimed "against the vile practice now so much in vogue among the better Sort, as they are called, but the worst sort in fact, namely, the sending their Wives to Mad-Houses at every Whim or Dislike, that they may be more secure and undisturb'd in their Debaucheries. . . ," and who expressed his opinion that these mad-houses should be regulated.

The practices of Benjamin Rush (Butterfield, 1951; Corner, 1948; Runes, 1947), the father of American psychiatry, were questioned by his enemies (e.g., Alexander Hamilton) and friends (e.g., Thomas Jefferson) alike. There were "lunacy panics" in England in the nineteenth century (Smith, 1981, p. 69) and a crusade initiated by a Mrs. Packard (Szasz, 1973) in Illinois against false commitments. For the most part, these objections to the practices of the Therapeutic State failed to restrain either its growth or its power. In the area of involuntary commitment, for example, where laws regarding substantive grounds and procedural safeguards had been passed, Scheff (1973) reported in his study of one midwestern state that the average psychiatric interview of the patient lasted 9.2 minutes; and when the expert favored commitment, the decision was pretty much automatic.

This state of affairs has changed rapidly. Morton Birnbaum (1960) proposed "the right to treatment." He argued that if a person is involuntarily committed for treatment and fails to get (adequate) treatment, this amounts to cruel and unusual punishment and a deprivation of liberty without due process and equal protection, which violates the Eighth and Fourteenth Amendments of the Constitution. Cases such as *Rouse v. Cameron* (1967), *Wyatt v. Stickney* (1971), and *O'Connor v. Donaldson* (1975) brought to the court's attention troubling facts and questions regarding treatment. Did these hospitals provide a humane psychological and physical environment? When a hospital provided one psychiatrist for 5,000 patients, could adequate treatment exist? And were phrases such as "milieu therapy" merely euphemisms for "no treatment" at all?

The cause of patients was being championed by litigants and by critics within the mental health professions. Kittrie (1971) proposed a "therapeutic bill of rights" for patients; Ennis and Emery (1978) wrote an American Civil Liberties Union handbook on *The Rights of Mental Patients;* and Thomas Szasz (1982) has proposed the use of a "pychiatric will" to protect ourselves from unwanted, future interference on the part of psychiatry in the name of benevolence.

A companion to the "right to treatment" issue is the "right to refuse treatment" (Finkel, 1984b). As the Therapeutic State grew, so did the variety and potency of its treatments. Behavior modification, using contingent reinforcers and punishers, held out the promise for greater symptom management. Electroconvulsive (shock) treatment and psychopharmacological drugs promised faster relief from mood disorders (e.g., depression), thinking disorders (e.g., psychotic thoughts), and aberrant behavior. Psychosurgery, whereby a microelectrode is implanted deep within the brain, offered hope that violent, aggressive behavior could be controlled. Yet the promises of these potent techniques were challenged by patients and their lawyers on psychological and constitutional grounds.

In *Kaimowitz v. Michigan Department of Mental Health* (1973), psychosurgery was challenged. In *Rogers v. Okin* (1979, 1980, 1981) and *Rennie v. Klein* (1979, 1981), the courts granted a qualified right to refuse psychotropic medications. In *Knecht v. Gillman* (1973), the Iowa Security Medical Facility was enjoined from injecting nonconsenting residents with apomorphine, a morphine base, vomiting-inducing drug, as part of an aversive conditioning program aimed at controlling behavioral problems. And *Wyatt v. Stickney* (1971) set some limits on the use of behavior modification programs. As Finkel (1984a) commented:

> Our skillfulness, particularly in the area of treatment, has wedded the courts to mental health professionals with the thread and hope that therapy will set the courts and allegedly mentally ill free from their respective disorders. The promise has not yet panned out. Involuntary treatment and hospitalization have not been effective remedies, and their failures have led patients back to the

courts, where they assert their right to treatment, or to be free. Our more potent treatments, such as drugs, electro-convulsive therapy (shock treatment), behavior modification, and psychosurgery, have led patients back to the courts, this time asserting their right to refuse treatment. Therapists and patients, the community and the courts, find themselves entangled and confused like never before. (p. 124)

Even as we pause in matters of criminal insanity, as legislators, jurists, and mental health professionals contemplate the smorgasbord of proposed changes that have been offered (Arenella, 1983), psychologists have been entering the courtroom in a new capacity—to present research findings regarding jury size, eye-witness identification, sensation, perception, motivation, confessions, and almost any and all matters psychological (Loftus & Monahan, 1980). We can already see a future that promises more psychologists in the courtroom, not fewer.

At the same time, there is discernible and refreshing change in the courtship: both parties, law and psychology, seem more willing and ready to examine their assumptions, expectations, practices, and ethics (Fitch, Petrella, & Wallace, 1987; Grisso, 1987; Rogers, 1987b; Slovenko, 1987). The inevitable "morning after" has dawned. When one awakens and discovers a marriage entered into blindly, a number of options are available. Some would favor a divorce, others would woo and pursue more vigorously, and still others would rethink (Fersch, 1980). I believe it is important for both parties to rethink. Justice no can longer afford to be blind in matters of divestment; "medicalization" of its most vexing problems and therapizing them away have not worked to the best advantage of all concerned. Our principles underlying punishment and treatment need reexamination. The rights of the defendant-turned-patient need to be weighed against the rights of the victim and the community. And Psychology, the first profession, must come to grips with what it can and cannot do.

The twentieth-century healer stands today at ancient crossroads: "the healer's knowledge, powers, and desire to help leads to the therapeutic path, yet the 'right' to traverse that path and the 'correctness' of that path have been called into question" (Finkel, 1980, p. 2). The practices of defining and diagnosing mental illness, of predicting dangerousness, and of treating both, need to be scrutinized; so, too, do the limits of benevolence (Gaylin, Glasser, Marcus, & Rothman, 1978). For the healer to heal thyself requires an ethical examination to disentangle questions of fact from questions of value.

> Disentanglement does not necessarily mean divorce: a separation may be healthy in order to analyze our practices, ethics, and conceptions, our language and intent; a separation may also provide the time to examine what each can do well, what promises we can keep and can't, and what we may reasonably expect from the other. Psychology and law can relate, do relate, and in some sense, must relate. We still search, in action and reflection, for the sane, common ground." (Finkel, 1984a, p. 124)

II

Background Issues—Basic Concepts, False Hopes, and Erroneous Beliefs

4

The Concept of Mental Illness (Disease)

The historical courtship and developing contention between the disciplines of law and psychology finally seems to have produced an understanding that "insanity" is a legal, not a psychiatric, concept. In the process of differentiating "insanity" from "mental illness," a corollary has emerged and gained the status, in some quarters, of a self-evident truth: the corollary asserts that mental disease is a medical concept, and one that the medico-psychological expert is uniquely, if not solely, qualified to address. Some are no doubt content with this decoupling. After all, the error of the alienists—of conflating "the two quite distinct concepts" (Moore, 1984) of *legal insanity* and *mental illness*—has been undone, and now each discipline can deal with and decide matters that fall within its own special province. But like Neville Chamberlain's "peace in our time" proclamation, there are reasons to suspect that the forecasted era of detente is an error of naive optimism.

Skepticism arises principally on two counts. First, the concept of "mental illness"—how it is understood and what it implies—remains shadowy yet central in the various insanity tests of today. A second reason for skepticism concerns the relationship between "mental illness" and "legal insanity." Since *some relationship* still exists between the two, as the various insanity tests denote, we still have the unsolved problem of specifying the nature of that relationship. An acknowledged decoupling of "mental illness" and "legal insanity" does nothing, in and of itself, to either define the former or specify its relationship to the latter.

This chapter begins by spotlighting the concept of mental disease. Three broad questions will be pursued. What is the meaning of "mental disease"? How has "mental disease" been related to "legal insanity"? And how should "mental disease" relate to "legal insanity"?

THE PROBLEM OF DEFINING MENTAL DISORDER

The concept of mental disease has its own problems; for one, it seems stubbornly resistant to definition. The most recent *Diagnostic and Statistical Manual of Mental Disorders* (DSM-IIIR; 1987) of the American Psychiatric Association has this to say regarding the basic concept of "mental disorder":

> Although this manual provides a classification of mental disorders, no definition adequately specifies precise boundaries for the concept "mental disorder" (this is also true for such concepts as physical disorder and mental and physical health). . . .
> There is no assumption that each mental disorder is a discrete entity with sharp boundaries (discontinuity) between it and other mental disorders, or between it and no mental disorder. (pp. xxii)

This lack of definition bedevils the discipline of psychology as well. The beginning student who opens an abnormal psychology text is apt to find plenty of discussion regarding abnormality but little in the way of a clear definition. The psychologist who opens the *American Psychologist*, the premier journal of the discipline, and reads the article by Smith and Kraft (1983) entitled "DSM-III: Do Psychologists Really Want an Alternative?" finds disclaimers and disparities, but finds neither a clear idea as to how to define mental illness nor a formulated approach for nosological taxonomy.

The lay person may find this lack of definition difficult to comprehend. Conservative estimates regarding the scope and extent of mental and emotional disorder reveal that *"at least 15 per cent* of the people in the United States will experience serious emotional problems *during any given year"* (Gallatin, 1982, p. 3), which translates into 30 or 40 million people. With numbers as large as these, and with these conservative figures reflecting only *serious* problems, it is likely that the lay person knows someone or is the someone with problems. With firsthand knowledge, along with some culturally ingrained beliefs (e.g., "mental illness is like physical illness") and popular images evoked by phrases such as "nervous breakdown," lay individuals are likely to possess their own understanding of what mental disorder is. So why is it that the appropriate professions are having difficulty?

Fingarette's (1972) illustration comparing the idea of mental disease with the idea of inadequate vision may help in understanding the difficulty. Let us say we wanted to determine if Jones has inadequate vision or not. We might start by referring Jones to the relevant medical professional, the ophthalmologist. The ophthalmologist, through examination and testing, reports back to us the degree to which Jones' vision deviates from the standard (norm) and in what ways it deviates. The ophthalmologist may also tell us whether the deviation results from problems associated with the cornea, pupil, iris, lens, the muscles that control the lens, the retina, choroid coat, and so forth. But has the professional told us whether Jones's vision is inadequate or not?

As Fingarette (1972) puts it,

> The question whether vision shall be considered adequate depends on the context of the use of that vision. Adequate vision for a ditch digger may not be adequate for a jeweler; and even a jeweler may have tunnel vision, a condition that does not substantially hinder his repair work but renders his vision inadequate for driving a vehicle. The medical condition of the eyes in each case may be the same, but the social task varies. Inadequate vision is thus in part an occupational concept. It is also a concept that can be rooted in public policy. For example, Jones may have adequate vision to drive in a community that is willing to take great risks and that has poor public transportation; whereas he may have inadequate vision in a community where public transportation is excellent and cheap, and where public policy favors minimizing risk. In either case the medical condition of Jones is the same. (p. 38)

When we move from analogies to the real thing, the problems of defining mental illness compound. One reason is the "behavior" itself. When we look at the symptoms and signs associated with mental disease today, we are no longer looking at just the extremes of deviancy (e.g., epileptic seizure, mania, depression, hysteria) that seemed so self-evidently bizarre. As we move away from the extreme of behavior toward the more "normal" end of the spectrum, discriminations become more difficult and our confidence in what is and is not mental illness declines. Such a movement has occurred in the area of psychopathology.

In the twentieth century, conditions called "personality disorders" and "transient situational personality disorders" found their way into the literature (DSM-I, 1952) and waiting rooms of psychiatry. When DSM-II (1968) was published, a new group of disorders, "behavior disorders of childhood and adolescence," was added. DSM-II also added a curious and contradictory category, "conditions without manifest psychiatric disorder and nonspecific conditions," which included such subtypes as "social maladjustment," "marital maladjustment," and "occupational maladjustment"; the inclusion of this category blurs the distinction between normal and mentally ill even further. With the advent of DSM-III in 1980, the pages of the manual more than tripled, and the number of newer and milder conditions increased again. Whereas some of the conditions in the manual are associated with physical causes or concomitants (e.g., Organic Mental Disorders, Substance Use Disorders), more are not. Thus, for most people who seek and come in contact with a mental health professional, "it is probably fair to say that they seek help mostly for irregularities of thought and feeling which result from irregularities of thought and feeling" (London, 1964, p. 17). As thoughts and feelings become the more dominant symptoms and clinical foci, and as behaviors tend to be more ordinary than extraordinary, the problems of defining and differentiating normal from abnormal becomes more difficult.

One difficulty is the problem of *context*. In Fingarette's example of inadequate vision, context makes a difference: the same degree of visual impairment is evaluated differently if the context is ditch digging, jewelry repair, rural driving, or urban driving. "Context" plays a considerable role in diagnosing mental illness, as the following examples illustrate. Consider a student on campus seen talking feverishly to himself. An observer might excuse the behavior as probably a case of last-minute cramming for an exam, a debate, or an oral report. But noting the same behavior, this time in an elderly woman on a street corner feverishly engaged in a monologue, may lead the observer to hypothesize more quickly about "abnormality." "Context" plays a determining role in the following examples.

> Overly aggressive behavior may be labeled as abnormal if the child is a girl, but not if the child is a boy. Shyness or withdrawal may be a problem if the child is a boy, but not for a girl. . . . Drug taking may or may not be labeled abnormal depending upon the subculture, streetcorner, or campus on which it is observed. . . . Promiscuous behavior may or may not be labeled abnormal, depending upon the city, state, or country in which it occurs. (Finkel, 1976b, p. 24)

And so on. A relativistic position (Mechanic, 1962) emerges: it is not just the behavior, but the behavior against the backdrop of context, that determines "whether a deviant act is evaluated as criminal, corrupt, or ill" (Finkel, 1976b, p. 24).

One context that is especially germane to diagnosing mental illness is the psychiatric hospital. Lewis Carroll's (1970, p. 89) dialogue between Alice and the Cheshire Cat, while talking about and taking place in Wonderland, could have applied equally as well to the psychiatric hospital.

> "We're all mad here. I'm mad. You're mad."
> "How do you know I'm mad?" said Alice.
> "You must be," said the Cat, "or you wouldn't have come here."
> Alice didn't think that proved it at all. . .

David Rosenhan (1973) tried to prove Alice's point by having eight sane people (pseudopatients) try to get themselves admitted to different psychiatric hospitals by complaining that they were hearing voices of a sort. They were all admitted. The plan was for each of them to then act perfectly normal and try to get discharged "essentially by convincing the staff that he was sane." Hospitalization lasted from seven to fifty-two days for the eight pseudopatients. Of special note here, in light of the issue of context (Fleischman, 1973) is the fact that the staff began to interpret certain behaviors of the pseudopatient, such as note taking and verbalizations that they were feeling fine, *as symptomatic* of schizophrenia.

Rosenhan's work leads us to a third problem—that of the "labeler." Rosenhan's pseudopatients got themselves admitted to the hospital; in a sense, the pseudopatients labeled and diagnosed themselves by appearing at the hospital. But many individuals who become patients in psychiatric hospitals get there in other ways. A dramatic example of one of those other ways is what the Secret Service and St. Elizabeth's Hospital staff call "White House cases." Consider the man who approaches the White House gate, insists on seeing the President of the United States, is angry that the President has not answered his last 243 letters, and says something to the effect that "If I don't get an answer, something is going to happen and you'll be sorry." This individual stands a good chance of being transported to a psychiatric hospital for evaluation and possible admission. The point is that *before* the psychiatrist gets to make a professional diagnosis, a prior "diagnosis" *has already been made.* In this case, the first diagnosis and labeler is the Secret Service agent. But it could be, in other instances, a family member, neighbor, storekeeper, policeman, general practitioner, clergyman, or spouse.

In an article entitled "The 'Last Straw': The Decisive Incident Resulting in the Request for Hospitalization in 100 Schizophrenic Patients" (Smith, Pumphrey, & Hall, 1973), the authors categorize these 100 incidents leading to hospitalization into three groups.

> Behavior was seen as (a) *actually or potentially harmful* to the patient or others, ("threatened to hit husband," "attacked mother with a gun," "choked a child," or "cut wrists in a suicidal attempt"); (b) *socially unacceptable* because of its embarrassing, disgusting, or puzzling nature, ("nude" in a public park, "ate raw chicken," "spit on the neighbors," or "irrational about radar"); and (c) *indicating mental illness and requiring treatment* in a mental hospital, ("thought he was losing his mind and begged his mother to take him to the hospital," "referred by her doctor because of hallucinations," or the husband knew she "was very ill when she accused a man in a car following her and misidentified the driver as Frank"). (p. 71)

Let us look at one example from above, the individual who "ate raw chicken." In a different culinary context, alongside steak tartare, raw oysters, or at a Japanese sushi bar, the individual may go unnoticed. However, in this example, someone did notice and that someone did make a judgment regarding mental illness. But was it a palatable or a psychiatric judgment?

What of other behaviors? "Refusing to eat" may be a sign of mental illness to some but an example of envious self-control to another. "Wandering," in the eyes of the poet, lover, or vagrant, may be judged differently than it would be by a storekeeper. The same goes for irrational talk, inexplicable behavior, uncontrollable crying, using obscene words, and so forth. Some behaviors are regarded with more alarm by family members than by citizens in the community, whereas for other behaviors, the reverse is true. The police (Bittner, 1973) arriving on the scene of a domestic quarrel may not see "mental illness" or the need to take someone to a hospital, whereas a family member may be convinced that it is the right and only course to take for someone so "disturbed."

The labeler's perceptions and interpretations are not only relevant for an admission to a hospital decision, they are also relevant to a formerly discharged patient seeking to remain at liberty. Miller (1967) noted that one factor that related to recidivism (the return of the patient back to the hospital) was the "tolerance for deviancy" displayed by significant others. If others view the person's behavior only as "odd," "quirky," or "eccentric" (i.e., "Well, that's the way he is"), they are more likely to let him be; if, on the other hand, they view the behavior as "symptomatic of disturbance," then they are more likely to want to send this former patient back to the hospital.

To summarize, reaching a diagnostic decision regarding mental disease is a complex process. The judgment takes in "behavior" in the widest sense—what is seen and what is inferred; it involves context; and it involves labelers, their perspectives, and their tolerances. But more, as was the case in inadequate vision, it involves values and issues that appear to take us beyond what is merely psychiatric.

MENTAL ILLNESS: A MEDICAL OR CROSS-DIMENSIONAL CONCEPT?

We thus arrive at a question: Is "mental illness" a medical concept or, as Fingarette (1972) puts it, a "cross-dimensional concept" (p. 37)? If the answer is "a medical concept," then it follows that mental illness falls within the area of expertise of the medico-psychological specialist, thereby reaffirming the alienists' preemptive claims of hegemony. But if the answer to the question is that "mental illness is a cross-dimensional concept"— where medical, legal, occupational, social, political, economic, actuarial, and moral factors play a part—then it follows that the medical perspective is but *one* view on this complex matter, rather than the solely authoritative view. An implication of this cross-dimensional answer is that Psychiatry's dual claims—of expertise and sole expertise—are subject to challenge.

Psychiatry's claim of a special expertise and, thereby, a continuing role in insanity cases, is embedded in the American Psychiatric Association Statement on the Insanity Defense (1982):

> The American Psychiatric Association is not opposed to legislatures restricting psychiatric testimony about the aforementioned ultimate legal issues concerning the insanity defense. We adopt this position because it is clear that psychiatrists are experts in medicine, not the law. As such, the psychiatrist's first obligation and expertise in the courtroom is to "do psychiatry," i.e., to present medical information and opinion about the defendant's mental state and motivation and to explain in detail the reason for his medical-psychiatric conclusions. . . .
>
> Psychiatrists, of course, must be permitted to testify fully about the defendant's psychiatric diagnosis, mental state and motivation (in clinical and commonsense terms) at the time of the alleged act so as to permit the jury or judge to reach the ultimate conclusion about which they, and only they, are expert. (p. 14)

From the cross-dimensional perspective, however, even the American Psychiatric Association's more modest assertions are subject to question. If "mental illness" is not solely a medical concept, then why must psychiatrists be permitted to testify as experts on the matter? Put another way, as "experts in medicine," what medical and essential knowledge do psychiatrists impart to the judge and jury when they are "doing psychiatry" in the courtroom? The questions are put forth, as are the contentions. We now turn to medicine's claim of expertise.

How did it happen that aberrant behavior, peculiar thoughts, and disturbing emotions came to be seen as *disease?* The advent of the medical, disease model has been attributed to the early Greek physicians (Zilboorg & Henry, 1941). Greek medicine represented a reaction to, and replacement of, an older "animistic" way of understanding. Where the animists' explanations invoked gods and demons, spirits and souls, Hippocrates and his fellow physicians would see disease. It is clear in the following quote attributed to Hippocrates that he was delivering a mocking eulogy to the animist healers while triumphantly announcing that the age of medicine had arrived:

> They [animist healers] use purifications and incantations and, it seems to me, make the divinity out to be most wicked and impious. . . If you cut open the head, you will find the brain humid, full of sweat and smelling badly. And in this way you may see that it is not a god which injures the body, but disease. (Zilboorg & Henry, 1941, p. 44)

Hippocrates' "disease model," articulated over 2,000 years ago, has had its critics. The twentieth century's most vocal and persistent critic of the disease model has been Thomas Szasz. He fired the first shot in 1961, with *The Myth of Mental Illness,* and the salvos have not ceased. In the preface to his 1978 work, *The Myth of Psychotherapy,* he writes,

> I unwittingly undertook an enterprise that soon assumed a life of its own. My initial aim was merely to demonstrate that mental illness was fake or metaphysical illness and that psychiatry was fake or metaphorical medicine.
> But there was no stopping. (p. xv)

Szasz believes that physical diseases exist, but fervently insists that mental diseases do not. He believes that the language of medicine and the "medicalization" of "problems of living" serve as "sacred symbols" (1976) that "manufacture madness" (1970): they turn scapegoats, witches, heretics, and dissenters into mental patients. For Szasz, beneath the mask, language, and practices of psychiatry lurks insidious control.

On the one hand there is the certainty of Hippocrates that mental illness is a disease and, on the other, the equal but opposite certainty of Szasz that it is not. Psychiatry's claims for expertise and standing in the courtroom, however, do not rest or collapse on whether it can confirm Hippocrates and refute Szasz for each and every instance of mental illness. Rather, its claims rest on whether or not psychiatrists can *inform* the court about the mental and motivational state of the defendant at the time of the act in a specialized way that is beyond what amateur and armchair psychiatrists could do. Furthermore, this specialized opinion must be derived from a recognized and accepted body of facts. Thus, when psychiatrists "testify fully about the defendant's psychiatric diagnosis," as the American Psychiatric Association argues that they should be allowed to do, the court expects that such diagnoses will be reliable, valid, and relevant to the matter at hand. The diagnosis of "schizophrenia" will be used to illustrate the problems, questions, and issues that surround psychiatric diagnoses and, with that, psychiatry's claim of special expertise.

SCHIZOPHRENIA

Two college students, both taking a course in abnormal psychology, meet an elderly woman on a street corner talking to herself. They decide to engage her in conversation. They notice that it is difficult to follow her thoughts: her "associations" seem to jump from one topic to the next without apparent connection. They also notice that her "affect" does not seem to be connected with the particular associations. Her words and conversation seem to have a private, "autistic" quality to them. And that her emotions seem to flip-flop between extremes, presenting an "ambivalent" picture. The first student, remembering Bleuler's (1950) words regarding schizophrenia (i.e., "association," "affect," "autism," and "ambivalence" were primary symptoms of schizophrenia, for Bleuler), announces to his friend, "She's schizophrenic!" The second student, having just read the Introduction to DSM-III, replies, "No! She's an individual with Schizophrenia." With knowing, confident smiles and an agreed-upon diagnosis, the friends move on.

But *what* do they know? And have they informed us and explained to us the mystery of this elderly woman's behavior in some enlightening, specialized way? We shall see. The first point we should see is that the interrater reliability between the two student's diagnoses is high; in fact, the reliability here is perfect. We should not ignore this because the reliability of psychiatric diagnoses has been questioned in the professional literature for more than three decades and because in the public's eye today, the spectacle of the "battle of the experts" in insanity trials continues to raise questions about the reliability of expert diagnoses. The American Psychiatric Association's *Statement on the Insanity Defense* (1982) is both cognizant and responsive to this perception. It states that "to some extent the public appears confused," but that

> unfortunately, public criticism about the "battle of the experts" fails to recognize or acknowledge advances in psychiatric nosology and diagnosis that indicate a high degree of diagnostic reliability for psychiatry—80 percent or so—so long, that is as psychiatric testimony is restricted to medical and scientific, and not legal or moral issues. (p. 7)

As for the APA's claim of 80 percent or so reliability, the *Hinckley* trial represents somewhat of an embarrassing exception. To quote from Alan Stone (1984):

> The DSM-III diagnoses offered by the three psychiatrists for the defense included schizophrenia, schizotypal personality disorder with psychosis, and borderline and paranoid personality disorder with psychosis. A diagnosis of major depressive episode was considered also tenable, but it was suggested that this was secondary to the schizophrenic disorder.
> The defense psychiatrists also mentioned as appropriate diagnoses, even though not included in DSM-III, schizophrenic spectrum disorder, process schizophrenia, simple schizophrenia, pseudoneurotic schizophrenia, and ambulatory schizophrenia. The psychiatrists for the prosecution confined themselves to the DSM-III classification, but they diagnosed narcissistic personality disorder, schizoid personality disorder, mixed personality disorder with borderline and passive/aggressive features, and dysthymic disorder. One can only sympathize with the jurors. They would have needed to be sequestered for a week with Robert Spitzer (Chairman of the APA's DSM-III task force) just to digest the nosological jargon. (pp. 84–85)

As for the 80 percent claim, Stone concludes that "Hinckley apparently fell into the 20 percent nonreliability category" (p. 91).

So, returning to our two students, at least we know that their diagnosis was reliable. But reliability is, in ways, the least informing element to a jury; after all, in the realm of astrology and horoscopes, knowing someone's date of birth gives us a perfectly reliable way of diagnosing which of the 12 zodiac signs fits the individual; it is the validity of a diagnosis that is in question. And to explicate the validity problem, we return to our two students, who themselves have made a return visit, one week later, to that same "woman with schizophrenia," only this time she is not "the same woman."

At their second meeting, she displays *none* of the symptoms observed earlier: her ambivalence and autism are absent, and her associations and affect are not discernibly different from normal people. Both students, shaken by this turn of events, ponder the same question: Is she no longer schizophrenic, or has her schizophrenia gone into remission? Both, independently, come up with the same conclusion: she now has "schizophrenia in remission." Proud of their diagnostic acumen, and brimming with confidence, they share their observations and diagnosis with their professor.

The professor asks them why it is that they both reach the diagnosis "schizophrenia in remission" after the second visit, instead of concluding she has "no mental disorder." Although their eyes and ears detected not a trace of schizophrenia, they each mutter something about one week being too short a time for a disease to disappear.

"It's not plausible that it vanished completely; it's probably in the residual phase," they reply.

"What is the *it* you are talking about?" the professor asks.

"The disease," they answer, in a tone that indicates rising exasperation and a sinking feeling.

"But how do you know *it* is a disease? How did you determine that your diagnosis, the first or the second, was an accurate, valid diagnosis?"

How do we validate or confirm a diagnosis? An analogy to medicine is instructive. When medical doctors confirm their diagnoses, we typically mean the following: we mean that they have taken the patient's report of symptoms (e.g., pain, headaches) and/or their visible signs (e.g., rashes, lumps)—from which they arrive at a tentative diagnosis—and then they *relate* those signs and symptoms with *effects at a different level* of analysis (e.g., anatomical, physiological, biochemical, genetic). Using x-rays, CAT scans, blood tests, urine tests, pap smears, and the like, tests and devices for extending what we can see and know, these methods may then confirm suspected breaks, defects, and pathogens. When they do, we speak of an accurate, valid diagnosis.

Psychiatrists and clinical psychologists face a different set of problems in validating their diagnosis, and they employ a different set of methods from their medical counterparts. For one, clinicians are typically attempting to evaluate the mental (thoughts) and emotional (feelings) states of individuals, although these states are not directly observable to the outside evaluator. What can be seen and heard by the clinician are the responses, verbal and behavioral, that individuals emit. To get individuals to emit responses, psychiatrists and psychologists typically use such methods as an interview (e.g., a mental status exam) or a battery of psychological tests (e.g., Rorschach, WAIS, TAT, Bender-Gestalt, Draw-A-Person). The responses emitted must then be *related* to something else. What they are related to usually turns out to be what *other* individuals (e.g., clinical samples, normals) say and do. Here, then, is one difference. Whereas the person's x-ray picture shows whether a break in the bone exists, thereby relating this person's reported pain and black and blue skin to the broken bone beneath, the person's picture on the Draw-A-Person is related to the pictures of *others*. Instead of a comparison of the responses of the same person at two different levels of analysis, i.e., the medical analogue, we have a comparison between the person and other people at the same level of analysis.

Now we have a "best fit" problem. Do the person's responses look more like those who have been diagnosed previously as schizophrenic, or do they best fit with the productions of manic-depressives, or with brain-damaged patients, or with normals? Of course, the responses of each of those comparison groups has its own variability, such that not all schizophrenics, or not all "anything," will display the same, uniform picture; we can miss as we seek to match. But even if we do match, even if other diagnosticians agree with our match and we have a reliable diagnosis, what can we accurately say about this person's mental and emotional state? What predictions can we make abut *this person's* past, future, or current behaviors, and how accurate are those predictions?

The students interrupt, at this point, stating that if the Rorschach test confirms the diagnosis made from the interview, "then don't we have a valid diagnosis? And can't we then conclude and predict some things about the person's ego, id, defenses, and drives?"

"Wait just a moment," says the professor, "the x-ray and Rorschach are quite different. Whereas the x-ray shows whether a break in the bone exists, the Rorschach test allows only a cautious guess as to what goes on within the psyche. And bear in mind that when we peer into the mind we end up talking about *hypothetical constructs,* not physical entities. So how did you confirm the disease?"

"I guess we didn't. . . But does that matter? After all, a sizable faction in the field believes that schizophrenia is a disease. You had us read those co-twin studies (Gottesman & Shields, 1966), those adoptee studies (Rosenthal et al., 1968), and those high-risk studies (Mednick, 1970; Garmezy, 1971), and don't they all clearly point to an inherited factor? Surely that evidence confirms the disease point of view."

The other student interjects a contrary opinion, that of Szasz, who insists that there is no disease. To Szasz (1970) Bleuler was not the discoverer of schizophrenia and Kraepelin was not the discoverer of dementia praecox (i.e., the older term for schizophrenia); rather than discovering diseases, "they invented them" (1970b, p. 9).

"I think Szasz doth protest too much," says the first student.

"You've gotten off the point," says the professor. "The question I asked you did not concern either the general topic of schizophrenia or the 'nature vs. nurture' or 'syndrome vs. disease' controversies; what I asked you, and what a court would ask you to address, is the question of what you can tell us about this particular person-defendant's mental and emotional state at the time of the act. So far, all you've told me is that she was a 'schizophrenic' when you first met her and a 'schizophrenic in remission' the second time; and at no time were you able to verify her disease. But putting that aside, how does either of those terms explain the woman's mental state, emotional state, or actions to a judge and jury?"

"But she acts, thinks, and feels the way she does because she is a schizophrenic."

"No," says the professor, that is not an explanation." The professor's point is that the students have committed the "nominal fallacy," confusing a name with an explanation: rather than explaining the behavior, they have simply renamed it. Their "explanation" is similar to an answer "Because it's an elephant" to the question "Why does that big, four-legged creature with a trunk like peanuts?": it merely replaces a definiens with its definiendum.

The students now try a different approach. Still feeling that the label "schizophrenia" helps in some ways, they ask, "But don't we know more about the individual now that we have a diagnosis?" The professor returns their question and asks, "What is it you know?"

The first student, whose memorization skills serve him well, responds: "Well, we probably can guess that her contents of thought are different, with delusions, probably persecutory delusions, present. Being a schizophrenic, her form of thought is probably looser, jumpy, and idiosyncratic. Her perception would be impaired, and my guess is she has hallucinations, probably auditory hallucinations. Her affect would be inappropriate or flat, and her sense of self disturbed. She may have weak ego boundaries and not be able to separate her own identity from others. She has probably lost interest in things, and stopped functioning in ways; probably has pulled back from the world into her ideas and fantasies, and may lose contact with reality. If it's real bad, she may get rigid and go into a stupor.

How's that?" he adds, with his confidence returning.

"Not bad," says the professor, "for a listing of the characteristic symptoms, but, what do you know for sure? What would you swear to under oath?"

"I'm not sure I follow," replies the student.

"Well," says the professor, "if you could play back your listings of the characteristic symptoms, you might notice the number of times you used words like 'probably,' 'may,' and 'guess' and that what you were conveying was a general picture with a gamut of symptoms. But very few so-called 'schizophrenics' show the full gamet of symptoms, nor do they consistently display all of their symptoms at any one time. The general picture, replete with associated symptoms, does not necessarily fit this particular individual. And those symptoms that do fit at one moment may not fit at the next moment, day, or week, as you discovered quite recently after your second encounter with her."

"So you're saying I'm wrong," the student remarked.

"No, not necessarily wrong, but not necessarily right either. I'm questioning your 'certainty' and sense of confidence, and I'm wanting you to recognize correlations and generalizations for what they are, along with their limitations. In terms of validity, be it construct, concurrent, or predictive, you haven't made your case. That's what I'm getting at."

The professor questions the students, as a prosecuting attorney might, regarding the use, abuse, and meaning of the term "mental illness." If the concept is descriptive (i.e., designating a group of symptoms), rather than etiological, then we can say nothing about causation. As a descriptive concept, the term "schizophrenia" provides only a name for a collection of symptoms and adds nothing in and of itself beyond that. But forensic experts in court typically go beyond the label to *inferences* about mental and emotional functioning and to their implications for a defendant's motivations and actions. In this regard, the experts enter the dark and dangerous reaches of the mind, with no substantive footing and little in the way of construct validation to support their inferences; what little footing they have rests on weak correlations with the actions, thoughts, and emotions of others similarly diagnosed as schizophrenic. From there, it can be a slippery slope, or a free fall, into predictions regarding the defendant's past actions and intentions, particularly when those sorts of predictions in general have not received solid and consistent validation. If this represents the typical scenario and substance of expert testimony, then it becomes more understandable why some have called for limits or outright exclusions of medico-psychological testimony.

DEMEDICALIZING MENTAL ILLNESS

Judge Gerber (1984), in his recommendations concerning the insanity defense, notes the "ennui over the invasions of medical experts into the courtroom" and suggests that the insanity defense be reformulated "by purging the test of any medical ideology" (p. 85). Michael Moore (1984) suggests that

> the proper legal definition of mental illness, then, should reflect not medical classifications. . . If the issue is a moral one . . . then the legal definition of the phrase should embody those moral principles that underlie the intuitive judgment that mentally ill human beings are not responsible. (p. 244)

And Stephen Morse (1978, 1984) proposes "the Craziness Test," which demedicalizes the legal insanity test and "uses commonsense, ordinary language that can be understood by lay jurors and judges" (p. 317). His proposed test, along with his rationale, is as follows:

> The test is this: A defendant is not guilty by reason of insanity if at the time of the offense the defendant was extremely crazy and the craziness affected the

criminal behavior. From past experience, I know that suggesting this test produces reactions ranging from utter disbelief to profound shock. Immediate critical responses include the following: it is too vague; it gives juries unbridled
discretion and no guidance; it makes no mention of mental disorder; it will allow
too many acquittals. In response I shall argue that this test tracks the moral
issues with greater honesty and precision, is more workable, and will not lead to
the acquittal of more defendants than present tests or reformed versions of
present tests.

Legal insanity is a social, moral and legal issue, not a medical or psychiatric
issue. The question in insanity defense cases is *not* whether the defendant suffers from a mental disorder: The real issue that juries decide—no matter what
test is put to them—is whether the defendant's behavior related to the offense
was so crazy, so irrational, that he must be excused. The great virtue of the
proposed test is that it asks the real question directly without pseudomedicaliza-
tion. (p. 390)

The reformulations of Gerber, Moore, and Morse all share, to one
degree or another, a cross-dimensional view of mental illness. As a first
step, these reformulations decouple "mental illness" as a disease from the
legal concept of insanity. As a second step, there is a demedicalizing of the
concept of mental illness, along with a search to identify and extract the
proper dimension of mental illness as it relates to insanity. Moore (1984)
suggests that the *moral* meaning of mental illness, rather than the medical,
is the proper dimension; furthermore, the moral meaning is not, for him,
found in the texts and tomes of moral philosophy, but is to be sought by
"an analysis of that popular moral notion of mental illness" (p. 244) that
ordinary people possess. Morse also accents the moral dimension, and he
too seeks to put the question in moral, common-sense form to the jurors; in
turn, it is then the jurors' moral, common-sense, and intuitive understanding of mental illness that should guide them rather than
"pseudomedicalizations." While Morse would not bar psychiatrists from
the courtroom, he does support federal rule 413, which would prohibit
psychiatric diagnosis; the salutary effect of FR 413, as Morse sees it, is that
expert testimony would be more descriptive and behavioral, hence more
relevant for the jury's ultimate task.

After decoupling mental illness from legal insanity, and after demedicalizing and remoralizing the former, the two terms are recoupled
again, but on a new basis: both are now situated in the moral landscape of
crime, punishment, mitigation, and exculpation, as viewed by ordinary
citizens. This is where the law should move, say such advocates; a move
not to new ground, but back to the original ground from which insanity
laws sprung, before the medico-psychological tillers overturned and seed-
ed the soil with psychiatric diagnoses, blocking all else from view.

The medico-psychological experts, however, have not fled from the
courtroom and the insanity defense battleground. They have retreated,
somewhat, as the American Psychiatric Association's *Statement on the In-*

sanity Defense (1982) acknowledges, and this retreat has been underway since the heyday of Durham. The new battle line forms at *serious* disorders:

> The American Psychiatric Association, therefore, suggests that any revision of the insanity defense standards should indicate that mental disorders potentially leading to exculpation must be *serious*. Such disorders should usually be of the severity (if not always of the quality) of conditions that psychiatrists diagnose as psychoses.
>
> The following standard, recently proposed by Bonnie [1983], is one which the American Psychiatric Association believes does permit relevant psychiatric testimony to be brought to bear on the great majority of cases where criminal responsibility is at issue:
>
> "A person charged with a criminal offense should be found not guilty by reason of insanity if it is shown that as a result of mental disease or mental retardation he was unable to appreciate the wrongfulness of his conduct at the time of the offense.
>
> As used in this standard, the terms mental disease or mental retardation include only those severely abnormal mental conditions that grossly and demonstrably impair a person's perception or understanding of reality and that are not attributable primarily to the voluntary ingestion of alcohol or other psychoactive substances." (pp. 11–12)

Retreating and regrouping around serious disorders says a number of things. It says that psychiatry does have some special expertise to convey to the court about serious mental illness and that this knowledge about psychotic-like conditions does make contact with such legal concept as *mens rea*, diminished capacity, criminal responsibility, and most important, with legal insanity. It implies that we can now do what the nineteenth-century alienists were unable to do: that is, make certain connections between "mental disease" and "insanity," which, in the eyes of that sympathetic Victorian judge, James Fitzjames Stephen, the nineteenth-century medico-psychological expert could not do. In this regard, we now turn to modern twentieth-century efforts to establish such a connection and relationship.

THE HYPOTHESIZED RELATIONSHIP BETWEEN MENTAL ILLNESS AND INSANITY

We come now to the juncture where psychiatric terms meet their legal counterparts. Psychiatry speaks of "disorders," "syndromes," and "symptoms," whereas the law speaks of "insanity," "diminished capacity," and "*mens rea*." The problem, simply put, is that there is no easy translation or correspondence between the two sets of terms. Given that some relationship exists between legal and psychiatric terminology, how are psychological experts, lawyers. judges, and jurors to cross from one domain to the other?

A Mental Illness Threshold for Legal Insanity

The psychiatric idea that emerges for relating mental illness to legal insanity involves a *threshold:* individuals with certain types of mental disease that are not serious enough (i.e., disorders that are not ordinarily viewed as psychotic) would not be considered as qualifying for legal insanity; individuals with disorders that exceed the serious/psychotic threshold may qualify for legal insanity. This type of approach is seen in the ALI insanity test, which specifically mentions that repeated criminal or antisocial conduct does not qualify as grounds for an insanity judgment. The American Psychiatric Association *Statement* seeks to push the threshold line higher, to serious mental disorders, which, presumably, would be easier for experts to agree about and harder for the public to doubt. My own doubts concern three things: the disorders below the threshold, those above the threshold, and the threshold itself.

Considering disorders below the threshold, we have numerous instances in Anglo-American insanity law cases where such conditions have led to exculpation. Using DSM-II (1968), for the moment, there are historic instances of disorders classified under Neuroses, under Hysterical Neurosis, Dissociative Type, such as Amnesia (Schacter, 1986; Kopelman, 1987), Somnambulism (Fenwick, 1987), Fugue, and Multiple Personality, that have led to NGRI verdicts. Under Personality Disorders and Certain Other Nonpsychotic Mental Disorders, an insanity defense for Paranoid Personality, Explosive Personality, Pedophilia, and Sadism could be made, along with a number of cases that fall under Alcoholism and Drug dependence. Transient Situational Disturbance may also qualify, as might some of the Non-psychotic Organic Brain Syndromes. And some conditions that are not yet included in the diagnostic manual, like premenstrual syndrome (PMS) and menstruation *per se* (Harry & Balcer, 1987), are likely to find legal advocates willing to attempt an insanity defense for their clients. As DSM-III (1980) notes about DSM-II, "because psychosis was defined in terms of 'severity of functional impairment' and the 'capacity to meet the ordinary demands of life,' the psychotic-non-psychotic distinction was difficult to make" (p. 372). It still is difficult to make.

In DSM-III, there are likely to be a number of Organic Mental Disorders that fall below the psychosis line for either short or extensive periods of time. Under Schizophrenic Disorders, which had been classified in DSM-II as Psychoses, DSM-III now does not:

> DSM-III does not use "psychotic" as a fundamental basis for classifying the nonorganic mental disorders in order to avoid classifying the Major Affective Disorders as psychotic, since such disorders usually do not have psychotic features. (p. 373)

So in DSM-III, Major Affective Disorders may fall below the line. We still have those conditions of Psychogenic Amnesia, Psychogenic Fugue, Multiple Personality, and Sleepwalking Disorder below the line, as is Post-traumatic Stress Disorder. The Personality Disorders, some new, like Borderline Personality Disorder, and others renamed, like Intermittent Explosive Disorder, are still below-the-line candidates for legal insanity, as are Adjustment Disorders, Pedophilia, Sexual Sadism, Alcohol Abuse and Dependence, Substance Use Disorders, and Conduct Disorder.

In sum, all of the above "below the serious/psychotic line" disorders may be candidates for an insanity defense, given the right defendant and defense counsel and given the right support from an expert witness or two. All of these disorders, in diagnostic hindsight, might be qualified (with a fifth-digit code of psychosis) to push them above threshold. As that can occur, we see that it is not the disorder that is diagnosed that matters, but the qualifying amendments. We do not have, then, a system where disorders below the line are automatically not candidates for legal insanity.

The disorders above the threshold line are also problematic, on two counts. First, many of these disorders and the individuals who have them will function below the serious/psychotic line at certain times and under certain circumstances. The question, which a diagnosis *per se* does not answer, is: Was the defendant *at the time of the act* above or below the line? The second difficulty with disorders above the serious/psychosis line is that "psychosis" is not an across the board" state or condition: a patient in a psychiatric hospital diagnosed as psychotic may believe erroneously that the hospital staff is putting poison in his brussel sprouts to render him impotent, but nonetheless he may show good judgment in the eyes of the staff by regularly taking his medication. When we turn to a defendant in an insanity case who has been diagnosed as psychotic, the question is whether at the time of the act he was thinking and acting insanely or sanely. Was this a time when his perceptions were clear, his understanding sufficient, his judgment good, and his control adequate, or not? The term "psychosis" does not provide a certain answer, hence not all defendants diagnosed as psychotic will necessarily be legally insane.

The problem with a threshold line linked to diagnoses is that it simply does not work: it fails to demarcate disorders as consistently above or below the line; and even when we believe that a disorder is above the line and that the individual is psychotic, we must still *infer*, rather than deductively conclude, about the defendant's awareness. perceptions, thinking, feeling, and control at the moment of the act. A threshold such as this does not confer certainty.

A Judgment-Capacity Connection?

The psychiatrist and forensic expert might properly back away from claims of certainty and argue that what they can offer the court are probability statements—assertions about the defendant's mental, emotional, and volitional functioning that we have some degree of confidence in. These assertions, they might continue, are derived from clinical experience and empirical, correlational evidence; while they are neither causative nor certain assertions, they may nonetheless be informing to the jury. And in this light, a psychiatric diagnosis of mental disease is a first step. From there, for example, we can make inferences about the defendant's judgment, capacity for judgment, and degree of functional impairment. And in centering on the topic of judgment, the lexical threads of psychiatry draw closer to connecting with their legal counterparts. For embedded in those "cognitive" insanity tests, such as M'Naghten, the first part of ALI, and the Insanity Defense Reform Act of 1984, is the concept of judgment: Did the defendant, or could the defendant, make a realistic judgment of the situation and the nature, quality, and wrongfulness of his act, or was his judgment so impaired such that he did not know and could not appreciate? If experts can address and inform the jury as to the defendant's judgment in the psychological sense, then conclusions about legal judgment and insanity become but a natural extension.

There are problems in practice, however, that realistically limit such conclusions and "natural extensions" from the psychiatric to the legal domain; furthermore, these problems in practice reflect conceptual difficulties and disparities between legal and psychiatric approaches. To elucidate these limitations, we return to the psychiatric end of the judgment thread in order to follow its trail and unravel the dilemma.

On the psychiatric side, "judgment" is used frequently in connection with a wide variety of disorders. With organic brain syndromes, judgment may be impaired. With psychotic conditions (e.g., schizophrenia, paranoid states) judgment is frequently impaired. And in depression, in both its severe (e.g., manic-depressive illness, depressed type) and milder forms (e.g., depressive neurosis), depressed individuals may reveal faulty judgment in assessing others, themselves, and the future (Beck, 1972; Seligman, 1975). In fact, it is probably difficult to find any diagnosis where the case could not be made for some impairment of judgment. But before leaping to the unwarranted conclusion that everyone with a psychiatric diagnosis is impaired with respect to judgment (and therefore cannot be held accountable with respect to conforming to the law), let us take pause to note the following exceptions.

Depressed individuals may be better judges than their normal counterparts when evaluating a situation that is beyond control, yet may be poorer judges when control of the outcome is indeed possible (Alloy & Abramson, 1979). Paranoid individuals may display acute judgment in recognizing hostility in others, yet be obtuse when asked to judge their own hostility. The individual suffering from senile dementia may make poor judgments when sent to the grocery store to purchase a few items, but may be a perceptive judge when it comes to historical facts and the forces that shaped them.

What we begin to discern is that judgment itself is not necessarily a unified trait—either completely intact or uniformly impaired—but is a capacity that can be selectively functional or dysfunctional, and to varying degrees. How, then, does this selectivity and variability relate to the legal usage of the term?

"Judgment," when not used to designate an authoritative opinion, typically is used to designate a process or a capacity for forming an opinion or evaluating a situation by discerning and comparing. Oftentimes we are asking "Did the person, or could the person, evaluate his or her behavior *in respect to the requirements of the law?*" We see in this question that the "judgment" we are talking about is quite specific. It is different from judgment used in a social, business, or psychiatric sense. Whether Jones used good judgment in marrying Smith, in investing in a particular stock, or in deciding to terminate psychotherapy are questions that the law takes little interest in, although Jones, Jones's wife, Jones's business partner, and Jones's therapist may take great interest in them.

The law, however, moves from an uninterested to a disinterested party when Jones is caught for shoplifting. But Jones's lawyer notes that his client is no ordinary shoplifter, but a mentally ill and psychiatrically diagnosed individual. Unlike the ordinary shoplifter, who knew the law, yet, for some other reason, chose to break it, Jones's case is different. The ordinary shoplifter showed poor judgment, but it is a different type of poor judgment than in Jones's case. In the process of making a judgment and acting on it, the ordinary shoplifter may have weighed the law and the associated punishment against other motives (e.g., greed, poverty, retaliation, excitement, etc.) and decided to risk it. In evaluating this matter, we may decide that the ordinary shoplifter made a bad choice and showed poor judgment: he should have given more weight to the law and to his conscience and less to his competing motives. In his process of making this particular judgment we find fault. Yet typically we believe that the shoplifter *could have done otherwise,* as well as should have done otherwise: we infer *the capacity* to reach the lawful judgment and course of action.

Jones's lawyer argues that this is precisely where Jones and the "thief-of-the-mill" shoplifter part company. Jones's *capacity* to reach the lawful judgment and course of action has been impaired by mental illness. More than a faulty process, which Jones surely displayed, we have in the Jones case an *incapacity* that makes a crucial difference: it removes from Jones the ability to have done otherwise, an ability we attribute to the ordinary thief. Jones's lawyer is arguing that his client did not have a "free choice" in the way the shoplifter did, for his mental illness nullifies his once-present capacity. As a consequence, his act is one that can be pitied but not punished, since we cannot attach culpability to it.

The argumentation is fine; in fact, it has probably been made hundreds of times; what is not fine is the proof. When psychiatrists and psychologists take the stand as expert witnesses, they typically cannot furnish proof of an underlying disease or its connection to culpability. In the *Hinckley* (1981) trial, one expert, over opposition objections, presented CAT scan evidence of brain irregularities; this evidence, however, did not establish a causal relationship between those brain irregularities and either Hinckley's disordered thinking or his action of firing a pistol. In the absence of even this first-order relationship between disease and behavior, the expert is very far from being able to furnish medical proof regarding (1) where and how the disease physically impairs judgment, (2) where and how, within the brain, "judgment" is organized neurologically, and (3) how such impaired judgment affects behavioral sequelae. The lexical thread of judgment, starting at the psychiatric end running into the labyrinth of the brain, fails, at present, to emerge at the behavioral end to connect with its legal counterpart. A modern-day, forensic Theseus is not about to meet his Ariadne following this thread; at least, not any time soon. At worst, he may never, if some dualists are to be believed, for they regard the "pineal search" for a physical-mental link as a fool's quest.

The forensic expert, high-wiring on the thread of judgment, may claim that his assertions and psychiatric threads do not have to make substantive contact with the defendant's neurological network; rather, his traversing threads extend from the behaviors of the many to the behavior of the defendant; if he can show that others similarly diagnosed as the defendant have impaired capacity for judging, then he feels confident that his thread will support his weighty assertions about this particular defendant's judgment. But here we have a leap being made from the nomethetic to the ideothetic (Lamiell, 1981). In the nomothetic model, we deal with groups of individuals and seek correlates between that group and some behavior. In the ideothetic model, we deal with the individual and seek to explain that person's behavior. The Law, in an insanity case, is dealing with a particular defendant, and hence is operating in the ideothetic. The expert, however, is seeking to cross from the nomethetic to the ideothetic.

In trying to cross from the nomethetic to the ideothetic, the thread begins to unravel. Even if psychiatry found a correlation of .70 between schizophrenics and impaired judgment, nothing can be said with certainty about this particular schizophrenic defendant. Perhaps this defendant fell in the .30 group that did not show impaired judgment. And though the correlation ($R = .70$) appears high, the probability of a prediction being right ($R^2 = .49$) turns out to be less than 50%. The probability of being right drops even lower as we recall that "impaired judgment" is neither an across-the-board phenomena nor a consistent phenomena. What researchers measure and call "impaired judgment" when establishing the correlation of .70 may not be the *type* of judgment the law is weighing in terms of this particular defendant's judgment. Furthermore, there is no guarantee that a person showing impaired judgment at one testing time will show it the next time or did show impaired judgment at the time of the act.

In sum, generalizations about judgment may not be specific enough or relevant enough to the legal use of judgment; these generalizations do not warrant a high degree of confidence from one moment to the next; they warrant even less confidence when we go from group data to a specific individual; and, finally, they enjoy no hard neurological support at this time, which was the case in judge James Fitzjames Stephen's time.

A CONSCIOUSNESS-*MENS REA* CONNECTION?

Forensic experts are likely to press their case. If the thread of judgment proves too weak at this time, a tactical retreat to safer ground is in order. Some seek the safer ground in a consciousness-*mens rea* connection. Consciousness is a broader construct than judgment. In theory, consciousness gives rise to or makes possible a wide array of sentient activities that humans do: our awareness, perceptions, feelings, thinking, reflections, and judgments seem rooted in consciousness, the latter being necessary for the former. If experts can show impairment in consciousness—in the very basis of our mental functioning—then particular areas of functioning collapse.

The problem of "consciousness" is certainly one that has animated the discipline of psychology since its inception. In the late nineteenth century, Freud attempted to develop a model of "psychology" and "consciousness" on sound, neurological footing. If the model proved workable, then a deterministic and materialistic explanation for mental, moral, and legal thinking might be at hand. Freud (1974a) followed the thread of consciousness deep into his "Project for a Scientific Psychology" (1895), which was to be his "psychology for neurologists" (Fancher, 1973; Pribram, 1962). The thread ultimately ran out, and the founder of psychoanalysis, floundering amidst neurons and the mind–body pitfall (Nagel, 1974; Solomon, 1974), finally turned back to psychology and mentalistic explanations. So, too, have most expert witnesses. Yet many expert witnesses who walk along mentalistic threads in the courtroom do so with the materialistic hope (illusion)? that mentalistic heat signifies a physical hard wire beneath.

There are other experts, unabashedly dualistic, who believe that the crossing can be made on purely mentalistic grounds. These experts, like agile spiders, are content to weave an edifice of mental life for the jury, replete with stressors, impulses, defenses, and history; somewhere within this woven structure. they maintain, deep within the psyche, consciousness itself begins to crack and fragment, no longer holding itself together. With consciousness renting and splitting, the capacity for good judgment, undistorted perceptions, clear thinking, and responsible conduct diminishes. As a spider whose signal thread is cut and who does not respond appropriately to the fly caught within its web, analogously are mentally ill individuals deprived of their ability to act in legally appropriate ways. The therapeutic conclusion is not to punish the spider, but to repair its threads.

But the woven threads of the experts, spun from analogy and metaphor, fail in a *material* way to substantively support their airy connections. Those experts who seek to cross on such ethereal threads are advised to work with a net.

A Rent in the Self

The experts, still trying to hold their footing and standing in the courtroom, may choose to bypass the neurological quest entirely. "Why, after all," they might ask, "do we have to have a materialist basis for connecting psychological understanding to legal insanity? If we view the scientific/moralistic division between psychology and the law as bogus and, instead, see both disciplines as dealing with mental life from respective perspectives, then perhaps we can bridge the two using certain syntactical transpositions." In this vein, we turn to the Self, and a renting therein.

Let us start in the legal end, with terms such as "criminal insanity," "diminished capacity," and "*mens rea*," and see if we can translate them into satisfactory psychological equivalents. In my opinion, the best of such previous efforts is Fingarette's (1972), wherein he makes a distinction between the ordinary meaning of "the absence of *mens rea*" and a "more profound or radical kind" of absence of *mens rea* in insanity. Returning to the "ordinary shoplifter" to illustrate the above distinction, let us say that the prosecution wishes to prove that larceny has occurred. For larceny to be established, the prosecution is required to show that "unlawful intent" was present. But this defendant, who does not deny that he took the item, fervently denies that "unlawful intent" was in his mind; rather, he claims that his mental state was one that can be characterized as "preoccupied" ("absent-minded," if you like), and thus he lacked *mens rea*. But the shoplifter would most certainly deny that his absence of *mens rea* in this particular instance was an admission of insanity. As Fingarette (1972) notes,

> in the case of the insanity plea and in the case of childhood, the thesis of absence of *mens rea* cuts deeper than this: rather than amounting to a claim to be a responsible person under law who acted without guilty intent, it is in effect a claim that the person was not a responsible agent. (p. 164)

At this point, let us hold aside questions that relate to both childhood and mental retardation and focus more narrowly on the more typical cases involving insanity and mental illness. The reason for this distinction resides in the claim that could be put forward for both the child and the retarded adult—a claim that does not fit the typical insanity case—that the child or retarded adult never knew or never had the knowledge and moral appreciation that defines someone as a responsible, moral agent. In the typical insanity case, and *Hadfield*, *M'Naghten*, and *Hinckley* are examples, there is enough evidence to infer from past actions that the individual was once considered a responsible agent. But now he seems to have lost that status, with his once present capacity having somehow become defunct or diminished. How?

At this point, psychological explanations are usually offered. "He was unconscious of his motives." "Certain of his ideas were repressed, dissociated, or distorted." "His will was outside his control." But who, and what, is this "he"? One person, or two? A divided person is offered. Before we accept this psychological explanation and embellish it with metaphors of a divided "self" or multiple "selves," let us keep asking variants of the "how" question, such as "How has this divided self come about?"

The *unity of self* has presented philosophy and psychology with "an enduring dilemma" (Robinson, 1982a) that has by no means gone away; if anything, the issue remains alive, heated, and as confused as ever. Some of the current and historical confusion, as Robinson points out, stems from a failure "to make necessary distinctions" among such concepts as (1) *self*, (2) *self-identity*, (3) *personal identity*, and (4) *person*. Robinson's distinctions will be presented first, and then we will return to insanity and the question of how this rent or division of the Self has come to pass.

Starting with the concept of *person*, Robinson (1982a) writes:

> What is ordinarily meant by a *person* is a human being, often of unknown identity, possessing certain intellectual, moral, and social attributes not present to the same degree in the balance of the animal kingdom. Used this way, *person* refers to a collection of attributes shared by entities of a certain kind. It is not an answer to the question of *who*, but rather to the question of what.
>
> Personal identity, however, is an answer to the first of these questions. We can observe someone doing a variety of things and decide, in the absence of any biographical data, that the actor is a person. But to know *who* that person is we must go beyond the attributes that establish personhood. Thus, we will inquire as to name and occupation, address, social security number, fingerprints, credit cards, and so on. Following this investigation, which may move deeply into the details of this actor's life, we are prepared to assert that we now know the actual identity of the person—the personal identity. Note, however, that the person thus identified may be totally amnesic and therefore ignorant of the very identity we have established. In such a case, we would say that the person has a personal identity, but not *self-identity*. Nonetheless, the amnesic is not doubtful of existing (*cogito, ergo sum*). This person surely must be granted a self, and will claim as much whether we grant it or not. (p. 909)

With these distinctions made, let us return to the "split problem" in one of its forms: consider "self-deception." On this topic, Fingarette (1974) asks two questions: "Who can doubt that we do deceive ourselves? Yet who can explain coherently and explicitly how we do so?" Sartre (1974) calls the problem *mauvaise foi* (bad faith), and makes an interesting comparison between lying to yourself and lying to another. In lying to another, as opposed to merely presenting erroneous information that the speaker believes is true, the liar *knows* the truth: he must know the truth if his intention is to lie, and he does not hide this intention from himself. In short, the "liar" knows; the "lied to" does not. But in self-deception, the same person is both the "liar" and "lied to." Sartre (1974) writes, "It follows first that the one to whom the lie is told and the one who lies are one and the same person, which means that I must know in my capacity as deceiver the truth which is hidden from me in my capacity as the one deceived" (p. 72). How can this be?

According to Sartre, Freud's account of how this could be—invoking the unconscious—cannot work. The psychoanalytic interpretation, according to Sartre (1974), invokes the concept of the unconscious and hypothesizes a censor, "conceived as a line of demarcation with customs, passport division, currency control, etc., to reestablish the duality of the deceiver and the deceived" (p. 73). This division between conscious and unconscious, ego and id, cuts "the psychic whole into two. I *am* the ego but I *am not* the *id*. I hold no privileged position in relation to my unconscious psyche . . . . which means that I stand in relation to *my* 'id,' in the position of the *Other*" (pp. 74–75).

But this Freudian division and account does not work, and Sartre tells us why. This division between conscious and unconscious, or ego and id, is maintained by the censor. However, the censor does not repress everything from coming into awareness; rather, the censor is *selective*. Some ideas, memories, feelings, and drives are not repressed. In order to *selectively screen* (i.e., to pick one idea to repress but not another), the censor must *know*: the very act of selecting involves making a discerning choice, thus the censor must be aware. Using this Freudian account and Sartre's rebuttal, the defense attorney's claim that his allegedly insane client was "split, unconscious, and did not know" could be countered by the prosecution's claim "that he had to know in order to produce the very split."

Robinson's distinctions may help us here. The defense attorney is really speaking about his client's *self-identity*: from his client's subjective point of view, the client *identifies as himself* his conscious identity, while *disavowing* his unconscious identity. His lawyer would like the jury to believe that when you consider his *personal identity*, which can be arrived at "from the outside," so to speak, you miss the defendant's subjective self-identity. Furthermore, *personhood* can only be fully understood by considering this self-identity, and if this self-identity lacks the capacity for moral awareness and judgment, then we no longer have a responsible agent (person) that we can hold blameworthy.

The prosecuting attorney, using Robinson's semantic distinctions and Sartre's reasoning, would have the jury understand that the *self* is not split. This unity of the self then undermines the *self-identity* split that the defense proposes: put another way, the very act of trying to split the identity reveals awareness, discernment, selection, knowledge, choice, and the moral values that establish *personhood*—and with it, culpability.

Fingarette (1974) using Freud's last paper (1974b) and a different approach from Sartre, tries his hand at explaining self-deception. For Fingarette, the split in consciousness that occurs in self-deception is not the classical split between conscious and unconscious or between ego and id; rather, "the result of defence is to split off from the more rational system . . . a nuclear, dynamic complex. This nuclear entity is a complex of motive, purpose, feeling, perception, and drive towards action" (p. 93). Call it an ego-nucleus.

The reason for this split stems from an incompatibility between the current ego and the ego-nucleus. The incompatibility is "so great, relative to the integrative capacities of the Ego," that the Ego "gives up any attempt to integrate the ego-nucleus itself." In Fingarette's process, the splitting of the ego is "not something that 'happens' to the ego but something the ego *does*, a motivated strategy" (p. 94). The Ego has disavowed the ego-nucleus. The result is a *counter-ego nucleus.* Thus, to paraphrase Fingarette in Robinson's terms, self-deception turns upon the self-identity one accepts rather than the beliefs one has. If the self-identity one accepts does not avow some of one's actions, beliefs, and motives, then the necessary condition for moral action may be lacking.

While Fingarette's account is different from Sartre's analysis, and, as a process, makes more clinical sense than invoking the censor, it still does not get around Sartre's objections: Fingarette states that the ego is active (motivated) in the process. If the ego chooses to disavow rather than avow, it is responsible for bringing about the condition of not being morally accountable. So we arrive at a curious conclusion: on the one hand, at the time of the alleged criminal act, *personhood* has been so diminished that we no longer have a responsible agent, yet, on the other hand, during the psychic process of disavowal, we have a morally responsible person with an accountable self-identity choosing dissociation and diminution.

"Disavowing," which is at the heart of Fingarette's analysis, is not restricted to the mentally ill. Who has never said or heard the words "I'm not myself today"? We will hear it one more time, in the following example of Smith.

Smith, a businessman, with hopes riding on closing an important deal, loses out to a competitor. Disappointed, hurt, angry, even furious, he turns on one of his employees over a small matter and verbally abuses the chap. Coming home after this most disappointing day he is greeted by his spouse who has prepared a lovely meal. He grouses, pouts, and sulks throughout dinner. Wishing to be alone to read his newspaper, he finds the family dog once again under his feet and kicks "man's best friend" away. Later that evening, he offers "I'm not myself today" as an explanation.

While Smith's actions would not warrant criminal proceedings, they were certainly instances of "bad form": socially and interpersonally they fall outside the bounds of acceptable conduct. Smith's employee and Smith's dog whine and whimper, growl and grumble, and, for similar reasons, slink silently away. His spouse does not. Confronting him with his behavior, he offers the above excuse. While his spouse understands what happened today, she does not find his excuse acceptable. It is not acceptable, she tells him, to take his emotions out on her. There are other alternatives. But his lame retort is that it wasn't really "him."

In the language of disavowal and in the light of this chapter's topic, Smith is not *owning* his actions and his feelings. He certainly used poor judgment. Yet Smith is "normal," not mentally ill. However, to stretch this hypothetical example, let us imagine that in Smith's furious state he engages in homicidal fantasies about his competitor, and, upon leaving the office for home, runs right into his smirking competitor. We next see Smith being hauled into court on assault charges mumbling about not being himself.

A real-life case that bears directly on this matter is that of Kenneth Bianchi (*State v. Bianchi*, 1979), known as the Los Angeles "Hillside Strangler." In this case, the question of insanity turns on whether or not you believe that Bianchi had a "multiple personality," such that another personality (or personalities) unbeknownst to Kenneth did the act of which Kenneth was unaware, and hence, not responsible for. The experts disagreed. A whole issue of *The International Journal of Clinical and Experimental Hypnosis* (April, 1984) addressed the question of "multiple personality" in the Bianchi case.

In his analysis, John Watkins (1984) asserts that under hypnosis Bianchi manifested a multiple personality: "An underlying personality, 'Steve,' whose existence was apparently unknown to Bianchi, claimed responsibility for the 2 murders in Bellingham and those in Los Angeles," and that "the major personality (Ken) appeared to be amnesic to all of this." There were other tests performed, under and out of hypnosis, and another personality, "Billy," emerges. Watkins concludes that his diagnosis of multiple personality was strongly supported by the evidence, and he testifies for the defense that Bianchi was insane.

Martin Orne (Orne, Dinges, & Orne, 1984), on the other hand, based on his examination of Bianchi, claims that there were errors in Watkins' methods and conclusions and that the evidence does not corroborate multiple personality; rather, Orne (who testified for the prosecution) finds that Bianchi is a malingerer, simulating a multiple personality without being one; a man who engages in conning and deliberate deception, whom he diagnoses under DSM-III as Antisocial Personality Disorder with Sexual Sadism and whom he regards as legally sane.

Then there is Ralph Allison (1984), who testified as a court witness, who first concluded that Bianchi was a multiple personality and legally insane, but who then admits that "later events showed the diagnosis to be in error." He points out that the examining methods themselves could produce certain personality effects, as hypnotic suggestions, conveying the erroneous impression of a split psyche. He warns that "it may be impossible to determine the correct diagnosis of a dissociating defendant in a death penalty case" (p. 102) and concludes with a first-principle reminder "that the human mind can do anything" (p. 115). Perhaps a similar first-principle reminder could be uttered about the mental constructions, diagnoses, and conclusions of expert witnesses.

SOME CONCLUSIONS ABOUT THE MENTAL ILLNESS–INSANITY RELATIONSHIP

Clearly, twentieth-century psychiatrists, clinical psychologists, and forensic experts have not erased those doubts, voiced in the nineteenth century, about the concept of "mental disease" and its linkage to legal insanity. The conceptual bridges betwixt the two are more elaborated now, yet the supporting foundations remain suspect or flawed. The first conclusion is that a psychiatric diagnosis per se will tell the jurors nothing conclusively about the matter that they must decide. While some in the profession still believe in Hippocrates' conviction and the alienists' hope that our "science," rooted in "natural law," is capable of furnishing deterministic explanations that will supplant or set right our most difficult legal and moral entanglements, the evidence to date is not sufficient to warrant conviction. And in and of itself, it should not warrant either the conviction or exculpation of a defendant.

The second conclusion I wish to put forth is that there is no good reason why the medical concept of mental illness and disease cannot be replaced in insanity test definitions by a more common-sense meaning derived from the moral perspective of ordinary citizens; there is a virtue to this, as both Moore (1984) and Morse (1984) point out, in that both ends of the mental illness–insanity relationship will reside in the same moral sphere. In Chapter 7 I will deal with perspective of ordinary citizens through research findings, and in Chapter 11 I will seek to incorporate these understandings into a new insanity test. For now, the last conclusion concerns the place and role of expert testimony regarding mental illness and insanity.

My final conclusion is that I would not bar such testimony from insanity cases. Defense attorneys might argue that a prohibition on such testimony violates certain constitutional rights of defendants. But the type of testimony that is most informing is neither conclusions about sanity nor diagnostic nosology: what is more informing are descriptions of a defendant's behaviors and responses that can add to the other testimony that jurors hear, allowing them a fuller picture. As for inferences from behavior of the defendant (or from others similarly diagnosed) to the psychic life of this defendant, we must be cautious. "Inferences" seem to be a slippery slope that leads many an expert from low-level extrapolations to elaborated constructions of the mind before anyone can say "cross-examine." The expert's tether to facts and research findings, not strong to begin with, is likely to snap quickly with extension.

When experts construct for the jury the hidden reaches of the defendant's psyche, they may be performing a service of making the inexplicable and bizarre actions of the defendant seem understandable. But the experts might just as well be performing a disservice in the sense that these reasons and stories of the psyche might well be false stories, however interesting and elaborated they may be. The self, or self-identity, may rent; consciousness, avowal, and disavowal may be lessened, absent, or whole; judgment can be Solomon-like, poor, or nonexistent; and our capacity for acting responsibly can be full, diminished, or empty. All of these threads can be woven in a tapestry and story of the psyche. But the myths and metaphors do not to date unravel the Gordian knot of insanity. The danger is that these stories can give us the illusion that they do. The brakes on such unsupported tales should come, in the best of worlds, from the scientific and ethical integrity of the experts; if they do not, the courts and the legislators are likely to apply them for us.

5

Therapeutics for the Insane, Dilemmas for Therapists

Therapists and therapy surround both the issue of insanity and the erstwhile insane defendant-turned-patient. The Therapeutic State, with its rehabilitative promise, sends its emissary the therapist to administer therapeutics. Whereas the Law has been reluctant to turn the insanity *decision* over to the medico-psychological specialist, and that reluctance has increased of late, the courts have showed no such hesitancy in turning the allegedly insane defendant or the NGRI acquittee over to the therapists for treatment. If the allegedly insane individual is not competent to stand trial, then the therapist is called in to make him so. If the defendant is found not guilty by reason of insanity, then the acquittee is typically incarcerated in the custody of psychiatry until cured. And when the mental health professional says so, the defendant-turned-patient is set free. Or so it has been until Hinckley fired.

In the reverberating post-*Hinckley* times, the dispositive issue, the release decision, and the control of both are being reexamined. There are some who would favor not only demedicalizing the insanity test, but demedicalizing the pre- and postinsanity acquittal procedures as well. In line with this trend, the American Psychiatric Association's *Statement* (1982) on postacquittal procedures recommends a parole-board-like system that would take the release decision out of the exclusive hands of psychiatry. There are sound reasons for this relegalizing and demedicalizing move, with some of those reasons relating to clinical, ethical, moral, and legal dilemmas that face therapists in general, and those that work with involuntary patients in particular. For one, the Therapeutic State's long-standing promise of rehabilitation has not been realized, and the state of psychiatry today is no longer willing to reissue the old promise of a cure in every case. For another, psychiatry today is increasingly unwilling to play the part of policeman—the sole guarantor of the public's safety—when the therapeutics have ended but the danger has not. In retreating from its former promise and position, there is a growing awareness among therapists of their limitations and liabilities; in acknowledging the former, they seek to minimize the latter. However, the courts and the public have been slow to catch on to the limits of therapy, and, as for liabilities and responsibilities, neither the courts nor the therapists have been clear about either.

It is time now for those therapeutic promises and hopes, and those limitations and liabilities, to be examined. I believe these matters need to be understood because the insanity issue is more than just a test that defines a relationship between mental illness and exculpation; it includes procedures for handling the insane defendant after trial that rely on assumptions and presumptions about what therapy and therapists can do for the insane acquittee's state of mind and for the public's peace of mind. One set of issues concerns the nature of therapy, its "modes and morals" (London, 1964) and its effectiveness; another set of issues concerns the limitations, liabilities, and dilemmas that confront therapists. When both sets of issues are understood, the courts and the public will realize that the burden of insanity has not been laid to rest with a verdict, and therapists will realize the weight and dangers of carrying the freight.

THE REACH OF THE THERAPEUTIC HAND . . . AND THE SURETY OF ITS GRASP

That the "therapeutic hand" reaches the allegedly insane individual or the person found "not guilty by reason of insanity" cannot be doubted. But the pervasiveness of that hand may not be fully appreciated. The words of the American Psychological Association's Task Force on the Role of Psychology in the Criminal Justice System (Monahan, 1980), addressing only the psychological arm of the mental health profession (i.e., the other arms include psychiatry, psychiatric social work, and psychiatric nursing), portray a bigger picture.

> Psychologists are involved in virtually every facet of the criminal justice system. When a person is arrested, it may well be by a police officer who was screened by a psychologist before being hired and trained by other psychologists

in ways of handling such potentially hazardous situations as an arrest. Should the police officer use undue force or poor judgment in effecting the arrest, the officer may be sent to the department's psychologist for treatment.

The defendant may then be evaluated by a psychologist to determine whether he or she is competent to stand trial before a jury that other psychologists are in the process of selecting. If competent, the defendant may be examined by a psychologist to determine whether he or she was insane at the time of the offense and so should be sent to a mental hospital for psychological treatment. At the trial, eyewitnesses to the crime may have their perceptions and memories challenged by a psychological expert. The fate of the convicted offender may rest in part on what a psychologist recommends to the judge in a presentence evaluation.

Should the offender be sent to prison, he or she may be classified by one psychologist for the purpose of being treated by another, and the treatment may not end until a third psychologist predicts that the offender can be released into society without risk of recidivism. Remaining free on parole may be contingent upon attendance at outpatient psychotherapy. (p. 1)

While the reach of the therapeutic hand is extensive, our focus for now narrows on therapy and on the effectiveness of this endeavor. How effective is therapy in general, and, more specifically, how effective is therapy likely to be with an NGRI acquittee? Will therapists cure insane patients like Hadfield, M'Naghten, and Hinckley of their delusions? Will they be able to reestablish in such clients good judgment, reality testing, and control? And, as an anxious community awaits, will therapists be able to return to the community a sound and safe individual? To answer such questions, we begin by looking at therapy, at its best.

THERAPY AT ITS BEST

In broad strokes, psychotherapy works best when the following conditions apply. First, let us start with a willing prospective patient, one who recognizes the need for help, believes that psychotherapy will help, and who voluntarily seeks it out. It helps, too, if the patient is anxious to some degree, motivated, and willing to commit time, energy, and financial resources to this endeavor. It also helps if the patient's disorder is mild rather than severe, acute rather than chronic. On the demographic front, someone with the YAVIS syndrome (Schofield, 1964; Zilbergeld, 1983), a patient who is Young, Attractive, Verbal, Intelligent, and Successful, will likely do best. The odds of successful treatment are improved still further when patients believe that they can take responsibility for their lives, actions, feelings, and thoughts (i.e., internal locus of control), are honest and ethical, and can articulate and define their psychological problems and therapeutic goals.

Such is the portrait, in somewhat crude outline, of the ideal patient. Upon quick assessment, though, we note that this ideal patient bears little likeness to the typical insanity acquittee. But on to the therapist.

Psychotherapy, for its success, surely depends on the right sort of therapist. At a minimum, we hope that the therapist is competent, experienced, honest, and ethical. Those Rogerian (Rogers, 1951) qualities of being genuine, accepting, and understanding are helpful too. We expect a good therapist to keep confidentiality, to fully inform the patient about treatment and seek the patient's consent, and to establish with the patient a contract for therapy. It also helps if the therapist believes and expects therapy to work. If the right sort of therapist interacts with the right sort of patient, and the "marriage" is a good fit for both, then success is likely.

But the ideal world and the real world are seldom the same, and, in the latter, therapeutic successes have been both modest and spotty: outcome studies (Bergin, 1971; Bergin & Suinn, 1975; Eysenck, 1952; Gomes-Schwartz, Hadley, & Strupp, 1978; Smith & Glass, 1977) on the effectiveness of psychotherapy indicate that psychotherapy is moderately successful, under certain conditions, but with particular groups of patients and problems, psychotherapy has either a poor track record or a quite variable one. The Joint Commission on Mental Illness and Health (1961) report stated that

> major mental illness is the core problem and unfinished business of the mental health movement, and that intensive treatment of patients with critical and prolonged mental breakdowns should have first call on fully trained members of the mental health professions. (p. xiv)

In the years since 1961, newer forms of psychotherapy have come into favor, and improvements in other treatment areas, such as psychopharmacological treatment in particular, have had dramatic effects on reducing long-term hospitalizations. But discharging patients from hospitals is not the same as producing cures, as the American Psychiatric Association (1982), cautions:

> First, the law should recognize that the nature of inhospital psychiatric intervention has changed over the last decade. Greater emphasis is now placed upon psychopharmacological management of the hospitalized person. Such treatment, while clearly helpful in reducing the overt signs and symptoms of mental illness, does not necessarily mean, however, that "cure" has been achieved—nor that a patient's "nondangerousness" is assured. (p. 15)

Despite therapeutic improvements on a variety of fronts, "curing" an insane acquittee hospitalized in a psychiatric facility is far from a sure thing. One problem is that our treatments have not yet produced high enough cure rates, particularly for severe disorders and for involuntary patients. A second problem is that the issue of therapeutic effectiveness is confounded by certain ethical and moral dilemmas endemic to therapy in general, and that these dilemmas become most acute in cases of involuntary treatment. To understand this confounding of ethics with effectiveness, let us look at those therapies that have improved, where far greater control is now possible than ever before.

Therapeutic Dilemmas

Beginning with psychopharmacological drugs, the last 30 years have brought great changes: where the 1950s saw the introduction of the first generation of psychotropic drugs, we are now seeing second- and third-generation medications producing more potent and specific effects. In the area of surgical treatments, the lobotomy, the brainchild of the Portuguese neurologist and neurosurgeon Egas Moniz (Szasz, 1973), has undergone considerable technological change: in the 1940s, Dr. Walter Freeman (Gaylin, Meister, & Neville, 1975) performed thousands of frontal lobotomies as an office procedure, inserting a probe into the skull above the eyeball; but in the 1970s, the microelectrode replaced the transorbital probe, sterotaxic brain mapping afforded the surgeon greater precision in placing the electrode at cites deeper within the brain, and psychosurgery developed. With increased and expanded use of behavior modification and aversive conditioning procedures, greater control over a patient's behavior became possible. In sum, chemical, surgical, and psychological therapies improved, but with that improvement has come "a clear and present danger" (Robinson, 1973).

There is a danger that our effectiveness is moving at a faster pace than our ethics. Improved and more potent therapies court dangers that less effective therapies never threatened. The possibilities of social control, social engineering, and the loss of human autonomy arise, as does a question regarding the limits of therapy (Kittrie, 1971). Richard Wasserstrom (Kittrie, 1971) addressed this question in his following remarks:

> Treatments, no less than punishments, are capable of giving rise to serious moral problems. If, for instance, a person can be treated effectively only by performing a prefrontal lobotomy or by altering in some other more sophisticated fashion his basic personality or identity, it might well be that punishment would have the virtue (and it is no small one) of leaving the individual intact. Imprisonment may be a poor way to induce a person to behave differently in the future, but imprisonment may, nonetheless, permit him to remain the same person throughout. In short, treatments as well as punishments may involve serious interferences with the most significant moral claims an individual can assert. Like punishment, treatments of the type contemplated will doubtless be imposed without the actor's consent. The substitution of treatment for punishment could never, therefore, absolve us from involvement in that difficult but unavoidable task of assessing and resolving the competing claims of society and the individual. (pp. 386–387)

Serious moral problems confront the therapist, particularly when working with a "not guilty by reason of insanity" client. If the client's 'crime' was heinous, public pressure becomes greater to make very sure that this fellow is truly, if not radically, changed before discharge is entertained. A therapist treating such a client may sooner consider more potent treatments of social control than he otherwise would with a client whose actions did not arouse public outrage.

On the one hand, therapists have at their disposal a variety of treatments, some potent, though problematic, and others that are moderately successful; on the other hand, therapists have patients who may not consent to such treatments. Moreover, therapists may have their own agenda as to what issues ought to be addressed in treatment (i.e., what thoughts, feelings, and behaviors ought to be changed), whereas their patients might have quite different agendas. Furthermore, patients may expect and insist that their therapists protect their right of confidentiality in order for therapy to proceed, whereas therapists may not be able to honor such a precondition absolutely. What happens, then, if confidentiality cannot be guaranteed, if a "therapeutic contract" cannot be established, and if consent to treatment is not granted? We may have a situation, then, where we have potentially effective treatments, but we do not have the ethical and moral right to proceed.

At this point, the ethical and moral dilemmas become acute. However, these dilemmas are not just restricted to the area of potent therapies with involuntary patients; rather, the position I take is that therapy, by its very nature, is an ethical–moral undertaking. Therapists who fail to appreciate the ethical–moral aspects of their practice court a greater risk of ending up in court defending themselves and their practices (Finkel, 1980). When the public fails to appreciate the ethical–moral dilemmas of doing therapy, therapists are likely to see themselves and their profession portrayed as ineffective, empty promisers. And when the courts fail to appreciate these dilemmas, therapists see hypocrisy and betrayal: employed by the courts to handle their most vexing cases, then punished by the courts for trying. To avoid these pitfalls, we next examine the ethical–moral nature of therapy.

THERAPY AS AN ETHICAL–MORAL UNDERTAKING

An older view of therapy, rooted in an analogy drawn between therapy and the "tinkering trades" (Goffman, 1969)—those service guilds whose members, like the watchmaker, television repairman, and orthopedic surgeon, *repair* watches, televisions, and bones—asserts that therapy is not a moralistic endeavor and that therapists should neither moralize nor act as moral agents. If there is morality here, it is of a minimal Darwinian sort (i.e., "things ought to work as they were meant to work"): as broken watches, televisions, and bones ought to be fixed and set right, so too should psyches. Beyond that, when morals intrude into therapy, they indicate "slip-ups," "countertransference" feelings, and value judgments—errors that should be corrected in supervision in order for the therapist to regain "objectivity" and maintain the appropriate therapist-patient "distance."

This older view, when pushed to absolutism, would claim that the therapist has no business becoming involved in any of the following areas: (1) the economic or political beliefs of the client; (2) making value judgments of the client; (3) preaching to the client; (4) dictating the "good life" to the client (London, 1964). This older view has also been losing favor in the light of logic and litigation.

In dealing with a therapy client, this amoral position leads to difficulties that watches and the like never raise. What does a therapist say to a client who (1) reveals that she has perpetrated a criminal act, such as a theft; (2) reveals that he has contemplated murdering someone; (3) states that her religious convictions are in conflict with her desire for an abortion; (4) lets it be known that he has cheated on his spouse, feels (no or extreme) guilt, and is asking for advice? In each of these cases and to the many more that could be added, how is a therapist to respond in a morally neutral way?

If the answer is to be silent, to not respond, then, in the words of Perry London (1964), the therapist is deceiving "both the client and himself" (p. 12). If the strategm is to be nondirective or indifferent (e.g., "why should I give a damn how you act?"), can this line be maintained if the client's "acting out" takes a fiscal form, such as not paying the therapist, or a physical form, such as ripping up the therapist's office or person? I believe that the therapist's moral and ethical position would quickly surface in these instances: "Contracts ought to be kept," "property ought to be respected," and "persons ought not to be harmed" would likely be voiced by the therapist.

The alternative view, that therapy is an ethical–moral undertaking, emerges, in part, from a fuller consideration and appreciation of the sort of therapeutic dilemmas that were raised in the preceding two paragraphs; but in larger part, the ethical–moral position emerges from an understanding about the very nature of the therapeutic enterprise (Fingarette, 1963). There is a fundamental difference between watches, televisions, and bones and psyches. As seen in Chapter 4, "The Concept of Mental Illness (Disease)," what we typically deal with in therapy are people whose thoughts and feelings are disturbed by still other thoughts and feelings. Some seek treatment because they perceive a discrepancy between the way they see themselves and the way they want it to be. Still others seek assistance for personal distress surrounding standards of conduct, human values, good and bad. Nicholas Hobbs (1965) summed it up this way: "Psychotherapy may be described as an intimate dialogue about moral issues as lived by the client" (p. 1508). And London (1964), who has called therapists "the secular priesthood," put it this way:

> It is specious to argue, as some therapists do, that moral concerns are simply manifestations of "resistance" and that the underlying dynamics of the client's situation never relate to moral problems. It seems viciously irresponsible

for the therapist to argue that, at such time, he must formally remove himself from the discussion by telling the client that the therapy session can be helpful for discussing "personal, emotional problems, not moral ones" (pp. 7–8)

The amoral position becomes difficult to sustain either conceptually or practically. This is particularly so for therapists who work with the insane. It is difficult, if not impossible, for them to insulate their work with their clients from societal and judicial concerns. The therapist may be employed by a state agency or paid by the courts. The therapeutic agenda may be to restore competency so a trial can proceed or to deter the insane individual by keeping him or her in a hospital for the protection of society: these therapeutic goals are not necessarily the client's goals, although they represent the wishes of others. If therapists respond to the wishes of others or, at a minimum, are pressured by these "external" expectations, they must confront certain ethical–moral dilemmas.

As an illustration of a recent dilemma, let us consider John Hinckley's springtime, 1987. Having been hospitalized 5 years, he sought permission to go home at Easter to visit his parents for a day. Hinckley's doctors agreed that he was improving and supported his request. The government, however, argued that Hinckley was still too dangerous, citing his correspondence with Theodore Bundy, a serial killer, as indicative. The media reacted. The *New York Times* called the proposed visit an "insane risk." The issue was no longer a medical, psychiatric matter, as an editorial in The *Washington Post* (May 8, 1987, p. A23) made clear: "Medically, Hinckley is ready to go home. Politically he is not," wrote Charles Krauthammer.

In his "Let Hinckley Go" editorial, Krauthammer notes that modern psychiatry attempts to get patients "back into society as quickly as possible"; in judging Hinckley's case against other hospitalized psychotics, Hinckley's 5-year stay was a long time; judging Hinckley's case against the average length of hospitalization for NGRIs reveals that Hinckley's stay already exceeded the average NGRI's stay by about two years (see Chapter 6). After the press and public uproar, St. Elizabeth's Hospital withdrew the request for the one-day pass for "administrative" reasons. This was not a medical or psychiatric reversal of opinion, claimed Krauthammer, but a situation where doctors retreat before politically unsettling winds. The doctors know that "the idea that John Hinckley, let out for a half-day visit, would be a danger to President Reagan or anyone else is preposterous." Krauthammer continues:

His Easter would have been more heavily covered than the pope's. The only risk of injury would have been to the camera crews fighting for good position.
The danger here was not to public figures. It was to public sensibilities that were shocked five years ago by Hinckley's acquittal. It wasn't that Hinckley was not ready for the outside. It was that the outside was not ready for Hinckley.

If the doctors at St. Elizabeth's Hospital truly believe that Hinckley was ready for this one-day step despite his unusual pen pal, then their "administrative" retreat raises certain ethical-moral questions, such as "Who is the client here?" and "Whose values, and what values, are being imposed?" The doctors are in a dubious position, having the problem of "role bastardization" (Chingempeel, Mulvey, & Reppucci, 1980). They are treators of Hinckley; Hinckley is the client. As employees of a public hospital whose funding Congress oversees, they have some allegiance to the hospital, to the District of Columbia government, and to Congress. In their functional relationship with the judiciary, they have certain obligations and duties to the court. Thus, in functioning in various roles, each with their own set of obligations, the therapist in cases like this must confront a number of ethical, moral, and value dilemmas. Admitting that therapy is an ethical–moral undertaking, however, tells us neither how to solve such dilemmas nor where to draw the line regarding the imposition of values. Historically and currently, therapists look for those ethical precepts that will either help them resolve or avoid such dilemmas. We now turn to a number of suggested precepts.

IN SEARCH OF ETHICAL PRECEPTS . . . AND EFFECTIVE THERAPY

How is a therapist to act responsibly? And when we speak of the therapist's "responsibility," what do we mean? Widiger and Rorer (1984) believe that the concept of responsibility needs to be differentiated by type, and they use Hart's (1968) distinctions of role, causal, capacity, and liability responsibility.

Role responsibility refers to the obligations and duties that are said to attach "whenever a person occupies a distinctive place or office in a social organization . . ." and to the responsibility "for the performance of these duties, or for doing what is necessary to fulfill them" (Hart, 1968, p. 213). As to the therapist's role responsibility, we could say that a therapist is responsible for being on time for appointments, staying awake, furnishing a bill for services, keeping confidentiality, not being sexually intimate with the client, and so forth. Ethical standards, both for the particular discipline and for the state in which the professional is licensed, enumerate some of the role responsibilities associated with being a therapist.

Causal responsibility means causing or producing certain consequences, results, or outcomes. "Not only human beings but also their actions or omissions, and things, conditions, and events may be said to be responsible for outcomes" (p. 214). Whether a therapist can be said to be responsible for the deteriorating or improving mental health of the client is a question regarding causal responsibility.

Capacity responsibility refers to the possession of certain qualities or abilities, such as "understanding, reasoning, and control of conduct" (p. 227). When we raise the question in insanity cases "Is the defendant responsible for his or her actions?" we are raising a question about capacity responsibility. Likewise, when we ask whether the therapist could have foreseen the client's forthcoming divorce, hospitalization, suicide, or murderous act, we are questioning the therapist's capacity responsibility.

Liability responsibility is being held accountable or given credit for what did or did not happen. Ethical liability may be determined by an ethical review committee; legal liability is determined by the courts. Are therapists liable and subject to judgments of damage for the treatment (or lack of treatment) an involuntary patient receives (e.g., *O'Connor v. Donaldson*, 1975), for the harm caused by patients of theirs to others (e.g., *Tarasoff v. Regents of the University of California*, 1976), or for the psychological harm that a client reports following sexual relations with her therapist (e.g., *Roy v. Hartogs*, 1975)—these are questions of liability responsibility.

The determination of liability responsibility is hinged, to a significant degree, on determinations of role, causal, and capacity responsibility. For instance, in cases of alleged malpractice, a topic that is creating increasing concern within the therapeutic community (Cohen, 1979; DeLeon & Borreliz, 1978) and the courts, four elements are considered: for a plaintiff to succeed in a malpractice suit, it must be shown, by a preponderance of the evidence, that (1) the therapist owed a duty to conform to some standard of conduct; (2) that the therapist breached that duty, or was derelict, by some act of omission or commission; (3) that the plaintiff did indeed suffer damage; and (4) that the action of inaction of the therapist was both a cause in fact and a proximate cause of the damage. Elements (1) and (2) relate to role responsibility, whereas element (4) relates to both causal and capacity responsibility (Widiger & Rorer, 1984).

Having thus defined the four types of responsibility, we turn to the ethical precept of a therapeutic *contract*.

CONTRACTS

Regarding contracts, the American Psychological Association's Standards for Providers of Psychological Services (1977), offers a rather vague, general guideline. It states that "there shall be a mutual acceptable understanding between provider and user," but acknowledges that "varying service settings call for understandings differing in explicitness and formality" and that some "settings require an open-ended agreement" (pp. 8–9).

From a behaviorist perspective, a loose, vague, open-ended, or implicit understanding may be viewed as a sure bet to produce ineffective therapy. Stuart (1975), who is a behaviorally oriented therapist, specifies in the contract the goals to be obtained and the techniques to be used; furthermore, he provides the client with literature references describing the techniques, as well as data from outcome research; lastly, he specifies a date by which positive results are expected, provides a monitoring system to track objectives, and warns about undesirable side effects. To a therapist from a different theoretical orientation (e.g., analytic, existential, client-centered), Stuart's efforts may be seen not only as too much, but as counterproductive.

Szasz (1965), who approaches therapy from a different theoretical orientation, sees a value in an open and vague contract: by the therapist not specifying the focus, frequency, and duration of therapy, this forces the client to assume greater control. Thus, Szasz's tack is aimed at increasing the client's causal and capacity responsibility. Yet Stuart's tack, while placing more role responsibility on the therapist, nonetheless is also aimed at increasing the client's causal and capacity responsibility. The behavioral therapist would maintain (Hare-Mustin, Marecek, Kaplan, & Liss-Levinson, 1979) that if the patient cannot be specific in defining a goal, "this challenges the therapist to help translate vague complaints into specific problems." But to an analytic or existential therapist, this is removing from clients their (role) responsibility and placing it on the therapist, which "would be wholly inappropriate, and, in fact, counterproductive" (Parker, 1976): instead of increasing the client's causal and capacity responsibility, you run the risk of making the client more dependent on the "oracular pronouncements" (Menninger, 1958) of the therapist, which can further "infantilize" the client. What you may end up with, says the analyst, is someone with less autonomy than before. The "debate" degenerates still further when the behaviorist (Skinner, 1971) rejoins that "autonomy" as a concept is empty, being merely a mythical remnant from a mistaken and bankrupt theory of human nature.

What we have, when the name calling subsides, are differing theories about therapy and self-responsibility (Applebaum, 1982). Each approach prescribes and proscribes a contractual stance for doing ethical, responsible, and effective therapy, and each differs from the other. Thus, which particular position one holds on contracts depends in part on the therapist's *theoretical* orientation.

There is another difficulty with a therapeutic contract quite apart from the therapist's theoretical allegiance. As Karl Menninger (1958) notes, the therapist and the patient are not equals in the contracting arrangement: the patient (i.e., the party of the first part) has far less knowledge about how therapy works than the analyst (i.e., the party of the second part) and oftentimes has no clear idea what his or her problems are; these two therapeutic facts of life leave the party of the first part vulnerable to playing second fiddle, while the therapist calls the tune. Goldberg (1977), in *Therapeutic Partnership*, gives an illustrative anecdote:

> When I asked an analyst acquaintance of mine whether she and her patients have some explicit agreement about what they are working on together in therapy, she gave me an incredulous look. This highly trained, intelligent, and kind

friend tolerantly pointed out to me that "neurotics don't know what they want! How do you expect them to work on goals in their analysis? Instead, I point out to them through my interventions what it is they are working toward." (pp. 3–4)

Therapists may end up defining the goals of therapy or get patients to shift their identified goals (i.e., which may be cast by the therapist as surface or superficial goals) to deeper, dynamic, and intrapsychic goals or to the explicit behavioral goals that the therapist already had in mind. It is easy, almost too easy, for the therapist to paternalistically decide what is truly in the patient's best interests and to bring these interests into contractual agreement.

Some therapists not only do not shy from this possibility, but welcome the opportunity. As M. Brewster Smith (1961) states, "the psychologist has as much right to posit values as any one else, in some respects more." Given the fact that the *values* are not detached from *causes* or *consequences*, the behavioral scientist may be uniquely qualified for elucidating that causal network in which a value choice is embedded. And Halleck (1971) notes that

every psychiatrist who has ever treated a patient has had some notion regarding the best kind of life for that individual, and every patient who has benefitted from psychiatric therapy has incorporated some of the doctor's values. (p. 34)

In the very process of defining his needs in the presence of a figure who is viewed as wise and authoritarian, the patient is profoundly influenced. He ends up wanting some of the things the psychiatrist thinks he should want. (p. 19)

It is apparent that whatever the psychiatrist does, he will either encourage the patient to accept the existing distributions of power in the world or encourage the patient to change them. *There is no way in which the psychiatrist can deal with behavior that is partly generated by a social system without either strengthening or altering that system. Every encounter with a psychiatrist, therefore, has political implications.* (p. 36)

The values of the therapist, which are, to some extent, shaped and influenced by society's values, intrude into contracting, into defining what the client ought to want and work on. If this is so in "voluntary, contractual therapy," how much more so is it in "involuntary therapy," where therapists hold an even stronger hand, controlling, as they typically do, when and if the patient will be released from the hospital and what privileges the patient will be granted while in the hospital? Will, for example, a therapeutic contract with John Hinckley not be influenced by the values of the therapist, the courts, and the public? And if a John Hinckley or a Daniel M'Naghten or a James Hadfield see their therapeutic goals very differently, how are therapists to act responsibly and whom shall they serve? Do the client's wishes come first, or is it the therapist's, or society's? The precept of a therapeutic contract does not provide the answer.

CONFIDENTIALITY

Another precept cited as essential for effective, responsible, and ethical therapy is that of confidentiality. The client has the right of confidentiality, and the therapist has the duty not to breach it, so the precept goes. Siegel (1977) has argued that there are no circumstances that ethically can justify the breaking of confidentiality:

> when we agree to "exceptional circumstances" under which the confidentiality of information about individuals is waived, we not only violate the civil rights of children and adults, but we violate our essential role as psychologists. (p. 5)

While Siegel highlights our role responsibility, others who favor absolute confidentiality cite causal responsibility, noting that our ability to effect change may diminish drastically if we violate confidentiality in any form. If clients cannot trust that we will maintain confidentiality, they may withhold certain facts, feelings, and fantasies in therapy, or may avoid therapy altogether.

The Law, however, has cited capacity and liability responsibility in a number of key cases and ruled that the therapists loyalty cannot be solely, or absolutely, to the client. In *Tarasoff v. Regents of the University of California* (1976), the California Supreme Court drew some limits on confidentiality, stating that

> public policy favoring protection of the confidential character of patient-psychotherapeutic communication must yield in instances in which disclosure is essential to avert danger to others. The protective privilege ends where the public peril begins. (p. 553)

The case in brief is this (Mills & Beck, 1985). Prosenjit Poddar, an Indian by nationality, was a graduate student at the University of California at Berkeley. In the autumn of 1968, he met Tatiana Tarasoff at a folk dance. They saw one another at social events, he kissed her on New Year's Eve and thought that the relationship was serious, but she told him it was not. He became withdrawn, spent hours listening to tape-recorded conversations he had made with Tatiana, and neglected his school work. Tatiana went off to Brazil in the summer of 1969. Poddar entered outpatient psychotherapy at the University.

During therapy, Poddar told his psychologist-therapist that he had fantasies of harming Tatiana, perhaps even killing her. The therapist also learned that Poddar planned to purchase a gun. Worried about the potential for violence, the therapist consulted his supervising psychiatrist. Citing Poddar's illness and dangerousness, the therapist sought to civilly commit him.

The campus police questioned Poddar about his intended behavior, and Poddar denied any violent intentions. The police left his apartment with a warning for him to stay away from Tatiana. Poddar dropped out of treatment, perhaps because his confidentiality was breached. The therapist took no further action. But Poddar did.

Tatiana Tarasoff returned from Brazil, and Poddar went to her home with a pellet gun and a butcher knife. He shot her, she ran from the house, he followed her outside and stabbed her to death. The parents of Ms. Tarasoff brought suit, claiming that the therapist should have warned Tatiana about the danger.

In *Tarasoff* I (1974), the Court ruled that therapists have a duty to warn potential victims. The Court seemed to be saying to the therapists, "You could have and should have predicted this violence [capacity and role responsibility]; you had a duty to control or prevent it [capacity, causal, and role responsibility]; and you failed to do so [liability responsibility]."

Therapists were in uproar. To the therapists, the courts had placed them in a Catch-22, a crossfire, where they can be sued by clients if they break confidentiality or sued by third parties for failure to break confidentiality and warn. Therapists did what many would do—they appealed.

The American Psychiatric Association, the American Psychological Association, and others asked the California Supreme Court to rehear the case; the Court agreed, and in 1976 *Tarasoff* II resulted. The Court replaced *Tarasoff* I's "duty to warn" with something else; The Court said that

> when a therapist determines or pursuant to the standard of his profession should determine, that his patient presents a serious danger of violence to another, he incurs an obligation to use reasonable care to protect the intended victim against such a danger. [The discharge of this duty] . . . requires the therapist to . . . take whatever steps are reasonably necessary under the circumstances. (p. 346)

Tarasoff II replaced a specific duty—to warn potential victims—with a vague one—to use reasonable care. The ruling left in place the assumption that therapists could predict future dangerousness accurately (i.e., that they have this capacity), an assumption that therapists continue to challenge in court (*Barefoot v. Estelle*, 1983) with empirical evidence (Beck, 1985).

Since *Tarasoff*, a number of other court cases, *McIntosh* (1979) in New Jersey, *Lipari* (1980) in Nebraska, *Davis* (1981) in Michigan, and *Peterson* (1983) in Washington, have affirmed a Tarasoff duty, while in a few cases, such as *Shaw v. Glickman* (1980) in Maryland, courts have stated that "the confidentiality of the psychotherapeutic relationship must override a duty to warn." The California court says that the "privilege ends where the public peril begins," whereas the Maryland court says that "the lips of the psychiatrist and psychologist have been statutorily sealed shut, subject solely to being unsealed by the patient or by the patient's authorized representative."

The law, to date, is unclear and varied from state to state as to confidentiality and duties to warn or to take reasonable care. Some of the cases have extended liability even when no specific victim was mentioned: if victims were foreseeable, or if a class of people were at risk, so too would be the therapist. In a case on appeal before the Fourth Circuit, *Currie v. United States* (Fisher, 1987), the court considered but ruled against imposing an affirmative *duty to commit* in North Carolina. Other courts in future cases, however, may rule otherwise. To keep confidentiality or break it, to commit or not to commit, to release from a hospital or not to release, these are the questions and the dilemmas therapists now confront (Baird & Rupert, 1987). And all of these matters confront therapists who work with insanity acquittees.

When Hinckley seeks release for a day, should his therapist break confidentiality if a judge asks the therapist to reveal the content of therapy sessions? Should Hinckley's private diary, notes, and correspondence be given to the courts over the objections of the patient? If Hinckley commits violence, are the therapists liable to a third party for failure to break confidence and warn, for failure to use reasonable care, or for failure to keep him securely locked up? The precept of confidentiality, torn and tattered by court rulings, provides the therapist poor cover and no sure answer. It is no wonder the American Psychiatric Association seeks to demedicalize and relegalize control of insane acquittees.

CONSENT

The situation is much the same when we examine the precept of "consent." *Consent*, in relation to both human experimentation and clinical work, has been recognized and codified in numerous ethical canons. In the Nuremberg Code of 1946 (Reich, 1978), the very first principle reads "The voluntary consent of the human subject is absolutely essential" (p. 1764). The Helsinki Declaration of 1964 reads "If at all possible, consistent with patient psychology, the doctor should obtain the patient's freely given consent after the patient has been given a full explanation" (Reich, 1978, p. 1770). The Helsinki Declaration of 1975 (pp. 1771–1773) follows up, affirms, and elaborates this point. And the American Psychological Association's ethical standards (1979) again affirm the point that there is an ethical obligation to "fully inform consumers as to the purpose and nature" (p. 5) of an intervention.

With all of these affirmations one might think that the principle of "fully informed consent" would be indisputable and inviolable. Not so. The Helsinki Declaration of 1964 recognizes cases of legal incapacity, where "permission of the legal guardian replaces that of the patient" (Riech, 1978, p. 1770). The Helinski Declaration of 1975 (p. 1772) offers a caution to doctors where a subject (or a client in therapy or a patient in a hospital) "is in a dependent relationship" to the doctor.

There are other principles mentioned that could conceivably clash with the principle of fully informed consent. For example, the following two sentences might be interpreted as allowing for "therapeutic discretion" in not fully informing a client: "Concern for the interests of the subject must always prevail over the interests of science and society." "Every precaution should be taken to respect the privacy of the subject and to minimize the impact of the study on the subject's physical and mental integrity and to the personality of the subject" (p. 1772). What happens when a therapist believes that obtaining a fully informed consent will have a deleterious effect on the patient's mental integrity and personality or believes that such a consent will worsen the therapeutic course? Meisel, Roth, and Lidz (1977) answer,

> If disclosure of certain information—especially the risks of treatment—is likely to upset the patient so seriously that he or she will be unable to make a rational decision, then the physician has the "therapeutic privilege" to withhold such information. (p. 286)

There are a number of therapists who believe that strict, ethical guidelines and patients' rights are interfering with effective therapy. Lebensohn (1970), who has written about the practice of "defensive psychotherapy" (p. 36), gives an example of an informed consent procedure that could strike fear, rather than hope, in the hearts of prospective patients. This procedure forewarns clients of the possibility of not getting better and even getting worse; it raises the possibility that clients may become more dependent on the therapist and more emotionally involved with the therapist; it warns of the possibility of divorce or suicide; and it informs that client that anything said may be used at an involuntary commitment hearing. Lebensohn, with self-evident black humor, then says, "Having properly executed the above form, you may now enter the private consulting room and feel free to tell the psychiatrist anything and everything that comes to mind."

As with the topic of contracts, there are some schools (Gillis, 1979; Goldstein, Heller, & Sechrest, 1968; Haley, 1973; Rabkin, 1977) of therapy that use deception and covert manipulation to achieve effective change. Jay Haley (1978), for one, justifies manipulation over honesty in stating that "it is unlikely that an honest sharing of understanding within a paid relationship solves the problems the patient in paying his money to recover from" (p. 208).

Moving from theoretical to practical objections, many therapists feel that the assumption that patients can give informed consent is unrealistic; the assumption attributes a degree of capacity responsibility to mentally ill patients that they may not possess (Moore, 1978). Several empirical investigations (Applebaum, Mirkin, & Bateman, 1981; Olin & Olin, 1975) have shown "that voluntary mental hospital patients had little idea what they had consented to or what the consent involved" (Widiger & Rorer, 1984, p. 510).

Coming closer to insanity cases, let us imagine a defendant, perhaps a modern-day Hadfield, who is found "not guilty by reason of insanity" and confined to a mental hospital in which he now languishes. Actually Hadfield did a little more than languish at Bethlem: he killed another inmate (for which he was never tried). Let us say that our modern-day, hypothetical Hadfield is not getting any better (i.e., his violence still exceeds societal bounds); and his doctor wishes to perform psychosurgery to reduce his aggression. The doctor types out a consent form, has the patient read it, or has it read to him, and asks the patient to sign it. The patient does so. Do we have a fully informed consent?

This was a central question in the psychosurgery case of *Kaimowitz v. Michigan Department of Mental Health* (1973). An even more interesting question, raised in the post-trial *amicus curiae* brief of the American Orthopsychiatric Association filed in *Kaimowitz*, is "*Can* an involuntarily confined mental patient give informed consent?" The *amicus curiae* brief contended that "legally adequate consent" required that three conditions be satisfied: that the person is competent, that the person understands the proposed procedure (i.e., the person "knows"), and that the consent is given voluntarily. The brief went on to argue that none of the conditions were met, but moreover, raised questions about whether they could ever be met!

In regard to competence, *amicus* argued that an individual who had resided in a hospital for years, where "all major and most minor decisions were made for him," and where "the institutionalization syndrome" was common, was likely to have "diminished capacity." Regarding the second criterion, could such a mental patient know, the question was asked, Could that patient understand the meaning of sterotaxic surgery, mind–brain intereactions, EEG recordings, and microelectrode literature? And finally, to the question of whether the consent was voluntarily made, without "any overt *or indirect* element of force, fraud, deceit, duress, overreaching, or other ulterior form of constraint or coercion," the *amicus* brief argued the patient's position in "an inherently coercive institutional environment" did not afford the individual the opportunity and freedom to bargain as an equal with the doctor.

These interesting questions and contentions lead to a curious conclusion. If in fact the amicus opinion—that such an individual could not give competent, knowing, and voluntary consent—was upheld (which it was not), then the type of individual who could potentially benefit from such surgery could never receive it; and the person who could give competent, knowing, and voluntary consent, would be the type of person who would not need it. From the vantage point of the proponents of psychosurgery, a potentially effective treatment could never be attempted.

While psychosurgery is controversial, rarely attempted, and still regarded by the courts as experimental, psychopharmacological treatment is not. To the contrary, psychopharmacological treatment is commonplace, growing in usage, and regarded as accepted psychiatric practice; yet it is around psychotropic drugs that we have the greatest controversy—one that pits therapists against patients and their lawyers—where patients' rights and patients' needs appear to clash. In no other area have "right to refuse treatment" (Finkel, 1984b; White & White, 1981) cases spawned so much heat and contention.

The consent issue is this: when patients are involuntarily committed to psychiatric hospitals for treatment, and their psychiatrists believe that psychopharmacological treatment will relieve and release patients from their symptoms and psychoses, do patients nonetheless retain the right to consent or to refuse to consent to such treatment? Lawyers for such patients have argued that patients retain the right to refuse to consent, and that right cannot be overriden except in select, extreme instances. A number of court decisions, such as *Rogers v. Okin* (1979, 1980, 1981) and *Rennie v. Klein* (1979), have affirmed that patients have a qualified right to refuse antipsychotic medication.

Psychiatrists have argued that professional and treatment consequences would be damaging to all parties. The psychiatrist Thomas Gutheil (1980) points out that what the patients' lawyers have won for their clients is "a sham freedom," a "freedom of psychosis," that will leave patients "rotting with their rights on." If the patient's right to refuse treatment becomes paramount and absolute, the patient's needs may go unmet. This puts the State and the treating psychiatrists in impotent, conflictual, and untenable positions. The State commits such an individual under *parens patriae* or *police powers* grounds for treatment aimed at ameliorating mental disorder and decreasing dangerousness, yet the State's interest can be thwarted by patients' rights. Psychiatrists, with their Hippocratic Oath to heal and to do no harm, become reduced to jailers and watchers— legally forbidden to practice their best treatment while watching patients deteriorate.

THERAPEUTIC LIMITS

When the State commits an insane acquittee to a psychiatric hospital for treatment, the mental health professionals are limited in what they can do. They are limited by their treatments' lack of effectiveness with seriously disordered patients; they are limited by their own ethical–moral obligations and duties (Ewing, 1987); and they are limited by the constitutionally asserted and legally affirmed rights of patients. The promise of curative treatment seems to be growing fainter, as the spectre of punishment begins to loom larger. If the therapists cannot cure, may not cure, or are forbidden to cure, then are our rationales for committing the insane acquittee reduced to false pretenses? Has the purpose of treatment been transformed in practice into preventive detention? And is this not punishment for someone found not guilty?

Uncomfortable questions like these have led therapists and the State back to court to unshackle both from their Promethean binds, and the courts have been listening. In *Youngberg v. Romeo* (1982), *Mills v. Rogers* (1982), and *In re Mental Commitment of M.P.* (1986), the courts have been granting psychiatrists their "professional judgment" to override the patient's constitutional right to refuse antipsychotic drugs when a legitimate State interest (e.g., treatment) can be shown. Psychiatry and the State have also made use of incompetency hearings to overcome patients' rights and resistances: when a patient is declared legally incompetent, a guardian (or Committee) is appointed with the power to give consent to treatment.

But therapists are not out of the legal-ethical-moral woods yet; in fact, they may have entered more deeply a darkening forest of issues where ethical guiding lights diffract and reflect contradictory therapeutic paths. Those simple guiding lines of yesteryear, like the one J. S. Mill (1930) drew at coercion or the one at paternalism (Beauchamp, 1977; Dworkin, 1972; Feinberg, 1973; Gaylin, Glasser, Marcus, & Rothman, 1978; Robinson, 1974), have not held. Therapists who work with involuntarily confined patients, NGRIs and others, treat and compel treatment because they believe it is in the best interests of the patient and the State; in doing so, they can cite clinical wisdom to support it, laws that permit it, and ethical precepts to justify it. However, support and justification for opposing such practices have been cited by patients, lawyers, ethicists, and therapists on the other side.

What is unarguable is that the practice of therapeutics as a very private matter—conducted behind closed doors, in strict confidence, out of the public's view, and away from legal scrutiny—is no more. We have passed the point where therapy's concerns could be kept insular from society's agenda or patients' litigation. While this may limit therapy's reach and impede its grasp, the world of therapeutics has not been dealt a fatal blow. The dire predictions following the *Tarasoff* decision, for example, that the Armageddon for psychotherapy was upon us or that the decision was "necessarily lethal to psychology" have not come to pass (Shah, 1977, p. 2).

What has come to pass is a noticeable change among therapists and mental health professionals toward recognizing their limitations and presumptions. This, I believe, is positive. Questions about what we can do, may do, and should do are being sounded. For example, in states that have the death penalty, it is not constitutionally permissible to execute someone who is insane. But should a therapist assist the state in diagnosing and treating such an individual in order to make him or her sane and pronounce him or her sane when the consequence is execution? Ewing (1987) argues that our healing ethics do not support such interventions. In another example, the presumption that confidentiality "must remain *absolute* and paramount . . . over all other societal interests" is being reexamined. As Shah (1977) writes, "Such ethnocentric zeal seems to demand that the entire society should accept the value and ideologies of psychotherapists. In other words, what is good for psychotherapists is good for society!" (p. 2)

What is good for therapists may not look all that good to patients or the public. What is good for society may not be best for either therapists or patients. What the NGRI patient desires as best may not match with either the therapist's goals or society's agenda. Some sorting and reconciling of various interests and limitations are in order. In this regard, the American Psychiatric Association's *Statement* (1982) reflects a healthy change:

> The American Psychiatric Association believes that the decision to release an insanity acquittee should not be made *solely* by psychiatrists or *solely* on the basis of psychiatric testimony about the patient's mental condition or predictions of future dangerousness. While this may not be the only model, such decisions should be made instead by a group similar in composition to a parole board. In this respect, the American Psychiatric Association is impressed with a model program presently in operation in the State of Oregon under the aegis of a Psychiatric Security Review Board . . . Confinement and release decisions for acquittees are made by an experienced body that is not naive about the nature of violent behavior committed by mental patients and that allows a quasi-criminal approach for managing such persons. Psychiatrists participate in the work of the Oregon board, but they do not have primary responsibility. The Association believes that this is as it should be since the decision to confine and release persons who have done violence to society involves more than psychiatric considerations. The interest of society, the interest of the criminal justice system, and the interest of those who have been or might be victimized by violence must also be addressed in confinement and release decisions. (pp. 16–17)

For the good of therapy and society, all parties need to define more clearly their objectives. In regard to insanity cases and their disposition, society needs to sort its competing and conflicting theories of punishment (e.g., retribution, deterrence, rehabilitation) and to learn what therapists can and cannot do. For therapists and the mental health professions, their attention cannot be directed at just the client and the various modes of therapy: the impetus to develop more effective modes of therapy must be matched by moral, ethical, and societal concerns.

Patients have certain rights, even those who have been found "not guilty by reason of insanity." What we wish to do and can do must be weighed against the rights of the individual. We may wish to change and rehabilitate individuals through therapy, and they may decline. Or they may wish to return to society but we may desire their continued incarceration. These are disagreements not only about modes of treatment or effectiveness, but about morals, ethics, and values. The development of new modes of therapy has enjoyed a head start, while the development of a sounder moral-ethical-value position strives to catch up; if it does, we will be that much closer to a saner and more responsible policy for the treatment of the insane offender. Such a policy is likely to be based not on promises, but on a recognition of limits.

6

Punishment and the Insane

"Punishment" and the "insane," two nouns linked in the title of this chapter, retain a curious, yet conflictual, connection. To some experts, be they jurists, psychiatrists, psychologists, or legislators, the linkage represents an oxymoron—a combination of contradictory terms: these experts, from a conceptual vantage point, indicate that when someone is found not guilty by reason of insanity, that verdict denotes that we do not find the person culpable or blameworthy; hence, no punishment should follow. Despite such utterances aimed at decoupling "punishment" and the "insane," there seems to be some visceral charge that draws them together.

This linkage was apparent when Hinckley asked to go home for a day at Easter and the press and public reacted with outrage. Krauthammer (1987) may have correctly identified the emotional, visceral linkage:

> In our hearts we have found him "guilty though insane," and he continues to pay for his guilt. Because he is insane, we cannot quite bring ourselves to put him in jail. Because he is guilty, we must punish him. Because he is guilty *and* insane, we let the psychiatrists administer the punishment of imprisonment. Psychiatry, complained the lawyers, turned the Hinckley trial into a circus. The law returns the favor. The law turns the asylum into a prison.

If Hinckley and other NGRIs are *guilty in our hearts*, then we can understand the furor around such verdicts and release from hospital decisions: this sentiment seems to be saying that the insane have not been

123

sufficiently punished, and they ought to be. If this is so, we can see that our conceptualizations and emotions on this matter are schizophrenically split. Repeated conceptual utterances that the two terms ought not to be linked fail to persuade the viscera, which says otherwise.

Should the insane be punished? Should they be exculpated from punishment? These two questions and this chapter lead us to explore both conceptual and visceral arguments. Why do we punish? What theories and rationales support the practice of punishment? And when may we punish? What conditions are necessary for us to justify punishing someone? These are the conceptual, philosophical questions. Alongside the proposed answers to these questions stands the insane. How does, and where does, insanity fit into this scheme of punishment? But we still have those emotionally charged reactions, that visceral linkage. What of that? It, too, I believe, has some conceptual substance to it that needs to be elucidated, rather than dismissed. We begin this topic by first examining some popular, but erroneous, assumptions regarding punishment and the insane.

POPULAR, BUT ERRONEOUS, ASSUMPTIONS

Those popular, *but erroneous,* assumptions are the following: (1) that the insane, through the insanity defense, escape punishment; (2) that a successful insanity defense is easily engineered; (3) that the insanity defense, unlike other defenses, places an unfair burden on the prosecution; (4) that the insanity defense is the only defense that considers the "mental state," or "the thought of man," which, as Chief Justice Brian said in 1477, "is not triable" (Hart, 1968, p. 188); and (5) that this defense represents a singular exception to the general rules of law.

We will examine each of these assumptions, along with the facts that might support or refute each contention. The first assumption is that the insane, through the insanity defense, escape punishment. This assumption, or fear, was voiced by several senators at the Hearings before the Committee of the Judiciary of the United States Senate (1982). Senator Howell Heflin remarked (p. 3) that "we had testimony in the subcommittee that if the *Hinckley* case had been tried, we will say in the State of Florida or the State of Pennsylvania or the State of Alabama, under the procedure there would have been no legal right to have detained him. He could have walked out completely." And Senator Orrin Hatch (p. 7) noted that

> a defendant who successfully convinces a court that he is insane . . . is surrendered to the jurisdiction of the civil authorities who place him in a mental institution until a panel of doctors, for reasons perhaps completely unrelated to legal obligations, such as overcrowding in the asylum, decide he should be

released. As the media has learned in the *Hinckley* case, this could occur within 50 days under such a system.

In testimony at the Hearings before the Subcommittee on Criminal Law of the Committee of the Judiciary of the United States Senate (1983), Barbara Weiner (1983/1980) reviewed the "present reality" of state laws regarding the individual found not guilty by reason of insanity.

> Today, in most states, once a defendant has been successful with his insanity defense plea, the options available to the criminal court judge are very limited. In a few states, commitment to a mental health facility for some period of time is automatic. In most states, the court must hold a hearing or request the prosecutor to petition for a hearing using the same standard of civil commitment as is used in the mental health role. (p. 1066)

Weiner goes on to say that

> in almost every state, the present system relating to the disposition of the individual found not guilty by reason of insanity is filled with barriers which make it difficult, if not impossible, for the criminal court judge to assure that the public safety is being protected. This system has four major problems: (1) the NGRI individual must meet the civil commitment standard; (2) the court is limited to either civil commitment or discharge; (3) in most states there is no option for court imposed outpatient treatment; and (4) there are no provisions for review of the discharge decision in the majority of states. (p. 1067)

While the senators express the fear and Weiner presents the problems, there is another side to the picture. From Weiner's own data, 23 states have automatic commitment following a finding of NGRI; in addition, 17 other states hold a hearing, typically a civil commitment hearing, following a NGRI; and furthermore, 29 states provide for court approval before release from a mental institution can occur.

But neither fears about the laws nor concerns about their limitations speak directly to what is, after all, an empirical question: How are the laws working in regard to NGRI? The best answer to this question derives from the empirical work of Henry Steadman (Steadman, 1980; Steadman & Braff, 1983; Monahan & Steadman, 1983), who presented his findings before the Senate Subcommittee hearings (1983). In one study of 225 New York defendants found NGRI, the average length of hospitalization was 3.6 years. It was also found that "the more serious the crime of NGRI, the longer they remain hospitalized." How does this compare to a felon found guilty for a similar offense? Steadman's conclusion is the following:

> Insanity acquittees may be hospitalized about the same length of time as comparable felons are incarcerated when NGRIs are the responsibilities of correctional agencies, but for somewhat shorter periods (6 months or less) when under the auspice of mental health agencies. (p. 372)

Let us summarize, to this point, and provide a context. In regard to the first assumption, the defendant who is found "not guilty by reason of insanity" is *not*, typically, set free. Many of history's most notable insanity defendants (e.g., Hadfield, M'Naghten) found themselves in psychiatric asylums for the rest of their lives and today's most prominent defendant, John Hinckley, apart from the fears expressed by Senators Hatch and Heflin and those expressed by the press, still resides at St. Elizabeth's Hospital.

However, it is possible to argue, and some have, that the insane still escape punishment *in principle*, if not in practice, since they receive *treatment* in hospitals rather than *punishment* in prison.

The "in practice" side of the argument is easier to rebut. The 'quality of life' within most state psychiatric hospitals, particularly for the involuntarily confined, is typically dismal; and it has been this way for centuries, save for a few periods where change and hope occurred (Bockoven, 1956; Deutsch, 1949; Foucault, 1973; Rothman, 1971). On a historical note, Foucault tells us that in the classical age of the seventeenth and eighteenth centuries, when criminals were thrown into hospitals along with the insane, it was the criminals who objected: when confronted by the maddening and miserable conditions of the hospitals, like those depicted in Hogarth's Bedlam images (Gilman, 1982), the criminals petitioned the authorities for separate facilities.

Twentieth-century images of state hospitals come in a number of forms: Frederick Wiseman's documentary film *Titticut Follies;* books, such as Goffman's *Asylums* (1961) and the Joint Commission of Mental Illness and Health's report (1961); articles, such as Kiesler's "Public and Professional Myths about Mental Hospitalization" (1982); and through courtroom testimony in the spate of "right to treatment" cases (Finkel, 1984c). From such sources we learn of inhumane psychological and physical environments, brutality, malnutrition, locked wards, institutionalization, apathy, the social breakdown syndrome, inadequate staff, and expenditures lower than what we spend to maintain prisons. When the facets are pieced together, the twentieth-century portrait that emerges of the involuntary patient within the landscape of the hospital is anything but "a peaceable kingdom."

The "in principle" side of the argument—that the NGRI defendants are "treated," not "punished"—will be examined more fully later in this chapter. For now, Thomas Szasz's words (1970a), represent the first challenge to such a view:

> Excepting death, involuntary hospitalization imposed the most severe penalty that our legal system can inflict on a human being: namely, loss of liberty. The existence of psychiatric institutions that function as prisons, and of judicial sentences that are, in effect, indeterminate sentences to such prisons, is the backdrop against which all discussion of criminal responsibility must take place.
> . . . In the final analysis, the insanity plea and the insanity verdict, together with the prison sentences called "treatments" served in buildings called "hospi-

tals," are all parts of the complex structure of institutional psychiatry, which, as I
have tried to show, is slavery disguised as therapy. (p. 106)

To summarize the discussion on assumption (1), defendants who successfully invoke the insanity defense seldom walk out of the courtroom as
free men or women. The far more likely scenario transforms the defendant
into a patient and transports him or her to a psychiatric hospital. In such a
setting, the patient is likely to spend 3.6 years, which, according to Steadman and Braff (1983), is close, if not comparable, to what felons for similar
crimes spend in prison; using another account, this time a Nader task force
report (Chu & Trotter, 1972) comparing patients at St. Elizabeth's Hospital
with felons in the Federal penitentiary, it was found that a much higher
percentage of patients than felons spend 5, 10, 20, and 40 years or longer
institutionalized. Given the state, staffing, and funding for most of the
facilities for the criminally insane, the deprivations experienced by the
NGRI patient are likely to match, if not exceed, what awaits the convicted
criminal in prison. Whether the time spend by the NGRI patient is slightly
less, equal to, slightly more, or considerably more than the defendant
found "guilty," there is one difference by which the felon benefits: the
felon knows the maximum time of his or her punishment, whereas the
NGRI patient's "therapeutic sentence" is typically indeterminate.

The second erroneous assumption is that a successful insanity defense
is easily engineered. The fact that this assertion has been uttered so frequently in the face of an almost complete lack of support warrants study in
its own right. One form of this assertion was made following M'Naghten's
trial, when it was feared that M'Naghten's "acquittal" would lead many
more defendants to plead insanity, while leading many more judges and
juries to accept this defense as excusing. As Walker's (1968) data show, the
frequency of accused persons per thousand pleading such a defense actually declined in the 10-year period following M'Naghten (1843), as did the
success rate for the defense.

The current evidence, while sporadic, presents a similar picture.
Steadman cites two studies, one in Wyoming and the other in Erie County,
New York, that address the success rate for such a defense in recent times:
in the former study, 1 of 102 cases (0.9%) was successful, whereas in the
latter study, of 202 cases in which the defendant pled insanity, 51 (25%)
were successful. Not only was the success rate low, but the frequency and
percentage of such cases were also quite low: extrapolations indicate that
very few felony arrests (0.17%) end up raising the insanity plea.

A variation of this second erroneous assumption that has been put
forth is that criminals who have committed the most heinous and harmful
offenses will be more likely to try the insanity defense to escape punishment. Steadman (Hearings, 1983) presents evidence from five states (Michigan, New York, New Jersey, Missouri, and Oregon) that report the types
of crime that are associated with an NGRI verdict. His conclusion is that

the "public perceptions that all NGRIs are heinous, bizarre murderers and rapists is highly inaccurate" (p. 372). Less serious crimes, minor crimes, and less serious assaults make up a sizable portion of acquittals in some jurisdictions. Murder and attempted murder are common, particularly in the urban states (e.g., Michigan and New York), but "rape and other sex crimes are very infrequent."

Still another variation of this assumption asserts that for this defense to work the defendant needs to be wealthy. Senator Orrin Hatch's statement, (Hearings, 1982) refers to the problem of the "rich man's defense" (p. 7). The amount of money spent in Hinckley's defense (the figure of $1 million was mentioned) was the subject of considerable editorial comment. At Daniel M'Naghten's trial, the defense—consisting of four lawyers, who called nine expert witnesses—was paid for by the mysterious and substantial sum of 750 pounds, which was deposited in M'Naghten's name at the Glasgow and Ship Bank. Whether M'Naghten or Hinckley's defense would have succeeded without such ample capital remains open to speculation.

If a case does become a "battle of the experts," the cost will usually be high. Most forensic experts do not give their services gratis. These services—time spent examining the defendant, writing up evaluations, conferring with counsel, traveling, and testifying—cost. In addition, we seldom learn how many experts were paid by the defense (or the prosecution) before the "right" expert witnesses were selected. But most successful insanity defenses do not involve a "battle of the experts." As Steadman notes (Hearings, 1983):

> Contrary to the "battle of the experts" in a few widely publicized trials, the norm is for one set of clinical examinations to be done with the court following the reports submitted. Basically, what the clinicians recommend, the court does. (pp. 368–369)

Let us summarize in regard to this second assumption. That the insanity defense is easily and frequently engineered by desperate, heinous, and well-healed defendants is simply not so. The "betting man"—and lawyers are often paid handsomely to be just that—would most likely stop a client from quickly placing his or her liberty or life on the long-shot bet of insanity; at a minimum, the lawyer would advise the client to stop and consider the following points before the wager is made. The minor point is money: if the trial becomes a "battle of the experts," which isn't often the case, it will typically be expensive. The major point, one of far greater importance to betters, bookies, lawyers, and defendants, is the odds: the best ballpark "guestimates" place "insanity" as a long shot. And a third point to consider is the consequence of a wager lost: the defendant who loses, particularly if the crime does not involve murder or the like, is likely to wind up in a psychiatric facility, with the period of incarceration likely to be longer than if he or she had just entered a plea of guilty and served time in a penitentiary. In short, "an easy out" insanity is not.

The third erroneous assumption is that the insanity defense, unlike other defenses, places an unfair burden on the prosecution. Actually, I believe there is a kernel of truth here, although I also believe that the chaff far exceeds the wheat.

The "burden of proof" issue, which has been a topic of great concern in both House (1983) and Senate testimony and in the new legislative proposals being considered, is linked with the "standard of proof" issue. To simplify, in the burden of proof issue, the question is, "Who has the burden of proof, the prosecution or the defense?" In an insanity case, must the prosecution prove the defendant was sane at the time of the crime, or must the defense prove that the defendant was insane at the time of the crime?

When it comes to the "standard of proof" issue, three different standards have been discussed: Whoever bears the burden of proof, must they prove their case "beyond a reasonable doubt," or by "clear and convincing evidence," or by the "preponderance of the evidence" standard? A further question that arises is, "What do these three standards mean?" If we were to rank these standards by severity or by how demanding they are, it is clear which is ordered where: "beyond a reasonable doubt" is the most demanding; "preponderance of the evidence" is the least demanding; and "clear and convincing" falls in between.

What seem far less clear and convincing are the dividing lines that separate one from another. In this regard, jurists and legal commentators have fallen back to percentage analogies and football similes: it has been said that "preponderance" is equal to 51%, or just enough to tip a scale; that "clear and convincing" is about 75%; and the "beyond a reasonable doubt" lies beyond 90%. Using the football simile, "preponderance" is like the team on offense moving the ball across the 50-yard line into their opponent's territory; that "clear and convincing" is like moving into field goal range; and that "beyond a reasonable doubt" is like scoring a touchdown.

Returning to the erroneous assumption—that the burden is on the prosecution and that this burden is unfair—we must briefly examine our legal history and the current state of affairs. In Anglo-American law, there is the presumption of innocence. In a criminal case, to overcome this presumption "the prosecution must prove beyond a reasonable doubt all elements of the crime charged including *mens rea*" (Hermann, 1983, pp. 14–15). In this historical light, a case involving insanity is no different than one involving larceny, premeditated murder, conspiracy, or numerous other offenses. In the United States, this presumption of innocence and the prosecution's burden has been established in *In re Winship* (1970) "as a matter of explicit constitutional right" (Hermann).

Currently, in half of the states as well as in the federal courts, once the defense attorney introduces some evidence of insanity, the burden of proof shifts to the prosecutor, who "is required to prove the sanity of the defendant, along with all the other elements of the offense including *mens rea*, by proof beyond a reasonable doubt" (Hermann, 1983, p. 15). However, in England, and in the other half of the states, the defense bears the burden of proving the defendant insane, usually by the preponderance of the evidence standard.

What are we to make of our current and historical presumptions, burdens, and standards? On the face of it, the matter of insanity appears to place no greater burden on the prosecution than does any other criminal offense, and, in about half the states and England, it places less of a burden. If the actual and factual legal state of affairs contradicts assumption (3), what accounts for the perception of unfairness and the clamor for change?

I believe that the perception of unfairness (and this is the kernel of truth I alluded to earlier) derives from two sources: first, there is a fundamental difference between the concept of sanity (or insanity), on the one hand, and other types of criminal intent; and second, that the disciplines of psychology and psychiatry cannot, in the present state of their "science," furnish proof "beyond a reasonable doubt."

When a case involves alleged insanity in a state where the prosecution bears the burden of proof, the prosecution must prove beyond a reasonable doubt that the person is sane. "Sanity," or "mental health" (see Chapter 4), has yet to be defined in a clear, precise manner. Given that we could probably extract examples of unreasonable, irrational, or seemingly inexplicable behavior out of thousands of actions that pass unnoticed from any individual's history, can we really prove beyond a reasonable doubt that this is a certifiably sane individual? This is often the question when relatives challenge a testator's will. It seems all too easy to present facts and examples that cast doubt upon the veracity of "I, Solomon Smith, of sound mind and body," particularly if the rest of the sentence reads, ". . . do hereby leave all my worldly possessions to my dog, Fido, who treated me more kindly than my miserable offspring." The prosecutor in the criminal case involving insanity seems to be in the analogous position of Fido's attorney, who must defend the sanity or competence of testator Smith.

Proving that Mr. X differs from the class of normal, reasonable people is different from proving that Smith is one of those normal reasonable people. Not only is the problem different and more difficult, but the experts available to the prosecution—psychologists and psychiatrists—cannot furnish proof beyond a reasonable doubt. This became clear in the case of *Addington v. Texas* (1979), which involved involuntary commitment standards; the court came up with the "clear and convincing" standard because psychiatry was unable to meet the "proof beyond a reasonable doubt" standard. Whether it be predicting dangerousness or diagnosing mental illness, the profession's accuracy, reliability, and validity do not come close to doubt-erasing, touchdown-scoring levels.

As for an extra point, we can deal with erroneous assumption 4 relatively quickly. The assertion that the insanity defense is the only defense that involves "mental states" and the "thought of man" is simply untrue. In a case of larceny, the prosecution had to prove that a larcenous intention existed. Premeditated murder cases involve proving that intention was present. Conspiracy, recklessness, and negligence cases demand inquiry into the thinking of the defendants.

The fifth assumption, that the insanity defense represents a singular exception to the general rules of law, also proves fallacious. "Insanity" does exculpate a defendant, but so do other conditions: defendants in cases involving accident, automatism, self-defense, duress, and murder in the line of apprehending a suspected felon have been exculpated too.

These five popular assumptions, by at least the preponderance of the evidence, prove to be erroneous. But the fact that they have been raised repeatedly over a lengthy historical span, sometimes in the face of clear and convincing contradictory evidence, is indicative, in my opinion, of that deeper emotional/visceral linkage. When taken as a whole, these assumptions connote that something appears to be unfair when it comes to insanity; that through a legal system of laws and procedures that are inappropriately attuned, perhaps, the insane escape too easily a fate they properly deserve—their just desert of punishment.

But do the insane justly deserve punishment? In the next section, we explore some fundamental questions about punishment in general and then take up the matter of how insanity fits into the general scheme of things.

WHEN MAY WE PUNISH?

This question can be stated in a number of ways. One alternative is "Who may be punished?" Still another way of establishing the focus of this subsection is to ask "What conditions have to be met before we may punish?" These questions all relate to what Hart (1968) calls the *distribution* of punishment.

HARM

One answer to the question can be stated as follows: Punishment is contingent on a *harm* occurring. If someone injures, assaults, or murders another, a harm has occurred, and we typically punish the offender. The amount of punishment (which is a corollary issue in Hart's distribution category) is usually proportional to the harm done.

As soon as this answer is offered, exceptions come to mind. In the Hadfield case, King George III was not injured (i.e., Hadfield's aim, as his beliefs, proved to be untrue), yet Hadfield was tried on the charge of treason. Something other than harm appears to be the relevant element. We would probably agree that the trial of Hadfield should have proceeded not on the grounds that harm was done, but that harm was *intended*.

Before shifting to another proposed answer, some additional difficulties for the harm notion ought to be mentioned. One difficulty arises when, to disinterested parties, a harm seems apparent, although the interested parties (i.e., including the victim) claim that no harm was committed. The example of a mercy killing comes to mind, as does the sale of heroin to a terminally ill cancer patient in constant pain. The law, in bringing charges in cases such as these, might well sidestep the "objective–subjective" debate as to harm and invoke, rather, the principle that a criminal act (that which violates a law) has occurred, thereby justifying punishment.

When we speak of the amount of harm determining (through some rule of proportion) the amount of punishment, we run into some complications and exceptions. An individual whose actions, either through accident or negligence, led to the death of hundreds, may be punished less severely (or not at all) than one who, through premeditation, takes one life. Thus, whether punishment follows, and in what amount, is not necessarily dependent on harm or the extent of the harm.

A MORAL WRONG

Another answer to the question "When may we punish?" asserts that punishment should follow a moral wrong. This linkage between punishment and moral wrongfulness was the basis of ecclesiastical law (see Chapter 1), where culpability for sin was the foremost concern. If we were to look back still farther for the origins of this linkage, we would probably find our Anglo-American origin in the biblical "in the beginnings." That earthly laws (with their associated punishments) codify divine laws, commandments, and injunctions—morals—was recognized and expounded by many. The great Victorian jurist James Fitzjames Stephen said it quite clearly and forcefully in the following passage quoted from Hart (1968):

> Stephen, like his successors today, emphasized the interdependence and interpenetration of law and morals, not only as a fact to be observed but as something we should foster and intensify. In his view the object of the criminal law could not be stated either in the old Utilitarian language of deterrence or in the new language of reform and rehabilitation. He insisted that the criminal law did and should operate to "give distinct shape" to moral indignation, and

hatred of the criminal. Because the criminal law has this function "Everything which is regarded as enhancing the moral guilt of a particular offence is recognized as a reason for increasing the severity of the punishment . . . the sentence of the law is to the moral sentiment of the public what a seal is to hot wax." This is of course strong stuff and it would be surprising to find our judge repeating today Stephen's assertions concerning the moral rectitude of *hating* criminals, nor would they speak as Stephen did about the duty of the judge to express that desire for vengeance which crime excites in the healthy mind. Nonetheless, Stephen's view of the relation of criminal law to morality and what may be called his expressive or denunciatory theory of criminal punishment is with us still. (pp. 169–170)

It is not only "with us still," it is still giving us problems. Take, for example, "lying." I do not know of any moral system that does not see "lying" as a moral wrong, yet the law seldom cites lying as a criminal offense. In the case of lying, law and morality are not inextricably tied; and where they were once tied, as in blue laws (e.g., statutes regulating work, commerce, amusements, and the selling of alcohol on Sundays), the repeal of such laws amounts to a legal severing of those ties.

Not only is it the case that not all moral wrongs are legal offenses, but for some legal offenses it is difficult to perceive or attribute moral wrongfulness. Take, for example, some of the regulatory laws that have been enacted: laws that require a county sticker on a motor vehicle or a license to practice barbering. Would we feel comfortable pointing a finger, pronouncing moral guilt, and punishing someone for barbering without a license or driving without a sticker? I think not, although this can be debated (*Proprietary Articles Trade Assoc. v. Atty Gen. for Canada*, 1931).

If morality and criminality are not coextensive, then "when a moral wrong has occurred," like the previously offered answer, "when a harm has occurred," does not provide a consistent answer to the question "When may we punish?"

A Criminal Act

Given the disparities between moral and legal proscriptions, another proposed answer focuses on the latter as the basis for punishment: whatever is *legally* defined as a crime may be punished. But this simple, if not circular, answer creates its own set of complexities and exceptions. Legislating what is a crime is easier than determining if a criminal *act* has occurred. The key word is "act," which, as we will quickly see, is legally, psychologically, and historically thought of as distinct from mere "motion" or "behavior."

In the eighteenth century, in his *Lectures on Jurisprudence or the Philosophy of Positive Law*, John Austin (1885) set forth the distinction between "act" and "movement": "The bodily movements which immediately follow our desires of them, are the only human acts, strictly and properly so

called. For events which are not *willed* are not *acts* . . ." (p. 414). In Austin's
account, the *will* is the key element, and when it is present, we speak of
voluntary *actions;* when it is not present, we have involuntary movements.
For Austin, voluntary actions are punishable, but not what is involuntary.

This distinction makes apparent sense, particularly when we think of
accidents and reflexes. If a man accidentally falls down a flight of steps and
injures someone below, we are apt to excuse rather than punish him for
the crime of assault. The person who, when startled or stung by a bee,
reflexively jumps or flails his arm, thereby striking another, is similarly not
subject to punishment. The adage "accidents will happen" covers and
excuses such instances.

We begin to have qualms, perhaps, when we realize the number and
types of cases that appear to qualify as "not voluntary acts." The *Model
Penal Code* (2.01(2) at 24) establishes four categories:

> (a) a reflex or convulsion; (b) a bodily movement during unconsciousness or
> sleep; (c) conduct during hypnosis or resulting from hypnotic suggestion; (d) a
> bodily movement that otherwise is not a product of effort or determination of
> the actor, either conscious or habitual.

An "automatism" case in England involving Esther Griggs fits within these
categories (Walker, 1968, p. 168). When two constables responded late at
night to a female voice crying, "Oh, my children! save my children!" they
and Esther discovered that she threw her baby out of an upstairs window,
through a pane of glass. Esther reported she had been dreaming that her
little boy had said the house was on fire and that what she had done was
with the view of preserving her children from being burnt to death. A
grand jury refused to find a true bill against her, so she never went to trial.
In short, no *act* occurred, hence no criminal action was involved; without
criminal action, punishment is precluded.

The Griggs case presents some problems for Austin's distinction. Esther Griggs' statement reveals *willful,* purposeful, intended action: a series
of behaviors (e.g., reaching for the baby, picking up the baby, carrying the
baby to the window, and throwing the baby out) was voluntarily initiated.
This seems quite different from a bee sting reflex or a fall down the stairs;
however, the end result is the same. What is not the same, however, is the
element of *will.* In the Griggs case, the element of *will* was present, although the argument was that her will, awareness, and mental state were
distorted by the nightmare, thus we still do not have an *action.*

Griggs and other such cases reveal, in my opinion, the false distinction
between *actus reus* and *mens rea.* Historically, jurists have referred to two
separate and distinct phases of a trial. The first phase (*actus reus*) consists of
determining if a criminal act has occurred (Did Mr. Jones fire the gun, and
did the bullet from that gun strike and kill Mr. Smith?). When the *actus reus*

phase has been determined, the trial proceeds to the *mens rea* phase, where considerations of premeditation, provocation, passion, insanity—the mental elements—are brought to the fore. But the Griggs case, among others that deal with amnesia, fugue, or somnambulism (*e.g., Fain v. Commonwealth, 1879; Regina v. Tolson, 1889*), reveals that the mental element has to be considered in the *actus reus* phase, because a determination that an *action* occurred is dependent, in Austin's account, on such dark and murky concepts as the will, consciousness, and mental state of the defendant.

Hart (1968) states that "what is missing in such cases is a minimum link between mind and body . . ." (p. 92). I would add to that statement "some minimum link between an aware mind and body." But even with the addition, we still have problems, as contemporary psychological, physiological, and neuropsychological notions reveal. For example, we may voluntarily decide to take a drive in the car on the highway, but are we always aware, or fully aware, of turning the wheel ever so slightly to keep within the lane? We aren't aware, in the main, nor could we be; and if we were, the experience would be overwhelming and detrimental for performance. But just because we are not aware of most proprioceptive cues or adapt and habituate to the constancies of the road, we would not, ordinarily, excuse a driver who crashes his car into another. If the driver claims "But I wasn't aware!" someone would quickly respond "But you should have been aware!"

What emerges from this discussion is an *awareness:* that simply defining punishment as contingent on a criminal act *necessarily* leads us to further considerations. Our perception and judgment cannot rest on what is seen (the behavior), but must travel farther along that darkening road inward—a road leading to intentions, will, awareness, consciousness, and the mental state—which provides the psychological, albeit infirm, ground for deciding if what we saw was an *act* (or an act) or not.

MENS REA—INTENT

Using outward conduct alone (i.e., only the observable behavior) leaves us with too many problems and exceptions. Traditional Anglo-American thought demands more than outward behavior for conviction and punishment. Perhaps the closest we've come toward using only outward behavior are "strict liability" cases. "Strict liability," also called the objective theory of liability, has been attributed to Justice Holmes (Hart, 1968). For Holmes, the law does not need to discover what a man intended; rather, we can impute the intention "that an 'ordinary man,' equipped with ordinary knowledge, would be taken to have had in acting as the accused did" (p. 38). While "strict liability" may make the legal task of determining culpability easier, "it is generally viewed with great odium and admitted as an exception to the general rule, with the sense that an important principle has been sacrificed to secure a higher measure of conformity and conviction of offenders" (Hart, 1968, p. 20).

Using outward conduct alone also fails in cases where *there is no outward conduct* yet the absence of action is an offense. This situation arises most frequently in cases of negligence, where an action did not, but should have, occurred. While the concept of negligence as a basis for criminal liability has been debated, with Glanville Williams (1961) and Jerome Hall (1960) arguing that it serves no purpose and should not incur liability, most commentators take the position that negligence does have a proper place within the legal scheme of things; the law, given the number of statutes involving negligence "on the books," would seem to affirm the majority opinion. Something more, then, is needed—something we could pin our punishments to when action is either absent or insufficient.

Mens rea ("an evil mind," "a guilty mind," "a vicious will," "a state of mind," or "a specific intention"), a concept currently replete with meanings and rife with disagreements, was the inner element that Archbishop Wulfstan inserted into the secular, strict liability laws of pre-Norman England. But *mens rea*, broadly construed as "an evil mind" or "a vicious will," runs into some of the same difficulties that "a moral wrong" did: where we were in doubt before as to whether a legal offense was also a moral wrong, now we are in doubt as to whether a criminal offense implies, or even requires, an evil mind.

Retreats from the broad, general, and morally laden meaning of *mens rea* have been widely sounded, and more restrictive, morally neutered definitions have been offered. Austin (1956–1957, p. 1), for one, restricted *mens rea* to the elements of knowledge of the circumstances and foresight of the consequences. Thus, if the accused realized that he had a gun in his hand and not a melon, and if he was aware that in his gunsight was a man and not a tree, then we could infer that he had knowledge of the circumstances. If he realized that firing a gun at a man could lead to injury or death, then he had foresight of the consequences. If both were present, then so was *mens rea*. The term *mens rea* is not mentioned in the M'Naghten Rules, but its meaning, in the narrow, neutered sense, is clearly embedded: by using the phrase "to know the nature and quality of the act he was doing," the framers of the Rules were incorporating a meaning of *mens rea* similar to that of Austin. Dr. Turner, who wrote *The Mental Element in Crimes at Common Law* (see Hart, 1968), also restricted *mens rea*: for Turner, *mens rea* consisted of two elements—voluntary conduct coupled with foresight of the consequences of conduct.

Even if we restrict the meaning of *mens rea*, skimming it to a bare intention denuded of moral overtones, it still does not completely cover the question of when we may punish.

The Victorian judge, James Fitzjames Stephen, said that to punish bare intention "would be utterly intolerable: all mankind would be criminals, and most of their lives would be passed in trying and punishing each other for offences which could never be proved" (Hart, 1968, pp. 169–170).

Typically, at that point, we fashion an answer using the elements of a criminal act, a harm, and *mens rea*. The answer goes something like this: We may punish when a criminal act occurs and an intention to commit that act can be inferred. The severity of the punishment is usually proportional to the degree of harm, seriousness of the criminal act, and heinousness of the intent. In my opinion, particularly when the question of "insanity" is raised, this answer fails.

A Capacity

The argument that something is needed beyond *mens rea* (intent) and a criminal act has been put forward by Fingarette (1972). The element that is missing is captured by the term "capacity." To distill this subtle substance, along with its meaning and significance, we will mix the element of negligence and the case of Hadfield, and sift.

"I wasn't thinking," or "I didn't mean for it to happen," are the common defensive utterances of persons confronted after their actions have produced accidental, inadvertent, or negligent damage. In terms of the elements we have already discussed, these agents are staking their defense on the fact that they did not have the requisite intent or state of mind (*mens rea*) necessary for punishment, or, that under *actus reus*, no voluntary action occurred. But when we think of negligence we are implying something else. Using an example provided by Hart (1968), let us examine two sentences: "He negligently broke a saucer" and "He inadvertently broke a saucer."

> The point of the adverb "inadvertently" *is* merely to inform us of the agent's psychological state, whereas if we say "He broke it negligently" we are not merely adding to this an element of blame or reproach, but something quite specific, viz. we are referring to the fact that the agent failed to comply with a standard of conduct with which any ordinary reasonable man *could* and *would* have complied: a standard requiring him to take precautions against harm. The word "negligently," both in legal and in non-legal contexts, makes an essential reference to an omission to do what is thus required: it is not a flatly descriptive psychological expression like "his mind was a blank."
>
> By contrast, if we say of an agent "He acted inadvertently," this contains no implications that the agent fell below any standard of conduct . . . crudely put, "negligence" is not the name of "a state of mind" while "inadvertence" is. (pp. 147–148)

The reason that "negligence" is incorporated into the law and should be, according to Hart, is because we don't accept the excuse "I didn't think." Our quick rejoinder is "But you should have!" To quote Hart: "*if anyone is ever responsible for anything*, there is no general reason why men should not be responsible for such omissions to think, or to consider the situation and its dangers before acting" (pp. 151–152).

The implication, which I believe is quite clear, is that ordinary men and women have the *capacity* to think and consider; furthermore, we expect them to exercise this capacity. This is the very issue and heart of the matter of "insanity," particularly when we decide to exculpate. In excusing such defendants, we are saying that *they do not have such a capacity*, or that *they are unable to exercise their capacity*, by no fault of their own. I add the phrase "by no fault of their own" to incorporate a point put forward most persuasively by Fingarette and Hasse (1979). Their point can be seen through the example of the drunk driver. Intoxicated individuals may claim that at the time of the crash their capacities were "inoperable"; the courts, however, can counter with "yes, but by your own prior choices and actions you brought that incapacity about." In short, "you should have thought and considered," and the failure to do so amounts, at a minimum, to negligence.

In switching from the case of negligence to that of Hadfield, we will reach, as the Hadfield jury reached, a similar finding. Hadfield's defense could not have succeeded on either *mens rea* or M'Naghten Rule grounds. Hadfield's intent was not only evident, it was admitted. He bought pistols; he found out that King George III was to be at Drury Lane; he went there with the purpose of killing the monarch; he stood up in the theatre, aimed at the King, and fired; he knew that what he was doing was wrong, by legal standards, and knew that apprehension and punishment would follow. He had "intent" (*mens rea*). Yet he was found "not guilty."

I believe that the jury in the Hadfield case reached the right conclusion. Hadfield's attorney, Erskine, brought out Hadfield's delusion and the war wound of his head, and wove a picture of "motives irresistible." But to focus on "motives" is to miss the point, as the Attorney General of the United States, William French Smith, did, in his testimony before the Committee on the Judiciary of the United States Senate (1982). The Attorney General, representing the views of the administration, finds a flaw in "introducing motivation into the determination of guilt or innocence." A moment later in his testimony, he states that "Ordinarily, under our law, the reason or motivation for such an act is irrelevant to guilt" (p. 28). I believe he is wrong on several counts.

First, motivation is a relevant factor when it comes to determining guilt or exculpating. When we exculpate on grounds of "self-defense," "necessity," "duress," or "accident," we have typically inquired into the motivation of the defendant and found it to be understandable, not punishable.

My second disagreement with the Attorney General's position is that it misses the central issue in insanity cases: it is not "motivation" that has been introduced, but evidence that the individual's *capacity* to perceive and weigh, to think and consider, is defective. When Erskine engaged in his courtroom grandstanding by rubbing Hadfield's head wound and inviting the jury to inspect the visible membranes of Hadfield's brain, he was literally and figuratively showing that Hadfield's "capacity" was shot.

When it comes to a defendant in an insanity case, the "capacity" argument cuts deeper than does the absence of *mens rea*: rather than claiming that the defendant was "a responsible person under law who acted without guilty intent, it is in effect a claim that the person was not a responsible agent" (Fingarette, 1972, p. 131). The very "capacity" that makes for a "responsible agent"—the "capacity" we assume to be present and expect to be exercised when negligence is the issue—*is in question*. When Attorney General Smith recommended the *mens rea* thesis only— "mental disease or defect would constitute a defense only if the defendant did not even know he had a gun in his hand or thought, for example, that he was shooting at a tree"—he was averring to a position that the Hadfield jury had already shot down and that Erskine rejected with finality in uttering that "no such madness ever existed in the world" (Robinson, 1980, p. 42).

WHY PUNISH?

The preceding section addressed the question of *when* may we punish. This section, which addresses the *why* question, seeks to articulate the justifications used to defend the practice or exemption of punishment, particularly with regard to the insane individual. Every insanity defense test and trial has consequences. A defendant may be set free, imprisoned, or sent to a psychiatric hospital. The victim, or victim's family, along with the press, populace, and professional community, may be assuaged or enraged. Whether, in the aftermath, we feel that justice has been done, or undone, depends in part on whether we feel that our underlying and oftentimes competing justifications for punishment or its exemption have been supported or abrogated.

The question we face is twofold: "What do we want to have happen, and why?" The first part of this question is typically easier to answer: when a crime has been committed, we want punishment to follow. The second part of the question, dealing with "why," is far from clear, with reasons for wanting to punish an individual being numerous and varied. The victim of the crime, or the victim's family, may want revenge, or compensation, or both. Others might champion punishment as a way of satisfying the public's thirst for revenge and the public's demand for reprisals. Still others demand punishment as a way of satisfying a deity or tradition. Some feel that the public has been harmed "either because one of its members has been injured or because the authority of the law essential to its existence has been challenged or both" (Hart, 1968, p. 22), and that inflicting punishment on those who have voluntarily harmed others is right. The denunciatory theory of James Fitzjames Stephen pronounces punishment to give "distinct shape" to our moral indignation and hatred of the criminal: thus "the sentence of the law is to the moral sentiment of the public what a seal is to hot wax." And the "choosing system" idea says that laws and punishments are *offered* to all individuals, giving us a choice to obey or pay; inflicting punishment, then, is society's obligation in upholding its part of the reciprocal system.

Of all the rationales and theories offered to justify punishment the two most widely cited positions are those of *deterrence* and *retribution*. One way of distinguishing between theories is on the basis of whether they are oriented toward *past* or *future* action. The *deterrence* position is oriented toward the future and considers the protection of society to be the prime objective. The advocate of deterrence, by a utilitarian calculus of sorts, justifies our laws and punishments by invoking the greater good for the greatest numbers and claims that our punishments are in place to deter the future likelihood of crime. The *retribution* position is oriented toward past actions, or, more properly, the "moral evil of misconduct." The retributivist holds that if someone voluntarily commits an offense, then punishment to match the wickedness of the offense (i.e., the return of suffering) is itself morally just.

Complicating the picture still further is the *rehabilitation* position. When nineteenth-century alienists and medico-psychological experts began to enter the insanity dialogue, and as the "new criminology" (see Chapter 3, "The Courtship of Law and Psychology") gained ascendancy, a discernible shift from punishment to treatment (i.e., the process of divestment) occurred. But the rise of rehabilitation has, in turn, complicated and muddled the "why we punish" picture still further. When a defendant is given treatment, the advocates of retribution take umbrage, feeling that a crime and a moral wrong have gone unpunished: from the retributivist's point of view, the defendant not only fails to get his or her "just deserts," but instead, is handed "a piece of cake." The advocates of deterrence are no less satisfied than their retributivist rivals when the rehabilitationists carry the day; the utilitarians warn us of the consequences—more crime, more insanity pleas, and more public outcry—and they're typically right, at least on the last point.

In today's light, Hart's (1968) comment, that the "general interest in the topic of punishment has never been greater than it is at present and I doubt if the discussion of it has ever been more confused," (p. 1) still seems to hold. I think this assertion is true for the following reasons: for one, as Hart puts it, most instances of punishment reflect "a compromise between distinct and partly conflicting principles" (p. 1); for another, our faith in the reasonableness and workability of any one rationale, be it retribution, deterrence, or rehabilitation, has been severely shaken; still another factor is that the motive of revenge, or compensation, has been unfairly and perjoratively cast and is thus often left out of the decision-making process; and finally, insanity defense tests and trials typically afford only two choices—to treat or to punish—with a result being that we cannot do both. Let us examine these points.

RETRIBUTION

Our confidence in retribution as a justification for punishment has been shaken on several counts. Hegel's (1952) curious locution in defense of retribution, that "the immediacy superseded in crime leads, then, through punishment, i.e., through the nullity of this nullity, to affirmation, i.e., to morality" (p. 248), has been challenged on logical and pragmatic grounds. How and why does this "moral alchemy" of a crime followed by a punishment lead to a restoration of a moral balance? Those who challenge the death penalty, for example, question whether society is healed or made morally stronger when the state punishes by taking life. The opponents of the death penalty, contrary to Hegel's assertion, argue that society and morality are weakened when the state repeats, in the name of punishment, the very crime of taking a life.

Retribution rests on the belief that "X broke the law and could have kept it"; but that belief, predicated on the assumption that we are all responsible agents, has been under near constant attack ever since the nineteenth-century alienists entered the insanity dialogue. The likes of Forbes Winslow and Henry Maudsley claimed that disease nullifies responsibility, turning lunatics into pitiable, but not punishable, machines. Twentieth-century critics, such as B. F. Skinner and Lady Barbara Wootton, change the arguent but continue the attack. Skinner, in his provocative work *Beyond Freedom and Dignity* (1971), claims that the notions of "responsibility" and "autonomous man" are relics of an outworn and incorrect psychology; of more pragmatic importance, which, after all, is the behaviorist's bottom line, is the fact that these notions offer the behavioral scientist and concerned public "little help" *in controlling* the problems of crime. Lady Wootton (1960), for slightly different reasons from Skinner's, also favors eliminating the notion of responsibility. For Lady Wootton, an individual's responsibility or capacity to resist temptation and crime lies "buried in consciousness, into which no human being can enter" (p. 232). "No human being" also includes psychiatrists, who, Wootton feels, cannot reliably distinguish the sick from the healthy, and who do not enjoy "the public's confidence to a degree which gives any expectation that they might be entrusted with virtually the last word on what may be a matter of life and death" (Wootton, 1959, p. 236). What she proposes is a forward-looking system in which "the whole idea of responsibility" disappears.

The critics and critiques of retribution, from the alienists to Skinner to Wootton, all rely on strong *pragmatic* grounds to solidify their arguments. Yet retribution rests first and foremost on absolute, rather than pragmatic, considerations. Take as an illustration Kant's claim "that meeting the moral evil of misconduct with suffering is . . . good *per se*, so that, even on the last day of society, the murderer not only may but must be executed" (Hart, 1968, p. 75). For Kant, one of the strongest defenders of retribution, it is the "good *per se*," not the Skinnerian and pragmatic "good because it works," that is essential; even if there is no tomorrow, there would still be reason, in Kant's mind, to punish. But how many of us would hold to an absolute defense irrespective of pragmatics? If we found, for example, as the historian and surveyor of prisons John Howard (1784) did, that a prison did not mend morals or that a system of punishment based on retribution not only failed to deter crime, but actually led to an increase, how many of us would not want to compromise our justifying principle of retribution with something else?

DETERRENCE

The Utilitarian justification for punishment, *deterrence*, based on "the old Benthamite confidence in fear of the penalties threatened by the law" (Hart, 1968, p. 1) to control criminal conduct, faces a growing skepticism. The nineteenth-century alienists predicted that deterrence wouldn't work with the insane. You could lock Hadfield up for life, the alienists would say (which was done), and you still would have Bellingham, Oxford, and M'Naghten. But the skepticism extends beyond the limited class of insane or potentially insane individuals. The questions for the deterrence position are, Does it work *in general*, and can it serve *on its own* as a reasonable justification for punishment?

Twentieth-century criminologists, judges, legislators, and the public are confronted with the high recidivism rates for individuals who have been punished. That time served in prison (punishment) seems not to lead the individual to the "straight and narrow" path but back to crime, the courts, and prison is a saddening and sobering fact. It also casts a skeptical shadow across the Utilitarian's bright hope. And when state's enact tougher sentencing, or the death penalty, only to find that the rates of murder and serious crime do not drop, the Utilitarian's justification is further eroded.

As retribution is a moral and conceptual position most vulnerable to pragmatic attack, deterrence, the more pragmatic justification, faces its stiffest challenge on conceptual and moral grounds. Let us take two admittedly far-fetched examples. Suppose a community is suffering because so many individuals double-park; as a result, commerce is impaired and people are inconvenienced. The community decides that a greater deterrence is needed, so that the new punishment for drivers who double-park is to have their legs amputated. A Draconian measure, to be sure, but one that will surely get the attention of drivers. And probably, with only a few administrations of punishment, the problem will be brought under control. But even if the punishment served to deter and thus served the majority, there is still the question of whether it would square with our notions, i.e., retributionist notions, that punishment fit the crime. Would we stand for such a policy *even if it worked?* I think not.

In the second example, the Utilitarian lawmaker notes that more people die from drunk driving accidents than from murder; in terms of frequency and outcome, the former is a more serious problem for society than the latter. The lawmaker decides to propose a change in the scale of punishments, making the penalty for drunk driving greater than that for murder. Would the public support such a change, even if the majority benefited? Again, I think not. And the reason this measure would fail to attract public support I believe is that it does not fit with a commonly shared scale of proportion of punishment—a scale that weighs the gravity of offenses along moral, not pragmatic, dimensions. So even it if could be shown that the world would be a better place for most if all deterrent advocates were executed, the retributionists would no doubt smugly rise to their mistaken and condemned brethren's defense, thereby saving deterrent souls with retributionist largesse.

REHABILITATION

If retribution and deterrence have had their problems, the same (and more) can be said for rehabilitation. Our faith in rehabilitation, be it for the criminal in general or the insane defendant in particular, has been shaken. Our cure rate for the seriously disturbed patient (and the insanity defendant typically falls within this class) remains one of the major disappointments in the mental health profession. And the criminal, whether called just that or a "psychopath," "sociopathic personality," or what have you, has remained stubbornly resistant to psychotherapizing. Some researchers and therapists who have looked at the criminal personality (Yochelson & Samenow, 1976) and attempted to peer inside the criminal mind (Samenow, 1984) now tell us that criminals are different, are not victims, choose evil, and do not reform under classical therapy. In sum, the Therapeutic State has failed to deliver on its promise.

One of the problems with rehabilitation is that it typically masks and incorporates other operating motives. Individuals may advocate treatment (e.g., "that guy belongs in a hospital, not a prison"), but being held involuntarily anywhere also satisfies deterrent and retributivist motives. The particular individual is taken out of society and placed in the netherworld of the hospital where he or she cannot hurt those on the outside; not only is the individual deterred, but this "treatment" may also deter others, if psychiatric incarceration was the guaranteed consequence; such individuals also pay for their prior actions and intentions by forfeiting their liberty, thus satisfying in some part, retributivist motives.

Conceptually, rehabilitation stands apart and distinct from deterrence and retribution: the latter two are reasons for *punishment*, while rehabilitation's *raison d'etre* is *treatment*. But practically, rehabilitation is oftentimes a contaminated mixture of motives. We see this most clearly when psychiatrists, those rehabilitationist gatekeepers, release the insane defendant-turned-patient too quickly (i.e., according to the beholding eyes of the press, populace, and legislators). This point was just the concern of Senators Helfin and Hatch, who were quoted at the beginning of this chapter. That legislators fear that the courts have passed all control over the defendant to the therapists, *and shouldn't*, implies that there is still something "legal" at stake here.

So, too, does the recent American Psychiatric Association *Statement* (1982). In recognizing that "the decision to release an insanity acquittee should not be made *solely* by psychiatrists or solely on the basis of psychiatric testimony . . ." (pp. 16–17), the APA is reversing those preemptory and exclusionary claims that the alienists of yore had put forth. In now recommending a "quasi-criminal approach," it is implicitly recognizing that something "legal" and not just "therapeutic" is at stake here. The APA's recommendation for a "multidisciplinary board" invites other voices beyond the therapeutic to join the discussion and decide the issue.

What I believe is happening is a recognition that rehabilitationists have failed to exact the amount of punishment that deterrent or retributionist advocates desire. "Divestment" may occur, but there are strings attached and obligations other than treatment to fulfill. In short, "it's fine that you treat them, but keep them. The community isn't quite ready to accept them back. The fear is too great, and the punishment too little."

THE PROBLEM OF HAVING ONLY TWO CHOICES

Something is amiss here. I think the problem will become clearer if we contrast "insanity" with some of the other exculpating defenses, such as "accident," "self-defense," "necessity," "duress," "provocation," or "homicide in the line of arresting a felon." While all of these defenses can lead to exculpation, they are not all alike, particularly in regard to our empathy and understanding. If a bank teller, confronted by a bank robber's gun, threat, and demand, turns over the money, *we* understand the teller's response; we don't punish the teller for giving away what wasn't his; rather, we empathize with the real, human dilemma that confronted him. We can put ourselves psychologically in his place. For the individual who kills in self-defense, we can also understand and empathize. In other words, the actions of these individuals are not only legally excusable, but seem psychologically reasonable, understandable, and easy to empathize with. Not so, for the insane defendant. "I wouldn't think that way," or "I would have done something different," or "I would have never let myself deteriorate that way," or "but I would have thought of the consequences," are more likely thoughts and utterances when insanity is the exculpating case.

Judge Bazelon wrote in the *Durham* (1954) decision that "our collective conscience does not allow punishment where it cannot impose blame." Yet I think there are a number of insanity cases where we do exculpate— because of limited choice—where doubt and blame have not been laid to rest in our collective conscience. The *Hinckley* case is a prime example. In the hearings before the Senate Subcommittee on Criminal Law (1983), the Subcommittee took the unusual step of inviting *Hinckley* jurors to give voluntary testimony. Below is an excerpt from one juror's testimony. (pp. 159–164)

Senator Spector. You say you cannot pinpoint it.

Ms. Copelin. You cannot pinpoint. You know a person has a disturbance or has an illness. But you cannot say to what degree it is, not a layman, not me anyway. You just cannot pinpoint it because at one time they are saying or doing one thing and another time they are doing something altogether different.

One time maybe you could say well, OK, I know this person is sick. And the next 5 or 10 minutes or the next moment they can change altogether. But it is still mental illness. You cannot prove they are not mentally ill. And you cannot prove they are completely sane.

. . . .

We went in and we argued. We knew that the gentleman was guilty of his act, but we also knew there was a mental problem. But we could not do any better than what we did on account of your forms.

Senator Specter. On account of what?

Ms. Copelin. The form.

Senator Specter. The form?

Ms. Copelin. The form. You know, the forms where you have guilty, not guilty.

. . . .

Senator Specter. So, you are suggesting that, if they are guilty but insane that they ought to be detained for a long period of time even though you decided that they were insane at the time?

Ms. Copelin. Yes. I think they should get the help that they need and also punishment for the act they did.

. . . .

Senator Heflin. In other words, if you had had another alternative choice—

Ms. Copelin. Correct.

Senator Heflin. (continuing) then it would—

Ms. Copelin. Yes. If I had had another choice, in fact if we all had had another choice, it would have been different now. It would not have been this way. Everyone knows beyond a shadow of a doubt that he was guilty for what he did. But we had that mental problem to deal with. We just could not shut that out.

The juror presents the dilemma: desiring to both help and punish (but not being able to shut out either the "mental problem" or the knowledge "that he was guilty for what he did"), how can a jury, faced with only two mutually exclusive options, do both? In the *Hinckley* case they could not. What they did do, I will argue, was reach the "best fit" verdict, given their limited options. The NGRI verdict, to the jurors, assures them that the "mental problem" will be addressed, whereas a guilty verdict gives no such assurance. And the NGRI verdict, as best jurors can predict, will lead to incarceration in a psychiatric hospital for a significant period of time. This incarceration, even if the professed rationale is treatment, nonetheless in practice deters this individual (and others, perhaps); furthermore, this incarceration can serve the retributive end of a just desert.

In the *Hinckley* case, and in other insanity cases, the NGRI verdict may not be a "clean" verdict: rather, it may represent a compromise of retribution, deterrence, and rehabilitation that mixes guilt, innocence, and mental illness in a way that best fits, yet fails to ultimately satisfy. This, I believe, is the rub and root of the emotional, visceral linkage of punishment and the insane. Understood in this way, this reaction is not just some irrational lust to punish. If a significant number of insanity cases are impure cases—where some degree of guilt is attributed to the defendant by jurors and the populace—then the frequently heard utterance "that the insane escape punishment," at least in the formal, legally acknowledged and sanctioned sense, is sometimes true.

REVENGE AND "WILD JUSTICE"

The *Hinckley* juror speaks about not being able to shut some matters out. Yet, in the adjudication process, some individuals have been shut out from input where once their wishes carried great weight. I'm speaking about injured parties, victims, and the families of victims. Under tenth-century Saxon law, crimes were personal wrongs and the injured parties quickly picked up the spear to avenge the wrong. The guilty party could either "buy off the spear or bear it"; thus the matter was either settled with a *bot* (compensation) or perpetuated in a feud; in either case, the matter was privately decided. But with the ecclesiastical input (see Chapter 1), personal wrongs become moral wrongs, and with that shift, the settlement of a moral wrong became a matter of public policy. For breaking the King's Peace a *wite* had to be paid. If the crime was so great that the payment was beyond the means of the wrongdoer, then the latter was obliged to accept imprisonment. Furthermore, *botless* crimes left the injured parties without adequate compensation; thus the injured parties had to rely on public justice to assuage their loss and mollify their vengeance.

As Kalven and Zeisel (1971) note in their classic study of *The American Jury*,

> It took several centuries of Anglo-American legal evolution for the rather sophis-
> ticated idea to emerge that the state is the other party in interest in a criminal
> case. For some purposes, however, it is characteristic of the jury to continue to
> see the criminal case as essentially a private affair. (p. 242)

So instead of Ronald Reagan, James Brady, and other victims v. Hinckley, it becomes the *United States v. Hinckley*. Victims retreat under criminal law as the State emerges as the aggrieved party. But the jury, according to Kalven and Zeisel's research findings, "does not entirely embrace" (p. 257) this idea.

When ordinary citizens feel, as I believe many do now, that justice has become so focused on the wrongdoer at the expense of the victim, then our faith in public justice is severely shaken (Sales, Rich, & Reich, 1987). The psychiatrist Williard Gaylin takes up this point in his book *The Killing of Bonnie Garland* (1982), where the community's sympathy and support for the defendant far outweighed that for the victim. When victims feel left out, and when the courts leave them out, we arrive at the subject of Susan Jacoby's (1983) work, *Wild Justice: The Evolution of Revenge*, to which we shall now turn.

Jacoby writes: "Justice is a legitimate concept in the modern code of civilized behavior. Vengeance is not" (p. 1). We have been taught, she maintains, with the help of contemporary psychiatry, to see "vindic-tiveness as neurosis" (p. 12) and the "urge to punish" (Weihofen, 1979) as representing something base and unhealthy. *The Crime of Punishment* is the offering of Karl Menninger (1966); it is also perceived by many to be the official position of the helping professions. With the word "revenge" be-coming pejoratively tainted, we learn to hide our motives (and forget our history) behind euphemisms: victims, while testifying at a trial, must fre-quently defend themselves against the charge that they are out for re-venge, and they typically defend themselves by falling back on the euphe-mism that they "are only seeking justice."

Have we forgotten our dramatic figures, such as Hamlet and Orestes, for example, who, with doubts in mind, nonetheless pursued revenge? Are they to be seen as merely players on one side of the proscenium arch and history, no longer enacting modern motives? Or are they simply replaced, as the theatre has been by cinema, so that now we have Charles Bronson in *Death Wish* and Clint Eastwood in his *Dirty Harry* exploits doing our vengeance vicariously for us?

Vicarious vengeance is neither a panacea nor a substitute for justice. That the criminal justice system seems both confining and out of step with significant public sentiment is a conclusion being voiced by more and more writers. In the press, such editorials as those by George Will ("Shocking Crimes, Astounding Sentences," December 11, 1983) and Colman McCarthy ("Crime, Punishment and Victims," December 17, 1983) take up this theme. George Will talks about the case of Dan White, who killed San Francisco's mayor, George Moscone, and supervisor, Harvey Milk. When White's sentence was issued, "a six-hour riot" ensued; and when he was about to be released on parole, tensions and discord resurfaced. Will writes, "In the increasingly peculiar annals of American law, Dan White is less notable for his lurid offense than his imaginative defense, the 'Twinkie defense'": in this defense, the responsibility (and blame for the alleged criminal acts resides, allegedly, within the junk food. George Will feels that the public's

> desire for proportionate punishment—for civilized vengeance—was frustrated by a court that compounded White's crime. He destroyed two persons. It destroyed him by treating him as just a tossed salad of impulses, without the human dignity that punishment presupposes. (page C7)

Will, who defends retribution and the principle of proportionality, criticizes the therapeutic ethos. He writes:

> The element of retribution—vengeance—does not make punishment cruel; it makes punishment intelligible, distinguishing it from therapy. But a "progressive" aspiration has been to make people feel guilty about certain sentiments, such as (concerning crime) outrage and desire for vengeance, that are essential for social decency. (page C7)

He concludes his editorial with a point and a warning: "When a community is demoralized—literally, de-moralized—by courts that frustrate the desire for moral symmetry between crime and punishment, vengeance becomes the business of vigilantes."

Vigilantism may or may not be on the rise, but what is clearly on the rise, as Colman McCarthy points out in his editorial, is the notion and policy of victims' rights. McCarthy writes that

> it has been slow coming; but in the past few years victims' rights have been increasingly established in the justice system in much the way that criminals' rights began to be recognized in the early 1960s.
>
> Victim-compensation programs are now operating in 39 states. Seventeen states require victim or witness services. In 15 states, judges must issue "victim-impact statements" at the time of sentencing. Ten state legislatures have passed bills of rights for crime victims. Last year Congress enacted the Victim and Witness Protection Act. (page A19)

We see today the springing up of new organizations, such as the Stephanie Roper Committee and Mothers Against Drunk Drivers (MADD), that seek stiffer, more uniform sentencing. This trend may be viewed simply as symptomatic, reflecting perceived shortcomings in the way we punish, or more significantly, as reflecting still deeper problems. The public's dis-ease, I suspect, signifies a more troubling disorder within our criminal justice system—an underlying confusion and clash among theories of punishment—and an all too often confusion and fusion between punishment and treatment. While this clash and confusion cuts a broad swath across our criminal justice system, the insanity defense stands centrally and symbolically in the scythe's path and the public's eye, an easy target to swipe at, more difficult still to fell. Like a stubborn, perennial weed it stands, its root and rhizome promising more offshoots if the surface is merely snipped. Yet this weed has weathered historical attacks before and has been cultivated and protected by many who see it as serving a necessary and consonant function within our system of justice. Do we cut it, cultivate it, restrict its growth, or hybridize? The next, and last, subsection of this chapter looks at some proposed future direction.

FUTURE DIRECTIONS AND DEAD ENDS

From the numerous proposals and recommendations for change (Arenella, 1983), I have selected two for further discussion at this juncture. The two proposals—the abolishionist position, which would eliminate the insanity defense, and Lady Wootton's position, which would eliminate "responsibility" from the determination of guilt—establish the extremes of the various and varied recommendations for future directions. Interestingly enough, these two approaches, deriving as they do from contrasting philosophical positions (i.e., the abolishionist position derives primarily from retributivists' concerns, while Wootton's position derives from Utilitarian values), end up with a similar outcome—the elimination of insanity as a formal defense. And both, because of conceptual and pragmatical flaws, lead to dead ends.

Let us look at Lady Wootton's (1959) ideas first. In this view, "moral responsibility" is supplanted by "the practical test of whether punishment will in fact deter the offender . . . For criminal responsibility we thus substitute 'deterrent efficiency and/or efficient punishability'. . ." (p. 248). Here, *mens rea* is in the wrong place. "*Mens rea* is . . . relevant only *after* conviction as a guide to what measures should be taken to prevent a recurrence of the forbidden act" (Hart, 1968, p. 194).

> Moreover, once judgments as to moral responsibility are eliminated, the definition of the mentally sick as those whose peculiarities are likely to yield to treatment by persons holding medical degrees becomes nothing more than a useful

practical device for settling who is to be dealt with by whom. (Wootton, 1959, p. 245)

Curiously, Wootton's recommendations are likely to lead to a situation she distrusts—decisions being made more and more by medical professionals and social scientists. Once we enter this morally neutral land, who gets treatment and who gets punishment, or who is a likely recidivist and who is not, is most apt to be determined by the experts. This result is the alienists' dream come true. But more, it is a nightmare for the advocates for the Desert Model (von Hirsch & Hanrahan, 1979), or even the Modified Desert Model (Monahan, 1982), who believe that sentences should be predicated upon the "principle of commensurate deserts," where the severity of the punishment is commensurate with the seriousness of the offender's criminal conduct. In the words of the columnist George Will, this "does not make punishment cruel; it makes punishment intelligible, distinguishing it from therapy."

The abolishionists' position—eliminating the insanity defense—not only fails to eliminate the problem, but actually compounds the difficulties. First, all of the exculpating conditions (e.g., self-defense, necessity, duress, accident) and mitigating conditions inquire into *mens rea*. To exclude one and only one condition—insanity—moves us dangerously close to strict liability for which there is still great odium; as Judge Bazelon noted in the Durham (1954) decision, "Our collective conscience does not allow punishment where it cannot impose blame" (p. 862).

If considerations of mental illness or defect (i.e., insanity) are legislated out of the typical *mens rea* phase of the trial, *mens rea* factors may come to play an increasing role in the *actus reus* phase: with the definition of a criminal act requiring intention, typical insanity defenses may be argued in the future as automatism cases. This point occurred in an Illinois case of *People v. Grant* (1978). The defendant was an epileptic, susceptible to both "grand mal" and "psychomotor seizures," and had consumed enough alcohol to trigger a seizure at the time of the incident in question. He was convicted of aggravated battery and obstructing a police officer. While the defendant raised only the defense of insanity, the Appellate and Supreme Court agreed that "he was entitled to raise the defense of lack of a voluntary act as well." As Hermann (1983) writes,

> The significance of the opinion lies, however, in the relationship between the defense of involuntary conduct and the defense of insanity as it was identified by the Illinois Supreme Court. Both defenses were viewed as relating to the ultimate issue of responsibility. Additionally, the court recognized that the existence of mental disease would be relevant to both defenses . . .
> The court went on to identify the relevant feature of the insanity defense and to recognize it as a nonexclusive alternative to the defense of involuntariness; the court observed: "Similarly, the insanity defense exculpates a person whose volition is so impaired during a state of automatism that he is substan-

tially incapable of conforming his conduct to the law. To that extent, the defense of involuntary conduct and the insanity defense are alternative theories at the disposal of a defendant whose volition to control or prevent his conduct is at issue." (p. 108)

Whether "insanity" is converted into the defense of involuntariness, or a jury decides to acquit anyway, the outcome in either case is not the "just desert" the abolitionist had in mind. In fact, it is worse. At least the "not guilty by reason of insanity" verdict usually allows for commitment to a psychiatric hospital. With a successful involuntariness defense, or an outright acquittal, the defendant walks out of the courtroom free and clear.

In my opinion, if the topic of punishment and the insane is to be set right, a number of points need to be recognized. These points are listed below.

1. The connection between responsibility and punishment needs to be maintained (i.e., the retributivist's concern).

2. Future-oriented considerations, such as predictions of the likelihood of recidivism, need to have a place, but that place is in sentencing and release decisions (i.e., the Utilitarian's concern, as well as the concern of victims and their families), not in the verdict decision.

3. For "insanity," its meaning and essence are best appreciated through the concepts of capacity and negligence. The question is, "Has this person the appropriate *mens* to function as a response-able individual with respect to the law?" The question is not, "Does this person lack the appropriate *mens rea?*"

4. I think that it is time to recognize, as "the Bluidy MacKenzie" did in the seventeenth century, that mental illness can be of the exculpating or *mitigating* variety, and this is best dealt with *formally*—through an insanity defense test for exculpation and a "diminished response-ability" defense for the mitigating variety.

5. Where that capacity is diminished, but not to the point of exculpation, there is some degree of guilt and this ought to be punished.

6. Incapacity or diminished capacity must be tied to the question of whether the defendant bears some culpability for that incapacity. This requires a wider focus for assessing culpability than just "at the moment of the act."

7. That therapy (rehabilitation) has limitations; it works best when the defendant desires it, rather than when it is forced upon someone; and it is not a substitute for punishment.

How these points are to be parlayed into policy will be taken up in the last section of this work ("Future Directions and Recommendations"). As we leave the background issues section, we turn next to some prevailing currents and probable consequences, where the layman, neuropsychologist, and, finally, the patient, get their due.

III

Prevailing Currents,
Unsettling Consequences

7

The Layman's (Juror's)
Perspective on Insanity

Insanity trials like Hinckley's and M'Naghten's have been high drama, public morality plays that provoke sound and fury. Headlining the cast of characters are the defendant and the victim,

> while under the marquee, eminent jurists, lawyers, and psychological experts compete for center stage spotlight. The press, the public, and political leaders, an attentive, although not always an appreciative audience, follow the drama to its denouement and verdict. . . .
>
> Upstaged and overshadowed by the more *dramatis personae* of the trial are the jurors, who are typically regarded as merely minor characters, when they are regarded at all. But all of that changes when these jurors bring in a nettlesome verdict; when that happens, the spotlight shifts, the jurors and their decision occupy center stage position, and the audience reacts—usually with a chorus of bewilderment, criticism, and ascriptions. The postscripts of two of history's most celebrated insanity cases, *M'Naghten* (1843) and *United States v. Hinckley* (1981) illustrate this reaction. (Finkel, 1988, p. 97)

Before proceeding to the jurors' understanding of insanity and their reasons for their verdicts, along with the public's maligning and misconstruing of both, some words about why this topic is important are in order. Up to this point in this book the spotlight has been focused on those eminent jurists and forensic experts of yesterday and today, on what they said and believed, and on the laws and cases they framed and argued. In this regard, this work has mirrored an insanity trial, where much is made of the role of the experts. The often-repeated phrase "a battle of experts" not only continues to be heard but is repeated in commentary form by experts writing on the topic.

It is not hard to understand why. In the trial of insanity, the words of the experts are everywhere. Through testimony, the psychological expert presents a diagnosis of a defendant's mental state and a description of psychic processes, which can be enlightening or befuddling, but which is almost certainly technicalizing. The lawyers for the defense and prosecution, through their briefs, argumentation, and closing summations, elucidate the nuances of law and doubt. Judges and jurists have their say, as they interpret points of law, frame the rules, and provide instructions. And our theories of insanity and our principles of punishment, which have been formulated and debated by our most eminent legal, philosophical, and psychological scholars, are cited and intoned. Yes, much has been made of the expert, but when all is said and done, is it really much ado about nothing? For when we get to the bottom line—deciding—it is the layman who becomes the arbiter of the case.

If we forget the perspective of ordinary citizens, if we forget that these citizens sitting on a jury typically decide the case, and, in that capacity, determine law, then we run certain risks. To view insanity as a matter of reconciling enduring legal precepts with advancing psychological knowledge, a position taken by the late Justice Felix Frankfurter in his testimony on the topic (Gowers, 1953), is, I believe, an error: for such a view omits from consideration the perspective of ordinary citizens. It is my position that our laws and legal tests of insanity must also fit with the common-sense perspective of ordinary citizens about what is right, moral, fair, just, blameworthy, and not. When laws, insanity tests, and expert opinion get too removed, abstract, or out of touch, we run the risk of jurors rejecting the law, nullifying judicial instructions, and, in effect, making their own law. This has happened historically, in England and in the United States, with certain capital offenses, seditious libel, and prohibition laws (Horowitz, 1985; Kalven & Zeisel, 1971). When we forget that the jury serves as "conscience of the community," we run the risk of creating new laws and high expectations, only to have them dashed in practice.

So now we turn to the jurors' perspective, but not directly. First I will present the jurors' perspective as construed by the critics. Then I will present some empirical evidence from jurors and mock jurors in order to evaluate the validity of the charges.

THE JURORS STAND ACCUSED

After M'Naghten's verdict was announced, the press reacted with criticisms, ascriptions, and accusations directed at the jurors and at ordinary citizens who sit on juries. The *Illustrated London News* decried the "natural tendency of society to refuse to contemplate them [assassins] in any other light than as acts of madness." *The Times* of London editorialist voiced the hope that "soft-headed" citizens and prospective jurors would not "twist and torture" minor incidents of peculiar behavior in the accused's background into "symptoms of insanity." Some critics complained that jurors could not comprehend the judge's instructions; others asserted that jurors willfully disregarded the judge's instructions. Lord Cooper claimed that jurors simply retire and ask themselves "Is this man mad or is he not?" no matter what instructions the judge provides (Moran, 1981, p. 13).

Following Hinckley's verdict, similar criticisms were heard and those harsh questions were asked once again. Is "insanity" too complex a topic to be left to ordinary citizens to decide? Did they fail to understand the instructions or did they willfully disregard them? Did they let their sentiments rule instead of reason? Were they confused by the parade of experts and their contradictory opinions? Were the jurors influenced by irrelevant, extralegal (Visher, 1987) concerns? The United States Senate Subcommittee's request (1983) of *Hinckley* jurors to testify to explain their decision itself connotes a certain bewilderment: How could these jurors reach an NGRI verdict, the senators may have been wondering, when millions saw the "crime" run and rerun on their televisions? After all, our newspapers reported that Hinckley *planned* his act and *intended* to murder, did they not? After hearing about plan and intention, and after seeing "the act" with their own eyes, how could they still "see" it as "insanity"?

All of these questions, those that followed *M'Naghten* and those that followed *Hinckley*, reveal beliefs and suspicions about jurors, about their intelligence, understanding, presumptions, biases, willfulness, gullibility, and naïvete. But these criticisms and calumniations in the absence of data are, at bottom, merely idle speculation. In the absence of data, "it is clear that we have no clear understanding about what jurors understand about insanity, or why they do what they do" (Finkel & Handel, 1988). Press editorialists and public officials may wish, as many have, that they could be "flies on the wall" of the jury room, but alas, that trick of transmogrification has yet to be perfected. With "fly on the wall" evidence unavailable, we turn now to the next best thing—empirical evidence from mock jurors and juries—to provide us a clearer glimpse of the juror's perspective on insanity.

EMPIRICAL EVIDENCE

INSANITY TEST INSTRUCTIONS

The seminal work in this area was reported by Rita James (1959a; Rita James Simon, 1967) as part of a large study of jury decision making that was conducted at the University of Chicago Law School (Kalven & Zeisel,

1971). In her work, an experimental trial was recorded, with the parts played by law school staff; the trial transcript was adapted from the case of *The People v. Monte Durham* and renamed *The People v. Martin Graham*. Regular jurors, drawn from jury pools, were the subjects, and they were assigned to one of twenty juries. All of the jury deliberations were tape recorded. Ten of the juries received the M'Naghten test of insanity (i.e., "right from wrong" test), while the other ten received the Durham test (i.e., "product of mental illness" test). Each juror and jury was asked to state a verdict—either "guilty" or "not guilty by reason of insanity" (NGRI).

Three questions were asked: "(1) How is sane behavior differentiated from insane behavior? (2) How is the testimony of the expert witness evaluated? (3) How are the instructions interpreted?" (p. 63) Looking at question (3) first, one of the results reported was that the instructions to the jury (e.g., either M'Naghten or Durham) did not produce different verdicts. The jurors did not ignore the instructions, contrary to what Lord Cooper maintained: quotes from jurors indicate that the particular instructions were cited and debated, but *construed* differently. Interestingly enough, jurors' interpretations of the instructions mirrored, in some ways, the historical and professional debates. The following two quotes from two jurors, both of whom had the M'Naghten test, reveal a narrow interpretation of "to know" for the first juror and a "broad interpretation for the second."

> I think he is a little insane, but I think he knew the nature of the act, knew he was doing something wrong. The judge's instructions point out that even though the man may have had perverted notions, if he knew what he was doing at the time he committed the act, he knew he was doing wrong, that's all we have to pass on. That's really our decision.

> He (the defendant) knew what he was doing in the sense that he knew how to get into the house, where to find the bedroom, what articles he wanted to take, but, he still didn't know the full significance of what he was doing.

Jurors who received the Durham test instruction also revealed considerable construing. As James notes, "Durham jurors appeared to have no more difficulty than the M'Naghten jurors in construing the instructions to suit their beliefs concerning the centrality of cognition" (p. 68).

James' (1959a) work informs us that jurors do comprehend and remember the instructions and that they neither ignore nor nullify the instructions. However, James' work (as with any empirical investigation) has some limitations that require further investigation. One limitation was the fact that only one case was used. Perhaps that particular case, with its one defendant with his one type of mental illness, lends itself to similar verdicts with either M'Naghten or Durham. Would the same results occur if a number of cases were used, with different defendants, circumstances, and disorders? A second limitation with James' work is that only two insanity tests were used. Perhaps if more test instructions were used we would see that some tests do produce different verdict patterns.

In an experiment by Finkel, Shaw, Bercaw, and Koch (1985), five different cases were presented to 132 mock jurors, with all the cases involving a defendant pleading insanity, but where the nature of the mental illness varied from case to case. In addition to deciding five cases, each juror was given one of six different insanity test instructions. The tests used were the "wild beast" test (WB), M'Naghten (M), M'Naghten plus the irresistible impulse addition (MI), Durham (D), the American Law Institute's Model Penal Code test (ALI), and the Disability of Mind test (DOM) developed by Fingarette and Hasse (1979). Thus, in this experiment, the historical array of insanity tests was widened, with tests covering more than 250 years of jurisprudential history employed.

The five cases involved an epilepsy case (case A), a chronic alcoholic case (case B), a split-brain commissurotomy case (case C), a paranoid schizophrenic case (case D), and a stress-induced case (case E). All of the cases, save case C, were loosely modeled after actual cases: for example, *People v. Grant* (1978) deals with epilepsy; *Driver v. Hinnant* (1966) with a chronic alcoholic; *Hadfield, M'Naghten,* and *Hinckley* all deal with paranoid schizophrenia; and the Francine Hughes, "burning bed" case (McNulty, 1980) involves a stress-induced mental condition. Case C, the split-brain commissurotomy case, is a hypothetical case, one that has been proposed and debated in neuropsychological and legal circles and that will receive detailed attention in the next chapter (see Chapter 8). Instead of using actual cases, five hypothetical cases were developed to control for many of the differences that exist among the actual cases.

In the five hypothetical cases, all of the defendants are female. Held constant across all the cases are the following concluding circumstances: all feature the defendant at a party where the host displays a pistol; an argument not involving the defendant then erupts and the pistol falls to the floor; all of the defendants pick up the pistol and fire; and in all of the cases, a victim is shot and killed. All the cases were presented to the mock jurors in written form. Each juror received a booklet containing the five cases in random order. Each case contained a summary of background facts brought out in testimony, including expert opinion on the defendant's mental state, and a prosecution and defense closing summary to the jury. The jurors did not deliberate with one another, as this research focused on each juror's opinion separate from the group processes that go on during jury deliberations.

Whereas James found no differences between two instructions (M'Naghten or Durham), the results of this experiment showed no overall significant differences among the six instructions. I think this is a remarkable finding, particularly when you take the following facts into consideration: (1) the historical time span between the "wild beast" test (1723), the first test, and the last test, the "Disability of Mind" doctrine (1979), exceeds 250 years; (2) that the 250-year period has been rife with contention and debate regarding which of these tests best fits with our legal and psychological notions of insanity; (3) that the tests themselves are quite different in terms of wording, phrasing, focus, and length; (4) that great efforts have been exerted with each "new" test to write and perfect a better test of insanity; and (5) that after each new test appeared on the legal scene, predictions were made that each would produce changes in verdict patterns (i.e., either liberalizing or restricting NGRI verdicts). "It is sobering and somewhat ironic to find that the particular test used does not seem to matter when mock jurors make judgments of guilt or innocence by reason of insanity" (Finkel et al., 1985; Finkel, 1982).

In a follow-up study, Finkel and Handel (1988) asked 263 mock jurors to render verdicts for four cases (cases A, B, D, and E, with case C omitted), but in this study, no insanity test instruction was used; rather, mock jurors were asked to judge these cases using "their own best lights." How, then, would the verdict patterns of jurors who do not receive any legal test compare with those verdict patterns of jurors who do receive a test? The answer is that they look quite similar. No significant differences were found between having no test instruction versus having an insanity test, and, further, there were no significant differences between the no test group of jurors and each specific test instruction group. In answer to the question "Do test instructions instruct?" Finkel and Handel conclude that they do not. It is not the case that jurors fail to make discriminations; quite to the contrary, as we shall shortly see; rather, the insanity tests *per se* do not produce discriminating verdicts.

Case-by-Case Discriminations

When we look at the verdicts (guilty or NGRI) *by cases,* the differences among the cases are large and significant. In Finkel et al. (1985), cases A, B, C, D, and E are judged NGRI by 69%, 13%, 48%, 68%, and 74% of the jurors respectively; in Finkel and Handel (1988), cases A, B, D, and E are judged NGRI by 59%, 18%, 71%, and 78% of the jurors respectively. These findings reveal that mock jurors make discriminations among the cases as to verdict and that these discriminations appear consistent from one study to the next.

In addition to the qualitative judgment of guilty vs. NGRI, Finkel and colleagues had mock jurors make quantitative ratings on a 10-point scale of (1) How responsible is the defendant for her mental condition; (2) What degree of mitigation does the defendant's mental condition warrant; and (3) How responsible is the defendant for the crime committed? Jurors' ratings revealed significant differences among the cases, with their quantitative ratings paralleling their qualitative verdict patterns. To illustrate, for variable 3, which asks about the defendant's responsibility for the crime, cases A, D, and E have the lowest ratings of responsibility (4.00, 4.40, and 4.11, respectively), whereas the defendant in case C is judged to have greater responsibility for the crime (5.59), and the defendant in case B is judged to have the greatest responsibility (7.88). Again, the parallel holds for the question of mitigating effects, where the higher score indicates more degree of mitigation: cases A, D, and E have scores of 7.34, 6.79, and 7.59 respectively, whereas case C is judged to deserve less (5.64) and case B, the least (3.54). For variable 1 (responsibility for their mental condition), the parallel begins to break down: cases D and E are seen as least responsible (3.38 and 3.23), cases A and C more responsible (4.13 and 4.08), and case B is seen as the most responsible (6.80).

Of note regarding both the qualitative and quantitative differences is the fact that the jurors' discriminations among cases do *not* coincide with the "organic vs. psychogenic" distinction. We might think that jurors would be more sympathetic with organic mental disorders (case A—epilepsy, case B—chronic alcoholism, and case C—split brain), reasoning that "how could they help it, it's in their brains," so to speak; but this is not the case. Recent evidence (Roberts, Golding, & Fincham, 1987) suggests that jurors are more likely to reach an NGRI verdict where the defendant is perceived as having a serious mental disorder (i.e., schizophrenia as opposed to a personality disorder) and where the act seems more bizarre. In sum, jurors seem to be making more sophisticated discriminations, assessing each case individually. This will be shown more clearly when we next examine consequences and sentencing.

In Finkel et al. (1985), mock jurors were also asked a series of qualitative and quantitative questions about disposition and release. This may seem unusual, since jurors typically do not sentence the defendant. However, the asking of these questions can be defended on several counts: for one, less formal accounts of jury deliberations (i.e., the Hinckley juror's testimony before the Senate Subcommittee) suggest that jurors do consider what should be done with the defendant (e.g., Should the defendant be set free, imprisoned, or sent to a psychiatric hospital?), and this consideration may affect the ultimate verdict; and by soliciting information about consequences, such as where jurors would send the defendant and for how long, we can get some guage on jurors' retributive, deterrent, and rehabilitative motives.

Mock jurors' judgments regarding consequences are quite interesting and quite different from what might have been predicted solely from verdicts. The consequences question read "Should the defendant be (a) set free, (b) imprisoned, or (c) sent to a psychiatric hospital?" Let us compare cases A, D, and E, which, in terms of verdicts, appeared similar (e.g., the NGRI percentages for the three cases were 69%, 68%, and 74%, respectively). When it comes to consequences, they are treated very differently. Jurors are quick to "set free" cases A (55%) and E (46%), but almost never in case D (1%). The option of "imprisonment" is typically associated with a finding of "guilt," which in turn is associated with judging a defendant to be responsible and culpable. While jurors use the imprisonment option 22% of the time for case A, they use it only 5% and 9% for cases D and E. It seems likely that those mock jurors who find case A's defendant guilty feel that her negligence ought to be punished. But reaching a guilty verdict does not uniformly mean that jurors want the defendant punished by being sent to prison.

Both prison and a psychiatric hospital can serve a deterrent function; the former fulfills the retributive motive while the latter is thought to fulfill the rehabilitative motive. For case A, the split between prison and psychiatric hospital is exactly even (22%, 22%), whereas in cases D (5%, 94%) and E (9%, 45%) the vast majority favor hospitalization. We will have more to say about the deterrent and rehabilitative motives and their relationship to the consequences options later. For the case B defendant, who was far and away most often judged to be guilty, 53% of the jurors would send her to prison, while 45% would send her to a hospital. For the case C defendant, who was judged guilty 52% of the time, only 16% send her to prison whereas 83% send her to a hospital.

To summarize, when jurors get a chance to express their recommendations about what should happen to a defendant (the consequences option), they make very different recommendations for each case. Some defendants are set free (case A, 55%; case E, 46%), while others are almost never set free (case B, 2%; case C, 1%). As to the prison and hospitalization options, again the patterns are unique for each case, and in several cases they differ from what would have been predicted from just looking at the verdicts. In general, the factor of "mental illness" moderates the "guilty verdict— therefore prison consequence." A guilty verdict followed by a prison sentence represents retributive and deterrent motives; a guilty verdict followed by a hospitalization sentence represents deterrent and rehabilitative motives, in the main, and it also can be construed as the "guilty but mentally ill" (GBMI) option. Mock jurors used this option selectively, as the Hinckley juror said she would have if the option were available, with significant differences resulting among the cases. This option was the most prevalent choice for cases C (68%), D (86%), and E (59%), whereas in cases A and B, guilty-to-prison was the preferred option by 78% and 61% of the jurors respectively.

When it comes to prison sentences, there are differences among the cases, but these differences just fail to reach significance. Case C receives the longest sentence (22.4 years), with case B receiving the next longest (17.8). Cases D, E, and A were sentenced to 13.7, 10.5, and 10.0 years respectively. The length of sentence for case C (and the fact that 29% set a "life" sentence for this case) may be explained by the antagonistic relationship between the defendant and victim (perhaps raising a premeditated motive for jurors), which is not present in case B, thereby making defendant C's crime a more serious offense; the difference (and direction) is not consistent with the degree of mitigation, since jurors found a less mitigating effect due to mental illness for case B.

"Psychiatric sentencing" is both more complicated and more foreign for jurors, with most of the mock jurors preferring to let the doctor decide. For those jurors who venture into this foreign realm, questions were asked regarding minimum and maximum sentences. Setting a minimum sentence may be interpreted as a deterrent protection for society. This interpretation appears to be confirmed, in that a significantly greater percentage of subjects will set a minimum sentence for cases B, C, and D than they will for cases A and E; and the length of sentence is also greater for those defendants who are perceived as dangerous. In fact, for case D, which, to recall, was judged NGRI (68%) and sent to a hospital (94% of the time), more jurors chose to set a minimum time, and it was the longest sentence (10.2 years). The setting of a maximum sentence can be interpreted as a protection for the defendant-turned-patient; this interpretation is consistent with the fact that for the "sympathetic" cases, A and E, more jurors will set a maximum stay than for the other cases.

Based on the empirical evidence presented so far, some tentative conclusions can be drawn regarding the accusations and charges that have been directed at jurors. Dispelling the views of Lord Cooper and the London *Times* editorialist, jurors make rather fine discriminations among cases in terms of responsibility and guilt and what to do about it. Their verdicts do not appear to reflect naïvete or simplistic thinking, and their sentencing decisions do not ignore retributive or deterrent concerns. Contrary to di Beccaria's (1880) classical criminology, mock jurors do consider individual differences, and the punishment or treatment that jurors prescribe seems to fit the individual, not the act alone divorced from its context.

The ancient adage, that "madness is punishment enough," is borne out *only* when the case is viewed sympathetically, as seen for cases A and E, where many jurors will set the defendant free. But madness is not punishment enough when jurors' attributions are less generous; in those cases, the defendant ends up in prison or a hospital, and in either case, they stay there for some time. John Howard (1784) reported the adage, that "a prison mends no morals," and the mock jurors in this experiment seem to agree: even when a guilty verdict is rendered, which is a judgment of responsibility and culpability, many defendants are sent to a hospital rather than to prison. Perhaps this reflects a dim view of prisons, or a faith in the psychiatric alternative, or both. However, there is another sense in which we can look at what these two options accomplish: a hospital stay can satisfy rehabilitative, deterrent, and retributive motives, whereas prison fulfills only the latter two.

As to the charge that jurors are biased—that they will reach an NGRI verdict because they have a "natural tendency" to do so—the research evidence fails to lend support. Finkel and Handel analyzed extreme verdict patterns where mock jurors' verdicts were either all NGRI or all guilty for the four cases. From the obtained probabilities of a guilty or an NGRI verdict for each case, it was possible to compute the expected probabilities of all guilty and all NGRI verdicts and to predict the number of jurors who would reach each extreme; this is analogous to predicting how many times four heads or four tails will come up if a coin is flipped four times and if you repeated the four flip series 263 times. If the coin or the jurors are biased, we should see significantly more extreme patterns than chance probability would predict. We do not. The expected numbers of all NGRI and all guilty verdicts are 15 and 6 respectively, and the obtained numbers were 18 and 6; these differences are not significant.

In another area of research that has bearing on the question of juror bias, that of jurors' decisions in capital penalty trials (i.e., choosing life in prison or choosing death), a study conducted by Stanford Law School students (Stanford Law Review, 1969) found that "attempting an insanity defense" was positively correlated with jurors choosing the death sentence. Ellsworth, Bukatay, Cowan, and Thompson, (1984) suggest that jurors may see the insanity defense as "a ruse and an impediment to the conviction of criminals" (p. 90). And in an experiment by White (1987) where he tested three different defense strategies, it was found that "jurors exposed to the Mental Illness defense were most punitive" (p. 120). In fact, the mental illness defense fared poorer than making no defense at all. These results suggest that if jurors do have a bias, it is not one that favors insanity.

SUBJECT VARIABLES

We know that jurors are being discriminative, but we also know that the legal test instructions do not account for these discriminations. The question is "What does?" A number of researchers have looked at "subject" variables: the education level of the jurors (James, 1959b); the jurors' knowledge of mental disease (Finkel et al., 1985); the age of jurors (Feild & Barnett, 1978; Finkel & Handel, 1988); and the gender of jurors (Finkel et al., 1985; Finkel & Handel, 1988). James looked at the status and competence of jurors and noted "for the fear that, although the jury numbers twelve, the decision or basis of power, rests with one or two 'strong men' we found no substantial ground" (p. 570). The more educated juror (e.g., college vs. high school vs. grade school) participates more, focuses more attention to procedure and instructions (while the less educated give more emphasis to testimony, personal experiences, and opinion), but there were "no significant differences . . . between the more- and the less-educated jurors in their ability either to influence other members of the jury or to be persuaded by them" (p. 563).

Finkel et al. (1985) looked at the subject variable knowledge of psychopathology. They used two groups of college students as their mock jurors: one group had taken an Abnormal Psychology course that covered in detail the mental disorders described in the American Psychiatric Association's *Diagnostic and Statistical Manual of Mental Disorders* (DSM-III, 1980); the other group had no such background. A comparison of the two groups revealed no significant differences in their NGRI and guilty verdict patterns.

While research with college students is easier to conduct, there are certainly questions about how generalizable these results are to adult jurors. Access to jury rolls is considerably harder to obtain since the work of James: some jurisdictions, by statute, or by *de facto* procedure, wish to protect jurors' confidentiality, and minimize the intrusiveness of social science investigators who may burden or bias potential jurors. James and the University of Chicago Law School project were quite fortunate to obtain subjects from jury rolls.

How would college students compare with lay citizens? Feild and Barnett (1978) put this question to a test in their study entitled "Simulated Jury Trials: Students vs. 'Real' People as Jurors." The results showed that students were more lenient than nonstudents in their sentences. At first look, this finding casts doubt on the generalizability of results from student to real-world jurors. However, Feild and Barnett write:

> While a statistically significant result in the present study raised a question concerning generalizability, a closer inspection of this finding suggests that it may be of little practical consequence. The omega-squared value revealed that only 3% of the variance in sentence length could be accounted for by the juror factor. Thus, it appears that the use of college students in simulated juror studies using written case materials *may* have only minimal effects on the external validity of results for the general population. (p. 291)

Finkel and Handel (1988) compared college students and adults, with their adults ranging in age from 22 to 84 (with a mean age of 45), and found no significant differences in their NGRI vs. guilty verdicts for any of the cases (p. 291).

Finkel et al. (1985) compared male vs. female college students, and Finkel and Handel (1988) compared male vs. female adults. There were some differences, but the results need to be interpreted cautiously since all of their cases involved a female defendant. Female college students produced significantly more NGRI verdicts than male college students, but this finding failed to repeat in the second study. Adult males were not significantly different from adult females as to verdict, although males were more variable: female verdict patterns across the age span showed remarkable consistency, whereas males were highly variable; again, though, we do not know if these results would repeat if the cases involved a male defendant.

In general, subject variables either do not produce significant differences (e.g., education level, knowledge of psychopathology) or produce small or equivocal effects (e.g., adults vs. students, females vs. males). Visher (1987) states that

> empirical studies . . . occasionally find that jurors' demographic characteristics—age, gender, race, and occupation—are statistically related to jurors' judgments of the defendant. But a careful look at these studies reveals that these factors . . . only account for a small portion of the variance in verdicts. (p. 3)

Saks and Hastie (1978) summarize by stating that "research findings suggest that jury composition has little influence on the outcome of a trial . . ." (p. 71).

A Swayed or Independent Jury?

Jurors are not swayed or led by one or two strong jurors, but are they swayed by expert testimony? The fear, first expressed following *M'Naghten*, and heightened following *Durham*, is that jurors would be swayed by expert opinion and testimony. Leifer (1964) concluded that in the face of increasingly "technicalized" expert testimony "which the jury cannot understand" (p. 818), jurors would yield their moral decision to the experts. And Goldstein (1967) put the concern this way: "Whether the psyches of individual jurors are strong enough to make that decision, or whether the 'law' should put that obligation on them, is open to serious questions" (p. 82). This "cattle being led to slaughter" image is certainly at odds with Sir Matthew Hale's stout confidence in the jury: "Yet the law of England hath afforded the best method of trial that is possible of this and all other matters of fact, namely by a jury of twelve men all concurring in the same judgment. . ." (Walker, 1968, p. 110).

A second accusation hurled at jurors in this regard asserts that jurors simply disregard such testimony. In her study, regarding this point, James (1959a) has this to say:

> There is little doubt that the jurors paid careful attention to the testimony of the two experts. In each of the deliberations, references were made to the testimony and strong opinions were expressed concerning it. . . . (pp. 65–66)

From the general tenor of the deliberations it may be concluded that the jurors neither wholeheartedly adopted the opinions of the medical experts as directives for their own behavior nor did they completely discount them. They did, however, clearly differentiate their own role in this procedure.

These results are reassuring in several ways. Jurors, in the vast majority of the sample, retain their independence: the fears following the M'Naghten trial's parade of experts, and the even heightened fear following Durham that the experts would now clearly have their way, are unfounded, at least according to James' findings. The results are also reassuring from the other direction: jurors are not ignoring the experts and sailing solely by their own lights; rather, they listen and weigh expert opinion regarding mental illness, yet clearly differentiate the question of mental illness from the legal question of insanity.

CONSTRUING

In an insanity case, the facts are rarely in dispute. No one, for example, disputed the fact that Hadfield, M'Naghten, and Hinckley pulled the trigger. What is in question, typically, is the interpretation of the defendant's behavior. How is it construed (Kelly, 1963)? The first question that James sought an answer to was "How is sane behavior differentiated from insane behavior?" This is in some ways the most intriguing of questions, and the one that relates most directly to this chapter's title; it is also the question whose answer is likely to confirm or refute *The Times* editorialist's view that jurors soft-headedly "twist and torture minor incidents of peculiar behavior . . . into symptoms of insanity." According to James (1959a), the jurors most frequently cited the defendant's behavior at the crime scene, notably, "the nature of the items he was attempting to steal" and, secondly, his "behavior when caught by the police" (p. 63). Of those jurors who found the defendant "not guilty by reason of insanity," here are a few of their comments.

> Look at it this way. If you were going to go out and break into someone's house, would you take the chance of breaking into somebody's house and getting caught and spending a couple of years in jail just to steal a cigarette lighter or a pair of cuff-links? (p. 63)

As to the defendant's position when caught, one juror said:

> The defendant was hiding in such a childish way, in a corner holding something over his face like an ostrich, his failure to resist arrest by fighting or running away was not the behavior of the normal criminal, who should have been aware of his situation and the consequences of being caught. (pp. 63–64)

Paradoxically, those jurors who found the defendant sane (and guilty) cite the very same behaviors, but construe those behaviors quite differently.

> If in broad daylight, with people watching him, he had thrown a brick through the window and then tried to enter the house, that would have indi-

cated insanity (i.e., uncontrollable, compulsive behavior). But here we have a case in which the defendant broke into an empty house in the middle of the night by fiddling with the lock.

As James remarks, "these actions indicated the defendant's ability to plan and carry out purposive behavior—i.e., "he must have been watching the house for some time and knew that it would be unoccupied" (p. 64).

As another juror who found the defendant sane and guilty noted:

> When he entered, he did so quietly and at a time when any ordinary burglar would think it safe to break in. Once he was in the house, he didn't turn on any lights, which again is normal for a burglar; and he was selective in the articles he stole; that is, he took small pieces that were easy to carry and negotiable.

As for his strange behavior on being caught, "guilty" jurors found this consistent with a "normal criminal," who may display "hiding, cowering, playing dumb when you know you're caught," which "is what they all do." What some jurors find silly, irrational, and evidence for the attribution of insanity other jurors interpret as clever (e.g., "perhaps the defendant was one step ahead of the police") and therefore interpretable as the actions of a sophisticated criminal.

The processes and factors used by people to explain the causes of behavior have been of particular concern to the attribution theorists (Jones & Davis, 1965; Kelley, 1973; Perlman, 1980). Observers (e.g., jurors) typically decide whether the cause of the behavior was environmental (i.e., he cowered and played dumb because he saw the police and knew he couldn't escape) or related to the actor's attributes, dispositional factors (i.e., he cowered and acted dumbly because he's irrational). In insanity cases, we are typically dealing with dispositional inferences. Moreover, we not only make dispositional inferences, but we try to fit these inferences into one or another of our images: for example, in insanity cases, we have images and assorted ideas about the "reasonable" individual and the "insane" individual, but, as James notes, her jurors were using still another image as a standard—that of the "reasonable criminal."

In James's study, where the defendant breaks into a house and attempts to take certain merchandise, the "reasonable" standard is not relevant: "reasonable" individuals do not do such things; therefore, the two operable images left are those of the "reasonable" criminal and the "insane" individual. In differentiating the two, the defendant's mental history may provide the facts from which differentiable inferences can be drawn. Indeed, jurors cite the mental history of the defendant, and, after the facts regarding the crime and the way he behaved when caught, it was the next most important point for the jurors. Yet, here again, the facts lend themselves to different interpretations and attributions. As James states:

> The mention of shock treatments was the decisive point in one jury for arriving at a verdict of not guilty by reason of insanity, because it was argued:

"shock treatments are given only as a last resort to people who are very ill mentally."

On the other side, the guilty-prone jurors interpreted things differently.

The defendant had consistently and effectively used insanity to gain the things he wanted and could not achieve any other way. When he wanted to be released from the Army and later from the Navy, "he began acting queerly." When the defendant did not receive the affection and attention he demanded from his mother, he threatened suicide. When he wanted to gain release from an institution, "he knew how to act." The guilty-prone jurors saw these actions as consistent instances of malingering behavior.

And the malingerer, who manipulates others by fashioning his behavior to get what he wants, is more closely allied to the "criminal image" than to the "insane and guileless" portrayal.

From this work, we can infer some "errors" and stereotypes that jurors bring with them regarding "insanity." For the guilty-prone jurors, there is the belief that "a crime against property rather than person" indicates sanity. "The implication is that when the insane commit antisocial acts, they commit acts of violence and not those in which personal gain might be a factor" (James, 1959a, p. 64). This is consistent with the theorizing of Jones and Davis, who find that acts that are high in *hedonic relevance* (i.e., acts with positive or negative consequences for the agent) and acts high in *personalism* (i.e., acts directed toward the defendant) are most apt to indicate the actor's intentions, which, in this case, would fit the criminal picture more than it would the insane picture.

Another error that can be inferred from the guilty-prone jurors' comments is that "manipulation," "craftiness," "cleverness," and "guilefulness" are not associated with the "insane." Are the "insane," therefore, "hapless," "bizarre," and "unfathomable" creatures, living in a world where neither reasonable nor unsavory thoughts and intentions exist (Roberts, Golding, & Fincham, 1987)? If this picture comes close to the jurors' image, it suggests that jurors may first try to fit ("twist and torture," in the words of *The Times'* editorialist) their attributions into the pictures of the "reasonable" man, and then the "criminal" man, and that failing to find a fit there, they find the "insane" man image to be the only sane alternative left.

Using the jurors' comments in James's work, I have suggested that jurors are attempting a "best fit" analysis, trying to decide which of the relevant images best fits the defendant. But in doing a "best fit" analysis, what factors or constructs are jurors invoking? Finkel and Handel's work (in press) provides some answers. Their mock jurors not only decided four cases, but were asked to cite the relevant facts that were determinative for them and to explain how and why those factors were important. There was an additional task: the mock jurors were then asked what would have to change for them in order to reach the opposite verdict; they were asked to identify those changes and the meaning of those changes.

A group of student raters then categorized all the factors the mock jurors cited, using a categorization schema that had been extensively pre-tested and that proved reliable. The categorization schema represents seven construct dimensions: one end of each dimension represents the guilty factor and the other end the NGRI factor. The seven NGRI construct factors are: incapacity; impaired awareness and perceptions; distorted thinking; could not control impulses and actions; nonculpable actions; no evil motive; and others at fault. The seven guilty factors are: capacity; unimpaired awareness and perceptions; clear thinking; could control impulses and actions; culpable actions; premeditation or malice; and others not responsible. A number of these constructs have been incorporated in the various legal tests of insanity; other constructs, which appeared relevant though not typically included in the historic legal tests, were also included.

Looking at the results, over 75% of the mock jurors cite multiple constructs as relevant and determinative of their verdict. These results tell us that the jurors' constructs are complex. Second, the results show that the jurors' constructs shift and change with each case; thus, jurors display flexibility in their construct patterns, rather than rigidly applying the same factors to each and every case. These complex and discriminative construct patterns rebut the critics' accusations that jurors construe naïvely, simplistically, and indiscriminatively; to the contrary, they reveal that jurors use complex, discriminative, and flexible constructs to reach a verdict.

When jurors reach opposing verdicts, are they nonetheless citing the same set of constructs, or do they cite different relevant constructs? For example, if jurors cite "incapacity," "distorted thinking," and "nonculpable actions" as their salient factors for their NGRI verdict, will jurors who reach a guilty verdict cite the polar opposite constructs of "capacity," "clear thinking," and "culpable actions" as their most salient factors? No, they do not. Jurors whose verdicts differ on a case "see" the case through a differing set of constructs.

These results, while gratifying to the supporters of jurors, do suggest some problems. For instance, if we project to the group deliberations of a jury where jurors disagree with one another, they will typically try to persuade others to change their verdict—to "see" it their way. In their persuasive appeals, however, they are likely to cite *their factors*, but these factors are neither most salient nor most relevant to the jurors they seek to convince. We may have an "apples–oranges" problem. Their disagreement as to verdict overlays an underlying *perspectival* problem—a disagreement in seeing and construing. This problem arose in Holstein's (1985) work: when mock juries came up with more schematic interpretations, the deliberations not only took longer, but the probability of a hung jury increased.

> As jurors argue a case, each may have formulated an opinion as to what really happened and which verdict is more appropriate. As the deliberation proceeds, jury members account for their verdict choices and persuade others of the correctness of those choices by presenting their versions of the case at hand. But all supporters of the same candidate verdict may not base their decisions on the same pictures of what was going on. Each juror might articulate his or her unique interpretation, which may conflict with that of another juror who supports the same candidate verdict. Consequently an inadvertent competition may arise between different interpretations that support the same verdict, yet, in some ways, contradict each other. Ultimately this may detract from the ability of any one of them to convincingly characterize the situation and sway opponents' opinions. (p. 94)

To reinforce this point, we return to the Finkel and Handel study (in press) and examine the responses of jurors when they were asked to reach the opposite verdict from the one they originally rendered. They were asked to identify the changes that would have to occur in the facts or the testimony in order for them to reach the opposite verdict, and, again, they were asked to explain the meaning of those changes. The construct pattern for those subjects whose original verdict was NGRI was compared with the construct pattern of those subjects whose opposite verdict was now NGRI. This comparison showed significant differences: thus, even when jurors are now reaching the same verdict, they are not construing the cases the same way.

When verdicts of jurors differ, we typically have a perspectival clash; even when these jurors attempt to view the defendant in the opposite light, their construals do not exactly mesh. Given these results, one may wonder why there are not more hung juries than there are. Finkel and Handel's work sheds some light on this concern. When they compared the jurors' original verdict with their opposite verdict, they asked the following question: will jurors, when reaching the opposite verdict, merely "slide" along their relevant and determinative construct dimensions to the other pole or will they "shift" construct dimensions? What they found was a significant "shifting" effect: most jurors showed a mixture of sliding and shifting, with only a small percentage of jurors using exclusively the same dimension in both their verdict and opposite-verdict reasons across all four cases. They conclude that jurors' perspectives are changeable rather than rigid, with the vast majority of jurors willing and able to slide and shift to a different point of view. This evidence suggests that jurors are flexible enough to listen to and consider alternative perspectives, and this may be an important factor in why there are fewer hung juries than one might expect.

Framing the Case

It has been argued (Lamiell & Trierweiler, 1986) that making an assessment—be it a judgment about personality, a diagnosis of a person, or a verdict of a defendant—requires the rater or juror to first *contextualize* the problem. In the case of insanity, the problem is typically framed for the jurors by the prosecution and defense's opening and closing statements, along with the judge's charge and instructions to the jury. In most insanity cases, and in most states, the choices the jurors have are two: NGRI or guilty. But what happens when jurors contextualize the case differently? This question is raised because several research findings (Finkel & Handel, in press; Kalven & Zeisel, 1971) indicate that some jurors do indeed frame the case differently.

The *Hinckley* juror's testimony before the Senate Subcommittee on Criminal Law (see Chapter 6) illustrates the problem. As Ms. Copelin remarked to Senator Heflin,

> . . . If I had had another choice, in fact if we all had had another choice, it would have been different now. It would not have been this way. Everyone knew beyond a shadow of a doubt that he was guilty for what he did. But we had that mental problem to deal with. We just could not shut that out.

The problem for the *Hinckley* jurors appeared to be this: the prosecution, defense, and the judge had framed the case as involving only two choices, NGRI or guilty, yet the jurors, in their contextualizing of the case, saw a third choice—where guilt and mental illness are combined—but this option was unavailable to them.

In the work of Finkel and Handel, even though the four cases were framed as an NGRI vs. guilty choice, 12% of the mock jurors contextualized the cases outside the parameters of an NGRI–guilty decision. Some saw the possibility of a "not guilty due to self-defense" or a "not guilty because it was as accident." Others saw the possibility of "guilty to a lesser degree," such as involuntary manslaughter or criminal negligence. And still others framed the cases in dispositive light, rather than in terms of past culpability: their focus was on future considerations (e.g., the need for treatment, whether the defendant was punished enough, whether society needed deterrent protection), and they seemed to approach the case "backwards," from a judicial point of view, deciding first where the defendant ought to end up and then figuring out which verdict was most likely to bring that outcome about.

To cite a particular example, let us look at case A, the epilepsy case, through the eyes of several jurors. Some see this case not as NGRI vs. guilty, but as a tragic accident; for these jurors, a direct "not guilty," a dropping of all charges, or never bringing the case to court in the first place are the alternatives they see and seek. For some of the jurors, they see the case as "guilty," but in a different way. Citing "culpable actions" as the main factor, they judge the defendant cuplable for stopping her medication for epilepsy without consulting her doctor and for using alcohol. These culpable actions, coupled with the absence of any motive that could be interpreted as indicating premeditation or malice, lead these jurors to seek (but not find) a "guilty to a lesser degree" option, such as criminal negligence.

In another example, Case E, the stress-induced case, a number of jurors seek a straight "not guilty" on grounds of self-defense. Some wrote, regarding the victim (the husband), "the bastard got what he deserved." These jurors note that the victim was violent, abusive, and malicious; that he provoked the defendant on numerous occasions. Even though the defendant did not have her "back to the wall," so to speak (i.e., the usual legal definition of exculpatory self-defense), these jurors want a self-defense, "not guilty" verdict. The point here was made by Kalven and Zeisel (1971), who found that when juries believed that the victim provoked or had contributory fault (e.g., was negligent or assumed a risk), juries, ". . . if given the option of finding the defendant guilty of a lesser crime, will frequently do so" (p. 254). They go on later to say that "these last cases suggest, albeit faintly, that the jury inclines toward a concept of reduced or diminished responsibility, under which insanity would mitigate but not exonerate" (p. 332). Based on Finkel and Handel's work, where insanity cases were studied exclusively, we have firmer rather than fainter ground for this view that jurors are inclined toward a mitigating option. Even stronger evidence comes from the work of Roberts, Golding, and Fincham (1987), where the researchers directly tested the NGRI vs. guilty choice against a three-choice schema (i.e., NGRI vs. GBMI vs. guilty); dramatic differences in verdict patterns resulted when jurors were given a third option.

As an aside, contextualizing differently is not solely a jurors' tendency. Judges, too, may take into account provocation and contributory fault and may employ the NGRI or other verdicts even when these verdicts do not seem to precisely fit the case. Packer (1987) who studied sane and insane murderers in Michigan, reported the following case:

> This case involved a young man, diagnosed by the Forensic Center examiner as not having a mental disorder, who killed an extremely abusive father who had recently threatened him. The case was decided by a judge who found the man NGRI and made specific note in his opinion of the extremely abusive family situation the defendant endured. Thus, the judge apparently used the insanity verdict as a means of exculpating a defendant who did not appear to warrant imprisonment but who did not qualify for any other exculpating verdict. (p. 34)

Finally, if we see the *Hinckley* jury's dilemma in terms of how they contextualized the case, then their apparently inexplicable verdict becomes more intelligible. The option they wanted was not *directly* available to them. If you cannot directly punish and mitigate, if you cannot formally acknowledge mental illness and guilt, then an *indirect* avenue may be sought, and found. In this indirect route, an established and sanctioned verdict, NGRI, now comes to stand for something else. From one vantage point, this may be seen as a corruption of the law, a prevailing current, and an unsettling consequence. But from the vantage point of Kalven and Zeisel (1971), we are reminded that the jury is "an institution which is stubbornly non-rule minded" (p. 375); this does not necessarily imply anarchy, they note, for the jury's "war with the law is thus both modest and subtle" (p. 495), allowing the jurors room for their sentiments, values, and sense of equity, whereby they "can bend the law without breaking it" (p. 498).

Jurors' Sentiments

The critics of jurors are not without ammunition. From the broad spectrum of empirical investigations into juror and jury behavior, the critics do find instances where sentiments, biases, and "extralegal" concerns intrude and affect jurors' decisions. For instance, when judges instruct jurors to disregard certain testimony, there is evidence suggesting that the "disregarded" testimony does affect jurors' verdicts. In another area, jurors regard eyewitness testimony more strongly, with less reasonable doubts, than social scientists say is warranted. There have been studies showing that when a defendant is likable, attractive, and appears to have attitudes similar to the jurors, the jurors tend to be more lenient. As Davis, Bray, and Holt (1977) put it, "from all these studies, one might conclude that the jury critics are correct in claiming that jurors are inappropriately influenced by 'extralegal' factors" (p. 330).

Finding that jurors are influenced by "extralegal" factors is not necessarily a damning indictment of jurors, however. Many of the critics make two assumptions that are questionable. The first assumption is that a finding of extralegal influence means that the jurors are not weighing the relevant evidentiary issues heavily enough. A study conducted by Visher (1987) that compared evidentiary variables against extralegal variables casts doubt on this assumption: the results showed that evidence variables explained 34% of the variance of jurors' judgments, while extralegal variables explained only 10% of the variance.

The second assumption is that extralegal factors are all irrelevant to the task and should not be taken into account. To assess this assumption, I first turn to the work of Kalven and Zeisel (1971), who formulated the "liberation hypothesis" to explain, in part, verdict disagreements between juries and judges. The liberation hypothesis recognizes that facts and values "are subtly intertwined" (p. 164), and that "disagreements arise because doubts about the evidence free the jury to follow sentiment" (p. 166). Said another way, "the sentiment gives direction to the resolution of the evidentiary doubt; the evidentiary doubt provides a favorable condition for a response to the sentiment" (p. 165). Kalven and Zeisel correctly anticipated that the critics of jurors and juries would find new ammunition from their findings and hypothesis.

When it comes to insanity cases, the liberation hypothesis is most likely to be operating at full strength, because the facts are seldom in doubt but the meaning of those facts is. Sentiments about negligence, whether the defendant is seen as having been punished enough, and when the punitive consequences of a guilty verdict seem too severe (Vidmar, 1972), do come into play. However, these intrusions of sentiment do not indicate that the jury is a "wildcat operation," say Kalven and Zeisel; rather, juries seem to employ "a delicate calculus" for resolving complex and competing value claims. "The upshot is that when the jury reaches a different conclusion from the judge on the same evidence, it does so not because it is a sloppy or inaccurate finder of facts, but because it gives recognition to values which fall outside the official rules" (p. 495).

We need to recognize that the law places upon jurors two contradictory obligations: first, the obligation to follow the court's instructions and second, "a protected power and privilege to override that obligation" (Kadish & Kadish, 1977, p. 308). This second function has evolved in Anglo-American law. Centuries ago, an acquittal verdict that was judged to be in error could lead to an "attaint" and punishment of the jurors; no longer: a jury's acquittal in a criminal case is now final. As Alexander Hamilton argued, "if the law gives them the power, it gives them the *right* also" (*People v. Croswell*, 1804, p. 345). As the Supreme Court recognized in *United States v. Spock* (1969), "the jury, as the conscience of the community, must be permitted to look at more than logic" (p. 182). As Kadish and Kadish (1977) remark about the Supreme Court's verdict in another case, *Duncan v. Louisiana* (1968), "the fundamental function of the jury is not only to guard against official departures from the rules of law, but also, on proper occasions, to depart from unjust rules or their unjust application" (p. 311).

There appears to be much ambivalence about this second function. Some see the jury's power to nullify instructions as an invitation to anarchy. Only two states, Maryland and Indiana, expressly inform juries that they have nullification powers; for juries in the other states, "they know this fact only on a *sotto voce* level" (Horowitz, 1985). But others see this "jurisprudence of law-breaking" as a virtue. Kadish and Kadish put it this way:

> By the counterposition of duty to comply and privilege to depart, the legal system has generated freedom in a very fundamental respect: the freedom of people not simply subject to the law, but, always within limits, independent of the law and capable of using that law for the ultimate ends of the legal system.

That consequence is itself a value, and makes possible adjustment to conditions
that could not have been foreseen with any clarity and hence could not have
been planned for in detail. (p. 318)

So if jurors appear to depart from the law and the instructions, as they
appeared to do in *Hadfield, M'Naghten*, and *Hinckley*, they may be invoking
their "legitimated interposition" (Kadish & Kadish, 1977, p. 316) power.
The public and the legal system may both desire jurors to have the power,
and, at other times, desire that they not use it. But as Kadish and Kadish
remark, you can "have it one way or the other but not both" (p. 312).

THE LAW'S VS. THE JURORS' CONSTRUCTS

A quick summary of the empirical evidence suggests that jurors have
neither a natural tendency nor a bias toward the NGRI verdict. Jurors listen
to both the evidence and the experts, yet they remain independent. Where
their sentiments intrude, these sentiments appear relevant to the issue at
hand, *as they frame the issue;* and this intrusion of sentiment serves the
legally sanctioned function of letting the community's conscience inspirit
the letter of the law. And we know that when jurors construe insanity,
their constructs are complex, relevant, and flexible. However, even though
the criticisms of jurors' decisions in insanity cases are largely unfounded,
there still remains a problem: the law's historic and current insanity tests
fail, when it comes to jurors' verdicts, to produce differences in those
verdicts. It is as if "insanity test instructions" and "jurors' verdicts" are
two separate, unrelated events. Why that is so, and why it is a problem,
will now be addressed.

When laws or insanity tests are perceived to be out of tune with the
jurors' perspective, the medico-psychological perspective, and even the
legal perspective, pressure mounts to change the rule before too many
nettlesome verdicts are returned. Such a pressure began to mount with
Hadfield, and the aim of that pressure was to change the "wild beast" test,
which was no longer perceived as in tune with the relevant perspectives on
insanity that existed in the early 1800s. The M'Naghten Rule was the
eventual corrective. But the expectations in framing the M'Naghten
Rules—that more NGRI acquittals should and would occur—did not come
to pass (Walker, 1968). And empirical evidence shows no significant differences in verdict patterns between jurors given the "wild beast" test and
those given the M'Naghten test, even though the language and constructs
of these two tests differ greatly. So the first problem is that insanity tests
are changed, in part, to produce differences in verdicts, yet that goal is not
achieved.

This failure to produce different verdict patterns repeats and repeats.
For example, when the M'Naghten Rules were amended by adding the

volitional test (i.e., the irresistible impulse addition), or replaced entirely by the Durham product rule, the expectations were that more NGRI acquittals would occur. The empirical evidence with mock jurors shows no differences, however. When Durham was replaced by the more defined and restrictive ALI test, the prediction was for fewer NGRI verdicts. Again, however, empirical evidence shows no change in verdicts. And now that the Insanity Defense Reform Act of 1984 has been passed, where the volitional arm of ALI was lopped off, expectations are that fewer NGRIs should occur. But empirical evidence (Rogers, 1987a) shows that this prediction is not substantiated. Finkel (1988, August) gave mock jurors either the Insanity Defense Reform Act of 1984 test, or the ALI test, or the "wild beast" test, or no test instruction at all. None of the four conditions produced verdict patterns different from the others.

The reason that expectations fail to be met in practice, I submit, has to do with the disparity between the law's constructs of insanity and the jurors' constructs. The law's constructs are embedded in the wording of the test. In the "wild beast" test, the accented construct is distorted awareness and perception. Former Attorney General William French Smith proposed that we should return to this standard and construct in his testimony before the Senate Committee on the Judiciary (1982):

> Under this formulation, the mental disease or defect would be no defense if the defendant knew he was shooting at a human being to kill him—even if the defendant acted out of an irrational or insane belief. Mental disease or defect would constitute a defense only if the defendant did not even know he had a gun in his hand or thought, for example, that he was shooting at a tree. (p. 30)

But this awareness–perception construct, from the work of Finkel and Handel (in press, b), turns out to be the most frequently cited NGRI factor (20.6%) only in case E, the stress-induced case; it ranks second in importance (16.6%) for the chronic alcoholic case (case B); third in importance (16.9%) for the paranoid schizophrenic case (case D); and fifth in importance for the epilepsy case (case A). As a guilty factor, it ranks fourth, fifth, fifth, and sixth for the four cases. In sum, this construct varies by case in terms of relevance, being less relevant far more than relevant.

If we do the same type of analysis this time comparing M'Naghten's accented construct, distorted thinking, with the jurors' relevant constructs, we find that, as an NGRI factor, this construct ranks second for case D, third for Case E, sixth for case B, and seventh for case A; as a guilty factor, it ranks second, second, second, and third. Again, the law's construct varies in relevance, being less relevant or moderately relevant, but never being most relevant as a jurors' construct. The irresistible impulse construct fares poorly also, ranking third, third, fourth, and sixth as both an NGRI and a guilty factor. Neither the irresistible impulse test alone nor in combination with M'Naghten, as in ALI, is likely to fit well with the jurors' constructs. And the Insanity Defense Reform Act of 1984 test, since it returns to *M'Naghten*'s "distorted thinking" construct in updated language, is not likely to fare any better than *M'Naghten*, and that is borne out by recent research.

A reason for why the expectations that follow from a new insanity test fail to be met emerges. The law's constructs fail to match well with the relevant and determinative constructs of jurors. And if anyone's constructs are judged as "naïve," "simplistic," or "irrelevant," it appears that that charge is more sustainable when it is directed at the Law, not the jurors. "Insanity," as jurors understand and construe it, is a multidimensional construct, or, in the vernacular of construct theorists, a *superordinate* construct. Furthermore, the particular *attributes* of insanity (e.g., distorted thinking, distorted awareness–perception, lack of control of impulses and actions) that have been incorporated into legal tests, and which may or may not be manifested by a particular defendant, appear to be lower-level constructs and not the *essence* of insanity, as jurors see it. Defendants can be judged "insane" whether or not they manifest clear or distorted perception, clear or distorted thinking, or control or lack of control of their impulses and actions. If a sound, coherent, and workable insanity test is our goal, then we must articulate the essence of insanity in such a way as to accord with our legal, psychological, *and* common-sense notions. Such a test has not yet been developed, in my opinion, but certainly ought to be.

One objection and counterargument that could be raised at this point goes as follows. Starting from the empirical evidence that one test works as well or as poorly as the next, this counterargument states that perhaps we should be content with this result. The system seems to work, regardless of the test, so let us accept the results, cut our contentious and futile efforts at building a better mousetrap, and lower our expectations. Advocates of this position may sound cynical, but they would argue that they are simply injecting "realism" into the discussion. If all of the tests work about the same because they are written in ways that allow jurors to employ their intuitive, common-sense notions of insanity, and if this is what jurors will do anyway, why fight it?

This argument is not without its problems. First, if advocates of this position wanted to be truly consistent, and less hypocritical, why not do away with even the pretense of a test? Since jurors reach the same verdicts with or without instructions, why not give them no instructions, save to decide as they will? No one, to my knowledge, in all of the Senate and House hearings following *Hinckley*, went that far. Both the advocates of changing the test and the advocates of leaving it as it is all implied that the Law and the public need *a standard*. Having an insanity defense without a test would leave a void for vagueness, one that could be filled too easily by caprice or whatever expert's or juror's opinion happened to gain momentary credence and ascendancy. This scenario renders the law mean-

ingless, creating law without letter or substance, which is what some believe happened with the Durham test, which was no test at all.

In rejecting this scenario, we believe that we can do better in the area
of insanity, and need to. What I turn to, in the final section of this chapter,
are some suggested directions that emerge from our historical failures and
empirical investigations; suggestions that move toward a sounder, saner,
truer, and more perspectivally consistent insanity test.

SUGGESTED DIRECTIONS FOR AN INSANITY TEST

Fingarette (1972), in his explication of the meaning of insanity, construes the M'Naghten Rule differently from most commentators. He suggests that the framers of the Rule had a deeper construct in mind when
they invoked the "defect of reason" phrase. He proposes that a fundamental "incapacity," as opposed to merely "distorted thinking," is closer to
what the framers had in mind, and he further believes that "incapacity" is
closer to the essence of insanity.

In his own proposal, the Disability of Mind doctrine (Fingarette &
Hasse, 1979), he adds a second construct, culpable–nonculpable, to the
capacity–incapacity construct. His point in doing so can be made through
an example. Why is it, we could ask, that ordinary drunk drivers do not
raise the insanity defense? Surely, at the moment they crash their cars into
other cars, they are not in "right mind," not perceiving clearly, or not
thinking clearly, yet we do not exculpate the drunk driver. It is not "the
moment of the act" that is determinative of culpability, but the *culpable
actions* of drunk drivers *before* the act, sometimes hours before. When they
chose to drink, when they chose to continue to drink, when they chose to
drink knowing that they would later drive—these are their decisions and
actions we find blameworthy.

What Fingarette and Hasse find short-sighted about insanity tests is
the fact that the tests themselves focus exclusively on the moment of the
act, but should not. While insanity tests do restrict culpability to the moment of the act, jurors do not. In Finkel and Handel's work (in press, b),
jurors do weigh prior actions: in the epilepsy case, it is not the defendant's
action with the gun in her hands that is blameworthy but the fact that she
stopped taking her medication a day prior to the act, without consulting
her doctor. For the chronic alcoholic, the fact that she chose to have a drink
is a culpable action for jurors. And that the paranoid schizophrenic chose
to stop treatment over her doctor's strong advice, that again is a culpable
action according to jurors.

When Finkel and Handel compared Fingarette and Hasse's two construct dimensions (i.e., culpable–nonculpable and capacity–incapacity)

with the jurors' identified constructs, they found that these two constructs ranked first in seven out of eight cases. They conclude that these two constructs offer "a promising future avenue for construing an insanity test that fits well with jurors' common sense constructs."

This suggested direction converges with the recommendations made by Moore (1984) and Morse (1984, 1985). Moore not only seeks to de-medicalize the legal definition of mental illness (see Chapter 4), but he seeks to place legal insanity in its proper moral context. He writes:

> If the issue is a moral one . . . then the legal definition of the phrase should embody those moral principles that underlie the intuitive judgment that men-tally ill human beings are not responsible.
> The legal definition of mental illness should thus draw on the moral tradi-tion that is the rationale for the defense. What is thus needed is an analysis of that popular moral notion of mental illness. What have people meant by mental illness such that, both on and off juries, they have for centuries excused the otherwise wrongful acts of mentally ill persons? (p. 244)

Moore goes on to state the question "Is the accused so irrational as to be nonresponsible?" (p. 244) He then remarks, correctly, as it turns out, that "one rather suspects that juries have long applied this criterion, irre-spective of the wording of the insanity test" (p. 244).

Morse also seeks to put the insanity test in a moral context and one that conforms to the intuitive constructs of jurors. He rejects pseudomedi-calizations as inappropriate, and he rejects legal and semantic debates, such as whether "appreciate" should be substituted for "understand," as a "distinction without a difference." He offers, instead, "The Craziness Test": "A defendant is not guilty by reason of insanity if at the time of the offense the defendant was extremely crazy and the craziness affected the criminal behavior" (p. 390). Morse maintains that "this test tracks the moral issues with greater honesty and precision, is more workable, and will not lead to the acquittal of more defendants than present tests or reformed versions of present tests" (p. 390).

While Morse's "Craziness Test" itself lacks a certain precision, it was meant to provocatively make a point. The same point Moore is making, I believe, and the one I have been attempting to draw from historical dead ends and empirical avenues. The point is that an insanity test ought to rest on moral principles. That it ought to correspond and articulate the com-mon-sense moral precepts that underlie jurors' constructs of insanity. That the test ought to be denuded of medicalizations or legalizations that tech-nicalize and obscure, that remove the issue from its proper moral base, and that make legal insanity remote from the ordinary understanding.

Another suggested direction is that the choices available to the jurors, which have traditionally been two (i.e., guilty or NGRI), be expanded. From the way jurors construe and contextualize insanity cases, it is clear that they oftentimes see other options as best fitting, but run into difficulties and end up with "curious" verdicts when those options are unavailable. In the seventeenth century, "the Bluidy Mackenzie" recognized that culpability was graded, as opposed to full or absent. Jurors, too, recognize degrees of culpability. While Norval Morris (1982) would not go this far in his recommendations, he recognizes the point:

> Choice is neither present nor absent in the typical case where the insanity defense is currently pleaded; what is at issue is the degree of freedom of choice on a continuum from the hypothetically entirely rational to the hypothetically pathologically determined—in states of consciousness neither polar condition exists. (p. 61)

And, finally, I would suggest that test instructions make some explicit connections with dispositions such that jurors understand the likely outcomes and procedures that follow from a verdict. By removing ambiguity and thus guesswork, where the guesswork may be off the mark, we reduce another source of verdict variability and peculiarity.

The dominant theme of this chapter has been that the perspective of the ordinary citizen, long overlooked in the long-running debate over insanity tests, needs to be included; furthermore, this perspective can serve as a sound moral basis for insanity, as jurors serve as the conscience of the community. If the alternatives are the nineteenth-century alienists' suggestion to let the medico-psychological experts decide, or the suggestion that judges, following the letter of the law, decide, my vote, based on empirical findings, is to stick with the delicate calculus of ordinary citizens.

8

Neuropsychological Perspectives on Insanity

A prevailing current, with most unsettling consequences for insanity and the Law, emanates today from neuropsychological laboratories. Today's current updates the nineteenth-century alienists' claims that responsibility would give way to disease, that conventional morality would be superseded by natural law, and that Law itself would be replaced by Medicine. A century ago, the best legal minds gave the alienists' claims careful consideration. When Henry Maudsley wrote, J. F. Stephen read. And Maudsley (1876) wrote that

> it is certain, however, that lunatics and criminals are as much manufactured articles as are steam-engines and calico-printing machines . . . They are neither accidents nor anomalies in the universe, but come by law and testify to causality. . . . (p. 28)

And after critically evaluating these claims, Stephen (1877) wrote,

> If medical men could tell lawyers precisely how A's mind was affected in relation to a particular act by the mental disease under which A was labouring when he did that act, the lawyers could tell whether or not the act was a crime; but this is just what medical men cannot tell. (p. xxix–xxx)

At this point, with all the advantages that hindsight and history have to offer us, we may opt for the conclusion that the alienists' claims were pure hyperbole. After all, the medical men of the nineteenth century could not furnish the proof that jurists were seeking. Maudsley (1876) admitted as much when he wrote, following his steam-engines and calico-printing machines analogy, that "only the processes of the organic manufactory are so complex that we are not able to follow them" (p. 28).

But that was then. *What if* twentieth-century neuropsychologists can show that the alientists' claims were not false, but simply premature? That the "processes of the organic manufactory" have been followed, and understood, and that the proof the nineteenth-century medical men could not furnish is now available. What then?

Then, the suggested directions I recommended in the preceding chapter (and those in Chapter 4)—that we demedicalize and remoralize the notions of mental illness and insanity—may already be dead ends. For if the neurosciences have truly advanced to the point some have claimed, then those moral notions may already be myths—antiquated, evanescent notions that evaporate amidst hard facts of our brain's functioning. Take, for example, the assumptions embedded in the law's "reasonable man" test, assumptions that were themselves on trial, along with Bernhard Goetz, for the actions that occurred on a New York subway in 1984. Richard Restak (1987), a noted neurologist and neuropsychiatrist, had the following to say about Goetz, the "reasonable man" test, and brain facts:

> As a neurologist and neuropsychiatrist with over a decade of experience in conducting pretrial interviews of individuals who have acted violently, the "reasonable person" argument seems an illogical and outdated approach to fully understanding events such as occurred on the New York subway in December of 1984 when Bernhard Goetz shot and injured four teenagers.
> On the basis of what I know about the human brain I'm convinced that there are no reasonable people under conditions in which death or severe bodily harm are believed imminent.
> Deep within the brain of every reasonable person resides the limbic system: an ancient interconnected network of structures that anatomically and chemically haven't changed much over hundreds of thousands of years. We share these structures with jungle animals . . . Moreover, the limbic system is capable under conditions of extreme duress of overwhelming the cerebral cortex wherein are formulated many of the reasonable person's most reasonable attributes, like interpretation, judgment and restraint. . . .
> The limbic system may also be responsible, many brain scientists are convinced, for sudden outbursts of rage followed by violence, the so-called "episodic dyscontrol" syndrome. . . .Emotions are not incidental and subsidiary to rational processes. Instead, the reasonable person, even at his or her most reasonable moments, is influenced by emotional processes. . . .
> Our legal system, however, has yet to accommodate these new insights, and continues to stress the "reasonable man" standard. . . . What comes across . . . is the utter ordinariness and predictability of the "reasonable" person. . . .
> The prosecutor's logic is this: Once Goetz coolly discerned that he was out of danger, he should have calmed down, put away his gun and awaited the

arrival of the police . . . such expectations are neurologically unrealistic. Once aroused, the limbic system can become a directive force for hours, sometimes days, and can rarely be shut off like flipping a switch. (p. c3)

Restak concludes that lawyers and judges love to ask and explore questions about what a reasonable man would do under such circumstances, but Restak claims that the question is the wrong one, not attuned to the neurological facts.

I'm convinced that they're the wrong questions—products of an outmoded mentality that places an overemphasis on empty intellectualization to the exclusion of those deep and powerful emotional currents of fear, self-preservation or territoriality that can surface in any one of us and overpower the cogitations of reason.

Granted that this isn't a pretty or elegant arrangement. But as long as our brain is put together the way it is, no one should be too confident that he or she would remain completely reasonable under conditions where their life is perceived to be in imminent danger. Moreover, this critical perception of threat isn't based on rationality. It's fueled by those limbic derived emotions that have promoted the survival of our species.

Isn't it preferable therefore to face up courageously to these sometimes frightening and unpleasant realities instead of pretending that questions such as those being asked about Bernhard Goetz can be answered by courtroom speculations about how a reasonable person would have responded in his place?

To expect reasonable behavior in the face of perceived threat, terror and rage is itself a most unreasonable expectation. (p. c3)

Now we arrive at the subject of this chapter: neuropsychological perspectives on insanity. Instead of a comprehensive review of what is an extensive and complex area, this chapter will focus on those findings that derive from split-brain commissurotomy work. The purpose in reviewing both the facts and the proffered claims in this area is to see whether a new insanity defense is at hand, waiting only to happen, and whether the nineteenth-century alienists' claims are about to be fulfilled; for if such a defense is at hand and these claims can be fulfilled, our sacred notions of responsibility, free will, and the reasonable person may turn out to be bankrupt, and the basis for insanity may have to be neurologically recast. We now turn to the case of split-brain madness (Finkel & Sabat, 1985).

SPLIT-BRAIN BACKGROUND FACTS

The earliest direct observations of the brain revealed that it is actually divided into halves, with each half appearing to be a mirror image of the other. "These two parts, or hemispheres, are tightly packed together inside the skull and are linked by several distinct bundles of nerve fibers, which serve as channels of communication between them" (Springer &

Deutsch, 1981, p. 2). These distinct bundles of nerve fibers that connect the two hemispheres are called *commissures*, the largest being the corpus callosum, with the number of fibers being in the order of 200 million.

The notion that the two, mirror-image hemispheres might not be *functionally* equivalent derived from nineteenth-century clinical work. In 1836, a French general practitioner, Marc Dax, presented a paper based on his investigation of more than 40 patients who suffered from *aphasia*, a loss of speech following some damage to the brain. Dax found that the damage in all 40 cases occurred in the left hemisphere. He did not find a single case involving right hemisphere damage alone. In the 1860s, Paul Broca presented more precise evidence that pinpointed the area involved in cases of aphasia. Broca then went further, as Springer and Deutsch (1981) point out, linking speech and brain function to handedness:

> "One can conceive," he speculated, "that there may be a certain number of individuals in whom the natural pre-eminence of the convolutions of the right hemisphere reverses the order of the phenomenon which I have just described." These individuals, of course, are left-handers. Broca's "rule" that the hemisphere controlling speech is on the side opposite to the preferred hand was influential well into the twentieth century. (p. 11)

In 1868, the eminent British neurologist John Hughlings Jackson proposed his idea of a "leading" hemisphere, a "precursor to the idea of cerebral dominance" (p. 12). To again quote Springer and Deutsch (1981),

> "The two brains cannot be mere duplicates," he wrote, "if damage to one alone can make a man speechless. For these processes (of speech), of which there are none higher, there must surely be one side which is leading." Jackson further concluded "that in most people the left side of the brain is the leading side—the side of the so-called will, and that the right side is the "the automatic side." (p. 12)

Jackson did not ignore the right hemisphere: in fact, he raised the question of whether perception might be seated in the right hemisphere. And there is evidence, again from patients with brain damage, that patients "with certain kinds of right-hemisphere damage are much more likely to have perceptual and attentional problems" (pp. 2–3).

Given the facts of hemisphere differences, speculations arose as to what would happen if the hemispheres were split. The nineteenth-century experimental psychologist Gustav Fechner believed that "something like the duplication of a human being would result" (Springer & Deutsch, 1981, p. 26). Fechner's views were challenged by William McDougall, a British psychologist. McDougall felt that consciousness would not be split, as Fechner surmised, but would remain unitary. "To make his point, McDougall volunterred to have his corpus callosum cut if he ever got an incurable disease" (p. 26). This debate between Fechner and McDougall remained untested, then, because Fechner considered the separation of hemispheres to be an impossibility. Twentieth-century research would prove him wrong.

The first operation on a human was performed in the 1940s by William Van Wagenen. Why, you might ask, did a neurosurgeon perform such an operation (a commissurotomy)? The answer was *epilepsy*, at least those forms of intractable epilepsy that failed to respond to other types of treatment. The rationale involved "the spread of epileptic discharge from one hemisphere to the other" (p. 25), an effect first observed in the brains of monkeys; if the epileptic discharge was spreading via the corpus callosum, then perhaps severing this commissure might contain the epilepsy. The first operations failed to alleviate the condition.

Then came the work of Ronald Myers and Roger Sperry, the latter winning the Nobel Prize for his work. The discoveries of Myers and Sperry, who worked with cats, led neurosurgeons Vogel and Bogen to reconsider split-brain surgery with humans, but with a difference: perhaps the earlier surgery failed because the other major commissures were not cut. In the 1950s, Bogen and Vogel performed complete commissurotomies on two-dozen epileptic patients.

How does a comissurotomized patient look? How does he perceive and think? Is his personality altered? Was Fechner right, or was McDougall? The answer, in detail, will be forthcoming. But first, some glimpses. After the scars of surgery heal, neither strangers nor friends are aware of any differences in the commissurotomized patient's appearance, behavior, or personality. But when brought into a laboratory, where, for example, sophisticated methodological procedures can present visual stimuli for less than a fifth of a second, differences do emerge. If the split-brain subject, a right-handed individual, looks straight ahead and the words HAT BAND are flashed for less than 200 milliseconds, something unusual happens: when asked what he saw, he says "band." Normal subjects report that they saw "hat band." The reason for this difference is that "hat" and "band" lie in different parts of the visual field, and different parts of the retina receive their stimuli. Due to the commissurotomy, "hat" is projected only to the right hemisphere, whereas "band" is projected only to the left hemisphere. Because the interhemispheric connections have been severed, information from the right hemisphere does not cross to the left, where the verbal system in right-handers is located.

One last glimpse. Since our hands are controlled by the opposite hemisphere, does a split-brain subject *know* what is in his left hand? Suppose we place an unseen object in the left hand, which would project to the right hemisphere but would not cross to the verbal center in the left hemisphere. What would the subject report? He reports that he doesn't know. We move closer to an insanity defense waiting to happen if the object in the left hand is a loaded pistol.

SPLIT-BRAIN MADNESS

This insanity defense possibility was suggested by the Nobelist Sir John Eccles (1980). Sir John referred to a hypothetical situation—"a commissurotomized person found with a 'smoking pistol' in his left hand and the bullet pierced victim near his feet" (Finkel & Sabat, 1985, p. 225). If he was called as an expert witness, Sir John remarked, he would testify for acquittal on the grounds of insanity.

On quick reflection, particularly when we consider that there are only two dozen or so split-brain individuals, we might be tempted to dismiss this possible happening as too implausible to worry about. Furthermore, it is unlikely that the number of cases of intractable epilepsy requiring a commissurotomy will rise appreciably. Thus the likelihood of Sir John Eccles' hypothetical case arising, now or in the future, appears remote.

On further reflection, though, the "odds" may drop appreciably if we consider a possible variation. What if the defense claims that the alleged murderer was suffering from a *functional* commissurotomy? That a drug, an altered state of consciousness, a developmental quirk, an environmental stressor, or a psychic shock produced a functional dissociation of the hemispheres. At the clinical level, multiple personalities (Lasky, 1982) suggest such a functional dissociation.

The functional dissociation possibility was suggested by two eminent researchers in the neural sciences, Gazzaniga and Le Doux, where, in their work *The Integrated Mind* (1978), they present the case of George. To quote from Finkel and Sabat (1985):

> George is a fine, upstanding citizen, a married man who believes in fidelity and who does not condone extramarital affairs. But suddenly (!?), George finds himself in bed with Molly (who is not his wife). How do the authors and creators of this example account for this inextricable tryst of fate? Gazzaniga and Le Doux rescue their adulterer from this moral bed of thorns by proposing a form of the split-brain insanity defense! Here is their comment. (p. 227)
>
> Why did George suddenly find himself in bed with Molly in the first place? What is the mechanism for eliciting a dissonant behavior from the beginning? The behavior was clearly contrary to his existing (verbally stored) belief about such matters, and normally the verbal system can exert self-control. The reason we propose is that yet another information system with a different reference and a different set of values existed in George, but because it was encoded in a particular way, its existence was not know to George's verbal system and therefore was outside of its control. (p. 156)

Keeping in mind that George's "dissociation is *functional*, not physical, a top-notch lawyer, armed with such an example, embedded and wrapped in scientific respectability, might indeed employ such a defense to acquit his Jekyll-and-Hyde-like client. Albert De Salvo, the Boston Strangler, was one such Jekyll-and-Hyde-like client, as his lawyer, F. Lee Bailey (Bailey & Aronson, 1971) notes:

> After knowing Albert De Salvo for half an hour, the average person would feel perfectly comfortable about inviting him home for dinner to meet the family. That was one of the pieces that fell into place in the puzzle of the Boston Strangler. It helped explain why he had been able to evade detection despite more than two and a half years of investigation. De Salvo was Dr. Jekyll; the police had been looking for Mr. Hyde. (p. 149)

With such a Jekyll-and-Hyde-like client, a lawyer might seek all possible evidence—including neuropsychological evidence—"that might suggest that Mr. Hyde was operating through the right (now-dominant) hemisphere, or some particular information system, unbeknownst to the good, but temporarily dormant, Dr. Jekyll" (Finkel & Sabat, 1985, pp. 226–227).

> And if he found such evidence, he would ask the jury, "Why should Jekyll, on the left, be left to hold the bag, serve the time, or have *his* hemisphere electrically fried for the actions of the "right" Mr. Hyde?" You can almost hear his closing summary.

Actually, the defense attorney would not have to work hard in fashioning a closing summary: he might, instead, simply quote the last paragraph of Gazzaniga and Le Doux's (1978) book:

> Such a state of affairs makes the job for society and its judges extremely difficult. To which self do they mete out their punishments? As it stands, judges are, metaphorically speaking, called upon to punish the whole town for the wayward actions of one of its citizens . . . Just as social programs work poorly on a whole town because they are inherently unable to anticipate all the separate needs and conditions of its citizenry, the personal directive toward the person is equally sloppy and inaccurate in hitting the mark—the self that is responsible for the action in question. (p. 161)

The "odds" drop still further when we consider the fact that professionals are entering the courtroom in a newer capacity: not only are professionals entering in their traditional role of providing expert clinical judgments, but now we have "trial by data" (Loftus & Monahan, 1980), where social scientists inform the triers of facts about psychological research. This *research expertise*, specifically as it relates to neuropsychological findings from split-brain research, may increasingly come to the court's attention. But unfortunately, "facts" and metaphors regarding differential functioning of our two hemispheres are proliferating faster than our understanding. As Michael Corballis (1980) noted in an article entitled "Laterality and Myth," there are a number of "pop" psychology assertions regarding "right as opposed to left hemisphere" modes of thinking that have been bandied about (Bruner, 1965; Ornstein, 1972; Witelson, 1977). "We are already hearing the argument that functional disparity between hemisphere explains East–West differences, cultural diversities, artistic creativity, perceptual problems, and reading difficulties in children" (Finkel & Sabat, 1985, p. 226). With the terms already in our vocabulary, if not our consciousness, it is only a small step to take to extend this "argument-explanation" to the criminal acts of man.

Before returning to specifics, a summary is in order. To quote from Finkel and Sabat (1985),

> "Facts" regarding hemispheric disparities are emerging rapidly; far more rapidly than any theory or agreed upon understanding of what those facts signify. Coupled with the above is the greater likelihood that psychologists will be presenting those facts to juries. Lawyers, who often orchestrate marriages as well as divorces, have a vested interest here; the marriage of the neuropsychological expert and his findings with the defendant and his hemispheres is waiting to happen; the result of this coupling is likely to be split-brain madness—a new insanity defense in which personal responsibility is questioned once again. (pp. 228–229)

THE ISSUE OF RESPONSIBILITY

The courts and the populace have had little difficulty with the totally insane individual. Such a person, actively psychotic with all areas of mental functioning severely impaired, leaves us with little doubt concerning responsibility. Such an individual is judged not responsible for his or her actions, and a verdict of "not guilty by reason of insanity" typically follows.

The problems and issues get stickier and murkier as we move from "total insanity" toward "temporary" and "partial" insanity. The larger public was introduced to the problem with Robert Louis Stevenson's fictional story *The Strange Case of Dr. Jekyll and Mr. Hyde* (1937), in which Stevenson explored a type of partial insanity in the year 1886.

> But Stevenson and fiction were already late. The crimes had long since been committed, with real-life cases (e.g., Hadfield, M'Naghten) already "on the books" and on the minds of legal, psychological, and philosophical thinkers of the time. At issue were the nature of mind, consciousness, personality, and responsibility. At stake, often enough, was a defendant's life, which, often enough, was staked to an insanity defense. (Finkel & Sabat, 1985, p. 230)

When it came to the mind, and more specifically, the insane mind, M'Naghten's lawyer Cockburn cited Isaac Ray as the authority. Ray (1838/1983) stated

> that the insane mind is not entirely deprived of the power of moral discernment, but on many subjects is perfectly rational and displays the exercise of a second and well-balanced mind, is one of those facts now so well established, that to question it would only display the height of ignorance and presumption. (p. 32)

But if there is a second well-balanced and rational mind along with a temporarily dominant but disordered mind, what can we say regarding *responsibility?* Is this half-rational, half-irrational person responsible, or not?

The answer is not yet clear. What is clear is that the number of clinical cases that could fit this situation is large and growing. No longer do we have to document *furiosius,* total insanity; now, dissociative states, delusions, and impulse disorders qualify. Using the terms of the *Diagnostic and Statistical Manual* (1987, 1980, 1968), we are talking about instances of Paranoid Disorder, Schizophrenic Disorder, Affective Disorder, Dissociative Disorder (e.g., Multiple Personality), and Conduct Disorder. And there may be more, when we consider that some conditions (e.g., premenstrual syndrome) currently discussed and debated, may be included in the near future. Thus, what started as an extremely unlikely possibility—a split-brain insanity defense—now may be adaptable for numerous and varied disorders (Schacter, 1986; Fenwick, 1987; Harry & Balcer, 1987; Kopelman, 1987).

> At the psychological level, the *commonality* that runs through these diverse disorders is *dissociation*—some part of consciousness and personality separated and disowned; what usually follows is an ascription about the dissociated psyche—that it has its own thinking, motives, passion, and will—but that when "it" acts, "we" remain *unconscious of it or unable to control it;* hence we are not responsible. (Finkel & Sabat, 1985, p. 232)

What now follows are three descriptions of dissociation, one from the psychiatric perspective, another from the realm of fiction, and the last from split-brain research.

Isaac Ray (1838/1983) wrote about the criminal and psychological act this way:

> The *particular* criminal act, however, becomes divorced in their minds from its relations to crime in the *abstract;* and being regarded only in connection with some favourite object which it may help to obtain, and which they see no reason to refrain from pursuing, is viewed, in fact, as of a highly laudable and meritorious nature. Herein, then, consists their insanity—not in preferring vice to virtue, in applauding crime and deriding justice, but in being unable to discern the essential identity of nature between a particular crime and all other crimes, whereby they are led to approve what, in general terms, they have already condemned. (p. 34)

In the fictional realm (Stevenson, 1937 pp. 289–290), Henry Jekyll spoke about the deep *trench* that

> . . . severed in me those provinces of good and ill which divide and compound man's dual nature . . . I saw that, of the two natures that contended in the field of my unconsciousness, even if I could rightly be said to be either, it was only because I was radically both . . . It was the curse of mankind that these incongruous faggots were thus bound together—that in the agonized womb of consciousness, these polar twins should be continuously struggling. How, then, were they dissociated?

"Dissociate them he did. And like Ray's description, Jekyll looked aghast upon the actions of Hyde as something now 'outside' himself"

(Finkel & Sabat, 1985, p. 233). From the realm of split-brain research, the Nobelist Roger Sperry (1966) has argued for a doubling of consciousness in split-brain patients:

> Everything we have seen so far indicates that the surgery has left these people with two separate minds, that is, two separate spheres of consciousness. What is experienced in the right hemisphere seems to lie entirely outside the realm of experience of the left hemisphere. This mental dimension has been demonstrated in regard to perception, cognition, volition, learning, memory.

> For Sperry, the impression of mental unity in split-brain patients is an illusion, a consequence of the fact that the two sides of the brain share the same position in space, the same sensory organ, and the same experience in everyday situations outside the lab. (Springer & Deutsch, 1981, p. 182).

Gazzaniga and Le Doux extend the split-brain findings to their hypothetical case of George and Molly. Finkel and Sabat (1985) describe it this way:

> George is split—dissociated—but into various informational systems, each with a different referent and a different set of values; one system can be unbeknownst to another, even more than Jekyll and Hyde were to each other; so George fondles and fiddles with Molly ("Are we to presume with the left hand?"), all out of the awareness of the right-handed, left-hemisphered verbal system.
> But "Lefty" knows.
> "Righty," on the other hand, says "I didn't know."
> We now come back to our starting point, the split-brain, which can be viewed as the ultimate dissociation—two hemispheres, information systems (selves?) incommunicable. These Jekyll and Hyde hemispheres or information systems, one holding the smoking pistol and the other holding to its ignorance of the act, both court acquittal.
> Let us hear the evidence. (p. 233)

WHERE PERSONAL RESPONSIBILITY ENDS AND BRAIN PROCESSES BEGIN

Sperry, Gazzaniga, and Bogen (1969) wrote a provocative paper on interhemispheric relations, commissures, and hemispheric disconnections. Many picked up on this work and extrapolated beyond the facts. As a result, facts were stirred with metaphor and "pop psychology" flowered. The excesses of "pop psychology" were reminiscent of the extravagant claims of the alienists a century earlier. Daniel Robinson (1976) urged caution in our claims and advised that we "economise in the use of the human nervous system for metaphorical purposes . . . before this loose talk about hemispheres, minds, selves, and culture becomes habitual." But the "loose talk" had already been unleashed, as the following simile of Ornstein's (1972) indicates: "The left hemisphere, like Western philosophy, is analytical, verbal, linear, rational while the right, like Eastern thought, is intuitive, non-verbal, non-linear, a-rational" (p. 73). Robinson, using the one-line rejoinder "the inference, I suppose, is that Orientals tend to be left-handed," attempted to limit such loose talk and thinking.

Gazzaniga and Le Doux, in their work *The Integrated Mind* (1978), were also mindful of the excesses and distortions of "pop psychology"; in fact, Elliot Valenstein's comment on the book's jacket is that this work is an "antidote to 'pop psychology.'" But Finkel and Sabat (1985) are critical, claiming that Gazzaniga and Le Doux frequently confused what they sought to clarify: they confused

> The relationship between the brain processes which underlie the variety of conscious states that make up human life, on the one hand, and the personal responsibility that the law ascribes to the owner of those brain processes on the other.

Let us unravel Gazzaniga and Le Doux's thesis

> in order to keep clear the theoretical leaps that are being made about split brains, split systems, and split selves. We may then proceed to show how the concept (issue) of personal responsibility is affected and undermined by such thinking. (p. 237).

These authors attempt to show, using an example cited by Gazzaniga and Le Doux, that the assertion that each hemisphere is in possession of *vastly different functioning* is not true, but an artifact of the nuances of the experimental methods used. Finkel and Sabat (1985) present the example, followed by a different interpretation.

> In Case I, the split-brain patient is given a "block design" task, where he is shown four cubes on each of which a pattern is painted, and a picture of a design which could be made by placing the cubes in the proper position. The patient is asked to perform the task using only one hand at a time and the elapsed time is recorded for right vs. left hand. It was found that the patients' use of the left hand (controlled via the right hemisphere of the brain) led to faster completion of the task than did their use of the right hand (controlled via the left hemisphere). The question remained, however, as to whether such a result was tied to the perceptual properties (hard-wired) of each hemisphere or to the production of a response via use of each hemisphere. As it happens, in Case II, when the use of somatosensory motor system is not required—when patients must match the pictured design as flashed (in less than 200 msec.—to prevent the effects of eye movements which would send information to *both* hemispheres) to left or right hemisphere exclusively with a choice of four other designs, the differences observed previously disappear. So, visual perception is not qualitatively different in terms of the use of the left vs. the right hemisphere. It is only the active manipulation of the blocks themselves coupled with ongoing visual perception that presents an indication of hemispheric specialization. To repeat, the right hemisphere and left hemisphere are capable of providing the observer with an accurate appreciation of the visuospatial aspects of the block design task. (p. 237)

Others, too, have reached the conclusion that the differences between the information-processing characteristics of the right vs. left hemispheres are not extreme. Corballis and Morgan (1978) asserted that the hemispheres do not differ in terms of the *quality* of the information they process (verbal vs. nonverbal, for instance) but in terms of the *extent* to which they process such information.

> If one examines the evidence, the most obvious characteristic of so-called right-hemisphere functions is that they are non-verbal. Otherwise, they constitute a fairly wide cross section of normal perceptual and cognitive functions. (p. 266)

However, as Corballis and Morgan point out, comparisons of the right and left hemisphere have shown that there is "residual language capacity in the right hemisphere of commissurotomized patients" (Gazziniga, Bogen, & Sperry, 1967).

A more recent piece of evidence on the capacity of the right hemisphere in a commissurotomized person has been provided by Sperry, Zaidel, and Zaidel (1979). In this study, the authors flashed test photographs, each containing a number of faces, objects, etc., to the subjects' right hemisphere via a special scleral lens (Z-lens). The lens, which moves with the eye and occludes the desired half-field of vision, allows stimuli to be presented to the right hemisphere during prolonged examination by the subject. Under these conditions, they included in an array of unfamiliar faces one familiar face, e.g., a family member, well-known social or political figure, etc. The subject was asked to point to the face he or she recognized, if any. These subjects, without hesitation, pointed to the familiar face, reacted to it emotionally, and with a minimum of cuing, identified it correctly. Sperry, Zaidel and Zaidel (1979) concluded that there is:

> . . . the presence in the right hemisphere of a well-developed sense of self and social awareness . . . The overall level of the right hemisphere's ability to identify test items and also the quality of the accompanying emotional and evaluative responses were of the same order approximately as those obtained from the right visual field and left hemisphere. Occasional discrepancies between the left field and right field responses were the exception rather than the rule, did not exceed the intrahemispheric range of variation from one test session to another, and in general can hardly be considered indicative of left–right differences. Taken together, the present data strongly reinforce the assumption that human subjectivity is basically much the same in the two hemispheres. (pp. 163–164)

The authors hypothesized that impressions or "auras" regarding the object of familiarity are transmitted from right to left hemisphere via brainstem mechanisms. But, even before verbal identification, when the stimulus is confined to the right hemisphere, the subject reacts, recognizes, and knows the identity of the familiar person or object. That the right hemisphere is not completely nonverbal was clear in instances in which subjects tried to "cross-cue"—they attempted to *write*, with the *left* hand, the person's name on their *right* hand so that the somatosensory information would be sent to the left hemisphere. Again, this lends support to the notion proposed by Corballis and Morgan (1978) that the distinction between the hemispheres is "one of degree rather than kind" (p. 261) and also lends support to the attempt to undichotomize the hemispheres' function put forth by Gazzaniga and Le Doux.

Although Gazzaniga and Le Doux attempt to undercut the left-right dichotomy, they discuss the hemispheres almost as if each half of the brain *had a will*, separate and apart from the other, not to mention the patient:

> . . . these data suggest that both hemispheres are capable of appreciating the visuospatial aspects of the block design task, but the right hemisphere is vastly if not absolutely superior to the left in constructing the perceived relations by manipulating the items appropriately. (p. 50)

That is, the left hemisphere isn't as good at the block design task as is the right hemisphere. This sort of language persists: ". . . it was not clear whether the right-hand deficit resulted because the left hemisphere did not know what a cube was . . ." In these examples we find two key points regarding brain function and interpretation (Finkel & Sabat, 1985, p. 239):

> (1) The hemispheric differences once observed are not a clear-cut, hard-wire feature of the brain; rather they are tied to contrived situations presented to subjects in particular experimental tasks. Under normal conditions, surgeons assert, the split-brain subject is indistinguishable from other people. . . .
>
> (2) The authors impute performance and understanding to the hemispheres rather than to the patient—person. Thus, in a quick linguistic legerdemain, we have certain experiences of the *self* found to be in the ownership of the brain's left or right hemisphere. If it can be argued that our experiences are owned by the brain's hemispheres or information systems, the actions that are called forth following those experiences can likewise be placed in the ownership of neural networks. (p. 239)

If our actions are caused solely by neural networks over which we have little to no control, "it is a small step to argue that the responsibility resides with neural information systems and not with the individual, who is merely the passive reflection of the workings of the neural networks."

WHAT SORT OF PERSONS ARE HEMISPHERES?

This question was posed by Daniel Robinson (1976). We will look at three different answers. The first answer, proposed by Puccetti (1973), claimed that a split-brain would reveal a split-mind, so that the two separated hemispheres leaves us as two persons. From this thesis we derive the neurophysiological underpinning to explain multiple-personality cases. The second answer does not find two distinct selves, but only a partial self in the minor hemisphere; this thesis does not accord this "partial self" "full self" status, since it lacks verbal and moral centers.

And the third answer is that we have *one mind, one person,* as "apparently split" and as "apparently whole" as on most days in and out of the laboratory, who processes information from both hemispheres, and who may be unaware (unconscious) of information to some degree, depending upon whether or not the callosum is cut. This position asserts that to confuse mind and brain, or to fuse mind–brain distinctions into one indistinguishable whole—the brain—runs grave risks. To paraphrase Robinson, "The consequence of treating these hemispheres as evidence of new persons will be to render the concept of person inarticulate." (Finkel & Sabat, 1985, p. 235)

The first answer, that of Puccetti, corresponds to Gustav Fechner's position. The third answer, that of one mind, one person, corresponds to William McDougall's position. Gazzaniga and Le Doux's thesis combines answers 1 and 2 in sophisticated yet troubling ways. For example, the two hemispheres-two persons thesis works well for multiple personalities only when the number of personalities is two. But there are clinical cases (Thigpen & Cleckley, 1957; Osgood, Luria, Jeans, & Smith, 1976; Lasky, 1982) that show three or more personalities; in these instances, where the number of personalities exceeds the available number of hemispheres, the thesis breaks down. But this is precisely the point where Gazzaniga and Le Doux's hypothesized "information systems" comes to the rescue. Multi-information systems can handle multi-personalities, but there is a price to pay for this shift: "the physical 'solidness' of hemispheres now gives way to the metaphysical 'elusiveness' of information systems" (Finkel & Sabat, 1985, p. 236).

When we leave the physical for the metaphorical, as we do in Gazzaniga and Le Doux's thesis, we run into some difficult yet basic questions. How many information systems are there? Where are they? And how are they anchored in place and in function to the two hemispheres? These are the sort of questions that face any theorist when hypothetical constructs are proposed; they are the same sort of questions that Freud faced when he first proposed, but later abandoned, his "Project for a Scientific Psychology" (1974a).

Gazzaniga and Le Doux's thesis also involves elements of answer 2—where only a partial self is believed to exist in the minor hemisphere. Now we have information systems, but it is unclear whether all information systems are *essentially* equal. On the one hand, the authors claim that the information system has a sense of self, with likes, dislikes, feelings, and values. But key attributes are missing from some information systems—verbal, moral, and inhibitory abilities—which not only make these information systems "minor," but not responsible as well.

"The case that was made for George's innocence in his adulterous relationship with Molly (referred to earlier) hypothesized that George's desire for Molly was housed in other information systems which had different values than did George's verbal system and which were unknown to the verbal side of George and therefore uncontrollable. But if both the dominant (left) and minor (right) hemispheres can have a sense of self (i.e., likes, dislikes, feelings, etc.), and if one *can* be aware (even without the dominant neural base for linguistic function) of nonverbal information, then the linguistic element (or lack of it) does not provide George (or Gazzaniga and Le Doux) with exculpation. George's right hemisphere and left hand, that information system which has, to paraphrase Sperry, a sense of self, feelings, moods, likes, and hobbies, also *perceived, planned, and took* Molly to bed, and *remembered* the morning after.

As empirical evidence shows, guilt, anxiety, and other emotions need not be transformed into verbal terms in order to be felt—either before or after the crime; if this was not so, all aphasic and mute individuals would have a "blank check" defense for anything and everything from adultery to murder. Even if we allow for the person's hemispheres to have likes and dislikes—that is, even if we put the responsibility in the hemispheres and hands, and out of *the person's,* the case for exculpation on the grounds of ignorance does not hold up. For, even if verbal systems do dominate our lives, it is still possible for nonverbal information to gain representation in awareness.

We believe Gazzaniga and Le Doux are making another fundamental error here.

> In their attribution of human psychological qualities to the hemispheres of the brain, the authors appear to be advocating a materialist position which has a long history of debate. Even in our time, the debate is far from settled, yet the authors impute *will* to a cerebral hemisphere. It could likewise be argued, from a dualist or from a multiaspect monist position, that it is *the whole person* who has a sense of self, not the hemisphere; it is the person who knows his own name and can indicate so if given limited means of responding, not the hemisphere. It is the person who has changeable and, at times, opposing feelings, moods, likes, and desires, and these can be inferred from the behaviors generated through the right hemisphere. It is the person who has changeable and, at times, conflicting goals and aspirations for the future, not his hemisphere(s). And it is the person—as a "union of opposites," as Jung (1970) might say—who possesses (and deserves) "conscious status"—and all the responsibilities that go with it . . .
>
> So, if the "smoking pistol" was found in the left hand, for example, the prosecuting attorney would surely ask *the* defendant, *through* his respective hemisphere channels, "How did the pistol get into your left hand?" If there are two selves, then one of them knows. The early claim that the minor hemisphere "which is not really of the full status of self" *does not know* or *barely knows* has not been supported by the preponderance of evidence. Hemispheric studies show that subjects can discriminate a gun from a guava melon, if given palpable means; that they can demonstrate awareness (i.e., "hand knowledge," to say the very least, or comparison and reflection, to say more), if given palpable means; and they can discriminate pulling the trigger from not pulling, for one, or firing rather than eating the gun, for another. The claim that the event, murder, or infidelity, was *unmeditated* by the left hemisphere is secondary to the fact that the left-hand—right hemisphere knew.

Gazzaniga and Le Doux claim, however, that this "meditation" by one information system did not pass from unawareness into awareness until after the person observed his own behavior because of a limited interaction with the verbal system. Thus because this meditation did not pass through the moral–verbal centers of the brain, there was little consciousness, and less conscience; this is but a variation on the minor hemisphere–minor self thesis. In short, we might have meditated actions without moral screening—leading, presumably, to action without inhibition because we did not know, in the verbal sense, what we wanted to do until we saw ourselves do it. We come back to Gazzaniga and Le Doux's closing remark about punishing the whole town (person) for the actions of the wrong side of the tracks (wrong self), which, not so implicitly, argues for acquittal. But they have also argued for a full self representation. Now it appears that this full self is not quite full, because it lacks access to the moral, or verbal, integrative system; hence the self cannot be held responsible for the actions that follow. (Finkel & Sabat, 1985, pp. 240–241)

We reject this claim and line of thinking. In so doing, we take some cues from literature and others from science. For a literary example, consider the statement of Henry Jekyll (Stevenson, 1937, pp. 293–295):

That night I had come to the fatal cross roads. Had I approached my discovery in a more noble spirit, had I risked the experiment while under the empire of generous or pious aspirations, all must have been otherwise, and from these agonies of death and birth, I had come forth an angel instead of a fiend. The drug had no discriminating action; it was neither diabolical nor divine; it but shook the doors of the prisonhouse of my disposition; and like the captives of Philippi, that which stood within ran forth. At that time my virtue slumbered; my evil, kept awake by ambition, was alert and swift to seize the occasion; and the thing that was projected was Edward Hyde.

Henry Jekyll stood at times aghast before the acts of Edward Hyde; but the situation was apart from ordinary laws, and insidiously relaxed the grasp of conscience. It was Hyde, after all, and Hyde alone, that was guilty. Jekyll was no worse; he woke again to his good qualities seemingly unimpaired; he would even make haste, where it was possible, to undo the evil done by Hyde. And thus his conscience slumbered.

It is clear to us from Jekyll's knowledge and actions that his assertion that Hyde and Hyde alone was guilty *is not true*. Jekyll let his conscience slumber; Jekyll took the potion, much like the person using his left and right hemispheres to put the gun into the left hand; Jekyll conducted this dangerous experiment, on himself, without safeguards. No, Jekyll is not free from responsibility.

Nor is George, the hypothetical man who suddenly finds himself in bed with Molly. We question the Gazzaniga and Le Doux equation of verbal system = awareness system = responsible system = controlling system, with its implication that what is nonverbal (a) may not be moral according to our verbal system; (b) is not responsible; (c) is not controllable unless accessible to the verbal system. . . .

This case for a split-brain producing a completely split mind—which is then "dissociated" from reflection, understanding, responsibility, morality, and control—has, in our judgment, *not yet been made*. Nor has the existence of "multiple mental systems" been established empirically. (Finkel & Sabat, 1985, p. 242)

SPLIT PSYCHES

The implications of Gazzaniga and Le Doux's thesis for the insanity defense are twofold. For the *mens rea* phase of the trial, this defense can be used to challenge whether the defendant *knew* right from wrong, *understood* the nature of his act (in the moral or legal sense), or could control his actions to conform to the requirements of the law. But this defense also has implications for the *actus reus* phase: using Austin's (1956–57) definition of an act, Gazzaniga and Le Doux's thesis can be used to challenge whether an *act* did indeed occur, as opposed to mere behavior. If information fails to pass through a verbal, moral system, are we left with concluding that the behavior emitted was involuntary? It would seem so.

Not only is this defense applicable to both the *mens rea* and *actus reus* elements of the trial, but the defense could be adapted to fit a wide variety of clinical disorders and syndromes. "Multiple personalities," of course, but "amnesia," "fugue," "somnambulism," "paranoid states," "post-traumatic shock syndrome" (e.g., Viet Nam flashback experiences), drug induced reactions, various types of epilepsy, and "premenstrual syndrome" (PMS) could be some of the potential beneficiaries of a split-brain insanity defense.

It we look at these diverse conditions for a common denominator, it would appear that "dissociation" cuts across all of these conditions. To deepen our understanding of "dissociation," we leave the neurological for the psychological level to explore split psyches (see Chapter 4). Let us start with what DSM-III (1980) has to say regarding Dissociative Disorder:

> The essential feature is a sudden, temporary alteration in the normally integrative functions of consciousness, identity, or motor behavior. If the alteration occurs in identity, either the individual's customary identity is temporarily forgotten and a new identity is assumed, or the customary feeling of one's own reality is lost and replaced by a feeling of unreality. If the alteration occurs in motor behavior, there is also a concurrent disturbance in consciousness or identity, as in the wandering that occurs during a Psychogenic Fugue. (p. 263)

If we examine the DSM-III definition of delusions, we see some commonalities with dissociation:

> in the former case there is a dissociation between certain thoughts (themes) and reality; in dissociation, there is split, gulf, and gap in consciousness, identity, or motor behavior; both conditions have periods of normalcy, or partial sanity, where one's thinking, behavior, identity, and consciousness appear "regular and ordinary"; and both feature denial, of some sort. (Finkel & Sabat, 1985, p. 243).

A similar commonality exists for the other disorders, syndromes, and conditions mentioned above.

How is this "dissociation" explained on the psychological level? In Chapter 4 we discussed Freud's psychoanalytic account of dissociation, in which he invoked the concepts and dynamics of the "unconscious," the "censor," "ego-splitting," "defensive rejection," and "repression" to explain what Sartre (1974) called *bad faith* (*mauvaise foi*) and Fingarette (1974) called *self-deception*. To recall, when someone is in bad faith, one is *both* the liar and the lied to; in self-deception, one is both the deceiver and the deceived. One problem with the psychoanalytic account can be formulated in the following question: If the ego aims to "hide" something from *oneself*, where do we "locate the inner" victim "of this secretiveness?" Fingarette (1974) writes:

> Is the impulse to be hidden from the id? This makes no sense, for it is the impulse *of* the id. Is it to be hidden from the superego? No, for it is typically the superego which perceives the emerging id deviation, and which typically initiates the defense by inducing anxiety in the ego. Is the impulse to be hidden from the ego? Surely not, for the ego is by definition that "agency" which takes into account *both* the impulse and the conflicting superego demands, and which then designs and executes the defensive maneuver. (p. 89)

Finding the inner "victim" presents a problem for the psychoanalytic account, but so does finding the "deceiver." Sartre notes that it just won't do to say that the deceiver is *unconscious*, i.e., it doesn't *know*. As Sartre (1974) states, "I must know in my capacity as the one deceived" (p. 72) and a few pages later he writes:

> If we reject the language and the materialistic mythology of psychoanalysis, we perceive that the censor in order to apply its activity with discernment must know what it is repressing. In fact if we abandon all the metaphors representing the repression as the impact of blind forces, we are compelled to admit that the censor must choose and in order to choose must be aware of so doing. (p. 76)

For both Sartre and Fingarette, the process of dissociation involves knowing and disowning; the process of forming a delusion involves knowing and disavowing. Fingarette (1974) states:

> The self-deceiver is one who is in some way engaged in the world but who disavows the engagement, who will not acknowledge it even to himself. That is, self-deception turns upon the personal identity one accepts rather than the beliefs one has . . . The paranoid is filled with destructiveness, but he disavows it; since the presence of destructiveness is evident to him, he eventually assigns "ownership" of that destructiveness to others. With this as his unquestionable axiom, and with "conspiracy" as his all-purpose formula, he interprets all that happens accordingly. In general, the self-deceiver is engaged in the world in some way, and yet he refuses to avow the engagement as his. Having disavowed the engagement, the self-deceiver is then forced into protective, defensive tactics to account for the inconsistencies in his engagement in the world as acknowledged by him. (p. 81)

The deceiver knows. If we accept this conclusion, then Jekyll already knew about the Hyde in him before drinking the potion. And George knew of his wants, desires, and passions before he "suddenly" found himself in bed with Molly. Both Jekyll and George, it appears, gave up on any attempt to integrate the ego-nucleus itself. Both treated "the unassimilable" as "Other." George saw it as *not-me*. Jekyll tries to split this *other-me* off, as Other, separate from the "I." Jekyll could have controlled Hyde (e.g., by not taking the potion, for one), but failed to do so. George "the finder" could have controlled George "the found," had he not failed to resist. Whether you give up on assimilating, failing to resist, or actively attempt dissociation—there is consciousness, responsibility, and culpability. (Finkel & Sabat, 1985, p. 244)

Given these instances of clinical, fictional, and hypothetical split psyches, two questions of interest come to mind. How "split" is the split? And are there unifying forces (or tendencies) operating? For some of the conditions mentioned at the outset of the subsection, the "split" is not complete. In drug-induced reactions, oftentimes the individual is frighteningly aware of the feelings, thoughts, and memories that arise, and aware that he or she is not feeling like "themselves." In PMS, many women report (Hobson & Rosenfeld, 1984; Sommer, 1984) feeling "down" and "irritable," unlike "themselves." And there is evidence from the multiple-personality literature that the dissociation is not complete. There may be one personality, dubbed the "coconscious personality" (Coleman, Butcher, & Carson, 1980), that continues to function subconsciously.

Looking at the "unifying forces" question, we might conclude, on a *prima facie* basis, that the very fact that psychotherapy is used attests to unifying forces. While psychotherapy comes in a variety of stripes, schools, orientations, and methods, certainly most forms advocate increasing awareness. Some therapists may help bring overlooked or ignored feelings, thoughts, memories, or actions into consciousness: from the psychoanalyst exploring a dream of free associations with the patient to a behavioral therapist asking clients to chart their behavior, therapists are working toward increasing awareness and increasing the "connectedness" between thoughts, feelings, and behavior. Other, less used methods, such as hypnotherapy, narcosis interviews, and automatic writing, also are used to increase awareness, communication, and ownership of dissociated parts of the personality.

Curiously, the split-brain literature provides an interesting example of the unifying tendency, called "cross-cuing" (Gazzaniga & Hillyard, 1971). Here is Springer and Deutsch's (1981) definition of "cross-cuing," along with their commentary.

Cross-cuing refers

. . . to patients' attempts to use whatever cues are available to make information accessible to both hemispheres . . . If, for example, the left hand is given a comb or a toothbrush to feel, the patient will often stroke the brush or the surface of the comb. The patient will then immediately identify the object because the left hemisphere hears the tell-tale sounds.

Cross cuing provides a way for one hemisphere to provide the other with information about what it is experiencing. The direct channels of information transfer are eliminated by the surgery, leaving the patient with indirect cues as the only means of inter-hemispheric communication in most instances. Cross cuing can often be quite subtle, testing the ingenuity of the investigators seeking to eliminate it from the experimental situation.

Cross cuing is generally not a conscious attempt by the patient to trick the investigator. Instead, it is a natural tendency by an organism to use whatever information it has to make sense of what is going on. This tendency, in fact, contributes further insight into why the common, everyday behavior of split-brain patients seems so unaffected by the surgery. (pp. 33–34)

As Finkel and Sabat (1985) state, it would seem that

some kind of cross cuing occurs in all of us: even the noncommissurotomized person tries to make sense, in a variety of ways, of the various pieces of his or her experience, such as the attempt to find sources of anxiety, love, etc. If it is, as it seems, *natural* to try to integrate information, what was George thinking as he prepared to have his immoral affair? Was he not troubled by an unknown source of tension or anxiety—especially given his highly-principled nature and given the tendency to integrate all the information we have about our experience?

Our functional commissurotomy, George, and his sidekick, the smoking-pistol-packing defendant, surely they got more than 200 millisecond looks at Molly and the soon-to-be-shot-victim. Even if George fondled Molly with only his left hand, cross cuing would no doubt allow the left-hemisphered, silver-tongued George to moan, "Mmmmm. . . ." (pp. 246–247)

We can only imagine what Mrs. George might have said after hearing George's excuse.

CLOSING SUMMARY, DELIBERATIONS, AND A VERDICT

The question that may be placed before a jury in the not-too-distant future is whether or not the existence of what we call a "functional split-brain" (or, what Gazzaniga and Le Doux call a multiple neural information systems approach) provides exculpation from personal responsibility in the commission of an illegal or immoral act. These multiple information systems are either the alleged causes or neural correlates of the fact that each person has many different aspects to his or her personality—aspects that are often at odds with one another. Each different aspect of personality (or each "self") is, thus, mediated by a particular neural network or information system. (Finkel & Sabat, 1985, p. 244)

The problem that is posed is thus: suppose George commits what is to his "conscious, verbal mind" an immoral or illegal act. George's defense, which is handled by Gazzaniga and Le Doux, seeks to exculpate George for the crime. Their defense is as follows:

George's desire to commit the act was mediated by a neural network that did not interact with the neural network that houses verbal abilities. Thus *the* George to whom we and others ascribe *personhood* and *the* George to whom *George* ascribes *selfhood* was unaware of those desires that were unbeknownst to him and unaware of the acts that followed. Semantically and legally, we should not even call them "acts"; they were simply unconscious behaviors, much like those of sleepwalkers (somnambulists) who engage in behaviors that they subsequently, when awake, do not remember. Like Esther Griggs (Walker, 1968)—who, during a nightmare, hurled her baby through a closed window from a house she thought was on fire, but was not—George's seemingly purposeful behavior also lacked critical awareness that nullifies criminality. As Esther Griggs did not go to trial, since no "criminal *act*" occurred, George also should not be charged for automatism. George did not know of his desire to commit the act until he watched himself do so. Therefore, we should not punish all of George for the wayward actions of one facet of his personality that hid itself from his verbal, conscious self.

The prosecution would certainly raise questions regarding both the theory and the alleged "facts." Finkel and Sabat have done just that. They note that the multiple-information-system approach is a *theory* (Gazzaniga, 1985), and a questionable one at that. They point out that

> the idea that each of the multiple information systems contains different motives, feelings, desires, ideas, and has a "different set of values" would seem inconsistent with "the authors' (Gazzaniga and Le Doux's) desire to un-dichotomize the brain. For although, in their book, they seek to remove the dichotomies from the operating characteristics of the left and right hemispheres, they put the dichotomies *back* in different information systems. The authors, and others discussed earlier, have shown that the hemispheres differ in terms of the *degree* to which they process certain types of stimuli. It would thus seem consistent to argue that the multiple information systems differ in degree and not kind as well. That is, a particular information system might be dominated by one or another motive, feeling, etc., but in essence all systems would have the same constellation of motives, etc., and not be totally deficient in, nor totally unconscious of any. This would be analogous to the finding on a larger scale that the right hemisphere is not totally deficient in linguistic processing ability. (Finkel & Sabat, 1985, p. 245)

A second point and problem for the theory is the fact that split-brain subjects know the contents of information sent to their right hemispheres in an intimate, subjective way; with this the case, on what basis do Gazzaniga and Le Doux argue that such awareness (e.g., "I feel guilty about something") would be absent in the normally intact person?

Normally intact people normally have conflicts with aspects of their personalities. The phrase "I don't like that particular part of myself" has been uttered by many. Yet we don't exculpate for crimes we commit with the disliked sides of the personality. Nor do we exculpate, typically, in negligence cases, when the individual says, "I just didn't think." Hart's (1968) rejoinder, "But you should have thought," counters and disqualifies this exculpating excuse. The real question for the functional split-brain insanity defense is not whether the defendant did not think: the defense would have to prove that the defendant *could not* have thought. This is analogous to the irresistible impulse dilemma: could the defendant control his or her impulses, or did he or she simply fail to resist them? Given the unifying tendencies (e.g., cross-cuing), the defense has yet to prove that George could not have known what he was doing.

Gazzaniga and Le Doux (1978) argue that George didn't know of his lust for a woman other than his wife (something he believes to be unprincipled) until this desire (this other information system isolated from his verbal system)

> . . . grabbed hold and elicited a behavioral act that caused great consternation to his verbal system. This other side of George was not known to him until a set of environmental and biological circumstances came together and elicited this new behavior. (p. 156)

Thus, he suddenly found himself with Molly.

This argument seems questionable on the basis of psychological evidence. But even if we put the psychological evidence aside and focus only on the behavioral level, their claim is still questionable. As Finkel and Sabat (1985) state,

> Even if it is true that we do not know of our intentions until we observe our own behavior, what did George think of his own behavior (and his reasons for it) as he watched himself (a) arranging to meet Molly, (b) driving to their rendezvous, and (c) approaching her when they found themselves alone? That is, we are being asked to believe that George never knew that he wanted to have an affair with Molly until after having emitted a variety of behaviors which brought him together with her—behaviors which had no special significance until he "*found* himself in bed" with her. And, given their mutual presence in bed, George only then concludes that he must have wanted her—for any number of reasons. (p. 246)

This possibility strains plausibility. Given the number of behaviors in the sequence, and given the "natural tendency" to cross-cue, the burden of proof falls on the defense to explain why cross-cuing did not operate, and could not operate, to bring George's behavior into awareness. The defense, in the prosecution's opinion, has not borne its burden successfully.

A DISQUIETING EPILOGUE

The arguments and issues are not closed. Nor is the functional split-brain insanity defense dead. Like Maudsley's claim a century earlier, perhaps the functional split-brain defense is premature rather than wrong. Time, after all, is on the side of the materialists: they may locate those hypothesized neural "information systems" and follow the "organic manufactory" in the near future. If they do, they'll be back, and the concept of "responsibility" will teeter.

> Legally, the sanity-insanity distinction rests on the concept of "responsibil-
> ity," which has been seen as a function of man's autonomous being. That
> "concept of responsibility," which has withstood blows in the past, has been
> taking a beating of late, most often at the hands, pens, and electrodes of psy-
> chologists of one stripe or another. The concept has been scorned and discarded,
> displaced onto the environment, projected onto others, and absorbed into one of
> the hemispheres or information systems of the brain; Skinner (1971) finds the
> concept outmoded, offering us "little help"; and although the phrenologist did
> not, "pop" psychologists and some neuropsychologists search for responsibility
> under the microelectrode tip, in a specific locale, or *in one hemisphere or the other*.
> Perhaps the greatest danger facing "responsibility" is from "underneath."
> Responsibility rests on man's autonomous being, his well integrated person-
> ality. But what if that being has a defect of reason, caused by "disease of the
> mind," which is believed to be the result of disease (or disconnection) of brain
> hemispheres? What then? (Finkel & Sabat, 1985, p. 245)

At that point, the moralistic perspective of the law may not be able to
withstand the scientific challenge, with the term in greatest jeopardy being
"responsibility." But the law and its terms incorporate the central values of
the community, and, as Fingarette (1972) makes clear, "responsibility" is
central:

> It is plain that our criminal law, in its fundamental orientation, reflects and
> embodies certain fundamental values of our society. In particular, it embodies
> fundamental and characteristic resolution of the community, that normally the
> state shall deal with all members of the community as responsible persons under
> the law. In short, it is a central value, and not a mere utilitarian convenience,
> that socialization of conduct in our society shall normally be *through* responsibil-
> ity under law. Our criminal law, founded as it is on the principle of individual
> responsibility, is not a mere means toward reducing antisocial activity; the in-
> stitution is itself an essential end for the society. For we do not want merely an
> orderly society; we want an order of responsible persons, responsible under
> law. And, of course, the essence of this idea is that individuals shall normally be
> held responsible and so assessed when charged with transgressing the law. If I
> am not treated as responsible when I break the law, then I am not responsible
> even for keeping the law. (pp. 56–57)

But if the neuropsychologists of today and tomorrow can do what the
alienists of yesterday could not—show that an individual's actions can be
fully explained without resorting to a teleological concept like "responsibility," then conventional morality may indeed give way to natural law.
Before such an upheaval occurs, the scientific "evidence" needs to be
scrutinized carefully. "Evidence" is subject to multiple interpretations.

> We can take the same evidence, for example, that split-brain patients cannot
> verbally express the workings of their right hemispheres, . . . and claim that
> this proves (a) that the right hemisphere lacks consciousness, (b) that the right
> hemisphere has consciousness, but that it cannot produce articulate speech, or
> (c) that the person has consciousness, and that it can be demonstrated through
> suitable methodology and questioning. That is, despite the clear fact that, under
> laboratory conditions, there are genuine gaps in the extent to which the split-
> brain subjects can unify their experience of events projected to opposite hemi-

spheres, the exact quality of their knowledge is not precisely clear in the objective sense.

In addition, contradictory evidence needs to be recognized and considered; for split-brain research, Zangwill (1976) does just that in the following quote:

> Neither Akelaitus, nor after him Bogen and Sperry, could detect any gross change in intellect, personality or general behaviour of the split-brain patient after recovery from the immediate effects of the operation. (p. 303)

And then there is the beginning of this story, which started with a hypothetical—a commissurotomized person found with a "smoking pistol" in his left hand and the bullet-pierced victim near his feet—but which, as a story, also had its own beginning. How did the gun get into the left hand? Who raised, aimed, and squeezed the trigger? These are the questions that need to be raised and answered by both researchers and jurors. It seems all too easy to limit our vision and awareness and focus solely on the immediate and the material at hand. It is troubling when our vision stops at the defendant's gun, hand, and hemisphere and fails to appreciate the mind that put the gun into the hand and that uses whatever hemisphere it is given to process, discern, judge, carry out its will and act. The split-brain individual also gives aid and comfort to the mentalists, when, through the natural tendency to cross-cue, we see, to paraphrase Clifford Beers' (1935) title, a mind trying to find itself.

What then is *the illusion?* That we are a mental unity or that we are divided selves or information systems? That we are, at our essence, responsible and mindful beings or, as the materialists would have it, when the ghost in the machine (Ryle, 1949) is removed, we are, as Maudsley put it, "as much manufactured articles as are steam-engines and calico-printing machines . . ."

> That the mind appears both split and integrated, an apparent unity at one time and dissociated at another, has been acknowledged long before multiple personalities and split-brain subjects made their debut. That we can be both rational and rationalizing, stern and merciful, judgmental and forgiving is our *mystery*, which will remain such . . . (Finkel & Sabat, 1985, p. 250)

long after this work closes.

In the meantime, both positions marshal their evidence. The final verdict has yet to be rendered.

9

The Patient's Perspective
INVOLUNTARY TREATMENT

THE PRELIMINARY ISSUE—COMPETENCE TO STAND TRIAL

Before an insanity trial begins, or, more generally, before any criminal trial commences, a preliminary issue must be addressed: Is the defendant competent to stand trial? To introduce this issue and its historical background, let us consider the English ritual and question that precedes a trial and a problematic, albeit rare, response. When the accused is asked the question, "How doth thou plea, 'guilty' or 'not guilty'?" what happens if the accused fails to answer?

If the accused's response is no response, the court has a problem. As Walker (1968) states,

> unless he uttered the necessary words, reverence for the ritual of the law made it unthinkable to proceed with the trial, with the result that he could not be convicted and executed. More important still to the Exchequer, his property would not be forfeit. (p. 220)

For an accused to have a veto power over a trial's commencing simply through his silence would seem to be an overly luxurious if not ludicrous indulgence; the impatient judge, juror, and jurist might prefer to revise, rather than revere, such a ritual. But if you revise the ritual by making it unnecessary for the accused to utter a plea, you run a risk of overlooking an important question and discrimination: Was the accused genuinely rather than stubbornly mute?

To find out if the accused was "mute of malice" or "mute by visitation of God," the English resorted to "a form of medieval torture" (Winick, 1983, p. 3), *peine forte et dure*, "which consisted of slowly pressing him to death under an increasing weight, unless his endurance gave out in the process and he consented to plead" (Walker, 1968, p. 220). While *peine forte et dure* was used as late as 1736, and not officially abolished until 1772, the practice was fatally flawed. The deaf and dumb individual who was mute by visitation of God, following a session of *peine forte et dure*, could only receive his vindication in heaven. Another method, less dire and *dure* in its consequences, had to be found for determining the status and competence of the accused.

The preliminary issue is not limited to only the deaf and dumb. Between the stubbornly and genuinely mute individuals fell the insane. Coke and Hale, in the seventeenth century, agreed that an insane person should not be tried if, in Hale's words, "before his arraignment he becomes absolutely mad" (Walker, 1968, p. 221). Hale recommended that "he ought not by law to be arraigned during such his phrenzy, but be remitted to prison until that incapacity be removed; The reason is, because he cannot advisedly plead to the indictment." Hale also recognized that an accused could become *non sane memory* after his plea but before the trial, and, in that instance too, he should not be tried.

Hale's position, which represented the common-law point of view, held that it would be patently unfair to charge individuals who could not plead or try such persons who could not assist in their own defense. The pleading and trial would have to wait until the accused's incapacity was rectified. Yet this recommendation left Hale and others uneasy. Sending the accused to prison, or, said another way, placing the accused in the hands of the prison doctor, gave the latter unusual power and gave the former a potential escape route. The prison doctor could refuse to certify a patient as competent, thereby preventing the trial indefinitely. A patient, knowing that a trial might lead to his guilt and death, might well choose to fake incapacity indefinitely.

Perhaps Hale was having such presentiments when he made the following recommendation:

> But because there may be great fraud in this matter, yet if the crime be notorious, as treason or murder, the judge before such respite of trial . . . may do well to impanel a jury to enquire *ex officio* touching such insanity, and whether it be real or counterfeit. (Walker, 1968, p. 221)

Hale's criteria were strict: for this deferment of trial to take effect, the crime had to be a capital offense and the accused had to be "absolutely mad." But Hale's strict criteria were soon liberalized. In the Frith case of

1790 (*R. v. Frith*), Lord Chief Justice Kenyon, who later tried Hadfield's case, used a more generous test than Hale's. Frith, who was accused of throwing a stone at King George III, began making deluded statements when asked to plead. Lord Kenyon addressed the following remarks to the jury:

> The humanity of the law of England . . . has prescribed that no man shall be called upon to make his defence at a time when his mind is in that situation as not to appear capable of so doing. For however guilty he may be, the enquiring into his guilt must be postponed to that season when, by collecting together his intellects, and have them entire, he shall be able so to model his defence as to ward off the punishment of the law. . . . (Walker, 1968, p. 224)

Kenyon did not require, like Hale did, that the accused be absolutely mad, but only that it appear that he could not make his defense; furthermore, according to Kenyon, the delay would continue until the accused collected his entire intellects, rather than rectified his incapacity. Even with Lord Kenyon's more liberal construction, collecting one's entire intellects might still take forever, thereby effectively postponing the trial indefinitely. While waiting for the intellects to coagulate, another possibility might come to pass, initiated by the prison doctor, that would effectively bypass the trial altogether. The doctor might recommend to the Home Secretary that the accused should be pardoned; if the Home Secretary agreed, and did so, the accused would not be returned to the judiciary.

While this "escape route mechanism" was in place, Walker notes that it was used infrequently up until the late 1860s. Nevertheless, its potential abuse was worried about, particularly when an Act of 1840 regularized "the transfer of insane prisoners to asylums." Mr. Justice Patteson expressed such a worry when he thought he was to try a man named Dwerryhouse (*R. v. Dwerryhouse*, 1847). Dwerryhouse had scalped a woman. As Walker (1968) reports counsel for Dwerryhouse

> produced an affidavit from the asylum governor to the effect that the accused was hopelessly insane and was unlikely to recover, and explained to Mr. Justice Patteson that the new statute allowed the Home Secretary to keep the accused in any asylum until he was fit to be brought before the court. "Where is that statute?" exclaimed the judge. "If justices of the peace were to pronounce upon a prisoner's insanity, a door might be open to the most grievous abuses. The proper tribunal to determine if he is in a state to take his trial is a jury. . . . A man might be put into a lunatic asylum and kept there until the witnesses were dead. We are too gingerly in acting about insane people." (p. 228)

Again, as with other aspects of the psychology and law courtship (Finkel, 1980), some members of the court were worried about being "had."

On this side of the Atlantic, the early American courts followed the Anglo-Saxon common-law approach in which a person's "understanding" was paramount in judging competence to stand trial. While the principle of competence was affirmed, the American courts began to recognize a constitutional as well as common-law basis for this right. The incompetency doctrine received its first constitutional recognition in the case of *Youtsey v. United States* (1899), where the court acknowledged that it "is not 'due process of law' to subject an insane person to trial upon an indictment involving liberty or life." Subsequent trials broadened the focus to include communicative abilities as well as cognitive capacity.

> The modern formulation of the competency standard, stressing both cognitive and communicative capacity, is taken from the Supreme Court's opinion in *Dusky v. United States* (1960). In *Dusky,* the Court approved as a standard for federal cases whether the defendant "has sufficient present ability to consult with his lawyer with a reasonable degree of rational understanding—and whether he has a rational as well as factual understanding of the proceedings against him." (Winick, 1983, p. 4)

The principle articulated in *Dusky,* supportable on both common-law and constitutional grounds, has been accepted in all jurisdictions. The Supreme Court has not only affirmed the importance of establishing competency at the start of the trial, but has spoken through opinions in a number of cases (*Drope v. Missouri,* 1975; *Pate v. Robinson,* 1966; *Wojtowicz v. United States,* 1977) that courts must be alert to changes in competency throughout the trial process, including through rendering sentence. Even where the defendant does not raise the issue, *the court must,* if there is evidence that "raises a bona fide doubt as to the defendant's competency" (Winick, 1983, p. 9). A failure to raise the issue violates due process and requires a reversal of a conviction.

PRAGMATIC AND POLITICAL CONCERNS

Given the importance of this issue, coupled with severe consequences (e.g., reversal of conviction) if it is not pursued, it is likely that the judge or prosecuting attorney, faced with what may conceivably be a mentally ill defendant, will raise the incompetency issue on arraignment even when the defense does not. On grounds of principle, they must. However, for the judge, prosecution, and defense counsel, pragmatic and political concerns may also weigh heavily in employing this principled "escape route," especially when an insanity defense is likely. For example, defense attorneys (Bailey & Aronson, 1971, p. 171) know that an insanity defense is risky, particularly with a capital offense. Even if they had a solid case, they are aware that juries "frequently are reluctant to acquit criminals on insanity grounds." A strategy that avoids a possible death sentence, gets the accused some help, and protects the public, may seem ideal. F. Lee Bailey presents the dilemma for the defense in the following quote regarding the Albert De Salvo, Boston Strangler, case:

> There were personal considerations, too. If an insanity plea backfired, I had an excellent chance of being known as a lawyer who'd taken a perfectly pro-

tected client and steered him into the electric chair. Quite possibly, some of my colleagues might start yelling that my license should be revoked for risking a client's life to get publicity. (Bailey & Aronson, 1971, p. 172)

The prosecution, too, has pragmatic and political factors to consider. Requesting a competency evaluation may be a way of preventing the accused bail opportunity. Regarding a potential and uncertain insanity case, particularly in states where the burden of proof is on the prosecution to prove sanity, the easier out for the prosecution may be incompetence: after all, the public wants the accused locked up and off the streets, so if that can be accomplished psychiatrically, without the risk of an acquittal and without the expense of a trial, this option may seem to be a "no lose" proposition. Both the prosecution and the defense can count this outcome as a "victory," and the trial judge can be spared what might be a lengthy, contentious, and possibly reversable case, all the while protecting the public's safety.

It seems too good to be true, save perhaps for the accused. Roesch and Golding (1980) reviewed studies of hospital admissions for competency evaluations between 1973 and 1977 and found a steady rise in the use of competency evaluations throughout the country. Steadman and Hartstone (1983) reviewed recent empirical findings on defendants found incompetent to stand trial (IST) and found that they comprise approximately 32% of the admissions of mentally disordered offenders; translating this percentage into numbers, the researchers concluded that "on any given day in the United States in 1978 there were 3,400 defendants in these mental health or correctional facilities adjudicated as incompetent to stand trial" (p. 41). In addition to the numbers, the speed of the average competency hearing was found to be 10 minutes, and when the psychiatrists decided that a defendant was incompetent, "the judge supported that decision 92% of the time" (p. 45). Given the percentage, numbers, speed, and likely outcome, Mr. Justice Patteson's expressed fear that "a door might be open to the most grievous abuses" seems, on a *prima facie* level, supportable in fact.

LANG, JACKSON, AND MOST GRIEVOUS ABUSES

Two cases involving deaf mute defendants will be discussed in some depth to present the accused-turned-patient's point of view. There is a caveat to note from the outset: neither Donald Lang nor Theon Jackson can talk or communicate; the former is described as illiterate, the latter as mentally defective, so their "points of view," presented second-hand through their legal counsel's motions, must be inferred. With this caveat so noted, we turn to the case of Donald Lang (*People v. Lang*, 1979, p. 351):

"For 14 years the State of Illinois has been concerned with what to do with Donald Lang, an illiterate deaf mute who has virtually no ability to communicate with other people in any recognized language system. Notwithstanding this severe handicap, Lang has twice been charged with murder, and the State insists that he poses an extreme danger to society. He is admittedly unfit to stand trial and has been held to be not in need of mental treatment and not civilly committable to a mental institution. His legal history for the past 14 years illustrates the nature and complexity of the problem.

Ernest Tidyman (1974), who has written a book about the Lang case entitled *Dummy*, introduced his subject this way:

> "I don't know about The Dummy," a Chicago detective said during the research for this book, "but every time he goes through a neighborhood we find a dead broad."
>
> He is a suspect personality.
>
> But Donald Lang is also deaf, mute, illiterate, probably ineducable now, possibly psychotic and perhaps brain-damaged by disease and accident in childhood. He is also an American black, which is considered an infirmity and a defect by a major segment of the community.
>
> He is nothing and nobody; he will never be anything or anybody. That may be the reason he is worth thinking about. (from introduction)

The beginning of Donald Lang's legal story starts in 1965, when the State charged him with the murder of a woman the police described as a "known prostitute." Judge Napoli, aware that Lang was deaf and mute, requested that Lowell J. Myers handle the case for the defense; Myers, besides being a fine attorney who had extensive experience defending deaf persons, was totally deaf himself. Myers was quick to recognize the trap that was about to ensnare his client. He realized that Donald Lang, who was found unfit to stand trial, faced an indefinite civil commitment since his client would, in all probability, never be able to meet the *Dusky* standards for "competent to stand trial." Myers "agreed to waive Lang's constitutional right not to be tried," but the request was denied (*People v. Lang*, 1967). From Myers point of view, Lang's constitutional right—his so-called protection—had ensnared Lang in a situation where he could not prove his innocence because he could never get to trial.

Two years later the superintendent of the institution in which Donald Lang was committed wrote a letter to Myers stating that "sign language training had been completely ineffective" and that "Lang was unlikely ever to become fit for trial" (*People v. Lang*, 1979, p. 351). Myers then "filed a petition for a writ of *habeas corpus*, contending that Lang was being imprisoned for life even though he had never been tried for or convicted of a crime." In *People ex rel Myers v. Briggs* (1970) the court held that Donald Lang, facing indefinite commitment, "should be given an opportunity to obtain a trial to determine whether or not he is guilty as charged or should be released." At that point, the State of Illinois dismissed the charges against Lang because the principal witness had died. Lang was released. Lang's troubles continued, but we will shift to the Jackson case before picking up the tale. At this point, note that if the court had not ruled that

Lang should have a trial even though he could not meet the *Dusky* standards, Lang would have languished in confinement indefinitely, even though the State had no case.

Whereas the Lang case was dealt with through State courts, the case of Theon Jackson reached the Supreme Court (*Jackson v. Indiana*, 1972). A second difference between Lang and Jackson was the charge: for Lang, the charge was murder; for Jackson, the charge was two separate counts of robbery, where it was alleged that in the first instance he took "a purse and its contents" valued at four dollars and in the second instance, that he took five dollars. Regardless of this difference in the seriousness of the alleged crime, Jackson, too, faced a lifelong commitment.

Jackson, a mentally defective deaf mute with the mental age of a preschool child, could not "read, write, or otherwise communicate except through limited sign language" (*Jackson v. Indiana* 1972, p. 725). The evidence from examining doctors—that Jackson "would be unable to acquire the substantially improved communication skills that would be necessary for him to participate in any defense" and that it was very doubtful that he could ever "comprehend the charges or participate in his defense, even after commitment and treatment"—led the Supreme Court to the conclusion that Jackson's commitment would not be a temporary one.

Counsel for Jackson argued that such a "life sentence" violated the "equal protection" and "due process" clauses of the Fourteenth Amendment. The argument, in short, is that if the pending criminal charges were absent, the State, if it wished to commit Jackson, would have to proceed "under other statutes generally applicable to all other citizens: either the commitment procedures for feeble-minded persons, or those for mentally ill persons."

Counsel for Jackson noted that these other statutes have tougher standards for commitment; it was thus easier for the State to commit Jackson as IST than it would have been otherwise. In addition, if the other statues were applied, it would be easier for Jackson to be released. Furthermore, had Jackson been civilly committed rather than as IST, he would be held at a different institution, "affording appropriate care" and be "entitled to certain privileges not now available to him."

The Supreme Court decision delivered by Justice Blackmun, held:

> 1. By subjecting petitioner to a more lenient commitment standard and to a more stringent standard of release than those generally applicable to all other persons not charged with offenses, thus condemning petitioner to permanent institutionalization without the showing required for commitment or the opportunity for release afforded by ordinary civil commitment procedures, Indiana deprived petitioner of equal protection . . .
> 2. Indiana's indefinite commitment of a criminal defendant solely on account of his lack of capacity to stand trial violates due process. Such a defendant cannot be held more than the reasonable period of time necessary to determine whether there is a substantial probability that he will attain competency in the

foreseeable future. If it is determined that he will not, the State must either institute civil proceedings applicable to indefinite commitment of those not charged with crime, or release the defendant. (*Jackson v. Indiana*, 1972, p. 716)

This decision in the *Jackson* case has been hailed as a landmark. As Steadman and Hartstone (1983) write, "from the standpoint of legal precedent there was no mental health case law in the 1970s of greater importance than *Jackson v. Indiana*. . . ." (p. 55) In the often quoted words of *Jackson*, the Court established that "due process requires that the nature and duration of commitment bear some reasonable relation to the purpose for which the individual is committed." (p. 738)

I believe that the *Jackson* decision has had a significant impact on the legal disposition and length of detention of ISTs. Studies (Steadman & Hartstone, 1983) of ISTs before *Jackson* frequently concluded that ISTs "were hospitalized for excessively long periods of time and that it was not unusual for persons found incompetent to stand trial to receive the equivalent of a life sentence" (p. 48). In a study by McGarry and Bendt (1969), the researchers found that 56 of 219 ISTs hospitalized in Bridgewater State Hospital in Massachusetts were competent to stand trial, yet they had spent, on the average, 4.3 years in the hospital. On the basis of this study and others, the Group for Advancement of Psychiatry (GAP, 1974) concluded that "all too frequently a determination of incompetence becomes a lifetime sentence to a hospital for the criminally insane" (p. 905).

Studies of ISTs after *Jackson* (Steadman, 1979; Roesch & Golding, 1977) show a considerably different picture. The average length of hospitalization for ISTs in one state was 2.6 years, with murder and rape averaging the longest time (e.g., 3.7 and 2.3 years respectively). Thus, "lifetime sentences" after *Jackson* may indeed be the thing of the past.

The *Jackson* decision also played a part in the last phase of the *Lang* case. When we last left Donald Lang, he was released from confinement in February 1971. But in July 1971, he was arrested again and charged with the murder of another woman. The same predicament arose (i.e., he was incompetent to stand trial and he would never achieve competence), but the court, using the *Myers* rationale, brought him to "trial" in what is referred to as an "innocent only" hearing.

A jury convicted Lang, and he was sentenced to 14 to 25 years' imprisonment. The appellate court subsequently reversed Lang's conviction, stating that though the evidence clearly established guilt, no trial procedures could effectively compensate for the handicap of a deaf mute with whom there could be no communication. (*People v. Lang*, 1979, p. 351)

But the Illinois Supreme Court remarked that

in *Jackson v. Indiana* the United States Supreme Court commented approvingly on such hearings and noted that some States have statutory provisions allowing an unfit defendant a trial at which to establish his innocence.

Whereas the *Jackson* decision was surely precedential, it neither addressed nor answered all the questions regarding incompetency. What was omitted from the Supreme Court's consideration of *Jackson*, and what we will take up next, is the question of how "competency" is defined, understood, and assessed.

CONFUSIONS OVER COMPETENCY

John Monahan (1980, p. v; Burt & Morris, 1972) quotes "a telling colloquy between a trial judge and a psychiatrist.
Judge: Doctor, is he incompetent?
Psychiatrist: Your Honor, he is psychotic!"
Monahan notes

> not only the inadequacy of the psychiatrist's answer, but the infelicity of the judge's question. To avoid dealing with complex and problematic questions of law, judges frequently solicit conclusory opinions from mental health professionals. Oblivious to the limits of their expertise, mental health professionals sink to the occasion. (p. v)

Putting aside for a moment the *way* competency questions are asked and answered, and turning, instead, to the *meaning* of competency, I put forward an assertion. The assertion is that the concept of competency has been poorly understood, vaguely defined, and indiscriminately equated with a host of related but separable concepts. In the not too distant past, as well as in the continuing present, "competency" has been and continues to be confused with "responsibility," "insanity," "psychosis," "mental illness," and "committability." While the picture is changing, the confusions, both definitional and pragmatic, are worth noting and understanding.

Twenty or so years ago, when a clinician was asked to assess someone's *competency*, the evaluator had two major problems: the first was an inadequate or absent definition of the term and, hence, only vague criteria; the second problem was that there existed no specific test or assessment instrument to do the job. When in doubt, as most clinicians were, they fell back on the "psychiatric interview" (i.e., the "mental status exam"). This "fall back" strategy, however, muddied the already murky waters in two ways: the assessment remained subjectively and impressionistically grounded, and the examination itself was the same technique clinicians typically used when asked to determine "mental illness," "committability," "insanity," "responsibility," and so forth; thus, confusions tended to compound rather than clarify. Steadman and Hartstone (1983) summarized the situation this way:

> . . . clinical evaluations for competency were the archetype of clinical decision making. With no specific guidelines, a mental health professional typically

would see a defendant for 30 minutes or less and on vague criteria recommend whether he or she could proceed with a trial. What such assessments often produced was grave confusion between competency to stand trial and criminal responsibility and between mental illness and fitness. (p. 42)

As an example of definitional fusion and confusion, let us examine "committability." Today, in most states, for a person to be involuntarily committed to a mental institution, that individual would have to meet the following criteria: (1) the person has to have a mental illness, and (2) as a result of that mental illness, the person has to be judged to be potentially dangerous. Both criteria must be present, and the second is related to the first. In some states, a third criteria is added: that is, given the conclusion that a person is (1) mentally ill, if that individual (3) is in need of treatment, he or she may also be committed. The exact wording differs for each state, but it is typically criteria (1) and (2), or, in some states, (1) and (3), that must be met. These criteria and their specificity have changed dramatically over the last 15 years as "mental health law" and cases came before the courts and legislatures. In former times, it was quite common for states to equate "mental illness" or "committabilitiy" with "mental incompetence"; thus, when an individual at an involuntary commitment hearing was judged to be "mentally ill" and "committable," that finding was frequently a simultaneous and automatic judgment of incompetence. In short, they meant the same thing.

The Supreme Court in *Jackson v. Indiana* (1972) was quite clear that they *are not the same thing*. The Court noted that Jackson did not have any formal commitment proceedings which "would be required to commit indefinitely any other citizen. . ." (p. 738). Not only did the Court make it clear that being declared incompetent did not automatically lead to commitment, but the Court also noted that release from involuntary commitment should not be contingent upon attaining competency: "The practice of automatic commitment with release conditioned solely upon attainment of competence has been decried on both policy and constitutional grounds" (p. 734). Thus, they are not the same thing.

Over the last two decades, many states have changed their statutes such that now two separate hearings, findings, and judgments are required. As Ennis and Siegel (1973) state,

In most states, the label "mental illness" means that the person so labeled is unable to take care of his *personal* affairs (his health, personal safety, etc.), and the label "mental incompetence" means he is unable to take care of his *business* or *legal* affairs (his bank account, taxes, or property, etc.). (p. 74)

Thus, appropriately separated, an individual judged mentally ill and dangerous or mentally ill and in need of hospitalization may still be competent; alternately, a person judged incompetent may neither need hospitalization nor meet the criteria for involuntary commitment.

Similar distinctions should be made between incompetent to stand trial (IST), on the one hand, and "responsibility" or "legal insanity," on the other. In this instance, the concepts not only involve different criteria, they involve different points in time: "responsibility for one's acts" and "legal insanity" concern the time just preceding and through the alleged criminal act; an IST judgment concerns the time from arraignment through sentencing. Furthermore, various judicial decisions have made the point that a finding of "mentally ill" is not a finding of incompetence (*Hall v. United States*, 1969; *United States v. Horowitz*, 1973); a finding of "severely mentally ill," even "overtly psychotic," is not a finding of incompetence (*Feguer v. United States*, 1962; *United States v. Adams*, 1969); and that prior hospitalization in a mental institution is not proof of incompetence (*Newman v. Missouri*, 1974). Yet, for all the legal, semantic, and definitional differentiations that have been made, confusions have, and still, occur.

In the *Jackson* case, the Supreme Court noted that the Indiana statute (Section 9-1706a) confused the competency–incompetency distinction with the sanity–insanity distinction. Whereas the Indiana statute deals with procedures and grounds for a trial judge ordering a competency hearing, the wording of the statute speaks of the trial judge having "reasonable ground" to believe the defendant "to be insane." "Insanity" and "incompetency" are not only linked and fused in legal statutes when they should be separate, they are similarly linked at times in psychiatric opinions, as the case of *Lynch v. Overholser* (1962) illustrates.

Frederick Lynch was charged with passing two bad checks "in the amount of $50 each with knowledge that he did not have sufficient funds with the drawee bank for payment." The trial judge sent Lynch to St. Elizabeth's Hospital in the District of Columbia where the assistant chief of psychiatry reported that Lynch was "of unsound mind, unable to adequately understand the charges and incapable of assisting counsel in his own defense." At that point, the psychiatrist was only commenting on competency. But 24 days later, the same psychiatrist went further: He wrote the court that Lynch had "shown some improvement and at this time appears able to understand the charges against him and to assist counsel in his own defense." If the psychiatrist had stopped at that point, no confusion would have resulted; but he did not. He wrote that Lynch "was suffering from a mental disease, that is, manic depressive psychosis, at the time of the crime charged," such that the crime "would be a product of this mental disease." His last statement was gratuitous: He not only offered "an opinion that was not asked for," but he offered "the Durham defense for the defendant—who had not asked for it" (Finkel, p. 143).

To repeat, "competency" deals with the accused's *present* capacity to understand the proceedings against him or her and to consult with his or her lawyer with a reasonable degree of rational understanding. "Insanity" refers to the *past:* specifically, that point in time when the alleged criminal act occurred, and it is addressed to the accused's capacity *then*. "Committability" criteria relate to *present* signs of mental illness coupled with predictions of either imminent danger and/or need for treatment (e.g., hospitalization in the immediate *future*. In the *Lynch* case, the psychiatrist first blurred the past–present (i.e., insanity–incompetency) distinction; he then added to the problem by blurring the present–future (i.e., incompetency–committability) distinction when he wrote that Lynch "may have further lapses of judgment in the near future" and that it "would be advisable for him to have a period of further treatment in a psychiatric hospital."

Whether this broad unrestrained psychiatric report had an effect on the judge's subsequent decisions is speculative, although the judiciary's general reliance (i.e., 92% of the time judges support the psychiatric decision) on psychiatric opinion, coupled with what specifically happened next in the *Lynch* case, leads one to believe that it had a significant effect.

To pick up the story, Frederick Lynch is brought back to court as competent to stand trial. Represented by counsel, he attempts to withdraw his earlier plea of not guilty and plead guilty. The trial judge, however, refuses to allow Lynch to change his plea! The judge, while acting within his discretionary authority, has complicated the picture by adding yet another distinction. From the defendant's point of view, Lynch is in a seemingly contradictory "no man's land" where he is, on the one hand, competent to stand trial, but on the other, not competent to plead guilty.

How are we to distinguish between competency to plead and competency to stand trial (Virginia Law Review, 1982), and who should make the determination? In the *Lynch* case, the judge made the determination, although the "how" remains unknown. There is, however a logically prior question: Should we make such a distinction? Winick (1983) and Roesch and Golding (1980) review more recent legal cases that bear upon the dual vs. single standard of competency and find that the courts are divided. Winick (1983, p. 8) asserts that most courts do not make a distinction but rather use the same standard of competence to stand trial (*Allard v. Helgemoe*, 1973; *Malinouskos v. United States*, 1974; *People v. Heral*, 1976). However, when it comes to competence to waive counsel and defend oneself, the standard of competence "is considered stricter than the general standard of competence to stand trial" (*Westbrook v. Arizona*, 1966; *United States ex rel. Konigsberg v. Vincent*, 1975).

Roesch and Golding's (1980) review cites the case of *Westbrook v. Arizona*, where the Supreme Court ruled that a determination of a defendant's competency to stand trial "did not suffice" as a determination of a defendant's competency to "waive his constitutional right to the assistance of counsel and . . . to conduct his own defense" (p. 34). In *Sieling v. Eyman* (1973), the Ninth Circuit extended *Westbrook* and held that "where defendant's lack of mental capacity lurks in the background" a higher standard should be adopted regarding competency to plead guilty.

Clearly, confusion reigns. The courts are divided over a single vs. dual vs. multiple standard of competency. Will there be one standard of competency that covers standing trial, pleading guilty, and waiving counsel, or will there be separate and hierarchical standards? We do not know, as yet. As to the question of who would make such distinctions, or, more important, *how* one would make such distinctions, the courts have remained eerily silent. There is much that is worrisome here, particularly if the courts turn to psychiatric opinion for the answers. As Steadman and Hartstone (1983) convey, the judiciary's

> reliance on psychiatric testimony would not be so alarming if evidence indicated that psychiatrists or other clinicians had a clear and accurate understanding of what it means legally to be incompetent to stand trial. In fact, the existing data strongly suggest the opposite conclusion. (p. 45)

Is there, then, any foundation worth its empirical salt for believing that psychiatry or psychology will be able to make even finer discriminations? We will take up this question shortly, but first, let us return to the defendant-turned-patient.

Where, then, is the defendant in all this? Well, Frederick Lynch found himself back in the hospital. He claimed repeatedly that he knew what he was doing in cashing the two bad checks for $50 apiece; he was ready to plead guilty and take his punishment, which would have probably been at most a year in prison; what he didn't want—hospitalization and an insanity defense—he got. Trapped in a psychiatric hospital with a defense he didn't want, Lynch fought back. A *habeas corpus* proceeding resulted in his release, but this relief was all too temporary; the Court of Appeals reversed the *habeas* finding, and Lynch was returned to the hospital. The Supreme Court would ultimately hear the case and eventually rule against this "improvident confinement," but Lynch did not live to see his victory of principle. In an act that may be regarded as either confirming his madness or confirming the maddening morass of the competency issue, "Frederick Lynch punned himself to death. He lynched himself" (Finkel, 1980 p. 147).

ASSESSING COMPETENCY

The *principle* that an accused must be competent for a trial to proceed is not in question. What is in question in this subsection is the *practical matter* of how "competency" is assessed and by whom. We begin with some legal guidelines and then move to recent efforts by the mental health profession to solve the assessment problem.

The *Dusky* (1960) standard is our legal starting point: the

> test must be whether he has sufficient present ability to consult with his lawyer with a reasonable degree of rational understanding—and whether he has a rational as well as factual understanding of the proceedings against him. (p. 402)

In many states, *Dusky* is also the stopping point. Two states that have gone further are New Jersey and Florida. New Jersey adapted the American Law Institute's Model Penal Code, which includes the defendant's "capacity to appreciate his presence in relation to time, place and things," along with seven criteria relating to awareness of the legal process. Florida statute follows a checklist approach and assesses 11 factors, most of which tap the defendant's ability to appreciate and assist in the legal process. Given the accent on appreciating the legal process and being able to confer and assist with counsel, a question arises as to the mental health professional's sole responsibility for making the assessment. As Roesch and Golding (1980) state, "the process of determining competency requires substantial interaction between mental health and the law" (p. 6).

The courts have traditionally turned to psychiatry to determine competency, although not without misgivings. Sir Matthew Hale's misgivings led him to recommend impaneling a jury to inquire as to whether the incompetency was real or counterfeit. In *Wear v. United States* (1954), the trial judge rejected defense counsel's request for a mental examination, preferring to make such determination himself: "In my opinion and from what I have heard of this case, I think the defendant is a malingerer." However, the Appellate Court reversed the decision and implied that detecting mental disorders not "readily apparent to the eye of the layman" required a special eye (Gobert, 1973). Psychiatry's eyes and competency, however, may not be up to the task. Kenefick (1968)

> ventured the opinion that a competency determination is a process whereby a psychiatrist applies a rule he does not quite understand to a person he scarcely knows in order to determine his fitness for an environment he has never seen.

Despite uncertainties, and with eyes and ears arguably open to potential pitfalls, mental health professionals have ventured forth to make competency assessments. We now turn to their more recent efforts.

When it comes to the efforts of the mental health professionals, the early literature featured attempts to develop a checklist (Robey, 1965; Bukataman, Foy, & de Graazia, 1971). McGarry and his colleagues (Lipsitt, Lelos, & McGarry, 1971; McGarry, 1973) went further, developing two quantitative measures, the Competency Screening Test (CST) and the Competency Assessment Instrument (CAI). The CST has 22 sentence-completion items in which defendants are given the start of the sentence and they must complete the sentence. Items include "Jack felt that the judge _____" and "The way a court trial is decided _____," and each item is scored 2 (competent), 1 (questionable), or 0 (incompetent). Roesch and Golding (1980), who questioned the CST's reliability and validity, are less reserved in their criticism of the test's scoring rules. They write:

> On one item, "Jack felt that the judge _____," a response such as "was right" or "was fair" would receive a score of 2, while responses such as "was

unjust," "was too harsh," or "was wrong" would receive a score of 0. This item is intended to tap the legal criteria of understanding and awareness of court process and the psychological criteria of acceptance of court process. Another item, "The way a court trial is decided _____," also designed to tap awareness and understanding of court process, is scored 2 if the respondent says "is by the evidence or "is the judge decides," but 0 if the respondent says "is open for improvement" or "is on the majority of opinion."

There are several alternative hypotheses one could make regarding scores in the incompetent direction. For example, past experience with the criminal justice system may result in an increased feeling of powerlessness to control one's outcome within that system. . . . An alternative and equally plausible explanation is that the respondent is giving an accurate response based on his own past experiences with attorneys, or on a sense that the outcome is beyond one's control so that a response would be futile. (pp. 60–61)

We can only imagine how Frederick Lynch might have responded to such CST items given his experiences and sense of powerlessness. Another criticism of the CST has come from Brakel (1974, p. 1116), who questions the high scores: he points out that scores of 2 on many items may be more ideal rather than real and raises the possibility that some respondents may be "playing the game" "whereas resistance to orderly participation in this morality play" is viewed as incompetence.

The other assessment measure developed by McGarry and his colleagues, the Competency Assessment Instrument (CAI), has been more sharply criticized than the CST. The CAI is a semistructured interview with five rating scales assessing (1) appraisal of available legal defenses, (2) unmanageable behavior, (3) quality of relating to attorney, (4) planning a legal strategy including guilty pleas to lesser charges where pertinent, and (5) capacity to disclose to attorney available facts surrounding the offense including the defendant's movements, timing, mental state, and actions at the time of the offense. Each item is scored on a 1 to 5 from "total capacity" to "no capacity." Roesch and Golding (1980) believe that "the reliability of the CAI has not been adequately studied. . . . More important, the lack of predictive validity support renders the CAI unusable in a decision making sense" (p. 65).

To summarize, while the development of assessment measures may be viewed as commendable step in the right direction, the checklists and quantitative rating scales designed so far still have a long way to go: their validity, reliability, and fundamental assumptions are open to challenge or have been inadequately tested. In addition, the basic direction of this work may be the wrong tack to take. The inclusion in these instruments developed by mental health professionals of more and more items designed to tap *legal* rather than *psychological* dimensions of competency raises questions about whether the test makers are themselves competent to ask, interpret, and score such items.

Who, then, is competent to ask, interpret, and answer the competency question? Mental health professionals or lawyers? The answer, sadly, may be neither. As Roesch and Golding (1980) note,

> mental health professionals in general, and psychiatrists in particular, continue to exhibit a marked tendency to equate psychosis with responsibility and/or competency, in spite of the fact that this is not in accord with *either* legal standard. (p. 16)

As for lawyers, Rosenberg and McGarry (1972) suggest "that many attorneys simply do not know what competency means. Of the 28 attorneys they interviewed, ten had no knowledge at all of the legal criteria which should be the basis of requests for evaluations" (Roesch & Golding, 1980 p. 50).

Roesch and Golding (1980) have offered a new direction—in competency assessment—a functional approach that "may necessitate the use of lawyers in the evaluation process" (p. 7)—which, based upon what we've already discovered, may be either the best or worst of both possible worlds. They believe that both lawyers and mental health professionals have something to contribute to competency assessment. To their credit, they make the case that "competency" is a construct that *"can never be fully reduced to a set of concrete operations and observational terms. . . . Thus no absolute set of facts is ever dispositive of competency"* (pp. 12–13). Their functional approach is an individual approach, which treats each defendant and case singularly. The question is, Can this defendant, given the particulars of his or her case, competently consult, assist, and comprehend? Their reading of *Dusky* leads them to believe that this is what the Supreme Court had in mind. This is debatable. And whether states will shift from a general test to a specific, functional approach has not yet been answered, although signs of movement in this direction have not been all that evident.

UNEQUAL PROTECTION

Once the competency issue is raised, legal and psychiatric processes are set in motion that in many jurisdictions place the defendant at a disadvantage. In comparision with other alleged criminals or those who have been involuntarily committed through civil means, potential or actual ISTs may not be receiving their equal protection. For example, once the court decides that a competency assessment is warranted, most jurisdictions mandate that the evaluation take place in a hospital, yet "inpatient evaluation is unnecessary for all but a fraction of defendants" (Winick, 1983, p. 10). To make one comparison, the civilly committed individual is entitled to treatment in the "least restrictive" locale, whereas the alleged IST is sent most often to the far more restrictive hospital. Making the comparison with other criminal defendants, most of these defendants would be released on bail or some other pretrial release provision, but the alleged ISTs suffer a deprivation of liberty by their usually unnecessary hospitalization.

Once the alleged IST is in the hospital, the evaluation period is usually more than 30 days and sometimes up to 80 days (Winick, 1983). While the *Jackson* decision specified that the period last no more than a "reasonable" time, the typical period for outpatient evaluation can be as little as several days or a couple of weeks; thus, the inpatient defendant spends more time being evaluated, suffers a deprivation of liberty, and runs a higher risk of being stigmatized because of the hospitalization.

If the defendant is found to be incompetent, many states provide for automatic hospitalization. Individuals not facing criminal charges but who are found to be incompetent are not automatically committed; rather, under the separation of incompetency and commitment decisions coupled with the "least restrictive alternative" doctrine, they are protected from automatic commitment; the IST, however, is not equally protected in many states. In addition, *where* the IST is hospitalized is often different and worse than would be the case for a civilly committed individual. Many states commit such defendants to maximum-security facilities for the "criminally insane," which typically results in a greater deprivation of freedom than would otherwise occur if the confinement were in an ordinary psychiatric hospital.

If one were civilly committed, the individual would have a statutory right to periodic review, with the burden of proof borne by the State. Not so, typically, for the IST. Even with the *Jackson* decision, "a 1979 survey found that almost one-half of the jurisdictions still permitted indefinite commitment without requiring periodic review" (Winick, 1983, p. 21; Roesch & Golding, 1979).

One unequal protection that may be justifiable concerns the "right to refuse treatment" (Finkel, 1984b). Committed patients and prisoners, through legal challenges, have been granted the right to refuse treatments under certain circumstances. Such treatments as psychosurgery, electroconvulsive therapy (ECT), aversive conditioning, and psychotropic medication have been challenged in court cases on constitutional, common-law, and statutory grounds. However, "even fundamental constitutional rights are not absolute and in appropriate cases must be subordinated to overriding state interests" (Winick, 1983, p. 17). In the case of ISTs, the state has a substantial interest in "the integrity of its criminal justice system" (Shapiro, 1974, p. 300) and, therefore, in bringing defendants to trial as speedily as possible. In Winick's (1983) words, this "would seemingly be counted as sufficiently compelling to outweigh the defendant's interest in refusing treatment necessary to restore him to competency" (p. 17).

How long may a state confine individuals declared IST before it must bring them to trial, release them, or initiate civil commitment proceedings?

The Supreme Court, in the *Jackson v. Indiana* (1972) decision, declined "to precribe arbitrary time limits"; the Supreme Court did, however, voice "substantial doubts" about the treatment the accused will get, "given the state of most of our mental institutions" (p. 735), in helping such a person to become competent. Others (e.g., Winick, 1983) have suggested 6 months as a sufficient time interval, since "this is the maximum length of time normally required to treat most civilly committed patients in hospitals" (p. 21). The average detention time for ISTs turns out to be 2.6 years, or five times as long as most civilly committed patients serve. But again, the state has a different interest in the two groups: for the IST, a charge is outstanding, and the state has an interest in bringing the person to trial. In the case of *In re Banks* (1979) the court held "that the state has no legitimate interest in incompetency commitment beyond the maximum sentence term authorized for the offense charged, and that confinement beyond this point would therefore violate due process" (Winick, 1983, p. 22). Some states (e.g., Louisiana, Massachusetts) have mandated the maximum sentence limit or a portion of the maximum sentence, such as two thirds (e.g., New York).

If the IST is restored to competency, brought to trial, and found guilty, does the individual get credit for the time spent hospitalized against the prison sentence? In most states, yes, although a few states do not give credit; thus, in the latter cases, the formerly incompetent but now competent and guilty person will likely spend more time confined than would an ordinary person whose competency was not challenged.

If an IST is released, are the outstanding charges dropped? One could make a case for dismissal on either due process or speedy trial grounds, yet most states do not dismiss the outstanding criminal charges. Furthermore, some states provide for the revival of the charges after they have been dismissed; one judge expressed the reason for this by stating that the court "is aware of many criminal cases where defendants have made seemingly miraculous recoveries after pending criminal charges have been dropped" (*United States v. Lancaster*, 1976).

To summarize, the IST defendant, when compared with either a criminal defendant or an involuntarily committed patient, is at a disadvantage in the following ways: (1) he or she is typically evaluated in a hospital rather than in a less restrictive placement and typically is not eligible for bail; (2) the hospital where the evaluation takes place is likely to be a maximum-security facility with fewer amenities and more restrictions; (3) the time of evaluation is longer than for commitment; (4) a committed patient has a 6-month review period while the IST has no specified time limit; (5) the IST is in a hospital typically five times longer than the committed patient; (6) the committed patient has a right to refuse treatment, whereas the IST's right may be overriden by compelling state interests; (7) in some states, the IST is not released even after the maximum sentence for the charge has been served; (8) in some states, the IST does not get credit for the time spent in a hospital applied to his or her sentence, if eventually found guilty; and (9) the IST's charges may not be dismissed, and may even be revived, following release. Unjustifiable unequal treatment seems to predominate (Gobert, 1973).

NGRI CONSEQUENCES

We have reached the penultimate point for the allegedly insane defendant. The preliminary issue of competence to stand trial was finally settled. Having been found competent to stand trial, the individual was sent from the hospital to the court. The trial concluded with a verdict of "not guilty by reason of insanity" (NGRI), which thereby erased the "allegedly." The NGRI individual now awaits the consequences.

The consequence that is most likely to occur is involuntary commitment to a facility for the criminally insane. This consequence comes about in one of two ways: automatically, as a result of the verdict and state statutes that mandate commitment, or through a commitment hearing initiated by the state. Barbara Weiner (1980), in her article and testimony before the Senate Subcommittee on Criminal Law (1983), noted that 23 states have automatic commitment following a finding of NGRI, while 17 other states hold a hearing to determine the consequence. Let us note what does *not* occur, typically: this defendant, who successfully pleaded an insanity defense and who was found "not guilty," rarely walks from the courtroom to the community as a free person. Unlike other defendants found "not guilty," the insane acquittee is not free. "Acquittal" is a word that is about to become a euphemism—an euphemism that provides little comfort and scant shelter before state interests that are about to fetter his or her freedom.

Is this outcome fair? Is the process by which this occurs *due process?* Are there defensible reasons, legally and psychologically grounded, to support this outcome? What are the states' reasons, and are they compelling enough to override the individual's right to be free from confinement? These are the questions we now take up.

The state's interest in retaining and restraining the NGRI are these:

> First, the state has an interest in deterring false insanity pleas by future criminal defendants; second, those acquitted may have a degree of culpability for an offensive act which civil committees do not have; and third, the acquitted patient may be more likely to injure others, since his conduct has already manifested itself in an antisocial manner. (Kirschner, 1978, p. 233)

Kirschner puts forth a fourth, "unexpressed reason motivating legislatures and courts":

An aroused public may want to do more than deter false insanity pleas, it might feel that retribution and isolation are so important that a person should be punished regardless of mental responsibility. Legislators and judges "notice" that people will be very upset if they perceive even an insane killer is to avoid punishment.

To this list of four I add a fifth: That the insane acquittee is seen as in need of treatment, such that involuntary hospitalization is the humane, benevolent, and therapeutic thing to do.

This list of five can be regrouped along familiar, traditional lines. Reasons 1 and 3 are deterrent motives: number 1 is to deter others, and number 3 is to deter this particular individual. Reason 2 reflects a retributivist motive. Reason 5 reflects a rehabilitative motive and is hinged to the state's *parens patriae* powers. And reason 4 reflects the political winds of an enraged populace, whose fear, anger, and desire for vengeance demand incarceration.

These reasons all have a history. The Saxon saying "buy off the spear or bear it" was one recommendation for dealing with the revenge motive of a victimized family or community. The Roman adage that "madness is punishment enough" is countered by the retributivist's claim that the madman isn't punished at all! When Parliament hastily passed the Insane Offenders Bill in 1800 following Hadfield's acquittal, the focus was on deterrence—both of Hadfield, since the bill incorporated language that would retrospectively apply to him, and of future insane acquittees. Queen Victoria's concerns following M'Naghten's acquittal were for future deterrence of incidents of both violence and insanity pleas, which she, as others, thought likely to increase, as well as for the present "fact" that insane acquittees who inflicted harm were apparently escaping their "just deserts." And the alienists and positivist criminologists of the nineteenth century voiced their therapeutic, rehabilitative wishes for control and cure.

All that is old hat. What remains is to assess whether the old hats wear well today—whether the reasons for continued confinement fit at a jaunty or jaundiced angle stop our NGRI's Fifth and Fourteenth amendment rights of due process such that, in the words of *Jackson*, "the nature and duration of commitment bear some reasonable relation to the purpose for which the individual is committed."

RETRIBUTION

The retributivists have relied upon the "principle of commensurate deserts" (Monahan, 1982, p. 103), namely, that "the severity of the punishment be commensurate with the seriousness of the offender's criminal conduct" (von Hirsch & Hanrahan, 1979, p. 4). In Monahan's (1982) words, "Seriousness, in turn consists of two components: the *harm* committed and the degree of the offender's *culpabiliity* in committing it." (p. 104)

Now, let us apply the principle and its two components to two cases we have already met, that of Donald Lang and Frederick Lynch. The *harm* Lang was accused of was murder; the *harm* Lynch was accused of was writing bad checks. Certainly, these harms can be discriminated and ordered in terms of severity by laymen or jurists, although it is arguable as to whether they can be precisely fixed on a scale of *absolute* crime seriousness. The seriousness of the harm, however, is not the important component where an NGRI is concerned; rather, *culpability* is. Our entire legal history regarding the insanity defense, save for rare and notable exceptions (see Chapters 1 and 2), is based upon the belief that insanity is an *excusing* condition: exculpating the insane offender is a judgment that *he or she is not culpable* and therefore *not punishable*. Hence, such a defendant, following an NGRI verdict, is not to be given a desert, for that would be unjust.

The moral ground upon which the retributivist seeks to punish evaporates when an NGRI verdict is returned. But what of the "aroused public" who wishes the defendant to be punished "regardless of mental responsibility"? They see a serious harm and criminal act having been committed. But popular judgments of seriousness

> may be untenable either because they contain factual misjudgments or because they involve moral judgments that do not withstand scrutiny . . . One should, in other words, *consider* the popular judgments, not necessarily abide by them. (Monahan, 1983 p. 105)

In the typical insanity defense case, *mens rea* is found wanting, thus no *criminal* act is judged to have occurred. In the atypical insanity defense case, or case of automatism, the judgment is that no *act* occurred, hence no criminal act. The public's judgment, therefore, becomes a misjudgment. If some in the public understand this but still wish to make a moral judgment and punish anyway, their reasons, like the retributivists, "do not withstand scrutiny."

At this juncture, retributivists and aroused citizens might say, "Wait a minute, we feel that this individual is partially guilty, does deserve some blame, and should be punished." My response would be, "O.K., but then you need to change the law whereby mental illness becomes a mitigating but not necessarily exculpating condition. Once you've done that, then you can assign some degree of blame and punishment for this 'new offense.'"

This is precisely what the Scottish jurist "the Bluidy Mackenzie" proposed in the seventeenth century (e.g., "diminished responsibility"); it is also what the English did in the Homicide Act of 1957; and it is similar in nature to the "guilty but mentally ill" (GBMI) option that is currently under consideration. If a defendant opts for this defense rather than the traditional insanity defense, there is an admission of some degree of culpability. If a jury finds a defendant to be GBMI rather than NGRI, that would be a judgment of partial culpability. In both instances, some degree of retributive punishment becomes permissible, and a "just desert" could follow. Whether the desert (von Hirsch, 1978) was "pure or less pure" (p. 623) (i.e., the Desert Model or the Modified Desert Model, where the latter might include deterrent and/or rehabilitative considerations), would be a matter for the legislature to decide. I would recommend this option to the public and retributivist as a way of legally and morally securing both sure footing and the desired consequent. I would strongly oppose, however, disguising and smuggling retributive motives and ends into either automatic commitment statutes following an NGRI verdict or into involuntary commitment and subsequent release decisions for the NGRI acquittee.

DETERRENCE

The state's police power, invoked when involuntarily committing a mentally ill and potentially dangerous individual, for example, legitimizes the state's interest in deterrence. Yet the state's right to proceed with deterrence is balanced against the individual's rights to liberty, to be different, and to be left alone. The state must make a clear and convincing case and must afford the individual procedural due process. When a state automatically commits an NGRI defendant rather than having to go through an involuntary commitment hearing, the substantive issues remain unproven while due process rights are ignored. Whether this unequal treatment of the NGRI acquittee under the deterrent rationale is defensible will be taken up shortly. Before that, we turn to the issue of deterring others.

Deterring others, which, in insanity cases, means deterring false NGRI pleas, is also a legitimate state interest. But whether the state can do this by confining those adjudicated as NGRI is another matter. The state has ways of deterring others: setting higher, swifter, and more certain punishments for offenses. But swift, certain, and weighty deserts are to be contingent on guilt, not to be inflicted upon the "not guilty." As Kirschner (1978) writes,

> allowing non-criminal confinement of the NGI for the purpose of deterring future insanity pleas does not avoid the problem of punishing the not guilty; in effect, it simply hangs "a new sign—reading "hospital"—over one wing of the jail house." Such a policy might run afoul of the eighth amendment prohibitions against punishing an individual for his status and not for an offense. (p. 271)

Returning to deterring the NGRI acquittee, comparisons with the civil commitment process are instructive. For civil commitment, mental illness and potential dangerousness are the criteria. Mental health litigation has brought to light the "void for vagueness" that surrounds "dangerousness," as well as the inability of mental health professionals to predict dangerousness accurately (Monahan, 1981). As a result, most states have rewritten their commitment statutes over the last 10 years in an attempt to define more precisely the nature, extent, and imminence of the danger. In addition, some states now limit how far back into an individual's life we can go in search of dangerous actions or intentions; suggestions of 30 days, 6 months, 1 year, and 18 months have been put forth (Ennis & Emery, 1978), but the net effect is clear: incidents indicating dangers should be relatively *recent* and *clear*.

In applying these lessons to the NGRI acquittee, let us keep in mind two points at the outset: first, the insanity judgment is a judgment about whether the person was a responsible person *at the time of the act;* second, the civil commitment decision involves a judgment of mental illness and potential dangerousness *at the present moment.* For the NGRI acquittee being automatically committed without a hearing, no assessment *at the present moment* has occurred. Defenders of this procedure are quick to point out though that the insane acquittee has already committed a dangerous and illegal act, where in the civil commitment case we are venturing uncertain predictions based on unclear "events." But "since recent overt acts evidencing dangerousness now seem constitutionally required before civil commitment can take place" (Kirschner, 1978, p. 273), the differentiating factor that separates a potential committee from a potential NGRI then becomes the prosecutor's discretion in deciding whether to proceed civilly or criminally. In short, the difference between the NGRI and the committee regarding overt dangerous acts may not be as great as defenders of automatic commitment maintain.

As to the imminence issue, the NGRI's dangerous act is by now history. In the United States, where trial delays are far more common and lengthier than in England, the NGRI defendant may come to trial over a year after the act occurred; where a competency hearing has been ordered, the delay is longer; and when a defendant has been declared incompetent and confined, he or she may spend 2.6 years in a hospital before the trial finally proceeds. Thus, at sentencing time, the time of the act may be years in the past; to use that historic act to assert dangerous *now*, at sentencing, may indeed exceed constitutional and statutory limits.

Furthermore, something else has occurred between the act and sentencing: that is, the defendant was judged *competent to stand trial.* Current competence may be presumptive evidence for doubting whether the defendant is currently mentally ill. Thus, doubt exists on two counts for the NGRI acquittee—the two counts that happen to be the two criteria for commitment: current mental illness and current evidence of an overt dangerous act. In my opinion, for the state to have its deterrent way, the state must overcome those doubts with clear and convincing evidence, with a defendant's due process rights protected.

There is another way for the state to effect deterrence. Call it "diminished responsibility," "diminished capacity," "GBMI," or what have you, it is the option that recognizes some degree of cupability along with mental illness. Once culpability is acknowledged, punishment can follow. A "just deserts" model may fix *the range* of punishment based on retributive motives; but with a "modified just deserts" model, there is room for deterrent considerations to play a part by moving the sentence "up or down" within the retributively fixed range. Monahan (1982) offered the following principle:

> Within the range set by the seriousness of the crime committed, the severity of an offender's sentence shall be proportional to the degree he or she reliably and validly can be predicted to offend again. (p. 112)

The problem, today, is with the reliability and validity of our predictions. Monahan would be the first to caution the deterrent advocates and mental health professionals that they have not yet achieved reliable and valid predictions. The number of studies (Kozol, Boucher, & Garofalo, 1972; Wenk, Robinson, & Smith, 1972; Monahan & Monahan, 1977), reviews of studies (*Baxtrom v. Herold*, 1966; Rubin, 1972; Ennis & Litwack, 1974; Cocozza & Steadman, 1976; *Addington v. Texas*, 1979; Monahan, 1981), and commentaries (Dershowitz, 1970; Steadman, 1975; Walters, 1981) on the accuracy of predictions of dangerousness lead to a disheartening conclusion for the deterrent advocate. To give free reign to professional predictions today would yield an unacceptably low rate of accurate predictions (i.e., true positives) and an unacceptably high rate of false positives (i.e., predicting someone to be dangerous when he or she is not). Today, when courts and legislatures are tightening the reigns on prediction as it is used in civil commitment proceedings, it would be unwise to proceed in the opposite direction in the criminal arena. Tomorrow's story has yet to be written.

REHABILITATION

To confine the NGRI for purposes of treatment is to therapeutically presume that benevolence—enforced benevolence—will rehabilitate the defendant-turned-patient. The presumption has not panned out. Effective involuntary treatment has been the exception; the rule has been that the NGRI spends, on the average, 3.6 years in the hospital, with longer times for the more serious harms (Steadman, 1980). The NGRI patients are likely to be sent to facilities for the criminally insane, which are often the worst in terms of therapeutic programs and staffing. When Justice Blackmun wrote the opinion in *Jackson v. Indiana* (1972), he raised "substantial doubts about . . . the rationale . . . that care or treatment will aid the accused in attaining competency . . . given the state of most of our mental institutions" (p. 735). In *Jackson* we were dealing with an IST situation, where the state has a compelling interest in providing treatment to bring the individual to trial; with the NGRI, there is less of a reason, and often even less treatment.

Involuntary treatment, particularly when brought about under the *parens patriae* rationale, is subject to challenge on legal and ethical grounds, and this has been happening at an increasing pace (Finkel, 1984b). Both the presumptions and naïvete of the Therapeutic State, along with the limits of benevolence, are under scrutiny by mental health professionals, judges, and jurists (Kittrie, 1971; Gaylin, Glasser, Marcus, & Rothman, 1978). One result has been the elimination of the need for treatment criterion for involuntary commitment from a number of state statutes over the last decade. Another result has been the number of right to refuse treatment cases (*Kaimowitz v. Michigan Department of Mental Health*, 1973; *Rogers v. Okin*, 1979, 1980, 1981; *Rennie v. Klein*, 1979, 1981) and their success.

NGRI patients, thrust in a hospital for the criminally insane against their wishes, and faced with the spectre of therapeutic control and social engineering for their own good, are likely to look a gift horse in the mouth and reject the benefaction. Therapy works best when it is voluntary. I believe therapy should be offered to the patient, but his or her declining should be respected. Thus, the rehabilitative reason for commitment must be removed as a primary rationale.

The therapeutic wish can have a place, but that place is a secondary one. Therapy can be offered to the committed NGRI patient, after a due process hearing has made him or her one. And therapy can be offered to the GBMI patient, whether he or she is imprisoned or hospitalized. But the offer should be extended free of coercion.

RELEASE

We have arrived at the final subsection of this chapter, and the "ultimate issue," from the NGRI patient's perspective: Does he or she ever, and under what conditions, get released? No other issue seems to provoke such strong responses. For the sceptic, cynic, and opponent of insanity defenses, the spectre of an NGRI being released reinforces their worst fears and suspicions. For the civil libertarian who sees the NGRI patient being treated unequally when it comes to release—having less protections then either criminals or civil committees—the discrimination is an anathema.

Let us begin with a recognition that the NGRI patient is "neither-fish-nor-fowl," but is "twice-cursed, as mad and bad" (Morris, 1983). Unlike criminally blameworthy, sentence-serving convicts, the NGRI patient does not, typically, have a fixed sentence with a date of certain release. In addition, granting parole to a prisoner "is nearly entirely within the discretion of administrative agencies, but once parole has been granted, substantial due process rights prevent arbitrary revocation of the parolee statues"

(Kirschner, 1978, p. 238); not so for the NGRI patient. The civil committee has periodic reviews, where the state must bear the burden of proof if recommitment is desired; the state also bears the burden of meeting the "clear and convincing" (*Addington v. Texas*) standard. For the NGI patient, judicial review may overturn a hospital's unanimous recommendation for release; the *habeas corpus* remedy, while available, places the burden of proof on the NGRI patient; and in some states, the state must meet only the "preponderence of the evidence" test to continue confinement of the NGRI. And finally, while the courts have increasingly used the "strict judicial scrutiny protection" for both convicts and committees, they have often used the less rigorous "rational basis" scrutiny for the NGRI patient. Thus, neither-fish-nor-fowl, he or she becomes both mad and bad and twice-cursed. The community may be glad, the NGRI patient sad, and angry. Yet the question remains, and is, "Does the curse get broken?" or "What is the right course regarding release?"

The first obstacle the NGRI patient faces when it comes to release comes from the hospital itself. As noted in *Jackson v. Indiana* (1972) and as poignantly brought to light in *Wyatt v. Stickney* (1972; *Wyatt v. Aderholt,* 1974), state hospitals often have neither the therapeutic program nor adequate staffing to promote psychological betterment. When it comes to the NGRI facility, the situation is worse.

> For example, a United States district court noted that only 3% of the patients at Farview State Hospital, Pennsylvania's maximum security hospital for the criminally insane, received any therapeutic-psychiatric treatment. (Morris, 1983, p. 75; *Dixon v. Attorney General*, 1971)

A report (Dukay et al., 1965) on Ionia State Hospital, Michigan's maximum security mental institution, found that "the over concern for security is evident everywhere, and this reflects the poor understanding of the mission of the hospital.. . ." A study of Arizona State Hospital found conditions "relatively bleak," but worst of all was the maximum security ward (Morris, 1983, p. 79). "A New York judge recently characterized institutions for the criminally insane 'as relics of abhorance of misdeeds of bygone eras'" (*In re Rose*, 1981).

As a comparison, Morris notes that

> in 1965, the median stay of patients in New York's maximum security facility for criminal order patients was a minimum of six to seven *years*. The average length of hospitalization in New York's civil state mental hospitals was four *months*. (p. 78)

A more recent review (Steadman & Braff, 1983) of New York NGRI hospitalizations showed that 40% of the NGRIs hospitalized between 1965 and 1976 were still hospitalized in 1978, with an average stay of 3½ years. As for New Jersey's Trenton Psychiatric Hospital, the United States Court of Appeals for the Third Circuit (*Scotte v. Plante*, 1981) described the living conditions at the maximum security wing as "subhuman."

Untherapeutic-like facilities, inadequate staffing, security rather than treatment orientations, and the absence of treatment plans and means all contribute to a situation where the NGRI patient is unlikely to be perceived as ready for release. However, staff attitudes and procedures may act as a deterrent to release in still another way, as a report prepared for the California Department of Mental Hygiene revealed (Morris, 1983 p. 76). This Packer Report noted an "unwritten 10-year rule" operating at Atascadero, California's maximum-security mental institution: the rule precluded NGRIs who had been charged with murder from being considered for outright release or transfer to a less secure facility for 10 years.

We know that the public perceives the NGRI as unpredictable and dangerous (Steadman & Cocozza, 1978). Even though the public's perceptions are frequently misconceptions, nonetheless, most citizens want the NGRI to remain in the hospital, and judges are often sensitive to public opinion. The 10-year unwritten rule seems to indicate that mental health professionals may also be sensitive to community and judicial wishes and, in effect, act them out. The motives would seem to be either retribution or deterrence, but both are inappropriate for different reasons: retribution, as we noted earlier, is inappropriate because the NGRI was found to be NG, and thus neither culpable nor punishable; and deterrence is inappropriate because the NGRI, at this point in time, has not been officially adjudicated as dangerous.

If the NGRI patient makes it past the hospital hurdle and receives a release recommendation, he or she still faces a number of obstacles imposed by courts and legislatures. The case of *United States v. Ecker* (1976, 1977) is illustrative. In 1967, Lewis Ecker "brutally raped and killed an employee of the United States Senate" (Kirschner, 1978). Ecker was found NGRI on both counts and committed to St. Elizabeth's Hospital.

> The Saint Elizabeth's Hospital staff on two occasions recommended conditional release programs for Ecker which were denied by the district court. In January of 1973, a conditional release plan was approved by Saint Elizabeth's which would have enabled Ecker to take advantage of vocational training facilities outside of the hospital grounds, and to visit his parent's home without hospital supervision. Judge Smith rejected the plan, and the rejection was affirmed in *United States v. Ecker* [Ecker 1]. The court was careful to note, however, that future approval of a comparable plan might be appropriate. Chief Judge Bazelon, writing for the United States Court of Appeals for the District of Columbia, expressed the view that the mere passage of time could settle many of the questions which led to the disapproval of the plan on that occasion.
>
> Over three years elapsed between Judge Smith's rejection of the conditional release plans involved in Ecker I and the 1976 court of appeals' decision in Ecker II. The appellate court in Ecker II was confronted with the district court's rejection of a hospital proposal for Ecker's staged reentry into the community.

Throughout each stage Ecker would live and receive therapy at the hospital. The district court rejected the release plan even though Ecker had met the conditions which Ecker I suggested were prerequisites to release, and the Government's psychologist agreed with the staff of Saint Elizabeth's Hospital that the plan should be granted. . . .

Ecker II followed distinctions made in the District of Columbia Code between the NGI and the civil committee for purposes of conditional release. Those civilly committed are entitled to release following a favorable administrative determination by Saint Elizabeth's Hospital. The NGI are entitled to release upon favorable administrative determination only if the court or United States Attorney pose no objection to the release program, or if the trial court finds than an NGI "will not endanger himself or others in the reasonably foreseeable future" under terms of the release. Ecker II held that an NGI patient would be entitled to the same release standard as civilly committed patients only after he had been confined for the number of years equal to the hypothetical maximum sentence which could have been imposed following conviction for the offense charged. . . .

Ecker II raises significant questions concerning constitutional requirements for release or conditional release of those not guilty by reason of insanity. The court tacitly places the NGI on a spectrum of culpability and dangerousness between the criminal convict and the civil committee. Consequently, it is permissible for the District of Columbia to erect obstacles to the release of an NGI which are not faced by civil committees. But the assumption that the NGI are on a different place on a spectrum of culpability and dangerousness than are the civilly committed seems inconsistent with the meaning of an NGI acquittal. (pp. 233–236)

The *Ecker* case raises serious equal protection questions.

Since the liberty right of the confined NGI is identical to that of the imprisoned and committed, it follows that distinctions in treatment of or procedural rights afforded to these three categories must be justified by reference to the differing state interests in confinement. (Kirschner, 1978, 261–262)

Let us set the *Ecker* case against the legal backdrop of *Baxtrom, Humphrey* (*Humphrey v. Cady*, 1972), and *Jackson*, where equal protection issues were central. In *Baxtrom v. Herold* (1966), a prisoner challenged a New York procedure

which transferred him from the custody of the Department of Corrections to the Department of Mental Hygiene upon expiration of his penal sentence. The Court held that the New York procedure violated the equal protection clause because it failed to give the same procedural protections to convicts ending their sentence that it gave to other categories of potential civil committees. In *Humphrey v. Cady* an individual was committed under Wisconsin's Sex Crimes Act to a "sex deviate facility" in lieu of criminal punishment. The statue allowed recommitment for an indefinite number of five-year confinements without a jury trial to which other civil committees were entitled. Following *Baxtrom* the Court held that Humphrey had been denied equal protection . . . . (Kirschner, 1978, pp. 264–265)

In the *Jackson* case, the Court also held that Jackson did not receive equal protection. Thus, for prisoners (*Baxtrom*), sex offenders (*Humphrey*), and

ISTs (*Jackson*), the Court has moved toward mandating equal protection. Is this trend, then, not applicable to the NGRI? Or are there compelling state reasons to discriminate?

One case that addresses these questions is *Bolton v. Harris* (1968), although the answers provided by the court are contradictory and the reasoning, muddled or absent. On the one hand, the court in *Bolton* found the District of Columbia's law mandating automatic commitment of the NGRI to violate equal protection. As Chief Justice Bazelon of the United States Court of Appeals (1968) noted: "A defendant who was insane for the purpose of responsibility at the time of the offense may not be insane for the purpose of civil commitment at the time of the verdict" (p. 647). The court recommended a new hearing (*Specht v. Patterson*, 1967). But when it came to release matters, *Bolton* "held that equal protection guarantees were not violated by the requirement that NGI acquittees undergo a judicial proceeding which was not required of civil committees" (Kirschner, 1978, p. 268).

The NGRI does face substantive and procedural hurdles in the way of release in many jurisdictions that committees do not face: extra procedural review steps, different burdens of proof, and different standards. When it comes to standards (Morris, 1983), "as of 1976, 18 states utilized release criteria that were more restrictive for insanity acquittee patients than for civilly committed patients" (p. 70). With standards like "restored to sanity," "cured," "no longer mentally ill," or "entirely and permanently recovered" being applied to disorders like schizophrenia, it is doubtful that many NGRI patients could qualify. But many committees with that disorder could not meet that standard either. Two points are important here: one is that the standard is discriminatory; and the second is that that standard is not relevant. Since the question for both the NGRI and the potentially dangerous committee is the same—Is he or she a likely danger now?—the standard should be the same, and relate to danger rather than to mental illness alone. Overall, different standards, burdens, and procedures seem unfair.

THE APA POSITION

The American Psychiatric Association's *Statement on the Insanity Defense* (1982) approves of the discriminatory treatment between civil committees and those NGRIs who were charged with violent crimes.

> In our view, it is a mistake to analogize such insanity acquittees as fully equivalent to civil committees who, when all has been said and done, have not usually already demonstrated their clear-cut potential for dangerous behavior because they have not yet committed a highly dangerous act. . . . The usual civil committee has not, however, committed nor will he commit in the future a major crime. Most mentally ill persons are not violent. By contrast, the "dan-

gerousness" of insanity acquittees who have perpetrated violence has already been demonstrated. Their future dangerousness need not be inferred; it may be assumed, at least for a reasonable period of time. (p. 15)

I believe this position fails to adequately recognize psychiatry's inability to predict dangerousness accurately. The statement above contains two predictions: first, for "the usual civil committed," the prediction "nor will he commit in the future a major crime" is offered; second, for the dangerous NGRI, the APA writes that "their future dangerousness need not be inferred; it may be assumed, at least for a reasonable period of time." The APA predicts a "true negative" (i.e., will not commit a dangerous act) for the committee and a "true positive" (i.e., assumes the NGRI will be dangerous) for the NGRI. What the statement ignores are "false negatives" and "false positives."

First, for the committee, factually we are seeing, because the legal statutes are demanding, more overt acts of dangerousness for those individuals who will become civil committees. If they have recent acts of overt dangerousness in their history, our confidence in the APA's "true negative" prediction declines. As an example, take two individuals, both paranoid and delusional, who believe their spouses are about to kill them; they pick up a kitchen knife and attack. In one case, because the spouse has quick hands or feet, the blow is blocked or the intended victim runs and escapes; in the second case, the intended victim is slow, and less fortunate. Because of a prosecutor's decision, this first case comes before the courts as a civil commitment case, whereas the second is an insanity case. We thus have a civil committee and an NGRI both seeking release. The APA statement makes differing predictions and seeks to establish different procedures for release. This discriminatory recommendation would seem to be based on classification rather than factual determinants.

The second prediction concerns the NGRI charged with violent crime. Studies of our predictions of danger referred to earlier note that psychiatrists greatly overpredict dangerousness, thus "false positives" are usually very high. Furthermore, and the APA statement implicitly acknowledges this, predictions of danger become even more hazardous after "a reasonable period of time" has elapsed. Given court delays, incompetency evaluations, and IST time, the reasonable period of time may have long passed; in such instances, *our predictions* become dangerous.

When we look at the APA recommendations, they move away from the old alienist position that mental health professionals alone should decide such matters. The APA is "quite skeptical" about that arrangement. As we have noted, it recommends the following:

. . . the decision to release an insanity acquittee should not be made *solely* by psychiatrists or *solely* on the basis of psychiatric testimony about the patient's mental condition or predictions of future dangerousness. While this may not be the only model, such decisions should be made instead by a group similar in composition to a parole board. In this respect, the American Psychiatric Association is impressed with a model program presently in operation in the State of Oregon under the aegis of a Psychiatric Security Review Board. In Oregon a multidisciplinary board is given jurisdiction over insanity acquittees. The board retains control of the insanity acquittee for a period of time as long as the criminal sentence that might have been awarded were the person to have been found guilty of the act. (pp. 16–17)

I have no quarrel with this recommendation *per se;* in being willing to share the power and responsibility for release decisions, psychiatry is acknowledging its current limitations and past failures. However, what can be implied from this statement by its absence is that for civil committees, "it is business as usual," where mental health professionals are solely responsible for release decisions. If this is the APA policy, it preserves the unequal, discriminatory treatment based on class.

My own recommendation would be along the lines proposed by David Wexler (1981). The review board or court-approved release is fine, but the crucial distinction for release procedures should be drawn between *dangerous* and *nondangerous* patients, not between committees and NGRIs. In this model, similar boards with similar compositions would make the release decisions for civil committees committed on grounds of mental illness and potential dangerousness and for NGRIs. This model does a number of things: it acknowledges the mental health professions' inability to predict accurately, at the present time; it incorporates community, victim, and the victim's family sentiments in the release decision; and it is nondiscriminatory, which affords NGRIs and civil committees equal protection.

A final comment on the APA Statement. It says:

We believe that neither the law, the public, psychiatry, or the victims of violence have been well-served by the general approach and reform of the last ten years, which has obscured the *quasi-criminal nature of the insanity defense and of the status of insanity acquittees.* [italics added] (p. 15)

It seems to me that if you acknowledge a *quasi-criminal nature of the insanity defense,* this acknowledgement seems inconsistent, given the APA's rejection of the "guilty but mentally ill" option. The GBMI option acknowledges a criminal, culpable, punishable nature for those defendants not adjudicated NGRI; it could set a retributive just deserts sentence range, with the final sentence moved up or down within the range based on rehabilitative and/or deterrent considerations. The APA notes that the GBMI "approach makes sense only if meaningful mental health treatment is given defendants following such a verdict" (p. 9); it remains dubious that this will occur. Yet our treatment record for NGRIs in facilities for the criminally insane does not have to be inferred; "bleak" and "subhuman" were some of the adjectives describing conditions and treatment that ranged from the abysmal to the dismal.

Treatment could be offered to both the adjudicated GBMI and NGRI patient. For the GBMI, it could be offered in prisons or in a special penal hospital. Whether the public and legislatures would be willing to provide funds for this endeavor, an APA concern, is yet to be tested. But let us keep in mind that this is the same public, and the same legislatures, that provide the current inadequate funds for NGRI facilities, staff, and treatment programs. Funding-level questions are of a different order than questions of consistency and equal protection; regarding the latter two, the APA's stand provides neither consistency nor equal protection.

IV

Future Directions and Recommendations

10

The Essence of Insanity

A DOGGED DILEMMA

Justice Oliver Wendell Holmes, Jr., once remarked that "even a dog distinguishes between being stumbled over and being kicked" (1881). Was Holmes intending to convey ironic admiration for canine certitude? We cannot say for certain, although Holmes was certainly well aware that our own ability to discern intent from accident, or sane intentions from insanely distorted intentions, has been dogged by doubt. Given our own all too human failings with these tough adjudicative discriminations, Holmes proposed a simpler principle and task. In advancing the principle of "strict liability," Holmes would restrict the adjudicator's purview to the behavioral and subsurface levels, rather than invite excursions into the subterranean depths of intentions and mind. One result of this restriction is that the extent of our inferences would be judiciously reduced to what could be obviously inferred by any "reasonable man." Instead of burrowing into the mind's darker recesses, where it is all too easy to err and lose our way, all we have to do now, says Holmes, is observe behavior and sniff the ground for telltale intentions.

According to his critics, Holmes was not only barking up the wrong tree, but he was leaving the reasonable man out on a limb, over a slippery slope. To see why, let us imagine what it would be like to live in a strict-liability world, where intention did not count and where punishment was contingent solely on behavior. In such a world, a waiter who spills some hot coffee on a patron faces assault charges. In a freak football accident, a defender hits the ball carrier with a jolting tackle; the tackled player's neck snaps, and the injuries prove to be fatal. In such a world, a charge of murder is brought. Other strange transformations result: a case of self-defense becomes a case of murder; an arithmetic error becomes tax fraud (Gerber, 1984). While these examples may be unlikely, even far-fetched, the uncertainty in this new behavioral world is not; it increases precariously. Faced with a new and unsafe world below, our reasonable man might well decide to apply the evolutionary brakes—choosing not to come down from the tree.

Actually, there is nothing new about this new behavioral world. It existed in pre-Norman England (see Chapter 1), where, under the secular Saxon system, "criminal responsibility" was hinged to harms, injuries, and the individual's behavior. But we have seen that this "behavioral view" of criminal responsibility was challenged and amended by the ecclesiastical position, which asserted that *mental* and *moral* elements must be considered and weighed before guilt could be established (Walker, 1968)

> . . . And if it happens that a man commits a misdeed involuntarily, or unintentionally, the case if different from that of one who offends of his own free will, voluntarily and intentionally; and likewise he who is an involuntary agent of his misdeeds should always be entitled to clemency and better terms owing to the fact that he acted as an involuntary agent. (p. 16)

The Norman conquest, carried out by the sword, soon plowed under the behavioral Saxon system and cultivated the principle that stands today—that "guilt in action" requires "guilt in intention." We recognize that "accidents will happen," and that necessity occasionally leaves us the unenviable choice of taking a life or losing our own. If we wish to endorse the position that excuses accidents, self-defense, and unintended harms, we must be willing to wrestle with the tough discriminations; and one of the toughest, surely, concerns insanity.

Our legal history since Saxon times reveals a commitment to this proposition that we ought to distinguish between those who knowingly commit crimes and those who simply "stumble" and to distinguish the mad from the bad. Ten centuries of Anglo-Saxon law confirm this commitment. But the fact that something has been so regarded for centuries merely reflects legal tradition, not justification. In a time when tradition is being questioned and calls for abolishing the insanity defense are being answered in some states, any new proposal upholding some form of an insanity defense must rest on reasonable justifications. The question then is "What principles and reasons support an insanity defense?"

IN DEFENSE OF AN INSANITY DEFENSE

Three different principled reasons for maintaining an insanity defense will now be examined. The first and oldest reason is based on the doctrine of *mens rea*. The second reason, championed by H. L. A. Hart (1968), rests on the distinction between voluntary and involuntary acts. The third reason, articulated most fully by Fingarette and Hasse (1979), involves the concept of *mens*. These three principles have been invoked as justifications for punishing those who break the law and for excusing those who are insane. Each will be examined in turn, and I will argue that the *mens* principle most closely reflects the essential problem of insanity and provides the soundest principled basis for retaining the insanity defense.

JUSTIFICATIONS FOR EXCUSING

From the traditional translation of St. Augustine's adaptation of Seneca (Hall, 1960, p. 72), the early meaning of *"mens rea"*—"evil mind" or "evil will"—expressed the immoral element of guilt and culpability. Later jurists tended to back away from the "evil mind" usage to that of an intention to bring about what is forbidden, harmful, and immoral. Other writers distanced themselves from the "immoral" to an "intention to do an act which is made criminal by statute." Other commentators, like James Fitzjames Stephen, believed that there was "no single precise state of mind common to all crime," but rather individual *mentes reae*. Thus, in the words of Sayre, *"mens rea*, chameleon-like, takes on different colors in different surroundings" (Hall, p. 75). Whether this protean *mens rea* is diluted, subdivided, disguised, or taken straight—the sense of an immoral, blameworthy intent survives.

One of the modern proponents of *mens rea*, Hall, offers the following generalization:

> the harm forbidden in a penal law must be imputed to any normal adult who voluntarily commits it with criminal intent, and such a person must be subjected to the legally prescribed punishment. (p. 18)

The key phrase in regard to *mens rea* is "with criminal intent." For Hall and for others, a criminal act and a criminal intent must concur (*"actus non facit reum, nisi mens it rea"*) for guilt to be established. It follows from Hall's generalization that if there was no criminal intent, there is no guilt, and this is a justification for excusing the insane defendant who did not criminally intend to do the act that is penal by statute.

One of the opponents of the *mens rea* justification is H. L. A. Hart. Hart (1963, 1964, 1968) argues that the doctrine of *mens rea* is neither a necessary nor a sufficient condition for making an action criminal. Hart points out that there are some offenses where "strict liability" applies (e.g., bigamy, the rape of a minor, passing a worthless check, driving on the left side of the road, exceeding the speed limit, selling narcotics, selling oleomargarine for butter, selling adulterated food products, selling liquor to minors or drunkards, and others); in these cases, intended or not, the mental element is irrelevant to conviction. As to the "morally wrong" part of *mens rea*, Hart (1968) notes that there are actions that if done voluntarily are criminally punishable, "although our moral code may be either silent as to their moral quality, or divided" (p. 90). Take, for example, laws that make it an offense to drive on the left side of the road in the United States, or the reverse in England; no *moral* wrong is involved here, only custom. Similarly,

> many offenses are created by legislation designed to give effect to a particular economic scheme (e.g., a state monopoly of road or rail transport), the utility or moral character of which may be genuinely in dispute. An offender against such legislation can hardly be said to be morally guilty or to have intentionally committed a moral wrong. . . . (p. 90)

And finally, Hart raises the nettlesome problem of negligence, where the law holds someone culpable for not thinking or intending before he or she acted. Whereas Hall would like to exclude negligence from statutory offenses, Hart would not, and the law clearly favors Hart's position. Given these offenses that cannot be accounted for on *mens rea* grounds, some other principle besides *mens rea* must be invoked to justify the punishment.

While Hart makes some telling points in his critique of *mens rea*, he fails to score a knockout. The defenders of *mens rea* can easily sidestep the criticism that the doctrine fails to describe accurately or fully the working of any known system of law. Hall and his defenders could simply rejoin, as Wasserstrom (1967) did,

> that one of the important, central, or illuminating characteristics of existing systems of criminal law is this insistence on moral culpability. . . . that the "core" cases of criminality in almost any legal system are cases of seriously immoral conduct that are proscribed by law. It is surely more than accidental, so this argument might go, that when we search for *clear* cases of criminal behavior we think first of murder, rape, robbery and similar immoral acts. The point is that the immorality or blameworthiness of the action does seem to be conceptually *connected* (but not, perhaps, necessarily) with most typical crimes. (pp. 95–96)

When we read the legal definitions of the crimes that seem to concern society the most (e.g., murder, arson, burglary, larceny, robbery, forgery, assault, etc), we find, within their definitions, phrases such as "with intent to burn" or "with malice aforethought" that establish the *mens rea* component as essential (Clark & Marshall, 1952). We can acknowledge that some offenses are *mala in se* (wrong in themselves), like murder, whereas other offenses are *mala prohibita* (wrong merely because they were prohibited by statute), like driving on the right or left side of the road, without abandoning completely the doctrine of *mens rea*. As Wasserstrom (1967) states,

> when we go through the typical criminal code it is more difficult than Hart appears to allow to find many criminal laws with even moderately severe penalties that do not proscribe actions that those exacting the statute thought to be immoral. . . . And if this is so, it seems to me, Hall could rightfully claim that he had identified a characteristic of criminal laws that may merit appreciable further attention. (p. 97)

To give Hart his due, what he offers is a *different* rationale for excusing than Hall's *mens rea:* where the *mens rea* position holds that "it is wrong to punish those who have not 'voluntarily committed a moral wrong proscribed by law,'" Hart's principle holds that "it is unfair and unjust to punish those who have not 'voluntarily' broken the law." Hart justifies his position by noting what we would lose in a strict liability world when the voluntariness of an act is not considered: we would lose predictability, for we cannot know when mistakes or accidents will occur, and, therefore, when we would be punished; we would lose control, since consequences would be inflicted upon us for actions that did not stem from our choices; and we would lose a crucial connectedness, which the law ought to make clear, between wrong choices and sanctions.

Now we may ask Hart the same question he asks of Hall: does his proposed justification for excusing conditions adequately cover any existing or ideal legal system? In addition, we ask a second, more specific, question regarding the subject of this work: Does Hart's justification adequately cover the issue of insanity? I believe the answer to both questions is "No." To explicate my conclusion, let me begin by looking at those cases that traditionally have been excused or justified.

To simplify, I wish to sidestep a historical and arguable distinction between justification and excuse; instead, I will list the grounds that have been cited historically (Clark & Marshall, 1952) as constituting either justification or excuse under one heading, that of "excusing conditions."

1. Public authority
2. Domestic authority
3. Prevention of offenses
4. Defense of one's person or property
5. Defense of other persons
6. Necessity
7. Compulsion, Duress
8. Accidents
9. Automatism
10. The acts of children
11. The acts of insane persons

Under "public authority," for example, we excuse someone who carries out a death sentence by a court; in addition, we excuse a person who has (a) killed to prevent another from committing a felony by violence or surprise, or (b) killed to suppress a riot, or (c) killed to effect an arrest for a felony or to prevent an escape. Under "domestic authority," we excuse from a charge of assault and battery a parent or other persons standing *in loco parentis* who gives reasonable correction to his or her child.

Let us apply Hart's principle of excusing *involuntary* acts to this list. Take a case of accident, where the head of an axe being used by a lumberjack flies off, killing a bystander; granting that negligence was not involved, the axiom of "accidents will happen" is sorrowfully uttered, and the lumberjack is exculpated. Clearly, the act is involuntary. Similarly, in a case of compulsion (duress), where a man is forced to aid in a robbery because his child is being held at gun point, we would say that he acted involuntarily and excuse him. And there are cases of insanity, particularly automatism (e.g., the hypothetical case of split-brain madness discussed in Chapter 8 or a sleepwalking case), where we might well believe that the act was involuntary.

When we look at some of the other excusing conditions, Hart's involuntary principle has to be stretched to fit. For example, take a case of "necessity," where someone on an already fully and dangerously loaded lifeboat or helicopter pushes off others who seek to board because of the threat to the safety of those already on board. The actor's actions lead to the injury or death of others. In the actor's mind, he chooses his course of action because the alternative is life-threatening to those already on board. Hart might argue that he really didn't have a choice and that his act ought to be construed as involuntary, but this certainly stretches, if not vitiates, the meaning of involuntary as "not subject to control of the will." In this instance, we might well prefer the *mens rea* justification on semantic, legal, and conceptual grounds: it would seem preferable to claim that the actor voluntarily acted on his intentions, but his intentions were not criminal. Here, the *mens rea* principle provides a sounder basis for excusing.

Now I introduce what I call "the Hadfield problem." The case, to recall, involved a defendant who intended to kill King George III and who voluntarily acted on those intentions. Although he was deluded, he nonetheless possessed *mens rea* (i.e., an intention to perform an act that was criminal), or individual *mentes reae*. Yet Hadfield was acquitted on grounds of insanity, a verdict which, I believe, was the proper one. But in this type of case, and here I could have easily substituted M'Naghten or Hinckley for Hadfield, both the *mens rea* position and the voluntary action position fail as justifications for excusing such a defendant. There is something fundamentally amiss in these type of cases that neither the *mens rea* nor the voluntarism principle captures.

No *Mens*

I believe that Fingarette and Hasse (1979) have provided the best understanding of, and justification for, an insanity defense in general, and for "the Hadfield problem" in particular. Their doctrine of "Disability of Mind" begins with a "maxim": "where there is no *mens* there can be no *mens rea*" (p. 200). They argue that the truly insane individual may well be able to act voluntarily (contrary to Hart's thesis) and may well formulate intentions, *mens rea* and otherwise, and act on those intentions (contrary to Hall's thesis), but something more fundamental is amiss. What to the insane person's way of thinking seems rational is flawed in a deeper way. The flaw lies in the "lack of capacity for rational conduct in regard to the criminal significance of the conduct" (Fingarette & Hasse, 1979, p. 218). In the absence of such a capacity we have a person who is not "response-able," and this, Fingarette and Hasse submit, "is central to what we wish to express when we speak of someone as 'out of his mind,' 'out of touch with reality,' 'mentally incompetent,' 'crazy,' or 'mad.'"

By way of explication, they invoke the concept of a "shared background-nexus," where members of society, through socialization and enculturation, come to share certain basic feelings, perceptions, customs, values, attitudes, and social skills. It is from this valuational background-nexus that the community perceives murder to be wrong in a moral sense (*malum in se*). We expect members of the community not to premeditatively murder or take a life with intent; we expect people not to rape, assault, thieve, commit arson, and so forth. Because this background-nexus is shared, we can adjudicate cases by raising and answering just a select few questions.

> We can ask: Did the person *know* (realize, believe) that the behavior was causing a certain harm (or likely to cause it)? Did the person *intend* to cause the harm? Did the person act *voluntarily?* Such questions are significant if we presume that, all the time the belief developed and the intent was formed, the person effectively shared, at least to some minimal extent, in the web of social learning and attitudes that give such beliefs and intentions their usual basic significance. (Fingarette & Hasse, 1979, p. 229)

At this point, we could raise an objection, which the authors raise for us, that not all members of society share those values. There are individuals and groups who "may be so alienated from the law and what it stands for as to hold that certain unlawful homicides [and other acts] are excusable, or even justifiable" (pp. 225–226). The authors use the examples of a violent revolutionary and an impoverished urban youth who "may feel no qualms of conscience" in turning to violence, looting, or murder; to such individuals or groups, the particular killing or thieving is justified or excusable. However, the authors believe that these individuals

> recognize that totally indiscriminate killing or thieving is wrong. Their "code" may be different from the code of law, but there *is* a code, a code identifying killing and taking the possessions of others as kinds of acts that call for excuse, justification, or special pleading of some kind. (p. 225)

This type of individual may be socially alienated, but the authors claim that such a person is not irrational; rather, that person is

> rational in regard to the law, even though—perhaps on moral or political or religious grounds—in disagreement with it . . . In sharp contrast is the person who does not sufficiently share in the background-nexus to perceive the nature of the issue—or even, perhaps, that there is an issue at all. Such a person is not rational in regard to law. (p. 226)

One other point about the background-nexus needs to be made. It is not required, for the attribution of responsibility, that individuals consciously reflect or deliberate upon the valuational background-nexus. In cases of second-degree murder or voluntary manslaughter, for example, we recognize the knowing, intentional killing of a person to be a crime, even where deliberation and malice were absent.

> Can we reasonably expect a person to refrain from indulging the impulse to kill—even *before* he has deliberated on the question? Of course, we can and do expect this. It is axiomatic that it is no excuse that one acted before one thought (though it may be less culpable then acting after thinking). Far from being an unreasonable demand, this is a simple, natural, and extremely common type of expectation. Human life could not go on if, before each and every act, we had to contemplate it and be explicitly conscious of the inherent *malum* or *bonum* of the act, and then deliberately choose whether to do it. (p. 228)

Thus, there is the expectation that individuals have a shared background-nexus and employ it, with or without deliberation; it is in this sense that we assume rationality and believe individuals to be responseable. Where, through the presentation of evidence to the contrary, we become convinced (i.e., at some, yet unspecified level of certainty—the standard of proof issue) that a person has not acquired the background-nexus, could not acquire it, or did acquire it but, through no culpable fault, cannot employ it, we would judge such a person as lacking the necessary *mens* and hence, not having the capacity for rational conduct.

The "capacity for rational conduct" idea has its historical origins. Fingarette (1972) points out that a key phrase from *M'Naghten*, "defect of reason," is often either overlooked or seen as "a piece of redundant rhetoric" (p. 198). Many commentators and users of *M'Naghten* exclusively cite the "not to know the nature and quality of the act he was doing, or if he did know it, that he did not know he was doing what was wrong" section. This is why, Fingarette claims, the *M'Naghten* test has been *mistakenly* viewed as the "right vs. wrong" test, or a "test of knowing." It is deeper than that, he asserts. The "defect of reason" phrase is an additional distinctive criterion, and it is the proper one. Because it has not been understood as such, it has commonly been dropped from the legal language actually used. But this has been a profound mistake. The defect-of-reason clause tells us that "know the nature and quality of the act" and "know that it is wrong" must be taken to apply with reference to the person's reason, his capacity for rational conduct. (Fingarette, 1972, p. 198)

Another historical root of the no *mens* position can be read from the writings of Issac Ray (1838/1983). Ray pointed out that insane individuals, even when deluded, often know what is morally right and wrong *in the abstract* and indeed may abhor murder *in general*. But insane individuals *dissociate* the general background-nexus from their *particular act*. It is this *dissociation* that is the "defect of reason," in *M'Naghten's* phrasing, or the "defect in the capacity for rational conduct," to use Fingarette's term. Ray, like Fingarette, goes beyond mere *knowing*, which can be viewed as a symptom of insanity but not its *essence*. The insane individual, then, like the child or the moron, may cite or parrot the appropriate moral edicts that are a part of our background-nexus, but as to the crucial question—Does he or she utilize them?—the answer is sadly "No."

What type of person would fit within this no *mens* category? The child, for one, who has not yet acquired the background-nexus of values, beliefs, and sentiments. Mentally retarded individuals whose IQ placed them in the Severe or Profound subtype would certainly qualify. An individual who was brought up in a radically alien culture to our own might also fit. As an illustration of this last case, Fingarette and Hasse (1979) use the example of "an adult from a backlands African village, completely steeped in the cultural lore about witches and witchcraft," who

> might emigrate to a Europeanized community and in "self-defense" attack someone who shows all the standard signs of casting mortal spells. Here, we may suppose, the background web of learning and attitudes is so different from the Europeanized norms and beliefs, so permeated with a different understanding of the world, that even the voluntary, knowing, intentional, and even premeditated killing of the "witch" simply does not have the significance it otherwise would. This immigrant is a grave social danger, but criminal condemnation hardly seems fitting. (p. 231)

As to insanity, we would include those individuals whose mental pathology has caused a temporary or permanent dysfunction of that capacity.

Having presented Fingarette and Hasse's no *mens* defense of an insanity defense, we can now compare and contrast this defense with other excusing conditions. When we do, we will find that "insanity" is quite different from most other excuses. Let us begin with a case of self-defense. A person under clear danger of losing his life at the hands of an armed assailant, retreats as far as he can and now finds that he is literally and proverbially back against the wall; his pleas and remonstrations have failed to stop the assailant, so now he is faced with the deadly dilemma of either firing his own weapon in self-defense or forfeiting his life; he chooses the former. His defense, naturally, is self-defense. In making this defense, he is admitting that he committed the harm that is made penal under law, but that the extraordinary circumstances and the lack of a surviving alternative warrant exculpation. To put it another way, the defendant is offering a reasonable and competing claim that he argues should supersede the "thou shalt not kill" commandment. His defense implicitly admits that he is a response-able person but that circumstances beyond his control placed this rational, responsible individual in a vexatious and tragic situation.

A similar defense is offered for the cases of duress and necessity. Defendants in these cases also admit, explicitly or implicitly, that they were response-able persons, but at the time of the alleged crime, they were caught in a maddening situation and made reasonable (excusable) decisions. In the case of accident, too, the defendant is claiming to be response-able; he maintains that he acted appropriately, not negligently, and could neither foresee nor forestall the subsequent harm. In cases of public authority, prevention of offenses, and domestic authority, defendants defend themselves as response-able individuals exercising a competing duty that justifies or excuses their actions.

When it comes to an insanity defense, however, the claim is quite different. Here, the defendant is claiming nonresponsibility. "The claim of nonresponsibility, however, is not the offering of an excuse. In offering an excuse, one responds to a legitimate accusation by offering a particular reason why one should not be condemmed" (Fingarette and Hasse, 1979). In the insanity instance, the claim is that "the whole apparatus—accusation, denial, excuse, justification, condemnation, and punishment—is misplaced and inappropriate." Put another way, the insanity defense "is not a challenge to the prosecution's case but a plea to circumvent the prosecutory process (entirely or in some limited respect)" (p. 209).

In this respect, the case for excusing insanity most closely parallels that case involving infants and children. In *A Treatise on the Law of Crimes,* Clark and Marshall (1952) state: "A child is not criminally responsible for his acts or omissions if he is of such tender years as to be incapable of distinguishing between right and wrong, and of understanding the nature of the particular act" (pp. 125–128). While the language sounds M'Naghten-like, I believe that the actual meaning is identical to Fingarette and Hasse's position regarding "response-ableness." Recalling Bracton's thirteenth-century legal writings on the age of discretion (see Chapter 1)—the age when a child knows "what was what"—Roman law set that age at 7, whereas thirteenth-century English law fixed it at 12. Modern accounts of common law typically divide the age span into three parts (see Clark and Marshall, 1952): (1) a child under 7, who is "conclusively presumed to be *doli incapax,* or incapable of entertaining a criminal intent, and no evidence at all can be received to show capacity in fact"; (2) a child between 7 and 14, who is "presumed to be incapable of entertaining a criminal intent, but the presumption is not conclusive. . ." and "may be rebutted. . ."; and (3) a child over 14, who is "presumed to be *doli capax,* and therefore responsible, unless he shows, as he may, that he was not of sufficient capacity."

The issue of whether the child is *doli capax* or *doli incapax* is the same as whether an allegedly insane defendant is "response-able" or not. In both cases, if there is an insufficiency of *mens,* there can be no *mens rea,* but it is the *mens* question, not the *mens rea* question, that is paramount.

If we accept this reasoning—that the justifying excuse for the insanity defense is different from the other excusing conditions, save for the infancy–child excuse—then an implication concerning the burden of proof follows. In criminal trials, the burden of proof is typically on the prosecution as to the factual and *mens rea* elements of the charge. The defendant tries to defeat the accusation, as Fingarette and Hasse (1979) state, "by offering disproof of the act, or by offering some specific excuse or justification, or by a showing that the act alleged in a particular accusation, even if it took place, would not constitute a violation of law" (p. 209). So in a case involving second-degree murder, for example, the prosecution must prove beyond reasonable doubt that the act occurred and that the culpable intent was present, even where the defendant is claiming duress, necessity, self-defense, or accident. And in many states (about half), the situation is the same with regard to an insanity defense. Yet this burden on the prosecution was roundly criticized following the *Hinckley* decision, with a number of the critics believing it to be unfair and recommending that it ought to be changed.

But the problem has been in locating a justifiable rationale for shifting the burden to the defense. Not liking the outcome of the case and believing it would have come out better had the burden been otherwise is not a justifiable rationale. On the other hand, a number of defenders of keeping the burden where it is, on the prosecution, were maintaining their position because to do otherwise seemed to be *arbitrarily* designating the insanity defense as a singular exception from the other excusing conditions; to them, the support for change seemed more heated than reasoned.

Now, however, if we accept the no *mens* basis for an insanity defense, we have a reasonable justification for shifting the burden of proof to the defense. For it is the defense that is asking that the normal standards and procedures for judging response-able persons *be set aside* in this particular case. It is not so much a plea to excuse as it is a plea to exempt. Given this distinction, it seems reasonable that this burden be borne by the defense.

With the burden now on the defense, the next question is "What standard of proof should be used? I believe, as Fingarette and Hasse (1979) do, that the "preponderance of the evidence" standard should apply. The other possible standards, "beyond a reasonable doubt" and "by clear and convincing evidence," are problematic, for different reasons. The "beyond a reasonable doubt" standard is not likely to ever be met when it comes to insanity or other psychiatrically related matters (e.g., involuntary commitment standards, competency to stand trial) because the state of our science (art?) is such that neither psychology nor psychiatry can furnish doubt-erasing evidence. The "clear and convincing" standard, as it falls between the "preponderance" and the "beyond," is beset by gray areas on both the near and far boundaries; and between the extremes there is less than a clear and convincing understanding of what "clear and convincing" really means. The "preponderance of the evidence" test appears to be the best choice.

If the *mens* issue is deeper and more fundamental than *mens rea*, then there is an implication for the order in which these topics ought to be dealt with at trial: the implication being that the usual order of things in a bifurcated trial—where establishing guilt (i.e., *actus reus* and *mens rea*) precedes a second trial on insanity—is backwards, in part. Judge Gerber (1984) recognized this problem in his critique of bifurcation. He wrote:

> The central thesis in this bifurcation proposal rests on the asserted evidentiary separability of guilt and mental state; that is, on the assumption that evidence of sanity can be segregated from evidence bearing on intention, knowledge, and recklessness. That is a dubious hope at best. (p. 78)

There is no reason why, in a bifurcated trial, defense counsel could not present evidence and expert testimony bearing on how the defendant's mental illness negates *mens rea*, in the first part of trial, and then turn around and present the same evidence in the second part of the trial as it bears on insanity. This would be redundant and time-consuming in practice, but in regard to principles, it would mean that "the insanity defense acts as a second wind or second string in the bow of a guilty defendant" (Gerber, 1984, p. 59), where it can be employed twice. Actually, as I will show later on, the insanity defense can be employed not twice, but three times: to challenge *actus reus*, to challenge *mens rea*, and to affirm insanity. This degree of redundancy and confusion, which can lead to quite different outcomes, can be avoided if we adopt the no *mens* rationale for excusing insanity and deal with that question at trial *before* the determination of guilt.

THE NEED FOR A UNIFYING DOCTRINE

So far, I have presented a case for retaining the insanity defense in some form. In addition, I have laid out an argument for defining the essential characteristic of legal "insanity" as an incapacitation of *mens*. In this subsection, I will present a picture of the legal landsↄↄpe of laws and proposals that cover allegedly insane defendants; it will be shown that this landscape is littered with diverse doctrines, terms, rules, and laws such that the picture of possible outcomes displays divergence and dissonance, calamity and contradiction. I will argue that what is needed is a unifying doctrine, where, to paraphrase Fingarette and Hasse (1979), (p. 8), the basic concepts are simple, coherent, and powerful.

To begin, let us put ourselves in the place of an attorney defending an allegedly insane client. What is our strategy? Depending on the country, state, or jurisdiction we are in, our defense may be based on "automatism," "involuntariness," "unconsciousness," "diminished mental capacity," "absence of specific intent," "involuntariness due to addiction," "infanticide," or just plain old "insanity." Let us take, as our example and client, Esther Griggs, who threw her baby through a window. She claimed (Walker, 1968) "that she had been dreaming that her little boy had said that the house was on fire, and that what she had done was with the view of preserving her children from being burnt to death."

We could argue this case many ways. We might opt for "automatism," arguing that she was acting under the influence of stimuli independent of conscious control. Under "involuntariness," we can argue that her act was not properly an "act" but analogous to a reflexive chain of behaviors ungoverned by her will or thinking. Under "unconsciousness," we could argue that there was "will," "intention," and "action" *of a sort*, but that they were cut off from her conscious mind and from reality. Under "diminished capacity," we could claim that she wasn't a fully responsible actor. Under the "absence of specific intent" plea, we could argue that she never intended to harm or kill her child. If she had been drinking before she fell asleep and hence to dream, we could make a case for "involuntariness due to addiction." If the infant was less than 1 year old, and if some degree of depression was noted in Esther, we could invoke "infanticide." And finally, we could argue that she was "insane."

Depending on the strategy we select, our argument may be (1) that no charge should be brought because no criminal act occurred (which is what happened); (2) that the *actus reus* cannot be established; (3) that the *mens rea* is lacking; or (4) that the *mens* is diminished or absent. Each strategy could yield a different outcome: (1) the charges may be dropped and the defendant set free; (2) the accused may be acquitted and freed because the *actus reus* had not been proved beyond a reasonable doubt; (3) the accused may be set free because the *mens rea* element had not been proved; (4) the person may be found "not guilty by reason of insanity" and set free, or sent for psychiatric evaluation, or sent directly to a psychiatric hospital; (5) the accused may be found "guilty of a lesser crime and sent to prison; (6) the accused may be found "guilty" but with "diminished capacity" and sent to prison, or a psychiatric facility, or first one and then the other. If she is incarcerated, the length of incarceration, be it in prison or a hospital, could vary considerably, as could the ultimate release decision.

We have by no means exhausted the options and outcomes that are possible under the current hodgepodge of laws and defenses. My own judgment is that this current condition is both bewildering and unwholesome, with the need for a unifying, coherent, and simpler doctrine becoming painfully apparent. What follows is an examination and critique of possible alternatives for dealing with the insanity defense: (1) strict liability, (2) abolition of the insanity defense, (3) *mens rea* proposals, (4) Lady Wootton's proposal, (5) H. L. A. Hart's proposal, and (6) fine-tuning the NGRI. In the next subsection, proposals for dealing with partial insanity will be reviewed. The question is "Which approach best meets the *unifying, coherent,* and *simple* criteria?"

STRICT LIABILITY

The "strict liability" proposal, while simple, is far from unifying or coherent. When we limit the purview to whether the defendant's actions caused the proscribed harm and limit the juror's inferences to what a reasonable man might ascribe, we indeed simplify the case, but we sacrifice an important principle—one that affords the defendant every opportunity to defeat the charge and prove his or her innocence. If the defense is restrained by law from presenting materially relevant *mens rea* or *mens* matters, our highly regarded principle of a full and fair trial is scuttled, and a defendant's life or liberty is lost beneath the sea of conviction. Once the floodgates of strict liability are turned on, mental elements will be shut off and ruled immaterial and irrelevant; under these conditions, the insanity defense will be only one of many defenses that is washed away. The damage from such a solution would be excessive and the price to pay intolerable.

ABOLISHING THE INSANITY DEFENSE

Abolishing the insanity defense also appears as a simple solution; but what this position has that strict liability doesn't is a greater number of supporters. Unlike the "strict liability" proponents, the abolitionist advocates seek to effect and eliminate only one defense, the insanity defense. But on principled grounds, we should ask the advocates for a justification for this singular treatment of insanity. On legal grounds, we should ask if this is sound. And on pragmatic grounds, we should question whether it is likely to work as advertised.

I don't find a compelling principled reason for the elimination of the insanity defense. Other excusing conditions, like that which excuses infants and children under 7, remain in place, resting, presumably, on good reasons; but now we choose not to apply or connect those good reasons to the singular case of insanity. For Isaac Ray, the failure or inability to connect "in mind" the general rule to the particular case was itself the essence of insanity.

On legal grounds, according to Judge Gerber (1984), "Washington and Mississippi are the only jurisdictions that have faced the constitutional issues squarely." In both states, the highest courts ruled that eliminating the insanity defense was unconstitutional, as it violates due process. The courts

> reasoned that sanity is a condition precedent to the capacity to form intent; it is therefore an essential element of guilt. Due process requires that when the issue of a defendant's insanity is raised the jury find the defendant sane at the time of the charged offense in order to return a guilty verdict. (p. 84)

As an expedient solution, this pragmatic *dissociation* (and elimination) of insanity from the rest of the excusing conditions is bound to run into problems. Defense attorneys who believe their clients to be insane are not likely to drop their best defense just because lawmakers, by legislative fiat, have made the insanity defense "out of bounds"; rather, they are likely to smuggle this defense in, using one of the other options, such as "automatism," "involuntariness," or "unconsciousness." If counsel is prevented in the *mens rea* phase of the trial from arguing for insanity, he or she can simply argue his or her case in the *actus reus* phase, challenging the prosecution's claim that an "act" occurred.

In a 1978 Illinois case, *People v. Grant,* an epileptic defendant was convicted of aggravated battery and obstructing a police officer. The defense raised only the insanity defense, with a witness, a physician, testifying that "the defendant was experiencing a psychomotor seizure at the time he struck the police officer, and that the defendant lacked the substantial capacity to appreciate the criminality of his conduct or to conform his conduct to the requirements of law" (Hermann, 1983, p. 107). The Supreme Court, in its review of the case, ruled that the defense was "entitled to raise the defense of lack of a voluntary act as well." The Court stated

> Similarly, the insanity defense exculpates a person whose volition is so impaired during a state of automatism that he is substantially incapable of conforming his conduct to the law. To that extent, the defense of involuntary conduct and the insanity defense are alternative theories at the disposal of a defendant whose volition to control or prevent his conduct is at issue. (pp. 558–559)

This is the third string of the bow that I referred to earlier.

I have a number of objections to the abolitionist's pragmatic solution, which, in general, boil down to the opinion that the solution simply won't work. To spell out the particulars, I believe that the insanity defense will be played out, but in a disguised form. If it is played out during the *actus reus* phase, as the Illinois Supreme Court states it could, the outcome, if successful, would be acquittal; this is decidedly *not* what the abolitionists had intended. Another possibility, which I don't find heartening in the least, is trying the case as something other than what it appears to be: for example, taking a case where the charge would be first-degree murder and where the question of insanity exists and trying the case as voluntary or involuntary manslaughter. Yet another disagreeable possibility is that an increase in plea bargaining will result. When the prosecution reduces the charges, both the "true charges" and the issue of insanity get distorted. I believe that this practice subverts justice and increases society's disrespect for the law. I, for one, would rather see a courtroom version of *Hamlet* played out—Did he premeditate, deliberate, and with malice aforethought kill the King? Or was he insane?—than witness *Hamlet* done as *A Comedy of Errors*.

MENS REA PROPOSALS

As illustrative of the *mens rea* proposals for handling insanity, I will present the formulations of Judge Gerber (1984) and Norval Morris (1982). What Judge Gerber recommends and defends is that "any and all special statutory tests for determining insanity" be abolished.

> In its place, insanity evidence should simply be admissible to the extent, if any, that it disproves the statutory mental state defining the crime that the defendant is being charged with; that is, to the extent that it disproves intent, knowledge, recklessness, or negligence.
>
> The abolition of a specific test language offends neither the Constitution nor case law as long as *mens rea* remains. . . . Such a device would reinsert the insanity defense into its proper historical context prior to *M'Naghten* and, at the same time, relate it properly to the narrowly defined Model Penal Code definitions of *mens rea*. From a medical standpoint, the abolition of all test language would recognize two things: first, the fact that insanity is not a rigid state but a matter of fluctuation in insight; and secondly, the fact that any legal test of insanity incorporating medical concepts is thereby limited to passing medical ideology and is therefore unable to accommodate changing theories of illness.
>
> No statement of a rule permitting relevant evidence of mental defect or disease on the issue of *mens rea* should be required. Relevant evidence on the mental element of a crime is already clearly admissible. A clear statement of the role of insanity evidence is required, however, to insure that the traditional tests do not survive and to indicate that such evidence relates only to the special *mens rea* requirement at the time of the criminal act. (pp. 85–86)

Norval Morris (1982) puts it concisely: the "ordinary *mens rea* principle can well carry the freight" (p. 65).

But can it? I do not believe so. Gerber (1984) takes up the case of delusion, but he fails to take it far enough to confront "the Hadfield problem." He states that delusions "disprove *mens rea* directly on its own terms, not via reference to insanity, because the intent and knowledge requirements of *mens rea* are not satisfied . . ." (p. 59). Gerber goes on to illustrate this point by using an oft-repeated but rarely seen example of an actor who kills his wife while thinking he is squeezing a lemon. Since he did not know that it was his wife, and did not intend to kill, "these factors directly disprove the existence of *mens rea* and result in an innocence claim for that reason alone, not because of any reference to insanity."

But what if the actor did know it was his wife, and did intend to kill her—*because of deluded thinking?* This is "the Hadfield problem," and this type of delusional thinking is more common and problematic than the lemon-squeezing variation. It is this type of delusional thinking that appears in *Hinckley* as well. Gerber's *mens rea* position cannot carry this freight. Neither can Morris's version, although Morris acknowledges the problem. Regarding this type of delusional defendant, who believes "he is commanded by God to kill, as Hadfield and some others believed. . . . He probably does not fall within any *mens rea* provisions . . ." (p. 69).

What Morris recommends to handle these admittedly problematic cases is to treat and sentence such cases as manslaughter instead of murder, and he cites the English Homicide Act of 1957 as a way of legislatively achieving that end. But this recommendation appears more expedient than sound. It creates a version of diminished responsibility, or partial insanity, to handle such an insane defendant. It perverts and changes the charge, since the case is not manslaughter; from the prosecution's point of view, the case is one of first-degree murder. To use Morris's (1982) words, I do not think this is "a sensible use of prosecutorial discretion" (p. 72).

These *mens rea* proposals are simple and unifying, but they fail to coherently deal with insanity. They miss the deeper *mens* problem that exists apart from *mens rea*. Furthermore, as in Morris's recommendation, they open the door to partial insanity without adequate justifications, and leave far too much room for discretion, be it the prosecutor's discretion in creating a new crime or the judge's discretion in sentencing such a crime. Both types of discretion are likely to lead to lead to disparate handling and sentencing of similar crimes, and when that happens, "equal justice" typically loses, and disrespect for the law increases.

LADY WOOTTON'S PROPOSAL

Lady Barbara Wootton (1959) has offered her own proposal for dealing with the insanity defense. Lady Wootton favors a forward-looking, rather than a backward-looking, solution: she proposes that we abandon the concepts of responsibility, culpability, and *mens rea* during the trial phase and decide the guilt–innocence question on the basis of fact; then, after the judgment is rendered, society should decide, using *mens rea* and psychiatric recommendations among others, what is the best course of action for that individual and for society. Instead of focusing on moral guilt and retribution, she would like us to deal with social management, deterrence, and rehabilitation issues. In effect, her proposal abolishes the insanity defense, since mental elements and the question of responsibility would be moot under her schema. The mental elements and the question of responsibility become germane only after the verdict, when sentencing is taken up. Under this curious proposal, then, insanity may end up being a mitigating or moderating factor with regard to the sentence, but it would not exculpate a defendant as it does under the traditional format.

Some background is necessary before critiquing Wootton's proposal. Wootton does not believe that mental health professionals can reliably define mental health or ill-health "in objective scientific terms that are free of subjective moral judgments" (1959, p. 227). "It follows," she writes, "that we have no reliable criterion by which to distinguish the sick from the healthy mind." She remains suspicious of psychoanalytic claims that reliable diagnosis of unconscious motives can be made, but only by those . . .

> who have themselves been psychoanalytically trained. It follows, therefore, that, if this criterion were used, the distinction between those who could, and those who could not, be held responsible for their misdeeds could only be drawn by trained psychoanalysts. In the present climate of opinion there is no sign that psychoanalysts enjoy the public's confidence to a degree which gives any expectation that they might be entrusted with virtually the last word on what may be a matter of life and death. (p. 236)

Wootton's proposal not only bars the psychological expert from having the last word, it also prevents the expert from having any word on motives unconscious or unconscionable, since motives are irrelevant under her adjudicative schema.

But this curious proposal may produce even "curiouser" results. For in the sentencing phase, where motives, responsibility, and mental states are to be considered, the psychological expert is likely to have the first word, the most important word, and perhaps, the last word on the matter. Let us say that the expert decides that the now guilty defendant no longer poses a danger to society and is no longer in need of treatment; thus, since on neither preventive nor rehabilitative grounds is there reason for keeping him or her incarcerated in any facility, outright and immediate release is recommended. The opposite result may also occur. A defendant who might have been either acquitted or sentenced to a minimal term under traditional procedures might now be kept indefinitely, and interminably, because a mental health expert believes this to be best for the defendant-turned-patient and/or society. The irony is that the mental health professional ultimately may have the final word under Wootton's proposal!

Moreover, to create an effective forward-looking system, we would have to have experts to assess whether the individual needs education or therapy or both, and whether society needs protecting. To determine if someone is amenable to therapy, we would have to consider whether this person is, and was, responsible. As Wasserstrom (1967) puts it, Lady Wootton's proposal "is founded upon a false hope," for "if the therapy or reform imposed on an offender is to be even rationally selected, it is obvious . . . that we cannot avoid seeking to determine what his state of mind was at the time he violated the law" (p. 120).

Lady Wootton's proposal fails for a number of reasons. It fails, like "strict liability" does, because it exempts evidence regarding mental elements during the trial phase when they ought to be considered. It fails, like the "abolitionist" position does, because it does not recognize that insanity and the mental elements are likely to be raised during the *actus reus* phase. And it fails, because unlike its hopes, it places undue and undeserved authority in the hands of the experts who were supposed to have less influence under her schema. Rather than advancing us into a forward-looking future, this proposal returns us to the early days of the nineteenth century, when the recommendations of the alienists upset, if not overturned, the court's justice. The question of responsibility needs to be faced, not finessed; under Lady Wootoon's proposal, the question is not answered because it is not even raised. The public, the courts, and defendants are ill served by avoiding the central question of whether this defendant is responsible for his or her actions; furthermore, giving the responsibility issue, which properly belongs to the courts and juries, to mental health professionals, educators, and social engineers, presages a paternalistic, therapeutic state (Kittrie, 1971) that has already been tried, and found wanting.

H. L. A. HART'S PROPOSAL

H. L. A. Hart has carefully considered Lady Wootton's ideas, and while he has been critical of some parts of her proposal, the thought of putting adjudication and sentencing on some basis other than retribution appeals to him. In putting forth his own proposal, he "seeks to develop and defend a middle position" on the punishment–treatment issue. But the scheme he comes up with seems "to commit him to a position even more radical than that of Wootton's" (Wasserstrom, 1967, pp. 112–113).

First, I will express Hart's (1964) misgivings. He is disturbed by Wootton's "strict liability" approach that the "proof of the outward act alone is enough to make the accused liable to compulsory measures of treatment or *punishment*" (pp. 21–22). Hart insists on the *moral* importance of legal excuses, because they "help to assure that we will not punish those persons who did not, in some meaningful fashion, intend or choose to do the action proscribed by law" (Wasserstrom, 1967, p. 115). Thus, even if you take, as Wootton does, a preventive orientation and incarcerate individuals in hospitals or other "places of safety" for the good of society and the betterment of the individual, such a step, since it involves a deprivation of liberty, requires a justification. And Hart does not find a satisfactory justification for Wootton's proposal.

On sociological and political levels, someone like Thomas Szasz (1970) would bristle at the idea of hospitalization and "places of safety" being viewed as treatment as opposed to punishment: when people are incarcerated involuntarily, says Szasz, they are being imprisoned and punished. While Hart, too, has a "sociological doubt" concerning Wootton's proposal, it is his moral objection that is most incisive. According to Hart, an accused has a right not to be used (for the benefit of society or his or her own betterment) unless the accused could have avoided doing what he or she did.

Given his misgivings and criticisms of Wootton's proposal, I find his own proposal all the more dumbfounding, for, in the words of Wasserstrom (1917), "Hart has virtually gone over to Lady Wootton's camp" (p. 124). Hart terms his proposal a "moderate" form of the elimination of responsibility. To quote Hart (1964):

> Under this scheme *mens rea* would continue to be a necessary condition for liability to be investigated and settled before conviction *except so far as it relates to mental abnormality*. The innovation would be that an accused person would no longer be able to adduce any form of mental abnormality as a bar to conviction. The question of his mental abnormality would under this scheme be investigated only after conviction and would be primarily concerned with his present rather than his past mental state. His past mental state at the time of his crime would only be relevant so far as it provided ancillary evidence of the nature of his abnormality and indicated the appropriate treatment. (pp. 24–25)

I find Hart's proposal, in some ways, more extreme than Wootton's, and all the more astounding because the author is H. L. A. Hart. He is the one who insists that we should hold someone responsible for acts of negligence; he is the one who argued, on moral grounds, for excusing conditions. Yet here he takes a position that nullifies only the insanity excuse. By removing the issue of responsibility from an insanity question, he, in effect, turns the matter into a "strict liability" judgment with palliative treatment to follow. So-called "palliative treatment" will not soothe a defendant who was not responsible (because of mental abnormality) when he or she committed the offense, but who was convicted anyway under Hart's proposal.

Whereas Wootton's proposal is similar to the "strict liability" position, Hart's proposal is similar to the abolitionist's position. Hart's proposal is thus subject to the same criticisms that were directed at the abolitionist position. Again, this exclusion of an insanity defense will not make the problem go away; rather, it will encourage the use of alternative defenses and special pleas that not only mask the true issue and muddle the law, but produce undesirable outcomes. If Hart is still in favor of not convicting someone who did not *voluntarily* act, then he is inviting defense attorneys to play out the insanity drama under the guise of *actus reus*. This position is not simplifying, coherent, or powerful; above all, it is not justifiable.

Summarizing to this point, the five positions previously considered (e.g., strict liability, abolition, *mens rea*, Wootton's, and Hart's) all, in different ways, eliminate insanity as a separate excusing condition. With the exception of the *mens rea* proposals, the other four remove the central question of responsibility from consideration prior to conviction. This, I believe, is not the way to go. We will next consider other alternatives that, at a minimum, seek to retain the insanity defense in either restricted, expanded, or modified form.

Fine-Tuning the NGRI

Under this subheading I've grouped a number of proposals for retaining the insanity defense but with procedural or substantive changes. As to procedural changes, proposals for changing the burden of proof (i.e., typically, to the defense) and proposals that would restrict the role and testimony of the psychological experts have been made. As to substantive changes, proposals for eliminating the "irresistible impulse" test, for returning to the M'Naghten "right from wrong" test, and for restricting the meaning of insanity to something akin to the "wild beast" have been put forth.

One general objection I have to fine-tuning approaches is that they seem, in the main, to ignore history's lessons. Another objection is that they do not deal comprehensively and in a unifying way with the hodge-podge of defenses and pleas currently available. And finally, they fail to deal with the historic question of partial insanity and the current issue of guilty but mentally ill.

For procedures and particulars, I am not opposed to switching the burden of proof to the defense. However, I am opposed to a purely pragmatic switch done simply to make it more difficult for an insanity defense to succeed. A more satisfactory reason, developed earlier in this chapter, is based on the view of insanity in terms of *mens,* rather than *mens rea;* in the former view, the defense must show that the normal assumption of a response-able actor does not apply. The role and extent of expert testimony will be taken up more fully in subsequent chapters; for now, it is enough to say that I believe the expert has something to offer, but it is neither the last nor the final word.

When we switch to the substantive fine-tuning proposals, I believe most miss the forest for the trees: they focus on an aspect of insanity, but miss the essence. For example, the volitional test of insanity (the "irresistible impulse") has been in dispute since the day it was proposed. Besides the not inconsiderable problem of differentiating impulses that are irresistible from those that the individual simply fails to resist, the dispute also centers on whether impulse control is the essence of insanity or merely a symptom. My own view coincides with that of Fingarette and Hasse, where the essence and problem of insanity involves *mens* and the response-able capacity to use the background-nexus. The truly insane individual may display irresistible impulses or may not; his or her actions may look irresponsible or they may not; but the central question remains, "Was he or she response-able?"

The problem with eliminating the irresistible impulse criterion of insanity, as I see it, is what remains. Typically, it is some version of the knowledge test, be it M'Naghten or the American Law Institute's version, as is the case in the Insanity Defense Reform Act of 1984. But from the response-able view of insanity, "knowledge," "will," and "control" are only aspects or possible symptoms of insanity, rather than its essence. Some proposals tinker with words, repeating anew the historical tinkering attempts that were tried and found wanting. We can chop and prune trees, but that approach does not guarantee that we have found the right forest.

Former Attorney General Smith's approach (i.e., "did not even know he had a gun in his hand or thought that he was shooting at a tree") pares away M'Naghten's knowledge criterion of insanity; what is left resembles the "wild beast" test of 1723, in that distorted awareness and perception become the criteria. But where does all this historical pruning leave us? In effect, it leaves us with an insanity test that fits no one. To illustrate, what sort of individual would fit Smith's description? That person would have to be profoundly disturbed in the area of perception, thinking, judgment, affect, and control. There are individuals, at times, who are actively psychotic with that degree of disturbance: some individuals on drugs such as PCP, others suffering from delirium, or others brought through emergency commitment procedures to a hospital might fit the Attorney General's description. But his description does not fit most current and historic cases of insanity. It certainly doesn't fit or solve "the Hadfield problem." Hadfield's attorney, Erskine, riddled the logic of the "wild beast" test, and his points would similarly puncture former Attorney General Smith's proposal (see Chapter 1).

In trying to restrict the insanity defense, the administration's proposal turns out to be a *de facto* elimination: "*de facto*" because the excuse exists without anyone to use it. This proposal, like the *mens rea* proposals, goes too far, I believe, for it would convict those who were not response-able but who nonetheless possessed enough wherewithal to know a gun from a lemon and a man from a tree.

PARTIAL INSANITY

"Partial insanity" may be described as the issue that won't go away, no matter how much we wish it would. To the opponents and critics of the

THE ESSENCE OF INSANITY

insanity defense, partial insanity is Pandora's box, *sans* hope: it opens the door of insanity to labyrinthine corridors, and from there, toward maddening deadends. On the other side of the aisle, there are those who believe that the partial insanity issue not only can be dealt with, but must be dealt with for the total picture of insanity to fall into sensible order. In between are those who favor an insanity defense in some form, but who remain opposed to partial insanity on principled or practical grounds. These middle grounders continue to maintain the legal position of Bracton, Coke, and Hale, a position that has become tradition by virtue of repetition.

But the traditional position has been cracking on both sides of the Atlantic, and from these gaps and fissures have sprung partial insanity progeny. The traditionalists are challenged to articulate *justifications*, not just history, in favor of aborting. The proponents of partial insanity progeny are similarly challenged to justify the birth and development of this line. We turn, in this section, to an examination of partial insanity progeny and to the arguments for and against.

In today's climate, the debate centers on those proposals for a "Guilty But Mentally Ill" (GBMI) option, a "diminished responsibility" or "diminished capacity" defense, and Fingarette and Hasse's "Disability of Mind" (DOM) doctrine, which includes a "partial DOM" verdict. The critics ask, "What legitimate purpose is served by giving the jury the option of returning a guilty but mentally ill verdict?" Peter Arenella (1983), who asked the question before a House of Representatives Subcommittee on Criminal Justice, answers his own query:

> All of the problems endemic to the insanity defense remain. Moreover, a special verdict of GBMI is not needed to ensure that the defendant who unsuccessfully raises the insanity defense will receive appropriate treatment because he can present evidence of present mental abnormality at the sentencing stage. Finally, giving the jury the GBMI alternative raises the distinct possibility that juries will avoid confronting the difficult question of whether it is just to hold the offender criminally responsible by returning a "compromise" GBMI verdict. I suspect that the GBMI verdict proposal is actually designed to assuage the public's legitimate concern over the possibility that dangerous defendants who are acquitted will be released prematurely from mental hospitals. Concerns about social control may justify reforms which would rationalize post-acquittal procedures. They do not justify convicting persons who were not responsible for their acts and sentencing them to a term of punishment based on culpability that is not present. (p. 118)

Before dealing with Arenella's critique point-by-point, a brief historical sojourn is in order to develop the rationale for a partial insanity verdict. Two seventeenth-century jurists, the Englishman Sir Matthew Hale and the Scotsman Sir George Mackenzie of Rosehough ("the Bluidy Mackenzie"), proposed different approaches regarding partial insanity (see Chapter 1). Hale acknowledged that there was "partial insanity of mind" but believed that such a person ordinarily has the understanding of a child of 14 (the age of discretion), and therefore that individual should be judged to be responsible. Thus, Hale reserved exculpation for the totally insane individual only.

To understand Mackenzie's position, let us start with his departure from historic and contemporary thinking: the issue is "temporary insanity." To Bracton, in the thirteenth century, a person who was temporarily insane could not make a legal contract. To Sir Edward Coke, "temporary insanity" would excuse the person from culpability *only if* the insanity was "total." Hale, too, adopts this position. But Mackenzie departs from this historic line of thinking and draws a connection between "temporary" and "partial" insanity. The linkage can be understood if we consider cyclical disorders, such as manic–depressive psychoses. In this disorder, we may see an individual who, during either a manic or depressive episode, may meet the "total" insanity criterion, but who, during a lucid interval, would not. If such a person, during the lucid interval, signed a contract, it would be valid, and if he or she committed a crime during a lucid interval would be held responsible.

Mackenzie takes a different view in that he considers fury "a sticking disease" (*morbus durabilis*): by this he means that even though the individual is in a lucid moment, the *disease process* is still operating. In short, the disease is different from its symptoms, and that even when symptoms are not manifested, the disease process nonetheless continues. Isn't it likely, he would ask, that the disease process affects, distorts, debilitates one's response-ability to some degree? In his own words (Walker, 1968), "for where madness has once disordered the judgment, and more where it recurs often, it cannot but leave some weakness, and make a man an unfit judge of what he ought to do . . ." (p. 139). He then proceeds to make his recommendation and case for "diminished responsibility":

> It may be argued that since the law grants a total impunity to such as are absolutely furious therefore it should by the rule of proportions lessen and moderate the punishments of such, as though they are not absolutely mad yet are Hypochondrick and Melancholy to such a degree, that it clouds their reasons. . . . (p. 139)

Modern commentators remain divided as to whether the law can and ought to grade responsibility and culpability and therefore proportion punishment based on degrees of mental impairment. The arguments, on both sides, raise logical, legal, psychological, and practical points. On the negative side, there is Lady Wootton (1960), whose views and proposals on insanity have already been presented. As for partial insanity, or diminished responsibility, she takes a dim view. For psychological experts to try to assess *diminished* responsibility "is not a matter of scientific inference, but a sheer act of faith" (p. 232). Rather than illuminating the defendant's psyche and shedding light on the court's and jury's shadowy considerations, the psychological expert, instead, makes "an enormous leap in the dark; a leap in fact from science to philosophy" (p. 230). Her conclusion as to partial insanity is the same as she reaches for insanity proper. "But on these issues neither logic nor common sense, neither science nor philosophy, can give firm answers. Behavior is observable: culpability, I submit, is not—unless by God" (p. 235). And her recommendation is the same:

> Ultimately, therefore, as I see it, there is no solution except that of allowing the concept of responsibility to wither away. . . . In this way, and only in this way, can all the contradictions be resolved, and all the unanswerable questions be avoided. Forget responsibility, and psychiatrists need no longer masquerade as moralists, but can return to their proper role of applied scientists analyzing causes, predicting developments and indicating methods of control. Forget responsibility and we can ask not whether an offender *ought* to be punished, but whether . . . he is likely to benefit from punishment. (p. 239)

I think Lady Wootton is wrong in her conclusion and contradictory in her recommendation. The concept of responsibility is central and essential to the law and to the community's retributive sentiment that punishment match the crime; and the crime is inextricably bound to intentions, culpability, and responsibility. Her hope for "firm answers" cannot be met, if she means by that phrase a guaranteed truth. But can it really ever be met in any case? Her alternative, behavioristic and simple, commits us to different errors and, in my opinion, more serious and frequent errors: instead of making fine discriminations as to responsibility and culpability, as an insanity or partial insanity doctrine commits us to do, Lady Wootton's proposition commits us to see an alleged criminal act only one way. And in her recommendation, where psychiatrists can return to their applied scientific task, we then ask them, after the verdict, to aid us with the partially insane defendant in determining if he or she could benefit from punishment. But to do just that, they must peer and leap into the defendant's dark interior. Again, Wootton's proposal asks them to do, after the verdict, what she is opposed to them doing before the verdict.

Richard Sparks (1964) is also against grading responsibility and mitigating punishment. He claims in his analysis that we cannot simply deduce from an appraisal of an accused's general mental impairment how much responsibility and culpability are present; yet he believes we can deduce this "in those few cases in which he is deranged as to be completely incapable of rationally controlling his conduct in any way" (p. 16). But it is not a matter of *deduction* in either the total or partial insanity instance. To expect deductions is to expect too much here. The relationship between mental illness and responsibility in particular, and between psychological and legal concepts in general, is not of the order of geometric proofs or logical syllogisms. Psychological experts who profess, and jurors who decide, make inferences, not deductions.

While acknowledging that mental illness comes in gradations, Sparks wishes, however, to maintain that responsibility is either all or none. Yet, he is aware that there are cases, like provocation, where "we say that the accused was 'less than fully responsible for his crime,' and merely mitigate or reduce his punishment accordingly . . ." (p. 17). While he argues that provocation is "in fact very different" from diminished responsibility, his argument is weak. He argues that in provocation we have "objective situations," whereas in diminished responsibility due to some degree of mental illness we have internal, subjective, unassessable factors. However, when we find someone guilty of a lesser crime because of provocation, we are making a judgment of blame. We are saying that no matter what the provocations were, we expect people to restrain themselves, "cool their blood," find a safer option, interpret the situation differently, etc: we are saying that their internal perceptions, interpretations, emotions, thoughts, judgments, and reactions could have been, and should have been, different from those that led to a criminal act. Provocation cases are not, as Sparks would have it, solely a matter of objective situational factors; in fact, internal factors are the most relevant when a jury brings in a guilty verdict.

Sparks makes a further point against "mitigation based on mental impairment": he claims that it "makes no sense on *any* coherent theory of punishment . . ." (p. 21). The only theory he notes (in a footnote) is utilitarian theory. He seems to have overlooked *retribution*.

George Dix (1971) offers some reasons for grading offenses.

> First, doctrinal consistency demands it. The law requires defined states of mind. If psychological abnormality of some type is logically inconsistent with these states of mind, fairness and logic demand that such abnormality be the subject of legal investigation. Second, psychological abnormality bears on "personal turpitude," and the law, if it is to maintain the community's respect, must grade its condemnation according to the moral turpitude of the offender as the community evaluates it. The need to have criminal law accurately express community condemnation therefore requires this investigation . . . Finally, formally recognizing the relevance of psychological abnormality would amount to a realistic accommodation of the inevitable. Triers of fact will continue to be confronted with the formal all-or-nothing choice of insanity defense in cases where reasonable man would seek a compromise. Rather than ignore this situation, the law would best serve its goals if it recognized the relevance of the psychological abnormality short of insanity and used formal doctrine to assist the trier of fact in considering such abnormality in a manner most consistent with the objectives of the criminal law. (pp. 332–333)

Thus, the debate that started in the seventeenth century over partial insanity continues today. We now turn to particular attempts to deal with partial insanity. First, we will take up diminished responsibility and diminished capacity, and then we will look at the proposed "guilty but mentally ill" (GBMI) option.

THE ESSENCE OF INSANITY   267

Diminished Responsibility and Diminished Capacity

Two different, but related, models of dealing with partial insanity are "diminished responsibility" and "diminished capacity." "Diminished responsibility," the seventeenth-century brainchild of "the Bluidy Mackenzie," was conceived in Scotland and adopted by the English three centuries later in the Homicide Act of 1957. "Diminished capacity," California's offspring, germinated in stages, through three cases (*People v. Gorshen*, 1959; *People v. Wolff*, 1964; *People v. Ray*, 1975). Both models, through different methods, deal with the nettlesome problem of partial insanity, and, in the opinion of their advocates, architects, and progenitors, the progeny were doing quite nicely. To the critics, however, the verdict was quite different. As Peter Arenella (1977) sees it, diminished responsibility and diminished capacity were "two children of a doomed marriage" (p. 827). I will first present the positions, then the contention.

Diminished responsibility was the model Mackenzie created to lessen and moderate the punishments of the partially insane. Instead of just two choices—finding a partially insane defendant *guilty* of murder or *acquitting* on grounds of insanity—a third choice is created: in this case, the defendant is found guilty of *culpable homicide* (in some countries, it is called "murder with extenuating circumstances"). In its method, the diminished responsibility model lessens the punishment by formally reducing the charges. So instead of the crime of first-degree murder, we might find such a defendent guilty of manslaughter, as is done in England, or some such lesser crime. And the method is "formal" as opposed to "informal": in "informal" methods of mitigation, judges use their discretionary powers to lessen the severity of the punishment for first-degree murder, or a Home Secretary recommends mercy; in "formal" procedures, the legislature sets the crime and the sentence, although the sentence may be expressed in a range (e.g., 10 to 15 years), with some discretionary latitude reserved for the judge.

There is a similarity and a difference here between this Scottish-British diminished responsibility model and what Norval Morris proposes in his modified *mens rea* model: Morris recommends a diminished responsibility option for the Hadfield problem, which is a case of total insanity, but, as to partial insanity, he will let *mens rea* carry the freight; the Scottish-British version allows for total insanity acquittals (i.e., an NGRI option), yet also provides, in addition, a diminished responsibility option for cases of partial insanity.

As for diminished capacity, this model "admits all evidence tending to show that the defendant *was less capable* than an ordinary defendant of entertaining the requisite intent" (Arenella, 1977, p. 863). Arenella argues that this model evolved from the narrow confines of *mens rea* to a "broader and more amorphous view of *mens rea*" (p. 846), which, at times, comes closer to a consideration of *mens,* not just whether a defendant had a specific intent, but "why and how he had entertained it" (p. 843). In other cases, this model involves subtle discriminations among different intents, such as in the *Gorshen* case, where malice was judged to have been present, but not premeditation or deliberation. The result of these deeper and hazier penetrations into intentions ends up in an outcome identical to diminished responsibility—guilt, but for a lesser crime.

The contentious issues regarding both diminished responsibility and diminished capacity can be summarized in the following statements. These two alternative defenses: (1) invite unlimited psychiatric testimony; (2) call for too fine, and too subtle, and too subjective discriminations to be made; (3) will supplant the insanity defense; (4) deal formally with matters that should be addressed informally at sentencing, rather than during the trial; and (5) run into problems when no lower category of crime exists. I will present the views of Arenella, who raises all of these criticisms, contending that these two defenses "contain the seeds of their destruction" (p. 863), and who recommends that they be abolished. Arenella's views will, in turn, be critically assessed.

Regarding issue (1), Arenella believes that the diminished capacity defense "opens the courtroom doors to virtually unlimited psychiatric testimony" (p. 835). The same criticism can be leveled at diminished responsibility as well. Furthermore, the expert testimony is likely to range too far and wide of the specific intent, *mens rea* mark, and too deeply into unconscious motives as to how and why a defendant entertained certain thoughts and carried out certain actions. This open-door invitation, in Arenella's opinion, is likely to produce what the *Durham* product rule unfortunately did: technicalized psychiatric jargon and arcane explanations that do "not correlate with any specific statutory state of mind requirement" (p. 847). He predicts that "far from bridging the gap between criminal law and psychiatry, the diminished responsibility model merely accentuates the inevitable conflict between the two disciplines" (p. 831).

On principled grounds developed earlier in this chapter on the "essence of insanity," I have argued that we should move off the specific intent, *mens rea* question, because that is not the essence of insanity; and it is not the central issue for partial insanity either. Also, limitations can be placed on psychiatric testimony and conclusions (e.g., the ultimate question and the test question), and I plan, in the last chapter of this work, to do just that. Furthermore, it is hard to see greater conflict between the disciplines of law and psychiatry, given what has occurred during the last 150 years. It is also possible that a third option might produce greater harmony, for several reasons: for one, psychiatrists would testify on partial insanity knowing that the outcome will be treatment and some mitigation of punishment and that this will occur without them having to stretch and exaggerate their conclusions to make an exculpatory case; for another, defense attorneys do not have to stretch their cases to get treatment and a lesser punishment for their clients.

Regarding issue (2), Arenella believes that approaches that call for ever more fine, subtle, and subjective discriminations are not the way to go. Can we really discriminate malice from premeditation and both from deliberation? Under diminished capacity, might we arrive at a strange conclusion—that someone would be insane in general but sane for specific intent? Arenella asks, "Is this an illogical result? How can the defendant be insane, and therefore entitled for a complete defense, and yet not qualify for what is considered a "partial" defense?" (p. 834). And in the case of *People v. Ray*, Arenella notes that

> the court indicated its desire not to burden the diminished capacity doctrine with 'fine distinctions' but its ruling requires the jury to make an exceedingly subtle, if not impossible, distinction between the capacity to intend a specific harm and capacity to understand the nature and quality of one's acts. (p. 844)

These kind of fine, subtle distinctions are likely to push psychiatric testimony deeper into the subjective, psychic interior.

Arenella's points are worthy of consideration, yet they are most pertinent to the particular cases of diminished capacity and responsibility, *as they are codified and interpreted;* his points, however, are not damaging to *a third option in general.* A third option might be clearly articulated for partial insanity that does not involve "exceedingly subtle, if not impossible," distinctions. In large part, these subtle distinctions arise because the courts and the law are still wedded to *mens rea*, which Arenella upholds. But this approach has not worked, and, in turn, has spurred the courts to search for new options. Arenella's recommendation, that we abort these two children of a doomed marriage and return to *mens rea*, entraps us again in a doomed marriage. This, I believe, is neither the desired outcome nor the only recourse available.

Issue (3), that the third option will supplant the insanity defense and be the "easy way out," can be evaluated by turning to the available data to see if this is so. Walker (1968) presents figures on England's diminished responsibility "experiment" for a 6-year period following its inception, and compares this with the previous years where the third option did not exist. He states that

> the steady fall in both findings of "insane on arraignment" [incompetent to stand trial would be the U.S. equivalent] and findings of "guilty but insane" [not guilty by reason on insanity] has been compensated by verdicts of "diminished responsibility," *but no more.* (pp. 158–159)

Arenella cites the same data but his conclusions are stated differently:

> Although there is insufficient empirical data to prove convincingly that the diminished responsibility defense has supplanted the insanity defense in En-

gland, studies indicated that as the number of diminished responsibility claims have increased, the number of insanity pleas have decreased. (p. 854)

But this is what should occur if the third alternative is working! Cases that are truly partial insanity cases and not insanity instances can now be dealt with through the third option of diminished responsibility, rather than being forced to fit where they do not belong—as insanity cases. Interpreting the data differently, we could say that diminished responsibility has supplemented insanity, not supplanted it.

Regarding issue (4), that the third option deals formally with what should be addressed informally, I find Arenella arguing in a contradictory manner: in one instance he seems to be opposed to greater subjectivity, but in recommending informal mitigation (i.e., judicial discretion), he is proposing a highly subjective, individualized approach that has been loudly condemned as leading to very disparate sentences for similar offenses. Advocates of the Desert Model (von Hirsch & Hanrahan, 1979) and the Modified Desert Model (Monahan, 1982) oppose unfettered discretion in setting sentence length. Monahan believes that formally fixing a sentence, "which allows some role to such crime control devices as predictions of recidivism" (p. 103), is likely to produce more equal justice to defendants and to potential victims than would an informal system where each judge could set the sentence. The informal system, by comparison, is far more subjective and variable than a formal one. A formal system created by statute and by legislators directly answerable to the citizenry would be my preference over an informal system controlled by individual judges who are appointed, and, perhaps, less attuned or more immune to the wishes of the populace.

Arenella (1977), it would seem, wishes for less subjectivity on partial insanity criteria, but commits himself to greater subjectivity in applying mitigation through sentencing. What criteria would judges be using? Would they be the same for each case? For each judge? And would we ever know? His fear that a formal treatment of partial insanity would weaken "the criminal laws' social control function" (p. 850) and foster "an irrational, individualized decision-making process" (p. 857) is far more likely to come to pass under his recommendations for informal sentencing.

Issue (5) is that the "diminished defenses" run into problems when no lower category of crime can be found. This is a problem, as Arenella rightly points out. If the crime is attempted robbery, for example, and we find grounds for partial insanity, what is the next lower charge? We run the danger, here, of finding or creating a charge that does not fit the crime. The case of Dan White (the Twinkie defense) is an example. To the citizenry of San Francisco who rioted following Dan White's conviction and sentencing, a verdict of guilt for "voluntary manslaughter" seemed to make no sense, and a sentence of seven years, eight months, minus time in jail before trial, with one third off for good behavior, seemed incredibly light. Evidence brought forth during the trial indicated that Dan White had motives (malice) for killing the Mayor, George Moscone, and Supervisor Harvey Milk; there was more than enough time for White's "blood to cool"; and his actions seemed planned and purposeful. To those who were outraged at the verdict and sentence, this seemed to be a case of first-degree murder—with malice, deliberation, and premeditation—yet the court comes in with a verdict (e.g., "voluntary manslaughter") that does not fit the crime.

There is another way to go than down: an alternative other than lowering the crime to deal with partial insanity is possible, and I will present that possibility in the next chapter, when we take up Fingarette and Hasse's (1979) "Disability of Mind" doctrine. For now, and to summate, the two children—diminished responsibility and diminished capacity—have problems. But the problems Arenella raises are with *the way* the third option is conceived and carried out in these two diminished models, *not* with the reasoning behind a third option. I do not believe that he has made his case for aborting the third option and returning to *mens rea;* rather, he has raised some substantial problems that a third option would need to overcome.

GBMI

In reviewing the testimony given before House (1983, 1984) and Senate committees (1982, 1983), it is hard to find anyone who did not express an opinion about the "guilty but mentally ill" verdict. Some opinions were favorable, but most were not. Those who were opposed to GBMI, in one form or another, believed that it was "an idea whose time should not have come" (Slobogin, 1985). But come it has.

Instead of reviewing each and every form of a "guilty but mentally ill" or "guilty but insane" defense, I will present, rather, the issues, questions, and criticisms a "GB" defense ought to address, answer, and rebut for this alternative to be workable. The following four broad questions serve to organize the issues and criticisms to be taken up: (1) Is the "guilty but . . ." defense a contradiction in terms, a euphemism for abolishing the insanity defense, or a transparent facade for treatment? In short, is it something other than what its advocates proclaim? (2) What should be the criteria for a GB defense? (3) How is GB differentiable from NGRI (not guilty by reason of insanity) and from guilty? (4) What are, and what should be, the consequences following a GB verdict?

The "contradiction in terms" criticism was stated by Robinson (1982b), who called the "guilty but insane" (GBI) option "oxymoronic." His point being that the term "insane," as it has been used and understood through centuries of legal discourse, has been associated with a "not guilty" verdict. It is contradiction, then, to have an option that proclaims, in its first word, "guilty," but, through its third word, "insane," unites "guilty" to "not guilty" in one verdict. To the critics, GBI does violence, through apparent ignorance, to years of jurisprudential understanding.

This criticism is less substantial than it sounds; in fact, it is simply semantic. If we call it "guilty but mentally ill" (GBMI) instead of "guilty but insane" (GBI), the criticism evaporates. But this "word juggling" rebuttal is more than just that. The term "mentally ill" reflects more accurately than "insane" the psychological point to be made—that mental illness comes in shades and degrees, and thus responsibility and culpability can be graded. Morris (1982) makes this point when he writes:

> Choice is neither present nor absent in the typical case where the insanity defense is currently pleaded; what is at issue is the degree of freedom of choice on a continuum from the hypothetically entirely rational to the hypothetically pathologically determined—in states of consciousness neither polar condition exists. (p. 61)

We have no problem with the idea of gradations of responsibility when we rank order and punish negligence, recklessness, and premeditation differently. In an analogous way, the advocate of a third option claims that a GBMI defendant is more responsible than a NGRI plaintiff, but less culpable than a defendant found "guilty"; furthermore, the advocate maintains, the law needs to see shades of gray, for that is the "psychological reality" of things, instead of only seeing black or white, sane or insane. Jurists like "the Bluidy Mackenzie" and James Fitzjames Stephen saw neither a problem nor a contradiction here. Nor do I.

Some critics however, see red, and suspect ruse, when the GBMI option is raised. In his prepared statement before the Senate Judiciary Hearings on the insanity defense, Randolph Read (1982) wrote, "The alternative verdict of 'guilty but mentally ill' has been, without a doubt, the most brilliant stroke yet by those who oppose the insanity defense" (p. 67). To this critic, and others like him, there is the suspicion (bordering on conviction) that the advocates of the GBMI option are really abolitionists in disguise. Instead of making a frontal assault on NGRI directly, the GBMI proponents are suspected of seeking to topple NGRI through subterfuge. Critics like Read warn that if the GBMI passes through the legislative and judicial gates, the Trojan horse will reveal its hidden agenda, and the NGRI citadel will be conquered and crushed.

While rich in allusion, this criticism is too sinister for my tastes. I, for one, am a card-carrying proponent of NGRI, and will defend the insanity defense *in principle* as fervently as the defenders at the gates; yet, I can also believe that a third option makes sense. I take the position that the GBMI option is intended to supplement the NGRI, not substitute for it. I have no doubt that its adoption will affect the number and percentage of cases that fall in the NGRI category, but this is as it should be if this option is working. Cases that were formerly judged to be NGRI but should not have been (because some culpability was present) can now be properly categorized and judged for what they are.

Some critics of GBMI believe that the intent behind this option is to provide treatment for those defendants who need it, and they regard a GBMI approach to achieve therapeutic ends as wrongheaded. Richard Bonnie (1982), in his statement before the Senate Judiciary Committee, said the following:

> In any case, I believe a separate verdict of "guilty but mentally ill," which has now been enacted in seven States, is an ill-conceived way of identifying prisoners who are amenable to psychiatric treatment. It surely makes no sense for commitment procedures to be triggered by a jury verdict based on evidence concerning the defendant's past mental condition rather than his present mental condition and potential problems. Moreover, decisions concerning the proper placement of incarcerated offenders should be made by correctional authorities and mental health authorities, not by juries or trial judges. (pp. 256–257)

And another critic, Robert Sadoff (1982), made a related point in his statement:

> One of the questions that my students at the law school have always asked is, "Doctor, what good is it if you treat somebody in a hospital under GBMI, and then send them back to a prison for confinement? What good has the treatment done?" or, can you really treat somebody in anticipation of their spending the next 15 or 20 years in a prison. I think there are very real, practical questions in that line. (p. 467)

Yes, there are "real, practical questions in the line," but that is the wrong line. And yes, the GBMI is "an ill-conceived way of identifying prisoners who are amenable to psychiatric treatment," but that is not, or should not be, the primary purpose of GBMI. Both of these critics, from a rehabilitative vantage point, find the GBMI poorly suited to the task. But the task or motive for the GBMI option, I submit, should not be rehabilitation. As I see it, the *primary* reason for having a GBMI option is *to punish* those who are culpable to some degree for acts that are criminal. GBMI thus serves, first and foremost, retributive and deterrent ends. Rehabilitation is a secondary end, at best; to my way of thinking, treatment is something that can be offered to a defendant serving time, but it should neither be made mandatory nor the primary reason for confining. We already have civil ways, through involuntary commitment procedures, of confining those individuals who are potentially dangerous, mentally ill, and in need of treatment. We should not misuse criminal procedures to serve those ends.

To summarize, an adequate justification for a GBMI option can be presented. The justification includes the following points: (1) the primary reason for having a GBMI option is to punish those who are culpable in part for their actions; treatment is an ancillary consideration; (2) the GBMI option serves as a supplement to, not a replacement for, NGRI; (3) the GBMI option neither contradicts itself nor jurisprudential understanding, as the principle of *mens rea* acknowledges and codifies gradations of culpability.

We now take up the second and third questions, "What should be the criteria for a GB defense?" and "How is GB differentiable from NGRI and from guilty?" Looking at one bill introduced in the United States Senate (S.2672), we find the following:

> A defendant is guilty but mentally ill if his actions constitute all necessary elements of the offense charged other than the requisite state of mind, and he lacked the requisite state of mind as a result of mental disease or defect.

This answer gives us very little. It is a *mens rea* answer (i.e., invoking the "requisite state of mind"), but we are left in the dark as to how this is different from *M'Naghten* or *ALI*.

Another Senate Bill (S.2780) offers a different answer:

> The defendant shall be found guilty but mentally ill if the jury or court finds that the defendant is guilty but at the time of the commission of the offense was suffering from some mental disease or defect that impaired his ability to conform his actions to the law.

This answer seems to use the "irresistible impulse" test or the "control test" portion of ALI as its starting point. But again, how do we differentiate the GBMI from the NGRI? Perhaps it is through the word "some." But is a jury informed enough by such a word or phrase ("was suffering from *some* mental disease of defect") to be able to differentiate? And differentiate "some" from what? Is the jury supposed to infer that a "guilty" person has "no" mental disease, or just "a little?"

Michigan, the first state to adopt the GBMI verdict, provides the following criteria:

> (a) That the defendant is guilty of an offense; (b) that the defendant was mentally ill at the time of the offense; (c) that the defendant was not legally insane at the time of the commission of that offense (Cahalan, 1982, p. 112).

Point (c) tells the juror that the GBMI is not legally insane (NGRI), while point (b) tells the juror that the GBMI is mentally ill; after that, it is up to the jury to differentiate. The criterion here seems to be some degree of mental illness, rather than a *mens rea* or control criterion, but beyond that, nothing else is offered.

Associate Attorney General Giuliani (1982) in his Senate testimony, states that a GBMI verdict

> could be returned only if the mental illness does not negate the defendant's ability to understand the unlawful nature of his conduct and does not negate his ability to conform his actions to the requirements of the law. (pp. 32–33)

Here the language invokes both *M'Naghten* and the ALI control test portion, yet we are left with a question: If the mental illness *does not negate* understanding or the ability to conform actions, why not a verdict of "guilty"?

In this brief review of proposed and enacted GBMI definitions, the criteria seem too vague; with this vagueness, differentiations become difficult. In addition, the criterion for GBMI differs from proposal to proposal: in one case, it is *mens rea*, in another, it is the ability to control, and in yet another, it is some degree of mental illness. My own recommendation is that the GBMI not be linked to a specific *mens rea* element or the ability to control one's actions; rather, like insanity, it should be related to *mens* (i.e., the response-able issue) and differentiated from both "guilty" and NGRI in terms of degree of culpability. This is likely to require more than a sentence or two for a jury to get a clear picture; it will probably require examples. After reviewing various GBMI proposals, my conclusion is that no proposal to date provides jurors with the discriminative clarity they need.

The last broad question to be taken up concerns the consequences of using the GB option. Breaking down the broad question into specifics, we may ask: Who may invoke the GB option? Is a GBMI verdict appealable? If a jury returns a GBMI verdict, where is the defendant sent? Who determines the sentence? How is the sentence determined? Who makes the release decision? And what factors are to be considered in a release decision?

Who may invoke the GB option? In my judgment, either the prosecution or the defense. The prosecution may raise it because GBMI is a "guilty" verdict, and the defense may raise it because it mitigates the punishment that a "guilty" verdict would bring. The prosecution is likely to raise the GB option when the defense is going for NGRI and when the prosecution agrees that mental illness was present but believes that some culpability also exists. If the prosecution is intending to prove the defendant "guilty" of the charge, the defense may go for GBMI, rather than NGRI, if counsel believes that some culpability was present but that the defendant's mental condition warrants mitigation.

The difficulty to be avoided is where the defense opts for GBMI but the prosecution goes for NGRI. This would be, in Moran's (1983) words, a "dramatic reversal of adversative roles" (p. 438). This strange possibility could come to pass for two related reasons: (1) if the prosecution believes that an NGRI verdict will ensure a longer. possibility indefinite, incarceration (hospitalization) than would a GBMI verdict and (2) if incarceration was mandatory following an NGRI verdict.

This would not be a healthy situation, for either the law or the defendant. It can be avoided in two ways. One way would be to legislatively prohibit the prosecution from raising the NGRI option, using the rationale that this option is an "acquittal," thus the prosecution cannot actively seek it. A second way of avoiding this difficulty would be to prohibit mandatory incarceration following an NGRI. This could be done through legislative act, or the judiciary may rule (as they have ample reasons to, in my opinion) that mandatory incarceration following an NGRI verdict is unconstitutional, as it violates due process and equal protection clauses of the Fourteenth Amendment. However it is done, it should be done.

Is a GBMI verdict appealable? If the defense was trying for NGRI, it should have the right to appeal since this is a guilty verdict and its consequence involves a loss of liberty for the defendant. If the defense sought the GBMI verdict, and received it, it should not be appealing the verdict unless new evidence is uncovered. The defense may wish to challenge not the verdict, but the sentence, and this should be possible.

If a jury returns a GBMI verdict, where is the defendant sent? This is a question for each state and jurisdiction to answer. Prison, hospital, or some new, combinative quasi-prison-quasi-hospital facility have been suggested. My own guideline would be to remember that a GBMI verdict is first and foremost a pronouncement of blame and culpability; since there is blame, some punishment should follow; treatment is a option to be offered, but the defendant reserves the right to accept or decline. Within this guideline, various facilities could theoretically serve the primary function; however, practical problems, such as funding, staffing, overcrowding, etc., as they affect most prisons and state hospitals today, may in fact leave little in the way of choice. The legislative body that considers and enacts a GBMI option must also consider the consequences, including the "where" question, and provide the courts direction and support.

Who determines the sentence, and how? I believe that the trial judge should determine sentence, not the jury. The judge, however, must have legislative guidelines and sentence ranges to work within, as opposed to free reign and unfettered discretion. Jurors will know, through appropriate instruction, what will happen to a defendant if they find him or her innocent, guilty, GBMI, or NGRI. For the GBMI verdict for a particular crime, a number of factors need to be weighted to reach a "just desert": the crime, namely, that "the severity of the punishment be commensurate with the seriousness of the offender's criminal conduct" (von Hirsch & Hanrahan, 1979, p. 4); the degree of culpability; predictions of recidivism, to the extent that they can be reliably made; and considerations of the victim, the victim's family, and community sentiment. This is a Modified Desert Model of criminal sentencing.

As to the release from incarceration question (Who decides, and on what basis?), this is a decision that should be reached by a parole board, not by psychiatric judgment alone. This position is consistent with the "guilty" aspects of the GBMI verdict. The parole board operates under judicial direction, with the judge setting the minimum and maximum sentence: below the minimum sentence, no action can be taken; once the maximum sentence has been served, the prisoner is released; within the range, the parole board, which may be multidisciplinary and include psychological expertise, can hear input from various sources who have vested interests, and weigh the factors involved. For those who hope that a GBMI verdict will allow for indefinite confinement, I would be strongly opposed; that, to me, would be a grave misuse of this verdict, as well as raising some constitutional issues of due process, equal protection, and cruel and unusual punishment.

As to what happens when the maximum sentence has been served yet some think the inmate needs more treatment or society needs more time without this individual in its midst, my answer is the following: as with any prisoner who served his or her time, society must grant release; if members of society still feel that a danger exists, then they can initiate civil commitment proceedings, *but the burden of proof is on those who initiate involuntary commitment proceedings, not the prisoner;* and the presumption should be, like it is in other civil cases, that the individual does not need to be hospitalized, unless the presumption can be shown to be false by the appropriate standard of proof.

AN UNASKED QUESTION AND CONCLUSION

In the above review of broad and specific questions dealing with the GBMI option, I find no proposal to date that satisfactorily answers these essential questions. Sadly, many of the proposals do not even consider these questions. This does not rule out the future possibility that a well-conceived and well-written GBMI cannot be created. What it does say is that it has not happened yet.

However, there is one question, a very important question, that has not been raised in regard to NGRI or GBMI considerations with one notable exception. The question involves a defendant's culpability in bringing about the mental illness or his or her incapacity as a response-able person. The exception is Fingarette and Hasse's (1979) Disability of Mind (DOM) Doctrine. The next chapter begins by raising this question, defends why it should be raised, and uses the DOM as a starting point for the development of a future test of insanity and partial insanity.

11

Toward a New Test for Insanity

CULPABILITY RECONSIDERED

When we typically speak about "culpability" in connection with insanity cases, we usually, if not exclusively, focus on *the moment of the act*. In lay terms, we ask, "Was the accused totally out of his or her mind at the moment of the act, such that he or she should not be held culpable, or was the accused capable of exercising rationality, and therefore culpable?" This is the question that has been asked by judges and answered by juries over 250 years of Anglo-American jurisprudence regarding insanity. In the traditional schema of things, the possible answers are two: nonculpable or culpable, with the verdict being either NGRI or guilty. If we add "partial insanity" to the discussion, a third question is asked: "Was the accused's capacity for rational conduct only partially impaired, such that, at the moment of the act, he or she was to some degree culpable?" If the answer is "Yes," then a verdict of GBMI or diminished responsibility or diminished capacity follows. But notice that the crucial focal point is the moment of the act, regardless of whether two verdicts or three are being weighed.

Does this make good sense? To Fingarette and Hasse (1979), who propose the Disability of Mind Doctrine (DOM), it does not. Let us consid-

279

er variations of a case presented in Chapter 7 (e.g., Case A, involving epilepsy and a death by gunshot). In the original version, the facts at the moment of the act are indisputable: the accused was having an epileptic seizure while holding a loaded gun; she loses consciousness, and involuntary contractions lead to the squeezing of the trigger; the bullet strikes someone, and that someone is killed. What was in dispute in this case was the culpability of the defendant *prior to* the fatal act (if it can be properly called an "act").

In dramatic terms, it is the *fateful* act, not the fatal consequence, that rivets our attention and commands our judgment. The fateful act in the *Iliad*, for example, is when Achilles decides to fight rather than sulk, and in *Hamlet*, it is when Hamlet answers, for himself, the "to be or not to be" question. The denouement, be it Achilles killing Hector and he himself being killed by Paris or Hamlet stabbing Claudius and, in turn, dying from the poison, is the fatal consequence of an earlier, fateful decision. Returning from the epic and classic to the insanity drama, the plot in Case A turns when the defendant decides not to take her medicine. Would it make no difference if she was (1) even more negligent in her decision; (2) reckless in her decision; or (3) intended such an outcome when she decided not to take her medicine? And in the other direction, would it not matter if she took every reasonable precaution? Surely it does matter. In insanity decisions, the moment of the act is not the only moment worthy of dramatic and juridical consideration, and yet, historically, our vision, scrutiny, and judgment has been constricted to only that moment.

For Fingarette and Hasse (1979), another question emerges: "Is the person, by reason of some earlier conduct, responsible for the occurrence of the offending act as a result of irrationality?" (p. 199). Said another way, is the person responsible and culpable for bringing about his or her mentally disordered state such that, at the subsequent moment of the act, he or she is not a response-able agent? Fingarette and Hasse draw a parallel to voluntary gross intoxication. It is not the moment of the act that primarily concerns us in these cases: for example, in the case of a car crash resulting from the actions of a drunk driver, we don't ask the defendant "Why didn't you brake sooner, or why didn't you stay in your lane?" No, we are more apt to ask a question about an earlier moment, such as "Why did you drink if you knew you were going to drive?" In terms of our judgment of culpability, it is the defendant's fateful action at that earlier moment that arouses our blame.

In a similar vein, Fingarette and Hasse ask us to look at, and evaluate in terms of culpability, the earlier actions or inactions of the allegedly insane or partially insane defendant. At earlier moments, when he or she was a response-able agent, did he or she act in ways, or fail to act, such that his or her mental condition deteriorated to the point of partial or total insanity? If so, then there is "culpability in the context of origin" (p. 211).

Fingarette and Hasse's view appears novel against the backdrop of our historic criteria of insanity; but in drawing the parallel to voluntary gross intoxication and to other cases of negligence, they defend their views against the charge that there is no precedent for such a position. For a precedent of a different sort, there is Aristotle's distinction between "vincible" and "invincible" ignorance (Hall, 1960): in the former instance, Aristotle finds a person ignorant but competent to acquire the necessary knowledge, and hence the person is held culpable for the harm committed as a result of ignorance; in the latter case, "the harm was done not only 'in ignorance' but also 'through ignorance'" (p. 368), and thus, since the person lacked the ability to acquire the necessary knowledge, there is no culpability. Obviously, mental illness is one factor that may undermine the ability to acquire the necessary knowledge. Extrapolating Aristotle's distinctions of ignorance to insanity, we would expect the philosopher to make a further distinction, as Fingarette and Hasse do, as to whether the allegedly insane defendant was culpable for bringing about his or her incapacity.

THE DOM DOCTRINE

In the proposed instructions to the jury under the DOM doctrine, Fingarette and Hasse (1979) ask the jury, after they have determined the guilt or innocence of the defendant in regard to each count, to make a determination regarding disability of mind. Three findings are possible: disability of mind, partial disability of mind, or no disability of mind. If the jury finds either for a disability of mind or a partial disability of mind, they go on to consider the "culpability as to the context of origin of the mental disability" (p. 267). The jury then decides as to the defendant's culpability or nonculpability. Thus, one of four DOM verdicts is returned: (1) Nonculpable Disability of Mind, (2) Culpable Disability of Mind, (3) Nonculpable Partial Disability of Mind, and (4) Culpable Partial Disability of Mind. This is an overly simplified presentation of the DOM doctrine, but it will do for now. We next turn to an illustration found in Fingarette and Hasse's work which I will use to elucidate some of the complexities that arise in assessing culpability.

> Illustration 4. The defendant, having just seen his child killed by a reckless driver, ran into his house, came back with a gun, and shot the driver dead. A plea of D.O.M. is entered. The jury finds that, as charged, the defendant did deliberate and did intentionally and with malice kill the driver. The defendant is Guilty of first-degree murder. The jury finds that the defendant temporarily suffered lack of mental capacity for conduct that was rational in regard to its criminal significance, and that this lack played a material role, but not the chief role, in the defendant's acting as he did. The D.O.M. finding is: Nonculpable Partial Mental Disability. The defendant's criminal condemnation and punish-

ment are mitigated. (Conceivably, the jury could find full Mental Disability—
thus precluding any punishment. But proper jury instructions are essential
here. They should, in this special kind of case, emphasize that the law does not
contemplate absolving members of the community from criminal responsibility
for anything they may wish to do, even to the extent of taking the law into their
own hands and killing others, just because they have been themselves caused
deep sorrow or anger or frustration. The jury should be reminded that although
we may understand and in a certain way sympathize with the actions of a
distraught parent, this is different from saying that the parent genuinely and
preponderantly lacked the capacity to take into account the criminal significance
of the act.) (p. 250)

First let us establish the jury's decision-making agenda. They begin by
considering the charge, and find the defendant guilty of first-degree
murder. Step 2 involves the DOM decision: Was there no, partial, or full
disability of mind? They decide that there was Partial DOM, although
Fingarette and Hasse note that they might have found for Full DOM. Step
3, the final step, involves culpability as to the context of origin of the
mental disability, and here the jury decides that the defendant was nonculpable. For the purposes of explication and critique, I will focus for now
on steps 2 and 3.

Both steps consider culpability, although the "culpability" is different
in a number of ways. Step 2 involves weighing and weighting the culpability at the moment of the act: the jury weighs whether culpability was
affected by DOM, and if it was affected, the jury weights the extent. In a
sense, the jury is asked to *grade* culpability. This is not unlike asking a jury
to decide among guilty, NGRI, and GBMI alternatives. Table 1 presents the
choices and corresponding outcomes. The jury then proceeds to step 3
only if they have found "no" or "partial" culpability at step 2. Table 2
presents the choices and corresponding outcomes for this second type of
culpability—context of origin of DOM.

Notice that the culpability choices are of a different type and number
at steps 2 and 3. At step 2, the jury grades culpability, whereas, at step 3,
they make an all-or-none, yes-or-no decision. Might not culpability for
bringing about the mental disability be also graded?

To develop my point, let us examine Fingarette and Hasse's illustra-

TABLE 1—CULPABILITY AT THE MOMENT
OF THE ACT

Gradations of culpability	DOM verdict
No culpability	Full DOM
Partial culpability	Partial DOM
Full culpability	No DOM

TABLE 2—CULPABILITY FOR BRINGING ABOUT
THE DOM

Culpable or not?	Final verdict
Yes—Culpable	Culpable Full DOM
	Culpable Partial DOM
No—Nonculpable	Nonculpable Full DOM
	Nonculpable Partial DOM

tion 4; I disagree with the "Nonculpable" part of the verdict. Since the authors do not give the reasons behind this decision, I have to speculate. Is the cause of the defendant's distemper, his partial DOM, to be attributed solely to the external stimulus—the reckless driver? I do not think so. While we can project ourselves and imagine how the father was feeling having just seen his child killed, the question to be raised is "But what was he *thinking* during the time he was running into the house, locating the gun, and returning to the scene outside? Presumably, he had time (10 seconds, 20, 30, a minute, longer?) to think, to insert his reason into the context and maelstrom of feeling. And can't we imagine ourselves or others having different emotional reactions? Stunned disbelief, numbness, weeping, sobbing, fright? Would we all immediately react with anger, vengeance, and retaliation? If we can conceive of a variety of emotional, cognitive, and behavioral reactions, then certainly some of the variance results from internal factors—the way the individual handles stress and his emotions—rather than placing the cause solely on the external stimulus.

Some might disagree with my speculation and point out that perhaps the defendant didn't think at all. But I would rejoin, as H. L. A. Hart (1968) would, that we expect the person to think. Even in cases of self-defense, for such a defense to succeed, a defendant must show that his or her "back was to the wall" and that there were no other options save taking a life or losing one's own. Fingarette and Hasse seem aware of this point when they add that

> the law does not contemplate absolving members of the community from criminal responsibility for anything they may wish to do, even to the extent of taking the law into their own hands and killing others, just because they have been themselves caused deep sorrow or anger or frustration. (p. 250).

So even if the precipitating cause is the reckless driver's actions, law and psychology recognize that individuals still bear responsibility for how they handle their feelings, react, and act; in addition, we expect people to think in such circumstances.

To return to my point, I believe it is possible to find individuals *partially culpable for bringing about their disability of mind.* The advantage of what

I have been calling "a third option," be it GBMI, diminished responsibility, or partial DOM, is that it provides jurors a gradation and another option that better represents "the way things really are," in some cases. I also believe that it is necessary to consider the second aspect of culpability—whether the defendant bears some culpability for bringing about his or her disability of mind. But the lines of consideration should be graded, as opposed to all-or-none. In my Case A, the epilepsy example, I can conceive of variations off the story that raise possibilities of intent, recklessness, negligence, or no culpability whatsoever for bringing about the DOM. A jury may likewise see "in-between" cases that fit neither the "culpable" nor "nonculpable" dichotomy.

I want to make it clear that Fingarette and Hasse have not completely overlooked this point. In their Instructions For The Jury regarding *culpability as to the content of origin of the mental disability*, they state that one of the following three variants should be used depending, upon the particular circumstances.

> a. *The Defendant Caused the Disability or Failed to Take Reasonable Precautions to Prevent It.*
> b. *Recklessness in the Context of Origin of the Disability of Mind.*
> c. *Intent, etc. in the Context of Origin of the D.O.M.* (pp. 267–269)

These three variations, roughly corresponding to negligence, recklessness, and intent (with the latter being a "Dutch Courage" situation where alcohol, for example, is used to bolster one's courage to act, all begin the same way: "The prosecution alleges. . . ." However, it is unlikely that the prosecution will allege anything about mental disability. The prosecution is typically trying for a "guilty" verdict on a specific charge. The prosecutor's job is to prove beyond a reasonable doubt that the defendant committed the criminal act (*actus reus*) and had criminal intent (*mens rea*). For the prosecutor to allege anything about disability of mind undercuts his or her own case. This creates a practical difficulty or two for Fingarette and Hasse. If the prosecution, in all likelihood, would not allege anything about a DOM, let alone *select* the gradation of culpability for the DOM (i.e., which of the three variants is read to the jury), how would the variant be selected, and who would select it?

Fingarette and Hasse recognize "that culpability in the origin of a Disability of Mind can be of various kinds and degrees" (p. 212) and apparently see a need to fix some gradation of culpability. Presumably, there is a difference between their "culpable as to the origin of that disability" and "culpable and reckless," and differences between these two and "culpability with intent." If not, why bother making distinctions? And presumably these different variants and verdicts lead to differing sentences based on differing degrees of mitigation. But it seems to me that Fingarette and

Hasse create an unusual schema for assessment. In regard to assessing whether a DOM existed, the jury decides; if there is a DOM, it is the jury again who decides whether the DOM is total or partial. But when it comes to culpability for the DOM in Fingarette and Hasse's schema, it is the prosecution who picks the degree of culpability, whereas the jury decides "yea" or "nay."

This assessment schema, I believe, is not likely to work or work well. As noted earlier, the prosecution will not, in all probability, raise the DOM issue in the first place, therefore allegations about culpability of the DOM will not, in all likelihood, be raised by the prosecutor. Perhaps the authors believe that the appropriate gradation of culpability (e.g., negligence, recklessness, intent) can be derived from the charge (i.e., the alleged crime), but this does not work. Take, for example, a case similar to that of *Hinckley*, where the charge is attempted murder. The prosecution will attempt to prove intent. This, however, does not imply anything about the type of culpability for the DOM. It is possible that the defendant was culpable with intent for his or her DOM (the "Dutch Courage" instance), but it is also possible that the defendant was culpable in a reckless way or in a negligent way; the alleged crime *per se* does not tell us which it was.

Furthermore, if you specify the type or gradation of culpability for the DOM, as the Fingarette and Hasse schema dictates, then the jury is in a potential bind: if the jury feel that the defendant was reckless or negligent as to the DOM, but the prosecutor asks them only whether or not they believe the defendant to be "culpable with intent," then their answer is likely to be "nonculpable DOM." Because the jury has only two choices, culpable or nonculpable, rather than being able to select a third option— less culpable (e.g., reckless or negligent) than the prosecution alleges, but still culpable in part for the DOM—they are faced with the lack of a third option dilemma all over again. This, I believe, is contrary to the authors' intent. I will subsequently suggest a different way out of this dilemma, but before that, we turn next to another complexity in assessing culpability for the DOM.

AN EXPANDING CONTEXTUAL UNIVERSE

When it comes to specifying "the moment of the act," we have little or no difficulty. Sometimes it is literally "a moment." At other times, some may wish to include seconds, minutes, or even an hour before within the circumscribed "moment of the act." All in all, there may be an occasional quibble, but in the vast majority of cases there is unanimity.

When we switch to the second type of culpability that needs to be assessed under the DOM doctrine, culpability as to the context of origin of the mental disability, the situation is quite different. What, for example, is the *context?* Where, on a time dimension, are we and the jury to focus? When did the context of origin occur? Minutes, hours, days, months, years before? And would 12 jurors be focusing on and evaluating the same contextual period? Would 12 experts? I doubt it.

Given that the context is not given, how and when it is defined is going to depend on the perspective of the evaluator, in part. For example, consider how the following psychological experts might define the contextual period. An expert whose orientation is existential, and who sees individuals making choices all along life's way, may focus on a narrow contextual period, perhaps right before or days before the moment of the act. An expert whose orientation is Sullivanian, may look further back in time to when there were indications of a breakdown in the self system, when "not me" feelings and parataxic or prototaxic thinking were evident, when the individual's reality testing seemed to show signs of dysfunctioning. A Freudian expert might wish to go much further back in time, to childhood, where personality, dynamics, fixations, and all manner and kinds of psychological defenses were forming. But we need not stop there. Birth and prenatal complications take us back to the womb doors, and in. The genetically oriented expert goes back even further, and the systems oriented therapist takes us back a generation or two, when scripts and patterns were laid down. All of this is enough to prompt a confused judge and jury to plead for a statute of limitations.

Even though Fingarette and Hasse call this type of culpability the "culpability as to the context of origin of the mental disability," this title is somewhat misleading. It can be inferred from their instructions to the jury that we need not necessarily go back to the *origin.* More precisely, their instructions ask the jury to weigh whether "the defendant caused the disability or failed to take reasonable precautions to prevent it" (p. 267). The second part may help the jury locate a contextual end point. As an illustration, take Case D in Chapter 7, where an allegedly paranoid schizophrenic defendant, who was being treated as an outpatient and who was told by her therapist that she needed treatment, nevertheless stops treatment and refuses to continue. Instead of asking experts and jurors to locate the origin of her schizophrenia, we can ask the jury to weigh her treatment refusal as to whether this constitutes a failure to take reasonable precautions to prevent what subsequently happened. Her treatment refusal occurred at a defined point in time, whereas the point of origin of her schizophrenia is far from clear and subject to disparate opinions.

But we are not out of the contextual woods yet. Nor have we avoided that forced march back through time to find the origin. Staying with Case D a bit further, what happens if some of the jurors believe that she is culpable for her decision to stop treatment but others believe that her treatment refusal *was a product of her illness?* For the latter jurors, her treatment refusal decision is indicative that she was not a "response-able" person *at that time* and that her "choice" was not truly a free choice. The former jurors, those who hold her culpable for her treatment refusal, see her as a "response-able" person who made an irresponsible, but free, choice. Now we have a dilemma. The jury may be hung on this matter, and stop there; or the jurors might decide to march back through time in search of some other incident to culpably evaluate. Whether they will agree as to where to stop, or agree when they do stop, is subject to conjecture. What may be clearer is the need to give jurors some guidelines or parameters. Should we, then. set some arbitrary time limit, like a statute of limitations, beyond which the jury must not pass on their search for causal–culpable connections?

A second difficulty with "context," in addition to specifying the time period, is the problem of what elements are included or excluded from the context. We have already seen an example of this in my critique of Fingarette and Hasse's illustration 4. I included in the context the defendant's reactions to his feelings, his thinking or failure to think following his child's death, and his capacity to control subsequent actions; Fingarette and Hasse, from what I can tell from their words, did not include this as part of their context. An even better example, which I have cited before (see Chapter 1), was the disagreement between Mackenzie and Hale regarding on-again-off-again cases of mental illness. If there were in a defendant's history repeated indications of mental illness (e.g., several hospitalizations), Mackenzie was more apt to question the individual's "response-ableness" in the lucid intervals (e.g., after discharge from the hospital). Hale, on the other hand, was more apt to focus on the lucid interval and the fact that the accused had been released from the hospital. Thus, in Hale's context it is the last lucid interval that counts, and the assumption would be that the accused is response-able, sane, and culpable for his actions. Within Mackenzie's view, however, the history of hospitalizations colors the context significantly and casts a different tone upon the so-called "lucid" interval. To summarize, Mackenzie and Hale include different elements in their respective contexts, or when they do include the same elements, they weigh them differently.

A third difficulty that might arise with this type of culpability assessment will be illustrated through a hypothetical example of extremes. We begin with two caricatures, one of a Freudian expert witness, the other an existential expert witness. The Freudian caricature takes the witness stand and the position that we are what we are, and act the way we act, because of causes that occurred in our childhood; furthermore, we are unconscious of these causes; it follows, then, that our allegedly criminal actions of today are determined by what happened in yesterdays that are little remembered or long forgotten and that we are neither responsible nor culpable for them. The existential caricature takes the other extreme, claiming that our actions result from our choices, which we are free to make. With that freedom comes responsibility; hence, we are always responsible and culpable for what we do. Although these are caricatures, there is a realistic point to be made. There may be some individuals, who, by their convictions about human nature, have already decided the case, and all such cases. For them, hearing the particulars of the case becomes an unnecessary waste of time, and if they sit on the same jury but on opposite extremes of the issue, a deadlock is likely.

To summarize, this second type of culpability assessment is subject to a number of difficulties: the problem of defining how far back in time the context extends; the problem of deciding what elements constitute the context; and the potential problem that prior convictions held by experts and jurors about human nature may turn this supposedly empirical task into a syllogistic Q.E.D. In addition, there is the problem of whether this second type of culpability is graded or dichotomized. In the face of such problems, one might be tempted to drop "culpability for bringing about the disability of mind" from consideration and assessment; but this would be hasty, the result of the perception that the problems are too many and too weighty.

In my opinion, the issue of culpability for bringing about the DOM ought to be assessed, despite the difficulties, for without this second type of culpability, the insanity matter would be incomplete. And with an incomplete picture come inequitable and unintelligible decisions that arouse outrage and disbelief. "How can it be" the public may ask and the press may editorialize, "that a defendant who should have and *could have* prevented his mental health from deteriorating to the point of disability of mind, was found to be 'not guilty' for the subsequent crime that resulted?" They are right in asking such a question. We do not find drunk drivers "not guilty," even though their mental disabilities at the time of the act are at least as great as those of the allegedly insane. People understand that fatal acts are often preceded by fateful decisions, and when they are, we hold such individuals accountable. To not do so in cases of insanity or partial insanity runs counter to our intuitive notions of what is right and fair.

It is important to be clear about an implication of this position. The implication is that each of us is responsible for our own mental health. We are expected to take care of our mental functioning such that our ability to be what the law presumes us to be—response-able individuals—does not debilitate. We are expected to keep our actions within the bounds of law, and this further demands that our thinking, emotions, perceptions, and judgment be maintained in minimal, response-able, order. When we recognize (and we are expected to recognize) that our own abilities and insights are inadequate to the task—that we are in danger of coming apart at the psychic seams, so to speak—then we should get ourselves help; that the alternative course, to do nothing, is unacceptable and inexcusable, and, at a minimum, may amount to criminal negligence if the actions that follow fall outside the bounds of law.

Closing an Escape Hatch

Fingarette and Hasse seek to prevent those defendants who have a full DOM but who nevertheless bear some culpability for bringing about their disability from escaping condemnation and punishment entirely. They state:

> To cause or unreasonably risk the occurrence of Disability of Mind—for example, by self-intoxication, or by failing to take prescribed insulin medication—is in effect to cause or unreasonably risk a state of mind in which one is inherently unfit to observe a reasonable standard of care. In short, this is to be responsible, at the very least, for what is by objective standards gross negligence in regard to any relevant criminal norms. (pp. 212–213)

They go on to state that

> We propose as fundamental, therefore, that the irrational state of mind at the time, if culpably induced, should provide no cover of excuse from the usual tests of criminal negligence or recklessness. This places a "floor" under any mitigation of condemnation or punishment where there is culpable Disability of Mind." (p. 215)

They intend to close this potential escape hatch through the extension of the common-law crime of *criminal negligence*.

> The common law provides for crimes of criminal negligence in regard to the causing of grievous bodily injury or death. But it is reasonable, in the context of D.O.M. offenses, to make explicit and clear by statute that a wider range of acts, when performed in a grossly negligent way, are criminal offenses. So, for example, the causing of substantial property damage (at some specified dollar level or above) should be a criminal offense if done with gross negligence. In this way, one who was culpably Mentally Disabled—grossly intoxicated, for example—and who caused such damage without any intent or even adequate awareness of what was happening, could still be held criminally culpable for the "floor" offense of criminal negligence, rather than being allowed to escape on the ground of absence of any *mens rea*. Similarly, one who breaks and enters at night, particularly with a deadly weapon, or who flourishes a deadly weapon in an assaultive way, should not be allowed to escape punishment by a showing of gross intoxication to the point where intent necessary for burglary, or for assault, can be doubted.
>
> As to such cases of extreme intoxication, the law should be made clear in appropriate statute: one who deviates grossly from a reasonable objective standard of care—as such defendants plainly have done—and who does so in ways that either constitute criminal harms or are peculiarly closely related to such harms, should be held criminally culpable. The only exception would be, of course, if the D.O.M. is nonculpable in origin, as it is not in the case of voluntary intoxication.
>
> Given a suitable range of such "floor" offenses of criminal negligence, the judge would then instruct the jury on the criminal negligence offense relevant to the case, and would do this, of course, as part of the normal sequence of instructions as to the counts on which the defendant may be found guilty.
>
> The result of the preceding approach is then, in a nutshell, as follows: If the defendant is found to have unlawfully committed the physical act or caused the particular result, as contemplated in the statute, the defendant must then either

be found guilty on one or more counts of intentional or knowing crime as alleged, or be found guilty of the relevant count of criminal negligence. There is no escape from this much". (pp. 246–247)

Fingarette and Hasse also seek to close the escape hatch in another manner—the way the verdict is reported. They note that

A person may be guilty of committing a specified criminal act, but not criminally responsible and hence not "guilty" in an accusatory-condemnatory sense. We have repeatedly alluded to the obscurity created by confusing the question of commission of the defined act with the question of criminal responsibility. The D.O.M. doctrine suggests a simple and total clarification of all these issues; the finding of a Disability of Mind should never be confusingly reported as "Not Guilty." If a defined criminal act was committed, this should be unambiguously reported by a verdict of "Guilty"; if there is not proof of all the elements, the verdict should likewise be unambiguous: "Not Guilty." If the defendant did commit the criminal act as defined by law, then the finding as to Disability of Mind, unconfused with the former question, should also be reported. Where the jury finds full Disability of Mind that is nonculpable in origin, this finding amounts to a finding of complete lack of criminal responsibility. It entails that even though the alleged act was proved, no criminal condemnation or punishment is warranted, and that the social problems posed should be resolved in a suitable, nonaccusatory process. (p. 209)

Let us examine the implications of these escape-hatch closings. There are three problems, as I see it: (1) the reporting of a full Disability of Mind that is nonculpable in origin as "Guilty, with Nonculpable DOM"; (2) that criminal negligence is dealt with in two ways—first, as a specific charge and crime, and second, as related to culpability for the origin of the DOM; and (3) the fact that Fingarette and Hasse retain the *actus reus* part of the trial in its traditional meaning, which, I believe, creates a sieve in their antiescape device mechanisms.

The first problem is similar to the "guilty but insane" (GBI) contradiction in terms: if you find that someone is "insane," you are, in historic, traditional terms, finding the person "not guilty"; if so, then the "guilty" part of the term contradicts the "insane" part. Similarly, if you find that a defendant had a full DOM, and further find that he or she was nonculpable for producing the DOM, then he or she is not culpable for either the criminal act or the disability of mind; the "guilty" part of the verdict makes little sense. In the authors' own words,

Where the jury finds full Disability of Mind that is nonculpable in origin, this finding amounts to a finding of complete lack of criminal responsibility. It entails that even though the alleged act was proved, no criminal condemnation or punishment is warranted, and that the social problem posed should be resolved in a suitable, nonaccusatory process. (p. 209)

But by calling the verdict "Guilty. . . ," more than a hint of condemnation and responsibility is implied. I believe that calling it "guilty" is an error. The nonculpable full DOM is truly a "not guilty by reason of insanity" (NGRI) instance.

The second problem is that negligence is dealt with two ways—as a specific charge and as relating to culpability for the DOM—and this complicates the insanity picture and the adjudicative decision making unnecessarily. It also contradicts the authors' expressed aims. First, it does not keep the basic concepts "few, simple, coherent, and powerful." Second, by making criminal negligence a separate charge, the authors create the type of diminished responsibility defense they oppose: they oppose a diminished responsibility defense that finds a defendant guilty but to a lesser charge; they stated that diminished responsibility should mean that the defendant is guilty but to a lesser degree to the same charge; but as it stands now, the jury has the option, which they may indeed exercise, of finding the defendant guilty of the lesser charge of criminal negligence. This floor crime undermines and contradicts the authors' intent and complicates, if not confounds, the jurors' task. I believe that it is best to deal with negligence at only one point—not as a specific charge, but as it relates to culpability for the DOM.

A third problem is the *actus reus* phase of the trial. As I have maintained and some courts have noted, the *actus reus* phase of the trial may also become insanity's battleground. This can happen because the legal and historic meanings of an "act" have included *intentional, mental elements.* This is likely to happen in cases of automatism, unconsciousness, somnambulism, fugue, multiple personality, dissociative conditions, hypnotic or trance-like states, epilepsy, and our hypothetical split-brain madness. In all such cases, the defense may well argue that no *act* occurred; it may also argue that no *actor* or *agent* was present or functioning. If the jury finds the defense's arguments persuasive, then, according to Fingarette and Hasse's system, they report that the defendant is "not guilty" on all counts and do not take up the DOM or culpability for the DOM issues. In short, their job is over if, in the *actus reus* phase, they find no "act." If there was neither an agent at the helm nor any "act to speak of, then there cannot be an act of criminal negligence. In sum, the "floor" beneath the floor crime falls through.

As long as the authors, the courts, and the law retain the historic meaning of *actus reus,* no coherent insanity doctrine is possible. I reach this conclusion because all potential "insanity" cases will not be treated and adjudicated in a similar, coherent manner. "Typical" insanity cases (i.e., those that are decided on the basis of intentions, motives, morals, thoughts, impulses, etc.) will be played out in the *mens rea* phase; but what I call "atypical" insanity cases (i.e., such as automatism, unconsciousness, somnambulism, epilepsy, functional split-brain, etc.), where the issue of "self-identity" and the questions of whether there was, in any meaningful, traditional, historical sense, an "act" or an "actor" will never reach the *mens rea* phase, let alone any consideration of culpability for bringing about this condition. Given the fact that the law allows both types of defenses (e.g., *People v. Grant,* 1978) and that psychiatric categories, judgment, and testimony provide the room, shadings, and interpretative leeway, it is all too possible to turn a "typical" insanity defense into an "atypical" one. This same problem shatters and defeats the abolishionist's illusion and hope that by eliminating *mens rea* considerations in insanity cases you have effectively eliminated the insanity defense. Not so. Rather, it only increases the likelihood that lawyers and psychological experts will make "atypical" insanity defenses in the future. This outcome would produce neither a coherent doctrine nor a full hearing and adjudication of the case.

In short, the flaws of *actus reus* infect the remedies, and Fingarette and Hasse's system suffers from this infection too. The authors wish to eliminate the myriad of special defenses that have pervaded the insanity landscape; they wish to create one schema for dealing with all types and cases where disability of mind is alleged; and they wish to create procedural steps, practical guidelines, and a theoretically sound rationale for putting the schema into operation. But the operation may never begin because the flaws and flooring of *actus reus* are built upon the quicksand of self-identity and intentions.

A NEW SCHEMA FOR INSANITY

DOM as an Affirmative Defense

I believe that the DOM defense (i.e., an insanity defense) must be an affirmative defense: that is, it can be invoked only by the defense, and it cannot be thrust upon a defendant by the prosecution or the judge. I reject the reasoning of the United States Court of Appeals in *Overholser v. Lynch* (1961) that approved the trial judge's rejection of Lynch's "guilty" plea. The Appeals Court stated that

> society has a stake in seeing to it that a defendant who needs hospital care does not go to prison and hence defendant and his counsel did not have absolute right to enter plea of guilty and preclude trial of issue of insanity. (p. 388)

I think this line of reasoning is fallacious. The court and trial judge were invoking a paternalistic reason (e.g., the need for treatment), but this was misplaced. Presumably, since Lynch was judged "competent to stand trial," he met the *Dusky* (1960) standards of having "sufficient present ability to consult with his lawyer with a reasonable degree of rational understanding" . . . and "has a rational as well as factual understanding of the proceedings against him." I interpret *Dusky* broadly, and believe that if Lynch possessed the rational and factual understanding of the proceedings, and could consult sufficiently with his lawyer, then the plea that he and his counsel entered should be taken as one that has been competently considered. My line of reasoning, which construes *Dusky* in this way, also implies a rejection of the Ninth Circuit Court's decision in *Sieling v. Eyman*

(1961), where the court held that "where defendant's lack of mental capacity lurks in the background," a higher standard should be adopted regarding competency to plead guilty (see Chapter 9 for a fuller discussion).

If "defendant's lack of mental capacity" *now* "lurks in the background," it should be brought to the foreground in the form of a "competency to stand trial" decision. That had been done in *Lynch*. The Appeals Court ruling on *Overholser v. Lynch* (1959) seemed to confuse *civil* with *criminal* concerns. The question of the need for treatment and hospitalization was confounded with the task of adjudicating on the alleged criminal charge of passing bad checks. The Appeals Court ruling, and their reasoning, confounded and reversed the priorities of these two tasks. To put treatment concerns ahead of adjudicating amounts to a prejudgment of the latter: the court seems to have concluded that the defendant was *not* "guilty," but rather "insane," and that treatment rather than punishment should follow. This preemptory and paternalistic decision denies, *de facto*, the defendant's competency and wishes. This is a mistake.

It is also a mistake for the prosecution to assert and foist this defense on a defendant who does not wish to assert it. The prosecution may be concerned—if a defendant pleads "not guilty" without raising an insanity defense and the jury brings in a "guilty" verdict—that the decision will be reversed on appeal; a reversal based on the notion that the defendant was not adequately represented or informed about alternative pleas. This fear of reversal should be dispelled by *Dusky*. Since the defendant was found competent by *Dusky* standards, the presumption should be that (1) alternative pleas were explained by counsel, (2) that the defendant understood the alternatives, and (3) that the defendant's selection of a plea was competently decided. For a "competent" defendant to come back, after-the-fact, on appeal and claim that "I didn't know or didn't understand," seems to be a case of a defendant trying to have it both ways. Either you are "competent" (and you know and understand) or you are not. It would seem that the prosecution could well enough refute such an appeal without having to "cover all bases" beforehand.

Appeals, treatment, and paternalistic concerns should not outweigh adjudicative concerns once a defendant has been found competent. The assertion of a DOM defense is appropriate only for the defense.

REDEFINING *ACTUS REUS* BEHAVIORALLY

In my schema, *actus reus* is de-animated, restricted, and redefined, such that intentions, awareness, foresight, consciousness, and internal mental states are not considered in this phase of adjudication. In addition, I believe we should restrict our view of the defendant in this phase to *personal identity*, which, as Robinson (1982a) noted, can be established even if the person is "totally amnesic and therefore ignorant of the very identity we have established." This last restriction keeps questions of *self-identity* out of the first phase of adjudication. What we are left with, then, is the defendant's *behavior* and whether the behavioral effects are criminal.

In this first phase the prosecution must show that a crime has occurred *from the behavioral level* and that the defendant did it. In a murder case, for example, the prosecution must show that the defendant pulled the trigger and, as a result, the victim died. The defense may try to show that it was not the defendant who pulled the trigger, but someone else, or that the victim died of natural causes. If the prosecution fails to prove its case beyond a reasonable doubt, then the defendant is found "not guilty" and freed, and the charges are dismissed. If, on the other hand, the prosecution does prove that the defendant's behavior caused a crime, the jury proceeds to the second phase, where intentions, mental elements and states, and disabilities of mind are considered.

This redefinition of *actus reus* has several advantages: subjective, internal elements are clearly factored out of this phase and, thus, what is left to consider is external, objective, and behavioral. Unlike the wider, traditional sense of *actus reus*, this view eliminates the possibility that charges will be dropped because of mental states or factors in this phase of the trial; thus, epilepsy, unconsciousness, and automatism cases will be looked into more deeply in the second and third phases of adjudication. This change ensures that culpability for bringing about the mental disability will be subsequently weighed.

THE *MENS* PHASE

In a trial where insanity is not at issue, the second phase of adjudication involves *mens rea*. It is here that the issue of specific intent is taken up. For example, the question might be "Did the defendant intend to murder?" The prosecution attempts to prove intent, whereas the defense tries to show that no criminal intent, or a less culpable criminal intent, was present. Defenses such as accident, necessity, duress, and self-defense— defenses that claim that no intent was involved, no criminal intent was involved, or that the intent was excusable because of extraordinary circumstances—all deal directly with *mens rea*. In this type of trial, the relevant issue to be evaluated—*mens rea*—is the same for both the prosecution and the defense.

When "insanity" is raised, the issues for the defense and prosecution may not be the same. The prosecutor who seeks a "guilty" verdict must prove intent; therefore *mens rea* is the focal issue for the prosecution. But for the defense attorney who seeks exculpation for the defendant because of a total DOM, or seeks mitigation of punishment based on partial DOM, *mens* is the focus. The prosecution must prove *beyond a reasonable doubt* that the criminal intent was present. The defense must show *by the prepon-*

derance of the evidence that the assumption of *mens* (i.e., that the defendant was a response-able person) is not warranted. Thus, in an insanity case, the prosecution and defense may be working at cross-purposes and under different standards of proof.

If the defense makes its case (i.e., demonstrates by a preponderance of the evidence that the assumption of *mens* is not warranted), then the prosecution's *mens rea* case must topple. Of the two issues—*mens* and *mens rea*—*mens* is accorded primacy. This is, after all, what happened in the 1800 case of *Hadfield:* the prosecution demonstrated intent (*mens rea*) by showing that Hadfield had a plan to kill King George III and that he enacted his plan; however, Erskine, for the defense, challenged successfully the *mens* of Hadfield; and if the *mens* is defective, then the *mens rea*, no matter how clear it be, is undermined from "below." *Mens rea*, in short, becomes irrelevant and moot when the *mens* of the defendant is shown to be disabled.

The prosecution, then, must work at two levels: it must prove *mens rea*, but it also must successfully challenge the defense's "no *mens*" argument or its own case will collapse. The prosecution can attempt to show that the defendant indeed had his *mens*; if the prosecution is successful at this (i.e., has made its case by a preponderance of the evidence), then *mens rea* becomes the determiner of guilt or innocence. The prosecution may, however, take another line: instead of trying to prove that the defendant's *mens* was whole and sound, it may try to show that the defendant's *mens* was disabled *only in part* (a partial DOM), while simultaneously claiming that the defendant was thus response-able and culpable in part. This amounts to a GBMI verdict.

Shifting to the jury's decisions regarding this phase of the trial, the first decision they face is the *mens* question: Was the defendant, at the time of the act, suffering from a disability of mind? If they believe, based on a preponderance of the evidence, that he or she was, then they face a second question: Was the disability of mind *partial* or *total?* If the jury believes that there was no disability of mind, then they take up the *mens rea* (intent) issue: Do you believe that the defendant intended to commit the act? Table 3 presents the question, decisions, and outcomes.

The context to be considered in the *mens* phase differs considerably from what is assessed in the *behavioral* phase. Here in the *mens* phase, facts and opinions brought out through testimony that bear on the internal state of the defendant, his or her thinking and feeling, intentions, motives, and impulses, and degree of consciousness are all fair grist for the jurors to weigh. So, too, is testimony that relates to the self-identity of the defendant and to whether he or she is to be seen as an "agent" or "actor" capable of "acting" in a response-able manner. What the constricting of the former *actus reus* phase does (i.e., changing to a *behavioral* phase), coupled with the changing and broadening of the former *mens rea* phase to a *mens*

TABLE 3—*MENS* PHASE QUESTIONS, DECISIONS,
AND OUTCOMES

Questions[a]	Decisions	
Was the defendant suffering from a DOM at the time of the act?	Yes	No
Was the DOM total or partial?	Total	Partial
Outcomes	Culpability phase	*Mens rea* phase

[a]The jury gets this question after they have completed the first phase of the trial—the behavioral phase—and answered "Yes" to the question "Did the defendant commit the behavior that is criminal?"

phase, is to bring coherence and procedural uniformity to formerly disjointed and disparate legal pathways. Under this schema, "typical" and "atypical" insanity cases are procedurally handled in like fashion.

CULPABILITY FOR THE DOM

This third phase of adjudication, which takes up the question of whether the defendant was culpable to some degree for bringing about the disability of mind, occurs only if a total or partial DOM was found in the second phase (the *mens* phase) of adjudication. There are two questions here. The first is whether the defendant is culpable *to any degree* for bringing about the DOM or not. The jury's answer is either "Yes, there is some degree of culpability" or "No, there is no culpability for bringing about the DOM." If the jury's answer is "No," then they have concluded their work. If the answer is "Yes," then a second discrimination must be made: the jury must further decide whether the defendant is culpable or only culpable in part for bringing about the DOM. This is akin to a "total vs. partial" DOM discrimination. When this decision is made, the jury's work is complete.

What are the advantages and disadvantages of this schema and procedure as compared to Fingarette and Hasse's? I see four advantages to this schema. First, it gives the jury three choices regarding culpability for the DOM—culpable, culpable in part, and not culpable—where Fingarette and Hasse's schema only provides two choices—culpable and not culpable. By providing a third choice and a middle ground, we place the issue of culpability on a continuum that corresponds, I believe, to the way people tend to view and grade culpability. People do make discriminations between premeditation and recklessness, between recklessness and negligence, and between negligence and accident, and each of us has a scale of culpability or can articulate one if asked in reasonable ways. For example, using a magnitude estimation procedure, we could ask people to grade the following crimes on a severity scale of 0 to 100 or assign sentences (in years in prison) to the following crimes: a death caused by (1) premeditation, (2) recklessness, (3) negligence, and (4) accident. While the numbers and the differences between numbers may be quite different among subjects, the *order* is likely to show consistently high agreement.

If we take a continuum and reduce it to an "either–or," "culpable–not culpable" dichotomy, we limit the response options of the juror; furthermore, the response options we provide may not include the one the juror judges to be the best fit. If this is the case, the juror is stuck. What does the juror do, then, when he or she believes that the criminal behavior was not the result of either premeditation or accident but does believe that recklessness or negligence was present? He or she has to fit an "in between" case into one of two extremes, "culpable" or "not culpable," because the correct choice for this juror, "culpable in part," is not available. The result of this limit on response options is a verdict that is "off the mark," appearing as either too severe or too lenient depending upon which errant choice the juror does make.

A second advantage to this schema over Fingarette and Hasse's is that the prosecution does not determine which degree of culpability instruction is read to the jury. This determination should be made by the jury rather than preselected by the prosecution. As I pointed out earlier, Fingarette and Hasse's position that the prosecution somehow determines which culpability instructions the judge reads to the jury is neither a likely scenario nor a workable one. Furthermore, it removes the decision-making function from the jury and places it with the prosecution, which I find objectionable.

A third advantage of this schema is that it eliminates the need for a separate charge of criminal negligence, which Fingarette and Hasse create as a floor crime to close an escape hatch. To explain, Fingarette and Hasse worry about the following verdict in their own schema: "Nonculpable DOM." My example of the "epilepsy case" (see Chapter 7) is illustrative. The jury may decide that the defendant at the time of the act did indeed suffer from a full DOM, and they may also decide, using the two choices that Fingarette and Hasse make available to them, that the defendant was not culpable (as opposed to culpable) for bringing about this condition. This verdict, "nonculpable DOM," warrants no punishment. Aware that this verdict might come to pass, Fingarette and Hasse foresee the need to prevent a defendant who may have been negligent (e.g., in the epilepsy case, the defendant stopped taking her medication without doctor's advice) from escaping punishment entirely. But the effect of this separate charge—criminal negligence—is to create a "diminished responsibility" situation that the authors oppose. In their footnoted comment on the case of *Fisher v. U.S.* (1946), they state:

For example, in *Fisher*, the Court makes plain that when it speaks of "partial responsibility" it means to indicate "responsibility for a lesser grade of offense." It is made explicit and very plain that the Court here has in mind the traditional theory—of which we have been fundamentally critical—that in order to establish "partial responsibility" one can only do this by finding absence of guilt for the graver crime charged, and finding guilt along with *full* responsibility for a lesser crime. D.O.M. verdicts would avoid such confusion. "Lesser responsibility" becomes just that—lesser responsibility for the crime actually committed. (pp. 200–201)

Contrary to Fingarette and Hasse's stated position, their schema does not avoid such confusion; rather their schema creates the very situation that they are fundamentally critical of—the finding of guilt for a lesser grade of offense. In my schema, the epilepsy example could be handled by a verdict of "DOM, culpable in part" to the original charge; with such a finding, some degree of punishment would follow.

The fourth advantage of my schema over that of Fingarette and Hasse's is that even with their contradictory floor crime of criminal negligence, their flooring collapses in just those cases (e.g., epilepsy, automatism, sleepwalking, unconsciousness) when we most want it to hold. What makes their flooring give way is their adherence to the traditional meaning of *actus reus*, which is itself a sieve that does not hold for further examination and adjudication some of the cases we are most concerned about. In my schema, *actus reus* has been redefined and narrowed to "behavior that is criminal." This narrower, behavioral meaning does not let "acts that are not acts because intention was lacking" to fall through the cracks; they are held for further scrutiny in the *mens* and culpability phase of adjudication, where DOM and culpability for the DOM judgments are made.

One disadvantage of my schema is comparison to that of Fingarette and Hasse's is that another choice, the discrimination between *culpable* for the (partial or total) DOM and *culpable in part* for the (partial or total) DOM, is put to the jury. As you add choices, you lower the likelihood of unanimous decisions. In my schema, a jury may be divided over whether a defendant is culpable or culpable in part for the DOM, which would not occur in Fingarette and Hasse's schema since this choice is not put to the jury. I believe that the benefits of the choice outweigh the disadvantages. The jurors' disagreement and vote should be reported to the judge; when the vote is not tied, the judge should be guided by the will of the majority; when the vote is tied, the benefit of doubt should go to the defendant. But even though the defendant gets the benefit of the doubt, he or she does not escape punishment: for both *culpable* and *culpable in part* judgments warrant punishment. The jury may be divided as to degree of culpability, but they are united in believing that *some degree of culpability is present*. It would then be left to the judge to set the sentence. Table 4 presents the phases and outcomes.

TABLE 4—THE PROCEDURAL PHASES OF THE TRIAL, CHOICES, AND OUTCOMES

Phases	Choices and outcomes									
Behavioral phase	No				Yes					
Mens phase					↓					
					D.O.M.					
			No			Yes				
					Total		Partial			
Mens Rea phase	Yes	Yesᵃ	No							
Culpability phase										
Culpable to some degree?					Yes	No		Yes	No	
Partial (P) or total (T)?					P	T		P	T	
	↓	↓	↓	↓	↓ ↓	↓	↓	↓	↓	↓
Verdictsᵇ	1	2	3	1	4	5	6	7	8	9

ᵃTo a lesser degree.
ᵇVerdicts: 1, Not guilty; 2, guilty; 3, guilty, but to a lesser charge; 4, DOM, partially culpable; 5, DOM, culpable; 6, DOM, not culpable; 7, partial DOM, partially culpable; 8, partial DOM, culpable; 9, partial DOM, not culpable.

Before taking up the next phase, which is sentencing, we need to return to an issue that was raised but not answered regarding a time limit on culpability considerations. The question was "How far back in a defendant's past should we look when deciding whether or not he or she is to be judged culpable to some degree or not culpable for bringing about his or her disability of mind?" To recall the previous discussion of this matter, it is quite possible that different experts and different jurors will focus their attention on different points in the defendant's past. On probabilistic grounds, we would predict that the farther back in the past one looks, the greater is the likelihood that we will find examples that are indicative of response-able, culpable choices. If we exclude certain cases, the type that Lord Coke (Winslow, 1843/1983) called "idiota, who from his nativity, by a perpetual infirmity, is *non compos mentis*" (p. 3), and cases where disease or physical trauma have rendered the brain and mental functioning deficient, such as Lord Erskine claimed regarding the gunshot wound to the head that Hadfield received during a war—then it is possible, on theoretical grounds, to argue that all psychogenic cases, some of whom are now insanity defendants, were once response-able and culpable. This is not what I intended to have happen using my schema, for this would effectively eliminate an exculpatory insanity defense in all such cases.

The intent behind this *culpability for bringing about the DOM assessment* is to ensure that the defendant's fateful actions—be they actions he or she took or actions he or she failed to take but should have taken—actions that are *causative* and *culpable*—are weighed by the jury. Fingarette and Hasse, writing about such prior, fateful actions, distinguish three types: actions that are indicative of negligence, recklessness, or intent. As an example, consider a man with the diagnosis "Bipolar Disorder, Manic" (DSM-III-R, 1987), or what DSM-II (1968) labeled "Manic-Depressive Illness, Manic type." He has had a history of repeated manic episodes and during those episodes he has been psychotic (i.e., "gross impairment in reality testing"); in addition, angry tirades have been typical. He has been hospitalized following the start of some of those episodes. He knows of his condition, his diagnosis, and is currently taking lithium to control the manic episodes and is in psychotherapy to learn new ways of dealing with his feelings. He knows that this is what he must do, and he acknowledges that lithium has controlled the manic episodes; yet, he misses the excitement, power, and self-confidence he used to have during such episodes and feels that he has been reduced to a timid, mousy personality.

Now, for the problem. His boss has been verbally abusive, demanding extra productivity and longer hours, while reducing his pay; these are facts and not distorted perceptions. He is angry and wishes to confront his boss to demand better treatment and pay, but fears that the lithium will blunt his emotions and undermine his confidence, so he decides to stop taking his medication without his doctor's advice and consent a week before his impending showdown. The showdown gets "out of hand," and he assaults his boss. In addition to the assault charge, we have a question of negligence regarding his fateful action of a week prior—his decision to stop taking his medication.

This example can be turned into a recklessness example with an additional change in the script. Let us add that to show his boss that he means business, he takes a loaded pistol with him, which he brandishes. Again, he assaults his boss, and this time he wounds him. In both cases, after the harm, he claims he wasn't "himself," wasn't aware of what was happening, was "out of his head."

To turn the example into an "intent" case, let us change the script once more. Now let us say that the man deliberates about committing the perfect crime—killing his boss and getting away with it. He premeditates a plan: he will stop taking his lithium, bring a loaded pistol to the showdown, and if a manic episode occurs, will kill his boss during his disability of mind; he reasons that exculpation should follow, since he will be "insane" at the time of the act.

My point, and the one my schema for assessing culpability for bringing about the disability of mind tries to address, is that *these prior acts* are causatively and culpably related to the "moment of the act" *act*, and should be weighed. But with such a weighing comes certain contextual problems. Such actions that we may designate as negligent, reckless, or intentional can be quite varied: choosing to stop medication or therapy without consultation or over the expressed warnings not to, using alcohol, failing to get help when help was advised and available, putting yourself in a dangerous situation or not taking the steps to remove yourself from same, and many more. No list of examples would ever completely cover all cases and possibilities.

Even within a single case, examples of actions and decisions that might be construed as causative, and possibly culpable, could number in the thousands, given that we impose no time limitation on a historical search.

An argument for a time limit, analogous to a statute of limitations, could be made for the assessment of culpability for the DOM issue on grounds that it would restrict possible culpable action to more manageable numbers. Such an argument might begin by noting that there are examples in the law of statutes of limitation. For example, in breach of contract or personal injury suits, a plaintiff must bring the suit within a legislatively defined time period. Justifications for such arbitrary limits typically invoke the need to set some finality to potential legal matters and to unburden the courts from having to adjudicate actions long since past. In involuntary commitment cases, where the state must show mental illness and dangerousness, there is a similar question about how far back in the defendant's past the state can go in presenting evidence of potential dangerousness. For an adult defendant, could the state present evidence regarding fights in the third grade to support the claim that he is dangerous now? Some states have legislatively limited the time interval for citing past actions as evidence for current dangerousness.

In addition to legislating statutes of limitation, attorneys may invoke the laws of evidence, particularly, exclusionary rules, to limit certain matters: for instance, in the Federal Rules of Evidence (e.g., FRE 402, 401), only relevant evidence—where "there is a logical relationship between the evidence presented and the facts sought to be proven at the trial"—is admissible (Loh, 1985, p. 23). A defense attorney might invoke such exclusionary rules if, in his or her opinion, the prosecution is wandering too far back in time in search of culpable actions.

Even though an argument can be made for a time limit, with statutes of limitation and exclusionary rules cited as precedents, I believe that the argument is flawed and that limits should be rejected. In brief, statutes of limitation and time limits on causation are limits of a different sort. To explain, let us take as an example the case of a group of citizens who discover that they all have developed the same kind of rare disease and furthermore believe that the disease resulted from the actions of a company that dumped certain toxic wastes too close to the local water supply. The dumping, let us say, occurred 10 years prior. The statute of limitation on personal injury cases typically applies to when you bring the suit in relation to when you discovered the injury and suspected causes. If you've known about the injury and suspected causes for years but did not bring legal action, your belated action may be too late (i.e., beyond the statute of limitation). But if the case is filed before the statute of limitation is reached, the fact that the dumping (the alleged cause) occurred 10 years ago is neither irrelevant nor moot. Causation is usually one of the elements of a tort and one of the elements the plaintiff needs to prove.

Let us return to the issue of culpability for bringing about the DOM and the problematic argument for a time limit. Any time limit established would be arbitrary; moreover, such a limit could be contrary to a scientific inquiry into causation. For example, a geologist tells us that the cause of why a diamond became what it is has its origin millions of years ago; the weatherman on the local news tells us that our weather today has been caused in part by solar flares of a year ago; and the courts award plaintiffs damages for the negligent actions of the company that dumped hazardous waste materials 10 years ago too close to population centers. In all of these judgments and claims, the time between cause and effect is not germane. The central question for the scientist or court is "Is there a causal relationship between event A and event B?"

Arbitrary time limits as to causation or culpability are just that—arbitrary; worse, limits run counter to the spirit of scientific inquiry that demands free reign to pursue the causative thread no matter how far back it goes. An arbitrary limit would lead to the same kind of historical mistakes, contentions, and short-sightedness that I seek to correct. For instance, in the history of the insanity defense (see Chapter 3), when the nineteenth-century medico-psychological experts, the alienists, were battling the courts for hegemony over insanity, one of their most frequently heard charges was that the law had "an entirely obsolete and misleading conception of the nature of insanity" (Smith, 1981, p. 16); furthermore, the alienists claimed that the law did not, but should, correspond to scientific, medical, natural law findings. To the scientist or medico-psychological expert of today, time limits on causality are likely to be regarded as foolish, certainly fallacious, and perhaps indicative of a delusion that itself is tantamount to insanity! The old charges and contentions between law and medicine are apt to be repeated anew if a time limit was imposed.

Yet some guidance for the jury in this matter is critical. Their attention needs to be directed to particular incidents, actions, and decisions to be assessed, rather than to be left to wander. This needed guidance is provided by the prosecution. The burden is on the prosecution to identify those actions and decisions of the defendant that they believe are indicative of culpability; beyond mere identification, the prosecution bears the burden of proving, by a preponderance of the evidence, that those actions and decisions are indeed culpable. The defense, to defeat the charge of culpability for bringing about the DOM, must challenge persuasively the prosecution's contention and evidence. In short, the adversarial system provides the jury the focus and the evidence, and the preponderance of the evidence standard becomes determinative.

SENTENCES AND CONSEQUENCES

There is both empirical (Elwork & Sales, 1985; Finkel, Shaw, Bercaw, & Koch, 1985) and anecdotal (Moran, 1981) evidence suggesting that jurors may not comprehend the judge's instructions to them. If this is true in general, the problem is likely to be exacerbated when it comes to insanity. This is likely because "insanity," as a legal concept, has been less clearly and consistently defined than other concepts (e.g., arson, assault, robbery, murder); as a result, the jurors' interpretations of the judge's instructions, like subjects interpreting a Rorschach card, are apt to show greater variability and subjectivity. Another reason deals with the clarity of the perceived consequence to a verdict: whether or not jurors decide on a "guilty" or a "not guilty" verdict in a murder case, for example, they are apt to have a fairly clear picture in mind of what will happen to the defendant; when "insanity" is to be decided, this is not the case. If jurors bring in a "guilty" verdict in an insanity case, will the defendant end up in prison or a psychiatric hospital? Will the sentence be fixed or indeterminate? Will doctors decide when he or she will be released, or will the courts? The situation is likely to be more unclear if jurors bring in an NGRI verdict. Will the defendant be set free, imprisoned, or hospitalized? Who decides, and how is it decided? The same questions apply to release. A GBMI verdict may be even more unclear. Will it be prison, or hospital, or both? If both, what order? Who decides? How is it decided?

We have two interrelated problems: the first is that we have questions without clearly specified answers; and the second is that we have evidence that jurors think about the consequences in their verdict deliberations, even when judges instruct them not to. In the matter of verdicts, consequences, and sentencing, the courts have proceeded in a logical, sequential manner: typically, the judge instructs the jury to assess culpability and bring in a verdict; the consequence and sentence to follow is then usually decided by the judge. While this procedure appears orderly and logical, it may be unreasonable on psychological grounds: it asks jurors to compartmentalize the verdict decision from the dispositional decision and to pay attention only to the former. This may be reasonable to ask; and it may be difficult if not impossible to do.

If jurors are thinking about consequences while they are supposed to be reaching a verdict, they may be confounding and contaminating their decision. There is suggestive evidence (Finkel et al., 1985) that some jurors may, in fact, be working "backwards": first deciding where they want this insane defendant to wind up (the dispositional decision) and then selecting the verdict that they think is most likely to bring this result about. I do not think that the solution to this problem lies in firmer, sterner instructions from the judge to the jury "to compartmentalize better."

On the contrary, I think that the instructions judges provide the jury ought to incorporate and spell out the likely consequences to each possible verdict. This strategy recognizes the "psychological reality" that verdicts and consequences are intimately related. Without authoritative information from the bench regarding consequences, jurors are left with their own assumptions, which may be in error. For example, take the case where two jurors both believe that the defendant needs psychological treatment and that the public needs protection. Juror A, let us say, believes that an NGRI verdict will set the defendant free; thus, Juror A votes for "guilty" to achieve the desired ends, because he also believes that with a "guilty" verdict the defendant will be sent to a hospital for treatment. Juror B, on the other hand, believes that a "guilty" verdict will lead to imprisonment and no treatment; furthermore, Juror B believes that the defendant will probably receive a "light" sentence and thereby be back on the streets too soon; Juror B thus votes for NGRI, believing that the defendant will get treatment and will be kept in a hospital for however long it takes to achieve a cure. Here we see the dangers of jurors using their own beliefs—beliefs not grounded in fact or enlightened by the court—to bring about desired consequences through particular verdicts.

Believing, as I do, that more information (not less or no information) needs to be provided to the jurors regarding the consequences of particular verdicts, I will now attempt to spell out the consequences for all of the possible verdicts in my schema.

Let us begin with those verdicts that do not involve a DOM, starting with cases where the prosecution has not succeeded in proving beyond a reasonable doubt the *behavioral* elements (i.e., what I have called the behavioral phase). In such instances, subsequent phases of the trial (e.g., the *mens* phase, *mens rea* phase, and culpability phase) are superseded, and a verdict of "not guilty" is returned. The consequence is outright release.

In cases where the behavioral element has been proved, and a DOM has been asserted, the *mens* phase is taken up. If the jury believes, by a preponderance of evidence, that no DOM was present, the case moves to the *mens rea* phase. Three verdicts are possible: (1) not guilty, (2) guilty, and (3) guilty but to a lesser charge. The consequence for each will now be discussed.

The first possibility (i.e., behavioral phase—Yes, *mens* phase—No (No DOM), *mens rea* phase—No) covers cases such as accident, self-defense, defense of other persons, necessity, duress, prevention of offenses, public authority, domestic authority, and the acts of children. In these cases, it has been shown that the defendants behaved in ways that might ordinarily be considered criminal, but because the *mens rea* was lacking, we judge them "not guilty." These cases are examples of where excusing or justifying reasons are cited to explain the defendant's behavior in noncriminal terms and where the jury agrees. With a "not guilty" verdict, the consequence is outright release.

The second possibility (i.e., behavioral phase—Yes, *mens* phase—No

(No DOM), *mens rea* phase—Yes) covers typical criminal cases that lead to a "guilty" verdict. The jury finds that the defendant behaved and intended to behave in a manner that is made criminal by statute. Such an offender, judged "guilty" by the jury, is sentenced by the judge. The sentence maximum or sentence range is fixed by the legislature, but the exact sentence is set by the judge (Orland, 1973). As to the legislatively established sentence range, it has been argued (Monahan, 1982) that

> under the principle of commensurate deserts, the severity of punishment is proportional to the seriousness of the offender's criminal conduct. Seriousness, in turn consists of two components: the *harm* committed and the degree of the offender's *culpability* in committing it. (p. 104)

It has also been pointed out that there is disagreement as to whether we can determine the absolute harm of given crimes and even more disagreement as to determining culpability. Even if these two retributive factors could be generally agreed upon, we are still left with a range. The Modified Desert Model would use utilitarian grounds for setting the actual sentence within the legislatively set range. Monahan (1982) provides the following principle:

> "Within the range set by the seriousness of the crime committed, the severity of an offender's sentence shall be proportional to the degree he or she reliably and validly can be predicted to offend again. (p. 112)

Thus, at sentencing, the judge may hear appeals and evidence from the defense and the prosecution to lower or raise the actual sentence within the set range. I would recommend that judges follow Monahan's principle in deciding.

The third possibility (i.e., behavioral phase—Yes, *mens* phase—No (No DOM), *mens rea* phase—Yes but to a letter degree) also leads to a guilty verdict, but to a lesser offense. For example, if the prosecution brings the charges of first-degree murder but fails to convince the jury that premeditation and deliberation were involved, the jury, if they are convinced that *intent* to murder was involved, may bring in a verdict of voluntary manslaughter. The "guilty" verdict to the lesser charge brings a consequent sentence. This sentence (a maximum or a range) is again established legislatively, with the judge fixing the actual sentence. As before, the Modified Just Desert principle should serve as the guide.

Now we come to the DOM verdicts, of which there are six: (1) disability of mind, nonculpable, (2) disability of mind, partially culpable, (3) disability of mind, culpable, (4) partial disability of mind, nonculpable, (5) partial disability of mind, partially culpable, and (6) partial disability of mind, culpable.

The first case, "disability of mind, nonculpable," most closely corresponds to the traditional NGRI verdict. It is a close rather than exact correspondence for two reasons: first, because a different notion about the essence and meaning of "insanity" is used here and second, because the historic usage of NGRI failed to consider culpability for bringing about the insanity (disability of mind). Given these two changes, we could predict that fewer cases would fall into this modified version of the traditional NGRI category than would historically be the case. This schema, although it renames it, does not eliminate the NGRI verdict from the legal landscape; fewer cases in this category will hopefully represent truer cases.

This verdict means that we do not hold the accused culpable for his or her behavior when the harm occurred, nor do we find the accused culpable for bringing about his or her mental disability. On retributive grounds, there is not reason to punish, hence there is no sentence. This does not mean that there is necessarily no consequence. For deterrent reasons, the state may seek to involuntarily commit the individual on grounds of mental illness and potential dangerousness. However, this should be a separate, civil matter and should not automatically be triggered by a "disability of mind, nonculpable" verdict. The criminal trial jury's verdict is a judgment regarding the defendant's behavior at the moment of the alleged criminal act and a judgment regarding earlier (possible culpable) actions; it is not a judgment as to current or future functioning.

Critics who favor automatic commitment following an NGRI verdict have put forth the claims that the past harm (i.e., the reason for the criminal trial) and the jury's judgment of DOM are *prima facie* grounds (if not proof) of mental illness and potential dangerousness. Defenders of a separate hearing (see Chapter 9) have countered these claims on legal and psychological grounds. Without reiterating this argument in detail, I believe that the "separatists" have the stronger case. Involuntary commitment statutes (including emergency commitment procedures) exist in all states, and that process may be initiated by the state, family members, police, neighbors, and others. In short, there is civil recourse when deterrent (i.e., society needs protection) and rehabilitative (i.e., the defendant needs help) needs are perceived. To automatically link current and future concerns (i.e., deterrence and rehabilitation) to judgments on past actions (i.e., retribution) would be a mistake.

The second of the DOM verdicts is "disability of mind, partially culpable." This verdict differs from the first, "disability of mind, nonculpable," in that the jury finds some degree of culpability for bringing about the DOM. When there is a finding of culpability—be it partial or full, be it at the moment of the act or before—there is guilt; hence, verdicts (2) through (6) are all "guilty" verdicts and loosely analogous to a GBMI verdict. With a "guilty" verdict comes a consequent sentence. To see what that sentence may be, or how it is to be reached, let us turn to verdict (3) to make a comparison.

For the third DOM verdict, "disability of mind, culpable," we also have a judgment of culpability and guilt; however, in this case, the jury believes that the offender is more culpable than the case (2) offender for bringing about the DOM. Let us take as a reference point the crime of voluntary manslaughter, where no DOM is involved and where the behavioral and the *mens rea* elements have been established to the jury's satisfaction. If the sentence for such a crime is 5 to 10 years, the culpability for the DOM factor lowers the sentence range. Lowers by how much? This cannot be specified precisely. A rule of thumb can be provided, however. In case (2), where the offender is only partially culpable, as opposed to case (3) where the offender is judged culpable, the sentence range would lower more; for case (3), the sentence range would be lowered, but to a lesser degree than for case (2). What I am invoking as a rule of thumb is the rule of proportion that "the Bluidy Mackenzie" suggested: that the punishment (sentence) be proportional to the degree of culpability. In terms of lowering the sentence range, the relationship to culpability is inverse: the greater the culpability, the less the sentence range is lowered. Within the lowered sentence range, the Modified Desert principle articulated by Monahan can be applied.

For DOM cases (4), (5), and (6), where there is a finding of "partial disability of mind," there is culpability of another sort. This judgment affirms that while there was a partial disability of mind at the moment of the act, there was also a culpable degree of response-ability present too: in colloquial terms, the offender was not completely "out of his or her head." This judgment implies that the offender had enough "wherewithal" to do otherwise, although his or her "wherewithal" was impaired or diminished to a degree. The rule of thumb for this culpability factor is that a "partial DOM" lowers the sentence range slightly, but not as much as a "full DOM."

For DOM case (4), "partial disability of mind, nonculpable," there are two comparisons that serve as relative anchors for establishing the sentence. Case (1), "disability of mind, nonculpable," serves as one anchor: in case (1), there is a full disability of mind and no culpability for bringing it about, hence no sentence; the "partial disability of mind" establishes some culpability, therefore the sentence range is lowered, but not to zero. The second relative anchor is case (5), "partially disability of mind, partially culpable": because there are two types of culpability (at the moment of the act, and before) for case (5), whereas in case (4) there is only one type of culpability (at the moment of the act), the sentence range for case (4) is lowered more than for case (5).

For case (5), "partial disability of mind, partially culpable," the relative anchors are cases (4) and (6) on one culpability dimension and case (2) on the other type. The sentence for case (5) would not be lowered as much as it would for case (2); and the lowering for case (5) would fall in between cases (4) and (6).

For case (6), "partial disability of mind, culpable," we have the case

that warrants the least amount of mitigation. The degree of lowering
would be less than case (5) and than case (3).

To summarize, when a DOM verdict results, the sentence is determined in the following manner: (1) the sentence range that has been legislatively set for the crime *had there not been a DOM* (i.e., where behavior and
mens rea were proved) serves as the absolute anchor or reference; (2) the
greater the culpability, whether it be at the moment of the act or before or
both, the less the sentence range is lowered; (3) the appropriate comparison cases would serve as relative anchors; (4) within the lowered sentence range, Monahan's Modified Desert principle should be employed;
and (5) case (1), "disability of mind, nonculpable," because it is a *true*
NGRI with no type of culpability found, becomes the only "not guilty"
verdict, and hence warrants no sentencing; it may, however, warrant a
subsequent involuntary commitment hearing, but that hearing is (a) not
automatic, (b) not decided by this court, and (c) not based solely on the
evidence from the criminal trial.

It should also be noted that for the "guilty" verdicts, cases (2) through
(6), once the sentence has been served, the person is set free. If the state
believes such a person to be mentally ill and potentially dangerous upon
release, it may initiate involuntary commitment proceedings. However,
this proceeding should not be made easier for the state by the fact that the
offender has been previously convicted, sentenced, and incarcerated;
rather, the presumption of sanity and the right to be free should be assumed, with the burden on the state to prove otherwise.

So far I have said nothing about therapy in regard to sentencing. I now
will do so. The reason for its late inclusion in this sentencing subsection is
that I believe a criminally imposed sentence serves first and foremost to
punish an offender who has been judged guilty and culpable. The punishment fixed by a sentence should be based upon retributive and deterrent
grounds. I have argued throughout this work that imposing treatment
through criminal sanctions is an error.

This is not to say that treatment has no place in this schema. What I
propose is that treatment be made an option, available to an offender
serving his or her sentence, but an option that can be declined. Presentence indications as to whether the offender will decline or accept treatment
and predictions of the likelihood of improvement should treatment be
accepted should have no bearing on the sentence. In this regard, this
schema is quite different from that proposed by Lady Wootton (1959,
1960). Whereas Lady Wootton has little faith in the abilities of mental
health professionals to illuminate matters of responsibility and culpability
during the trial, she puts great faith, at sentencing, in their abilities and
competencies to predict and treat offenders under involuntary circumstances. Yet empirical evidence as to accuracy of predictions and successful
therapeutic outcomes with involuntarily confined patients does not inspire
faith (Finkel, 1980).

Where treatment acceptance and success do have some bearing is at release, much like "good behavior" plays some part in determining parole decisions. The release question will be taken up in the last chapter. It is time now to address and guide the jury through instructions.

INSTRUCTIONS TO THE JURY

General Remarks

Instructions to the jury is a relatively recent phenomenon. As Elwork and Sales (1985) note, "prior to the end of the nineteenth century, jurors often decided questions of both law and fact. . . ." (p. 282). The 1895 U.S. Supreme Court decision in *Sparf (Sparf v. United States)* "differentiated the roles of the judge and jury. It became the jury's duty to apply the law to the facts of the case. The judge now had an affirmative duty to instruct the jury on the law" (Elwork & Sales, 1985, p. 282).

What happens if the judge instructs the jury but the jury does not comprehend the instructions? Elwork and Sales note that several state supreme courts have ruled "that the judge is responsible for ensuring that jurors understand the law" (p. 281). The responsibility for comprehensible instructions has been clearly placed on the judge; however, social science research has presented evidence that juries oftentimes fail to understand. These findings are disquieting in general, but they are likely to pose "noisier" problems when insanity is at issue. The definition of "insanity" typically has timbres and harmonics that are not present in the definitions of clear-toned common crimes; and the definition of insanity is a tune that has changed rather frequently over the last 250 years of jurisprudence: repeated changes and ambiguity *per se* are apt to affect understanding and comprehension.

Another point, which affects my DOM schema in particular, is that this type of case involves more steps, differing burdens, and separate issues than would be likely in "simple" crimes and cases. In short, the complexity of the case increases the likelihood that the jurors may not comprehend.

When we return to the social science data, certain factors emerge as having a significant effect on comprehension. Three factors that I find particularly germane here are (1) incomprehensible language, (2) the absence of written instructions, and (3) the timing of instructions. As to incomprehensible language, the DOM instructions will have to be written clearly, using terms and words that are understandable to jurors. When in doubt, the rule should be "use simple words." When abstract concepts are being defined, examples and analogies can help to concretize and link those abstractions to what jurors already understand.

Even with intelligible instructions, the number of issues to be adjudicated, coupled with their complexity, will necessitate lengthy instructions. The expectation that jurors will retain in memory those instructions is unreasonable. Forgetting, distortion, and misconstruing are more likely to occur, and deliberations are more likely to meander onto inappropriate topics. The case for written instructions is a strong one, particularly when it comes to DOM.

The empirical evidence regarding timing of instructions is less robust. Traditionally, the substantive instructions are given after all the evidence has been entered. Advocates of giving instructions at the beginning of a trial (in addition to at the conclusion of the evidence) suggest that beginning instructions may reduce confusion and help jurors organize the evidence and interpret the facts. Elwork and Sales (1985) recommend that substantive instructions "known to be relevant to a trial before it begins should be presented to jurors both before and after the evidence is presented" (p. 291). I would follow their recommendation. A shortened form of the instructions that follow should be read to the jury before testimony and evidence are presented.

INSTRUCTIONS

You, the jurors, have heard evidence and testimony in this case, [insert case], a case where the defendant, [insert name], has entered a plea of Disability of Mind. I will now tell you about your job in this case: about what decisions you will have to make. I will also give you legal guidelines to help you weigh the evidence and reach a fair decision.

THE BEHAVIORAL DECISION

As I have said, this is a case where the defendant has entered a plea of Disability of Mind. Your first decision, however, concerns the defendant's *behavior*, not what the defendant thought, felt, or intended. The first question that you will decide is "Was the defendant's behavior criminal?" Another way of stating the same question is "Did the defendant's behavior cause the harm that is a criminal offense by law?"

For you to answer this first question, you need to understand what the words "defendant" and "behavior" mean here. First, the "defendant" is that person sitting over there [indicates]. His (or her) personal identity is [insert]. We know the personal identity of the defendant even if the defendant is asleep, in a coma, unconscious, or in an altered state. We know the personal identity of the defendant even if he (or she) does not know it or is unable or unwilling to give it. For your first decision, you are not to consider the defendant's mental state or who the defendant thought he (or she) was. Again, the defendant is that person [pointing], who we can name and identify.

When we speak of "behavior" for this first question, "Was the defendant's behavior criminal?" we mean the defendant's movements, motions, and actions that an outside observer would see. For this first question we do not consider the defendant's intentions, what he (or she) wanted to do or not do, meant to do or not do; nor do we consider what the defendant was thinking or not thinking while behaving.

So the question again is "Did that defendant's behavior cause the harm that is a criminal offense by law?" It is up to the prosecution to prove, beyond a reasonable doubt, that the defendant's behavior was criminal. If, after hearing all the evidence, you have reasonable doubts as to whether this defendant committed the behavior, you should find the defendant "Not guilty."

If you are convinced beyond a reasonable doubt that it was this defendant who committed the behavior, then you should find the defendant "Guilty." If you find the defendant "Not Guilty," then your job is complete. With a "Not Guilty" verdict, the defendant is released. If, however, you find the defendant "Guilty," you will have two more decisions to make. I will explain those to you now.

THE MENS DECISION

The next decision you have to make concerns the defendant's mental state at the moment of the act. The question you have to answer is "Was the defendant, at the moment of the act, suffering from a Disability of Mind, and did that Disability of Mind play a significant role in the defendant's criminal behavior?" To properly answer this question, you need to understand the meaning of three terms: (1) the defendant, (2) "disability of mind," and (3) played a significant role.

First, "the defendant." For this question, all the evidence and testimony related to the defendant's mental state, his (or her) intentions, feelings, thoughts, and state of awareness are all relevant. Who the defendant believes himself (herself) to be also may be relevant. In short, whereas the behavioral question asked you to consider the "defendant" in a narrower, objective way, this question asks you to consider the "defendant" in a broad way, which includes subjective factors.

The second term to be defined is "disability of mind," which is a legal term, not a medical, psychiatric, or a psychological term. I will explain it to you by giving some background assumptions. As a result of living in our society, we expect adult citizens to share certain common values, beliefs, perceptions, and understandings. To believe, for example, that it is wrong to commit murder, rob, rape, or arson; to know it is wrong, even if we cannot recite the legal definitions of those crimes. We are also expected to control our actions, to not do certain things because some acts are not in accord with our values, beliefs, and understanding of what it means to be responsible, law-abiding citizens. The law does not expect each of us to consult our values before each and every act; that would be impossible; yet the law does expect its citizens not to commit illegal acts even if they do not consciously consult those societal values that we all possess. For example, when driving a car, we don't swerve across lanes but, rather, we stay in our own lane; we stay in our lane not because we are consciously, at every moment, consulting our inner rules of driving. We have learned those rules of the road, and we can recite them if asked, but those rules affect us even if we are not conscious of it. We have a *capacity* to be in touch with society's rules, values, beliefs, and common understandings that we have learned and incorporated.

A "disability of mind" is where that *capacity* is impaired to a significant degree. Some individuals, for example, because they were brought up in a radically different culture, or because they are very young children, or because they are profoundly retarded, may have never learned those values. Some individuals, like young children, may be able to recite some general values, like you should not steal, yet they are not able to connect their particular actions to the general values. These individuals, it might be said, do not have the *capacity* for responsible action. Some other individuals may have the *capacity*, yet because of impairment of their functioning, cannot use or fully use their capacity. When individuals have their capacity significantly impaired, the law calls this a "Disability of Mind." If the impairment causes a *complete incapacity*, we say that such individuals have a "Total Disability of Mind." Where the impairment causes a *significant but not complete incapacity*, we say they have a "Partial Disability of Mind."

The third term you need to understand is "played a significant role." The Disability of Mind, either "total" or "partial," must be *a major factor in the defendant's subsequent criminal behavior:* that is what "played a significant role" means.

Now, the question is "Was the defendant, at the moment of the act, suffering from a Disability of Mind, and did that Disability of Mind play a significant role in the defendant's criminal behavior?" If you believe that the defendant had a total or partial disability of mind, but you also believe that the disability played no role or, at best, an insignificant role, then your answer to the question is "No." If you believe that the defendant did not have a total or partial disability of mind at the moment of the act, your answer to the question should also be "No." If you believe that the defendant had a total or partial disability of mind and you also believe it did play a significant role, then your answer to the question should be "Yes."

The burden of proof for a disability of mind rests with the defense. The law assumes that the defendant is responsible. It is up to the defense to convince you that the assumption of responsibility is false. The defense must show, by a preponderance of the evidence, that the defendant did indeed have a disability of mind. What does "preponderance of the evidence" mean? According to the law, it means this: where two sides present evidence, the side that presents the stronger, weightier evidence has the preponderance. In this case, the defense has the burden to prove disability of mind that played a significant role and to present evidence to support its claim; the prosecution may present evidence to show that the defendant did not have a disability of mind or that it did not play a significant role; then again, the prosecution could choose not to present evidence either because it does not contest the defense's claim or because it feels that the assumption of responsibility has not been proved false.

What you, the jury, must do is weigh the evidence. If you imagine a perfectly balanced scale and put the defense's evidence on one side and the prosecution's evidence and assumption on the other side, the question is, which side has the weightier (preponderant) case? If, in your opinion, the defense has produced the preponderance of the evidence, then your answer to the disability of mind question is "Yes"; you believe that the defense has shown that a disability of mind played a significant role in the criminal behavior. If, in your opinion, the prosecution has the preponderance of the evidence, then your answer to the disability of mind question is "No"; you believe that the defense has not shown that a disability of mind that played a significant role in the criminal behavior was present.

If your answer was "No," then you have completed the *Mens* phase and you will go on to the *Mens Rea* decision. You will skip the *Culpability* phase, as that is no longer relevant.

If your answer was "yes, the defendant did have a Disability of Mind," then you must answer the next question: "Was the Disability of Mind 'partial' or 'total'"? Again, "Total Disability of Mind" is where the impairment causes a *complete incapacity* in one's ability to use one's values, beliefs, perceptions, judgment, and understanding of what the law expects responsible individuals to do and not do. A "Partial Disability of Mind" is where the impairment causes a *significant but not complete* incapacity in one's ability to use one's values, beliefs, perceptions, judgment, and understanding of what the law expects responsible individuals to do and not do. You will report your verdict as either (1) Total Disability of Mind or (2) Partial Disability of Mind.

A Total Disability of Mind verdict implies that at the moment of the act the defendant was not responsible. A Partial Disability of Mind verdict implies that at the moment of the act the defendant was less responsible than an ordinary citizen who had no disability of mind, but it also implies that he or she is more responsible than a Total Disability of Mind case because he or she did not have a complete incapacity. Thus, with Partial Disability of Mind there is some responsibility, some degree of blameworthiness, some degree of guilt.

CULPABILITY DECISION

So far, you have answered the following questions. Regarding the *Behavioral Decision* you answered the question "Was the defendant's behavior criminal?" with a "Yes" answer. Your verdict was "Guilty." Regarding the *Mens Decision,* you decided that the defendant had a "Disability of Mind and that it played a significant role in the defendant's criminal behavior." You also decided whether the disability was *total* or *partial.*

You now have a final matter to consider, which we call the *Culpability Decision.* When we hold someone "culpable," we judge the person's actions to be blameworthy. That person bears some *guilt.* In the decision you now have to make, the question is "Is the defendant culpable to some degree for bringing about his or her disability of mind?"

To help you understand this question, I will give you an example. Take a person who has had seizures and who has been diagnosed as epileptic. That person takes medication to prevent seizures from happening. Let us say that the person forgets to take his or her medication, drives a car, has a seizure, loses consciousness and control, and crashes. It may well be shown that at the moment of the crash the person had a total disability of mind. But what about the person's failure to take medication? Did the person's earlier action or inaction cause the disability of mind, and if it did, should we hold the person culpable? This is what you, the jury, are now to consider in this case.

Did the defendant, by negligence or recklessness, cause the disability of mind to come about, or did the defendant, with intent, cause the disability to come about? The other possibility is that the defendant was not culpable for bringing about the disability of mind: that the defendant did not intend to bring it about and did not show evidence of recklessness or negligence.

For this decision of culpability for bringing about the disability of mind, the prosecution bears the burden of proof. The prosecution must show, by a preponderance of the evidence, that the defendant was *culpable to some degree* for bringing the disability about. If the prosecution fails to convince you by a preponderance of the evidence, then you should find the defendant "Not Culpable." If the prosecution does convince you, by a preponderance of the evidence, then you should find the defendant "culpable to some degree."

If you find the defendant "culpable to some degree," you must make one further decision: Is the defendant "culpable" or "partially culpable"? A "culpable" verdict means that you believe the defendant *intended* to bring about this disability. A "partially culpable" verdict means that you believe the defendant was either negligent in his or her actions or showed reckless disregard for the consequences of his or her actions. "Partially culpable" is still blameworthy, but it is not as blameworthy as "culpable."

Thus, on the culpability decision, your verdict will be one of the following: "Not Culpable," "Partially Culpable," or "Culpable."

I will now explain to you the consequence of your decisions for the defendant. Given that you found a *disability of mind* (either "total" or "partial"), and you made a decision as to *culpability*, there are six possible verdicts: (1) disability of mind, nonculpable; (2) disability of mind, partially culpable; (3) disability of mind, culpable; (4) partial disability of mind, nonculpable; (5) partial disability of mind, partially culpable; and (6) partial disability of mind, culpable.

Verdict (1), "disability of mind, nonculpable," is the only verdict where the defendant is not given punishment. Having found a full disability of mind at the time of the act, and having found that he or she was not responsible for bringing it about, we do not find such a defendant guilty or warranting punishment. However, if the prosecution believes that the defendant today presents a danger to the community, the prosecution can petition for a new hearing, with a new jury, to consider whether the defendant should be committed to a psychiatric hospital for treatment.

For all the other verdicts, punishment is warranted. For verdicts (2) and (3), where it was found that the defendant had a full disability of mind at the time of the act and was either partially culpable or culpable, we hold such a defendant guilty, blameworthy, and warranting punishment for his or her culpable actions. Punishment is lessened somewhat because the defendant had a full disability of mind; but if he or she were culpable for that disability, the judge will set the punishment in proportion to the culpability.

For verdicts (4), (5), and (6), there is also punishment. Verdict (4) receives some degree of punishment because the defendant did not have a full disability of mind; verdict (5) receives a greater degree of punishment because the defendant did not have a full disability of mind and also because the defendant was partially culpable; verdict (6) receives still greater punishment because the defendant did not have a full disability of mind and because he or she was culpable.

Even though verdicts (2) through (6) receive some degree of punishment, the defendant will be given the option, in addition to punishment, of being able to receive treatment should that be deemed desirable and wanted. Your job as jurors is now complete.

Mens Rea Decision

To reach this decision point you have already concluded two things: (1) that the defendant did commit the behavior that is made criminal by statute and (2) that the defendant was not suffering from a disability of mind. You must now take up the *mens rea* question. For a person to be judged "guilty" for a criminal *act*, two elements must be proved beyond a reasonable doubt. The first, which you have already decided, is that the defendant committed the criminal behavior. The second element is what the law calls the *mens rea* element. [Since this is familiar ground for judges, they can complete the rest of the instructions regarding *mens rea*.]

A Concluding Comment to the Jury

Now that I have given you instructions as to what you have to decide, you will retire to deliberate. Because these instructions have been lengthy, you will all receive a written copy of these instructions to help remind you of the decisions to be made, the order, the burden and standard of proof to be used, and the key terms to help you reach a fair decision.

12

Law and Psychology—The Courtship Reconsidered

REMAINING MATTERS

My recommendations as to the insanity defense are not yet complete. In Chapters 10 and 11 the focus was on the *law*—on defining legally the essence of insanity in a psychologically intelligible way, which includes culpability for bringing about the disability of mind, and on writing test instructions and procedures for adjudicating the matter fairly and coherently. What has been left out, and what still remains, is the matter of the psychological expert. What role is the psychological expert to play during the insanity drama and after?

The psychological expert's role will be examined in four different contexts. The first context is as an "expert witness," and the guiding questions are these. Should the psychological expert be accorded "expert witness" status? Is the substance of this "psychological expertise" science, morality, or one disguised as the other? How far may the expert go in answering the ultimate question of responsibility? And is the expert intruding upon, or usurping, the jury's prerogative? Many of these questions were embedded in the last question the House of Lords put to the 15 Justices who fashioned, through their answers, the M'Naghten rules; however, the Justices, then, hedged their answer on this last question, and thus begged the question. It is time to address it foursquare.

The second context concerns the adversarial model (Horowitz & Willging, 1984) and process by which the criminal trial is conducted in the United States. In this model, it is claimed that "truth" will emerge in this point–counterpoint, prosecution–defense battle. Some have questioned whether this model is the best approach for arriving at the truth or presenting expert testimony, while others have asserted their convictions that it is not. The problems that the adversarial model present for the expert and suggested alternatives will be the second context.

When the DOM and culpability issues have been adjudicated, the defendant may find himself or herself imprisoned or in a psychiatric hospital. The psychological expert is still involved, albeit in different ways. In this third context, we return to the topics of rehabilitation, treatment, and therapy and to the issues of expectations, effectiveness, and ethics.

In the fourth and last context, that involving the decision to release the "insane" individual back into society, we have issues that involve procedures, standards, authority, and accountability; in all of these issues, the psychological expert has been a central character. Here, too, the question is "What role should the psychological expert play?"

In all four of these contexts—providing expert testimony, being an advocate in an adversarial process, providing psychological treatment, and deciding the release question—the psychological expert has experienced conflicts and criticism. In recent times, in the public press, before Congressional committees, and in psychological and psychiatric publications, the role of the expert has been sharply and critically questioned. But the longest-running criticisms directed at psychological experts come from the Law. At times, it has seemed like Law vs. Psychology. At other times, it has seemed like a courtship (Finkel, 1980). Throughout it all, "a passionate ambivalence" (Bazelon, 1982) is detected. These strong pulls, in opposite directions, create tension and contradiction. We see signs in some areas of pulling back, while in other areas it is full speed ahead. The symptoms of ambivalence are evident in the area of insanity, but they are by no means restricted to that topic; the ambivalence cuts across the whole of the relationship, a relationship that has grown dramatically, even as the doubts and discontents mount. We now return to that courtship which is both withering and widening, for it is the courtship and its contentions that provide the context, passion, and subplot for the insanity drama at center stage.

A PASSIONATE AMBIVALENCE

Judge David Bazelon, the fashioner of the *Durham* test of insanity and a judge who has been both receptive to and critical of the behavioral sciences, began his invited address before the American Psychological Association this way (1982):

> Over the years I have developed a passionate ambivalence about the behavioral sciences. As a federal judge for more than three decades, I have tried to open the courthouse doors—but never hand over the keys—to the insights you and your colleagues can offer. At the same time, both on and off the bench, I have also seen behavioral science at its worst. Sometimes his clothes have been visible, but all too visibly tattered. Some think me a disappointed lover. But I am told that it takes continued love to be able to feel continued disappointment. (p. 115)

We hear in Bazelon's words the passionate ambivalence: the invitation to come hither, the opening of the courthouse door, and the hope of insight, enlightenment, and help; but we also hear the echoes of fear—the fear of the gatekeeper of Ilium opening the doors for the enticing Trojan horse—wondering if the gift conceals a price and whether the keys and control will soon be lost.

As history tells us, Bazelon's fear is no mythical fancy. A century and a half ago the alienists were standing before those courthouse doors seeking entree, promising enlightenment. In 1838, Isaac Ray (1838/1983) spoke about Justice's closed doors and mind, an adherence to views that have "ceased to be supported by the results of more extensive and better conducted inquiries." Those "better conducted inquiries," of course, were those of the alienists like himself, the medico-psychological scientists. His hopes were plainly stated:

> In their zeal to uphold the wisdom of the past, from the fancied desecrations of reformers and theorists, the ministers of the law seem to have forgotten, that, in respect to this subject, the real dignity and respectability of their profession is better upheld, by yielding to the improvements of the times and thankfully receiving the truth from whatever quarter it may come, than by turning away with blind obstinacy, from every thing that conflicts with long established maxims and decisions. (p. 4)

If Ray was hoping for entree, an audience, and the opportunity to impart rays of wisdom, Forbes Winslow was hoping for much more. Winslow (1843/1983), writing in the year of M'Naghten, 1843, stated:

> The time, I hope, is not very distant, when there will be instituted for the investigation of cases in which it is important to establish the existence or nonexistence of aberration of mind a separate jurisdiction, presided over by persons whose attention has been specially directed to the study of mental aberration. (p. vi)

Winslow hoped for control: he wanted the jurisdictional keys to the insanity fiefdom in the hands of the medico-psychological scientists. The suitor seeks to penetrate the gates, but preeminence is the desire. Blind Justice, feeling she is about to be had, opens an eye and tries to shut the gates. Courtship interruptus results.

Bazelon is not the only one who has been disappointed, nor is he alone in recommending that we keep a watchful, wary eye open. The disappointment and disillusionment have been felt by psychology and psychiatry as well. Many mental health professionals have offered their expertise to the courts in the hope that such knowledge will elucidate "the truth." They have been disillusioned when they find that "the primary purpose of the law is not the determination of factual truth, but the authoritative resolution of disputes . . ." (Sperlich, 1985, p. 345; Loh, 1985). Alan Stone (1984), President of the American Psychiatric Association and Harvard University Professor of Law and Psychiatry, is a passionate critic of the Criminal Justice System. He writes:

> The American Criminal Justice System is ready to collapse under its own weight. The criminals, if they ever organized themselves into a union and refused to plea bargain, could bring the whole enterprise to its knees. My colleague, Alan Dershowitz [1982], has described the courthouse as resembling a Turkish bazaar more than a hall of justice. And no wonder—prosecutors as well as defense laywers are scrambling to make bargains; they have no choice.
>
> I said that the Criminal Justice System fails to protect the public, but all this deal-cutting results in another kind of failure, a corruption of the public's sense of justice.
> . . . .
> After this account you can understand my response to recent complaints in the United States that psychiatry and the insanity defense were corrupting the system of justice. My response was that the insanity defense is a pimple on the nose of justice but the patient is dying of congestive heart failure. (pp. 46, 48)

Stone by no means is critical only of plea bargaining. His list of criticisms (and I summarize only some) is a long one: that courts not only interpret the law, but make policy decisions, oftentimes masking or denying the latter; that courts contradict themselves; and that the Supreme Court "has turned its back on the mentally ill," deals with issues "in the narrowest possible way," has "no coherent policy and no clear direction," and "is ambivalent" (pp. 104–105).

Others in the medico-psychological sciences have complained about legal "ignorance" and "inertia" (Lochner, 1973), its incompetency and illegitimacy as policymakers, and its imperial, close-mindedness (Horowitz, 1977). Sperlich (1985) put it this way:

> From the perspective of the sciences, the law looks like this: It needs science to fulfill its key task. It controls the use of science. It forever complains about science. Frequently it ignores relevant scientific findings. Often it misuses scientific evidence and mistreats scientific experts. The question suggests itself: Why do scientists continue to cooperate? (p. 328)

Sperlich refuses to explore masochism as the answer, but, rather, suggests that "the answer may well be found in a genuine feeling of obligation and the hope that cooperation will produce important social benefits." The curiousness of the scientist and the pursuit of truth are other noble reasons and answers to the motive question "Why cooperate?" These are the "hooks" that keep us invested and involved in spite of the disappointments and disillusionments.

There is a paradox in these mutual disappointments. Stone (1984) puts it this way:

> The more the law has condemned psychiatric power, and the more it has criticized psychiatric expertise, the greater has been the demand for these discredited services. What is more, lawyers keep finding new uses for psychiatric testimony. (p. 106)

The same and more can be said for psychological expertise. The areas of involvement between law and psychology and law and psychiatry continue to grow. As the courtship withers, it paradoxically widens. Horowitz and Willging (1984) write that the "courts appear to have difficulty finding a middle ground between rejection of social science and dependency on it" (p. 360). The social, behavioral, and medical sciences have their own ambivalence and paradoxical reactions: the more frequent the rebuffs and the sharper the criticism, the harder we pursue. There is a qualification here, followed by another paradox.

When rebuffed and criticized, some in the mental health professions have halted, self-examined, and said, "O.K., you're right, this is something we do not know enough about or cannot do well enough." Predicting future dangerousness is a central example. The second paradox is that when the professions have demurred, disclaiming expertise, the courts have said "Yes, you do have such expertise, and may testify," as in capital punishment predictions (*Barefoot v. Estelle*, 1983); furthermore, as in *Tarasoff*-like cases involving "duty to warn" (*Tarasoff v. Regents of the University of California*, 1974) and "obligation to use reasonable care to protect" (*Tarasoff v. Regents of the University of California*, 1976) potential victims from a potentially dangerous patient's possible actions, the courts have said that therapists not only should be able to predict dangerousness (even though psychology and psychiatry have demonstrated that they cannot predict dangerousness accurately), but that they are to be held responsible, liable, and negligent for their failure to do what they claim they cannot do.

In short, even when those in the mental health professions admit that their powers are negligible—that their Cassandra-like clairvoyance cannot accurately discern the dangerous from the non—the courts have claimed otherwise. Whereas Justice Mosk, in his dissent, recognized that we have a curious wonderland v. reality problem here (all the more "curiouser" because of who claimed what), the majority of justices nevertheless opted for wonderland, ascribing to professionals powers they do not possess, standards that do not exist, and obligations that they may not be able to meet. Thus, even when the professions have tried to retreat, deeper involvement resulted.

A WITHERING AND WIDENING COURTSHIP

In Chapter 3 ("The Courtship of Law and Psychology"), I detailed the overt beginning moves of the courtship as it unfolded in the nineteenth century. The alienists, the forebearers of psychiatrists and forensic specialists of the twentieth century, came from varied settings: some were superintendents of asylums or owners of a private madhouse; others were in private practice or university settings; most were physicians. The influence they had varied from one practitioner to another, as did the views they expressed. But in 1841, a formal solidarity began "with the founding of the Association of Medical Officers of Asylums and Hospitals for the Insane" (Smith, 1981, p. 13). However, the Association's effectiveness as either a unified voice or as a pressure group was not immediately achieved. But in the 1850s, the Association began the *Journal of Mental Science* under the editorship of Dr. John Charles Bucknill. The succeeding editors, particularly Henry Maudsley, who was described as a "brilliant and arrogant man," gave the alienists a voice, a sense of unity, and, most of all, a mission—the universal scientific goal of truth.

The goal was grand, if not grandiose: "responsibility" was to be replaced by "disease," "morality" was to be superseded by "natural law," and Law itself would yield to Medicine. The alienists' agenda was never achieved, but its inroads and influences were significant; and in some areas, criminal law did relinquish its jurisdictional hold (i.e., the process of divestment) over many offenders, with "treatment" coming to replace "punishment" as the dominant construct.

The alienists were predominately clinicians, those who diagnosed and treated individuals, administered hospitals, and derived their notions from their applied work. Their method was primarily a clinical case history approach (Rosenhan & Seligman, 1984), and their knowledge and certainty grew by the addition of case upon case. From the accumulation of cases, they developed a taxonomy, and from there, made generalizations. This method and approach carried on into the twentieth century, but it was joined in the twentieth century by another strand—a method and body of knowledge that derived from experimental work done in psychological laboratories. This "new science" and new strand of psychological knowledge, because it came from experiments that were controllable and repeatable, could isolate causal elements whereas the clinical case history method could not; thus, the emprical knowledge that grew from this approach was regarded as sturdier and more reliable. Experimental psychology was growing rapidly. It was about to be brought before the courts and the Law. A boon, or a threat? The messenger was Hugo Munsterberg.

In 1908, Hugo Munsterberg wrote *On the Witness Stand*. In his Introduction, he stated that "now experimental psychology has reached a stage at which it seems natural and sound to give attention to its possible service for the practical needs of life" (p. 8). He was bringing that knowledge to the courts: knowledge about illusion, perception, memory, emotion, suggestion, and more—the psychological underpinnings of witness testimony. But he would go further, offering knowledge and analysis of the trial process itself, and conveying his astonishment "that the work of justice is carried out in the courts without ever consulting the psychologist . . ." (p. 194).

Munsterberg's work was quickly criticized by the legal profession. Wigmore (1909), a legal authority on evidence, fired back. Wigmore seemed to be responding to what he perceived as Munsterberg's admonition of the legal profession, as well as to the scientific basis of Munsterberg's contentions (Lipsitt, 1984). Munsterberg may have erred, as Terman (1931) suggested, "not so much in exaggerating the importance of psychology for law as in exaggerating the importance of the contributions at hand." The "contributions at hand" would grow dramatically. But Wigmore's criticisms also reveal the legal profession's defensiveness and fear: to allow the essential *moral* nature of the law "to be washed away in a river of swirling empirical 'reality'" (Horowitz & Willging, 1984, p. 358) was unacceptable, and to be vigorously opposed.

In 1935 Edward Robinson's *Law and the Lawyers* brought the underlying Law vs. Psychology contention to the fore. Robinson believed "that every legal problem was fundamentally a psychological one," and he "urged that psychological 'facts' be substituted for such legal concepts as intent, reasonable person, and precedent. This was the road law would have to travel in order to be a truly scientific discipline" (Horowitz & Willging, 1984, p. 7). Robinson's proposition, which was the alienist's agenda now supported by the methods of modern science, was still unacceptable to the law; to open the courthouse doors surely meant losing the controlling keys. However, the actual impact of experimental psychology on the law remained quite modest, despite the urgings of Munsterberg, Robinson, and others, until the Supreme Court's landmark decision in *Brown v. Board of Education* in 1954.

"Jesus Christ, those damned dolls! I thought it was a joke."

The comment, by William Coleman (Kluger, 1979, p. 321), then clerking for Justice Felix Frankfurter, refers to Kenneth Clark's studies, where he used dolls, some brown and some white, to show children usually preferred the white doll and rejected the brown doll, even when brown was their own color. These results, along with other empirical evidence from social scientists, were to have a significant impact on the "inherent inequality" of "separate but equal" education, the central issue in *Brown*. It was no joke. And if there were laughs, they were quickly and loudly drowned out by a chorus of legal criticisms. Professor Edmund Cahn (1955) was swift and pointed in his critique:

> I would not have the constitutional rights of Negroes—or of other Americans—rest on any such flimsy foundation as some of the scientific demonstra-

tions in these records . . . [Behavioral science findings] have an uncertain expectancy of life." (Horowitz & Willging, 1984, p. 324)

Again, amidst the now familiar contention and ambivalence, we have that fundamental question: Does social science research enlighten substantive matters before the courts or does it threaten to displace the moral basis upon which the law rests? Social scientists, it is clear, were not resting, and they continued to bring before the courts more and more demonstrations, with longer "life expectancies," that would firm the so-called "flimsy foundation."

From today's vantage point, the amount of social science research that has been brought to bear on legal matters is staggering, and the breadth of topics that have been investigated would amaze even Munsterberg. In the area of predictions, the social sciences are still involved in competence, insanity, and involuntary commitment; added to those traditional areas we now have social scientists involved in sentencing, in capital punishment decisions, in release questions, and in predictions of recidivism (Ewing, 1985; Teplin 1984; Bartol, 1983; Shapiro, 1974; Lipsitt & Sales, 1980). The predictive business has spun a profiling offshoot: profiles of potential Presidential assassins, skyjackers, dope smugglers, terrorists, serial murderers, and more (Pinizzotto, 1984; Ault & Resse, 1980; Porter, 1983).

Social scientists have investigated judges, jurors, biases, voir dire, jury size, instructions, group decision making, and more (Kalven & Zeisel, 1971; Davis, Bray, & Holt, 1977; Follingstad, 1985; Buckhout, 1979; Ellison & Buckhout, 1981; Kaplan & Schersching, 1980; Saks & Hastie, 1978; Cohn & Udolf, 1979; Bermant, 1985; Lockhart v. McCree, 1986; Amicus curiae brief for the American Psychological Association, 1987; Bersoff, 1987). They have investigated a host of issues related to witness testimony: perception, eyewitness identification, cross-racial problems, the effects of unconscious transference, memory, storage, and stress on recall, confessions, and interrogation techniques (Yarmey, 1979; Loftus, 1979; Wells, 1985; Kassin & Wrightsman, 1985; Zimbardo, 1967; Loftus & Monahan, 1980).

Social scientists have investigated the legal process and its aspects: the adversarial system, discretionary law, the order of presentation of evidence, persuasion, instructions to the jury (the type, timing and comprehension), the standards of proof, the burden of proof, and more (Thibaut & Walker, 1975; Elwork & Sales, 1985).

The above listing is far from complete, and the breadth and depth of empirical research keeps widening and increasing. That fearful swirling river of empirical reality has already become a rising sea; it is no wonder that some jurists see fearful visions of capsizing and drowning, of the law losing its moral moorings, drifting to the whims and currents of empirical tides. These dreaded visions and "thick-coming fancies" are also shared by some psychiatrists and psychologists as well. Daniel Robinson (1980), a psychologist, questioned, through the subtitle of his book on Psychology and Law, Can Justice Survive the Social Sciences? His conclusion is that it could not. The psychiatrist Thomas Szasz (1984) had reached the same conclusion years before.

Thus, along with the widening comes a withering of desire, and a wondering about what went wrong, about what *is* wrong. The clarion calls can be heard, but the urgings have been contradictory: a few recommend retreat, or cease and desist; others recommend full speed ahead; and some urge us to pause and rethink. In the next section, I plan to pause long enough to bring to the surface certain underlying values that are either unresolved or conflictual and to think over such matters at some depth. In doing so, I am following Judge Bazelon's (1982) advice to psychology: "Unveil *your* values. Unveil our values" (p. 120).

UNVEILING VALUES

Judge Bazelon (1982) began to unveil some values, starting with "the sins of nondisclosure." One such sin, according to the judge, is that when health professionals enter the court to testify in such matters as insanity defense and civil commitment, there is a tendency to offer conclusory statements. He writes:

> Conclusory statements are bad enough when they merely propound the scientific gospel. They become positively dangerous when they verge into naked pronouncements on the ultimate issue faced by the decisionmaker.
> What the public needs most from any expert, including the psychologist, is a wealth of intermediate observations and conceptual insights that are adequately explained. Only then can his or her contributions be combined with the communal sense of right and wrong to produce a decision. (p. 116)

What are the causes of this tendency toward overstatement, conclusions, and the airs of certainty? Why have the scientific experts seemingly forgotten for those moments on the witness stand their modesty and their ethical obligations to admit uncertainty? As Thomas Grisso (1987, p. 836) says, why doesn't the forensic expert state " 'I'm sorry, but my technology and empirical base do not allow me to testify confidently on that matter' " with frequency. Bazelon (1982) comes very close to answering the question:

> Experts should be more than modest. They should aggressively resist the pressures put on them to go beyond their expertise. Moreover, the uncomfortable truth is that the public's abdication of responsibility is never permanent. If you too eagerly accept an illegitimate mantle of authority, you are likely to be thanked one moment and bitterly chastised the next." (p. 118)

Authority—is that the answer? The reflective forensic expert ponders, Do we seek power, control, and preeminence? Perhaps. Certainly, we can search our history (see Chapter 3) and find confirming instances of the expert's reach for authority. But to what end? What does authority confer? The words "experts" and "expertise" offer another clue. Does the very act of testifying confer an expertise and status (i.e., "expert") that we do not truly possess or deserve, but nonetheless desire? Do we use the courts to not only sanction our legitimacy within the legal scheme of things, but to sanctify our place as "scientists"? Is the expert thus posing, or, in the words Shakespeare wrote and Angus spoke about Macbeth, "does he feel his title hang loose about him, like a giant's robe upon a dwarfish thief"? As Macbeth wears a giant's robe, do we wear an illegitimate mantle?

Bazelon also refers to "pressures." Are we pressured from the outside, from lawyers, from the adversarial process itself, to become partisans? Do we foresake the whole truth (Stone, 1984, p. 72), then, for the partisan truth? But Bazelon does not let us "cop" an insanity plea for our actions: We should resist such pressures, and he believes we can; thus, those pressures, no matter how great or tempting, do not amount to irresistible impulses.

Overall, Bazelon's criticisms and admonitions are rather temperate. In sharper contrast, however, are the following criticisms and unveilings received by forensic experts from within the profession. First, a statement from Thomas Szasz (1984)

> I would define a forensic psychiatrist as an honest doctor sent into court to lie for his masters. (p. 122)

Second, a statement from Alan Stone (1984):

> But I would claim that if forensic psychiatrists limited themselves to the standards of bench scientists, not only would they not testify about ultimate legal questions; their lips would be sealed in the courtroom." (p. 66)

These two quotes, conclusory statements both, are far from temperate. It is not that they were said but why they were said that is of concern here. What values and facts lie behind these conclusions? We next turn to three such value conflicts. The first is the conflict between science and morality, between an orientation rooted in "facts" and another that is rooted in values (Fingarette, 1972). The second value conflict has been phrased in various ways: as a conflict between free will and determinism, as a mind–brain conflict, and as a conflict between those espousing the necessity of the concept of a "self" versus those who seek a deconstruction of the self (Stone, 1984). The third value conflict is between a paternalistic orientation and one that touts autonomy (Gaylin, Glasser, Marcus, & Rothman, 1978). I will try to show that these three value conflicts—science vs. morality, free will vs. determinism, and paternalism vs. autonomy—are simplistic, confused, and, in some ways, either not the point or beside the point. This is not to imply that there really are no conflicts; rather, by examining these conflicts first in their starkest light, I hope to identify what those conflicts are really about.

SCIENCE (AND FACTS) VS. MORALITY (AND VALUES)

To stake out the moral position in stark and extreme form, I turn to the words of Alan Stone (1984), who quotes and summarizes the position of Immanuel Kant (Kant, 1978, p. 111):

> The most basic question is whether psychiatrists have true answers to the legal and moral questions posed by the law. Immanuel Kant, who after two centuries is still a dominant figure in the landscape of moral philosophy, had strong opinions about this question. He wrote, "concerning the question whether the mental condition of the agent was one of derangement or of a fixed purpose held with a sound understanding, forensic medicine is meddling with alien business." Kant would give a different meaning to the ancient designation of the forensic psychiatrist as an *alienist*. Kant also wrote, "physicians are generally still not advanced enough to see deeply into the mechanisms inside a human being in order to determine the cause of an unnatural transgression of the moral law."
>
> Kant's opinion was both that our science was inadequate and that as to moral questions, alienists were meddling in alien business. (p. 59)

To the scientist who is psychologically and philosophically sophisticated, Kant's view appears ironic and wrong. It is ironic, given the philosophic position he developed in his *Critique of Pure Reason* (1781–1953). Unlike Hume, Kant shows us the possibility of "pure" reason, of knowledge independent of all sense experience, and this possibility comes about through "the inherent structure of our minds, from the natural and inevitable manner in which our minds must operate" (Durant, 1954, p. 267). In short, and put perhaps in extreme, Kant places understanding, including moral understanding, on a psychological foundation. If our modes of perception and apperception and our categories of understanding are embedded in the very inherent nature of our mind, then those disciplines that specialize in the nature of mind should have a preeminent claim to be heard. To paraphrase and reach the opposite conclusion, we can assert that the alienist is delving not in "alien business," but into the central matter of mind, for which the alienist, by virtue of training and experience, is eminently qualified.

Another point of Kant's—that we cannot see into the mind, deeply or otherwise—is of course true; but it is also irrelevant and beside the point. The law requires, except in strict liability offenses, that juries assess what is in defendants' minds (i.e., *mens rea*) all the time. They do so in spite of the "fact" that this is impossible "at this time" (i.e., "that science has not yet developed that far, but it may"), and in spite of the assertion that this task is a metaphysical impossibility. The law is not engaging in "bad science," or "bad metaphysics," or "bad philosophy." Those conclusions reveal a misunderstanding regarding what the law is about. I turn to Herbert Fingarette's (1972) passage to clarify:

> Of course, each such judgment of another's mind has its particular limits, obstacles, and sources of deception. We never know everything that is in an-

other person's mind at any time. But this does not imply that we know nothing of what is in his mind ever. We are not always confident in our judgment, but this does not mean we never are. In fact, in the moment-to-moment routine of everyday living, we are usually entirely confident of our judgments in these matters. The fostering of an image of all these happenings locked up inside a person's mind, and the tendency to emphasize the occasional problematic case where we are in doubt about what someone has in mind, lead to the impression that we are always forced to guess, that we always and necessarily are forced to engage in "mere" (that is, unreasonable) inference in these matters. The undue emphasis on our fallibility nourishes the utterly unwarranted inference that our judgments should always be challenged because they are always in principle challengeable.

But the impression that we can only speculate or guess about these matters is a temporary illusion produced by emphasizing the metaphor of an inaccessible interior. In actual fact we do not usually have to guess or speculate about such unobservable events. We make our judgments according to all that we do see and hear, what we know about the surrounding circumstances in the particular case, what we know about life in general, what we have learned in our own experience and inner life. We are very often warrantedly confident, not merely guessing, in making such judgments.

As to the metaphysical denial that such a judgment can ever attain to absolute certainty, that it is always challengeable and therefore always dubious because, whatever our indirect evidence, we can never make the final check and look directly into another's mind, the law need not concern itself with such an abstruse and controversial doctrine. For the law has no need to claim, nor does it claim, that it is making a "metaphysically certain" judgment, whatever that might be. It is enough—indeed it is the usual and proper thing—for the law to judge a man's mind in the usual ways, in the only way we can and do judge, by reference to what men can observe and what men can know of life. If there is a reasonable doubt because of lack of adequate information, that establishes no metaphysical crisis but only one of the commonplace outcomes in a criminal trial. Concerning metaphysical certainty, the law is concerned with what has often been aptly termed "moral certainty," not the metaphysical kind. (pp. 82–83)

Fingarette situates the law in a moral and communal context separated from metaphysical morality. In so doing, the "ultimate unknowable mind" problem is not necessarily fatal. Moreover, claims like Kant's, or Chief Justice Brian's (Hart, 1968, p. 188) before him ("the thought of man is not triable," said in 1477), and Lady Barbara Wootton's (1960, p. 232) after (a man's responsibility lies "buried in consciousness, into which no human being can enter"), miss the mark and confuse the core, central issues; and being that these claims are not determinative, they do not bar the courthouse doors to the psychological, scientific experts.

We now switch to the other extreme, presenting the scientific position in its stark form. The scientific thesis maintains that law (with its concepts of "responsibility", "intent," "will," and others) rests upon unscientific, outmoded beliefs about human nature, when it ought to be based upon natural law and scientific findings. Moreover, science elucidates causes, whereas the law offers only teleological (and hence fallacious) explanations. To cling to explanations and doctrines that are outworn and unsupportable is both irrational and unreasonable. Furthermore, scientifically derived notions help us not only understand human nature better, but help us develop better, more efficient means of reducing, controlling, and treating antisocial activity. Thus, *the moral nature* of the law—based as it is on irrational fictions unsupported by facts, unable as it is to understand or control criminal acts—ought to be superseded by a value-free, morally neutral science.

The above scientific thesis oversimplifies, confuses its own nature as well as the law's, and finally misses the point. To begin my critique of the scientific position, I start with the claim that Science could create a more efficient schema for reducing, controlling, and treating antisocial, illegal activity. This claim reduces science and moral law to two competing and "different means to the same end" (Fingarette, 1972, p. 61). This is a misconception. As "different means to the same end," we can also include systems that feature tyranny, benign dictators, and Brave New World conditioners and drug dispensers; any and all of these may be highly efficient at controlling crime, perhaps more efficient than a scientific means, but we do not choose these systems. As Fingarette states, our system

> . . . reflects and embodies certain fundamental values of our society. In particular, it embodies a fundamental and characteristic resolution of the community, that normally the state shall deal with all members of the community as responsible persons under law. In short, it is a central value, and not a mere utilitarian convenience, that socialization of conduct in our society shall normally be *through* responsibility under law. Our criminal law, founded as it is on the principle of individual responsibility, is not a mere means toward reducing antisocial activity; the institution is itself an essential end for the society. For we do not want merely an orderly society; we want an order of responsible persons, responsible under law. (pp. 56–57)

We pay a price for this value orientation. But let us be clear that the responsibility orientation is a central value, not primarily a means and method for reducing criminality. Thus, science's evidence of its "superior effectiveness in reducing criminality would be irrelevant. No evidence could possibly suffice to justify such a substitution. . ." (Fingarette, p. 60).

The second and third claims of the scientific position are that science produces nonteleological, causal explanations. Both claims are marred by error. Fingarette identifies

> a very generalized and fallacious presupposition . . . that any statement characterizing human affairs that is not itself a scientific statement must be either a relatively inferior ("common sense") approximation to such a scientific statement or else must be abandoned as false, irrational, or meaningless. (pp. 62–63)

He draws an analogy to chess to make his point. Let us say that we ask the question "Why was black's pawn moved?" to a physicist, a neuropsychologist, and a chess grand master. Let us also grant that the physicist is able to give a complete explanation of the move in terms of masses, forces, inertia, and Newton's laws. As for the neuropsychologist, let us grant that he or she too can give a complete explanation of the move in terms of sensory input, nerve transmission, synaptic action, sensory-motor templates, and the like. Both the physicist and the neuropsychologist have furnished us scientific, causal explanations of the move, each at a different level of analysis, and both may be true; however, for the question at hand, both are irrelevant. It is the chess grand master's explanation, "to threaten white's queen," which provides us the most meaningful account of the move, even though it is teleological in that it invokes the player's intent. The first point, then, is that teleological explanations, whether they are uttered by chess players, ordinary citizens, or legal moralists, are neither irrational nor necessarily inferior to causal, nonteleological explanations.

Now let us take a closer look at the typical "scientific" explanations offered in court by forensic psychiatrists. These psychiatric explanations oftentimes employ "structural" terms, such as "id," "ego," and "superego," and "dynamic" concepts such as "drives," "defense mechanisms," "forces," "conflicts," and "energy." Many of the terms are borrowed and adapted from natural science, *but they are used in a teleological sense:* they are used to explain a defendant's thought, wishes, aims, and self-control. These so-called "scientific" explanations are really much closer to the teleological explanations found in law that invoke "knowledge," "intent," "guilt," and "motive" than they are to the physicist's explanations of "matter," "energy," and "motion." Psychological accounts may technicalize and modify traditional legal terms, but their explanations of human behavior are essentially of the same kind as those used in the law.

In a more direct way, what I am saying is that the typical explanations offered by forensic psychologists and psychiatrists are *not scientific explanations.* This does not mean, however, that they are inferior, irrational, or not useful. They may be extremely useful and illuminating. Fingarette states,

> the sense of illumination afforded by such an explanation comes from showing us, to our surprise, that behavior which had seemed merely bizarre, arbitrary, or incoherent takes on the aspect of meaningful, intelligible, purposeful conduct in terms of our ordinary understanding of human beings and human conduct. . .
> In short, the psychiatrist does not use a radically different mode of explanation from our usual one; on the contrary, he reveals that he is more skillful than we in grasping the meaning, in familiar and teleological terms, of conduct which is on its face meaningless, bizarre, or extreme. (pp. 87–88)

A number of conclusions and implications are apparent from this look at science vs. morality. For one, both the science and the morality sides have been confusingly cast in extremes, and the extreme views do not accurately reflect what the law is about or what forensic experts do. For another, the so-called "gap" between science and morality, when it comes to the explanations and practices of forensic and legal proponents, largely evaporates. Scientific explanations, by their nature, do not assume an exalted status, nor do teleological explanations, by their nature, assume an inferior, irrational status. Thus, the forensic expert has no preeminent claim because he or she claims to be practicing science; and just because his or her claims to science are unjustified does not mean that the forensic expert has nothing useful to contribute.

Free Will vs. Determinism

Again, as in the preceding subsection, we begin with extremes. The "determinist" position holds that every action is completely causally determined (Fingarette, p. 71).

> According to determinist views, the conditions at any moment, taken together with the relevant laws of nature, necessitate (nonpurposively) the conditions that will obtain at the next moment.

The "free will" position holds that

> when the will operates it is never causally necessitated (in the above deterministic sense) to operate as it does. In Aristotle's words, "For what lies in our power to do, lies in our power not to do" (Fingarette, p. 71, citing *Nicomochaean Ethics*).

Although these positions are in opposition to one another, they lead, for opposing reasons, to the same conclusion: "that any attempt to distinguish those acts a person did freely from those he could not refrain from doing is a misguided attempt that must lead to error" (p. 75).

The metaphysical doctrines of "free will" and "determinism" lead to a common conclusion, but that conclusion clashes with what actually happens under law: whereas the metaphysical positions see error in trying to differentiate "free" actions from "caused" actions, the law does make differentiations. How are these legal differentiations to be explained? Is the legal reasoning behind the differentiating in error?

The answer to this last question is "No." To explicate, what does come clear is that the law is not committed to either metaphysical doctrine; in fact, the law uses terms such as "caused" and "compelled" or their opposites, "free" and "uncompelled," in an *ordinary* context of moral assessment rather than referring to the metaphysical context of universal causality or freedom. As an illustration, we can turn to examples of excusing conditions under law, such as self-defense, duress, or necessity. A defendant pleading such a defense is not making a metaphysical case for causality (i.e., "I was compelled or caused to act as I did"), and the law is not excusing the defendant on metaphysical grounds; rather, the law is operating on a common norm—one that says that if person is placed in a believably threatening situation where he or she is in mortal danger if he or she refuses to act as he or she did, we cannot demand that the person act otherwise (pp. 80–81). To demand that the person act otherwise would be inconsistent with our reasonable expectations that derive from our common-sense understanding of human nature.

There has been confusion and conflict in court between forensic experts and their legal, jurist counterparts over the "free will v. determinism" question. Much of that confusion and conflict, I maintain, occurs because scientific experts confuse themselves and the courts by hiding or overselling their presumptions. By way of explanation, I begin with how science oversells determinism. One area of overselling is our deterministic theories of criminality (Wilson & Herrnstein, 1985). The sciences have found correlations between a number of factors (e.g., genetic, age, gender, intelligence, broken and abusive families, alcohol, heroin) and crime; using those findings, scientists have constructed various theories (e.g., genetic, psychological, sociological) as to the causes of crime, with much of that theorizing being deterministic. But correlational evidence is not the strongest sort of evidence: we may use it to make fairly reliable predictions about groups of individuals, but our reliability and confidence in our predictions drops when it comes to individual prediction, which is what a criminal trial is about; on a more fundamental level, though, correlational evidence does not yield *causative* conclusions. The scientist may adopt Cicero's comment that "the nature of law must be founded on the nature of man," but science has neither furnished the completed picture of the nature of man or the causes of crime, nor has it demonstrated that the legal concept of personal responsibility is not part of that picture.

When the forensic expert enters the courtroom and uses a deterministic theory of violence as if it was an unquestioned scientific fact to support his or her testimony, he or she oversells determinism and undermines moral responsibility. The forensic expert oversells again, and distorts, when he or she speaks of "psychic determinism" as if it was the same, nonteleological kind of determinism that the natural sciences invoke. He or she perpetuates the distortion by failing to acknowledge that certain psychiatric concepts, such as

> reality principle, adaptation, ego, superego, and id . . . embody tacit reference
> to the individual's moral views and attitudes, to his capacity to apprehend the
> moral views of society, and even to the psychiatrist's own moral assessment of
> the conscience of a particular person. (Fingarette, p. 105)

The end result of these distortions at trial is that the "bad" became the "mad," and moral failures in "personal responsibility" become causally determined "psychopathology." This is not the end result, however, because after the trial the distortions turn into contradiction and paradox: following the trial, the therapeutic experts now recommend treatment to restore the defendant's sense of responsibility and to bolster his or her controls—through a therapeutic process that "is itself in some way rooted in responsibility" (p. 60).

The overselling of determinism has another offshoot in the mind–brain controversy. Set in extreme form, if science can reduce "mind" to the matter and materialism of the brain, then mentalistic and legalistic concepts, such as "personal responsibility," evaporate (see Chapter 8). The materialist position has had a long run in psychological theorizing. Hippocrates looked at the brain and the Greeks looked to the humours to explain human behavior. The classical age physicans of the seventeenth and eighteenth centuries invoked biles, chemistry, mechanics, and metaphors to account for human nature. The nineteenth-century alienists looked for lesions and disease pathology to account for aberrant behavior. In 1895, Freud, in his "Project for a Scientific Psychology" (Freud, 1974a) sought to develop a model and reduce psychology to physical matter and energy; although he failed, particularly when it came to accounting for consciousness (Fancher, 1973), and subsequently abandoned the Project, science has not given up the materialist hope of giving up the ghost in the machine.

The neuropsychological quest of the twentieth century is the latest, but certainly not the last, attempt to explain and locate "mentalistic" notions in the hemispheres of the brain and in the chemistry of the synapse. If it all becomes matter, then the notion of mind does not matter. If it is reducible to differential functioning of the hemispheres of the brain, or brain "modules" (Gazzaniga, 1985), then an integrated mind or a unity of the self (which is endowed with responsibility) either is nonexistent or, in the "modular" metaphor, fractionates into so many "minds" and "selves" that we are left to conclude that "nobody is driving the bus." As an end result, we have no one to blame and hold morally responsible when the bus crashes.

In an important way, the determinist–materialist quest is irrelevant. Psychological and psychiatric "scientists," in doubt and insecure about their own scientism, have acted, it seems, on the mistaken belief that unless they offer deterministic causes and materialistic answers, they have nothing of value to offer the courts. This belief is an error, I submit, and because I believe so, I disagree with two of Robinson's (1980) recommendations regarding how the law should treat psychiatric and psychological testimony. He writes:

> 1. All statements regarding the mental state of the accused or of any party to litigation are to be treated as statements of belief or opinion. They are not to be accorded the status of evidence, are not to be admitted in evidence, and juries are to be specifically instructed not to take them as evidence.
> . . . .
> 3. In all cases in which psychiatric or psychological testimony is to the effect that the party at issue is diseased, the testimony must be accompanied by relevant biochemical or neurological findings. For purposes of justice, the term *disease* refers to a discernible pathological process in the tissues or organs of the body. The term "mental disease" is to be taken as a metaphor, not as a diagnostic specification. (p. 206)

My position is that psychology and psychiatry may have something of value to contribute at a criminal trial; this contribution will be less definitive than the determinist–materialist may wish, but that does not imply that it is useless and irrelevant; furthermore, the testimony will be based in part on values and about values, but that again does not discredit its worth. Let us turn to an insanity case to illustrate. When a psychiatrist or psychologist is called in to examine the defendant, the expert possesses certain skills (e.g., interviewing) by virtue of training that will aid in determining whether the defendant (1) is aware (knowledgeable) of certain community values, attitudes, beliefs, and expectations; (2) knows that those values are embedded in the law; (3) shares those values in the abstract; and (4) incorporates those values in practice. In this capacity and task, the psychological expert is acting like an anthropologist or sociologist. "This amounts to saying that, contrary to the protestations cited earlier, the psychiatric expert by virtue of his professional doctrine and training ought to be peculiarly well equipped to assess a person's knowledge "that he was doing something wrong." (Fingarette, p. 100)

I would qualify the last conclusion by adding that although the expert is "well equipped," he or she can be fooled by a simulator, malingerer, or a deceiver. In short, the expert may be confident in his or her conclusion, but he or she cannot be certain.

Forensic experts also may testify about the defendant's behavior, his or her actions and words, and draw inferences about his or her memory, perceptions, affect, and cognitions. This evidence may be quite valuable for the jurors who have to decide the legal matter. And in this task and capacity, what the forensic expert is doing is akin to the experimental psychologist in a laboratory with college sophomores investigating attention, memory, perception, or cognition.

The forensic expert's testimony takes him or her into questionable areas when he or she offers a diagnosis (see Chapter 4). The first point I wish to make is that a diagnosis involves more than the sum of symptoms comprising a disorder; the second point is that having a diagnostic label infers less than what some forensic experts imply; and third, on both points, experts have run into problems.

On the first point, a psychiatric diagnosis involves values as well as symptoms. A certain combination of symptoms (e.g., these behaviors, feelings, thoughs) may be rare, in a statistical sense, but that does not make it pathological; our values about normal and abnormal, healthy and unhealthy, and morally sound and morally repugnant determine whether we call the symptoms "mental disorder" or not. Some may dispute that values play any part in the DSM-III, asserting instead that the DSM-III is "value neutral." However, the debate at the extreme (e.g., whether we include homosexuality or only ego-dystonic homosexuality or neither in our nomenclature) only brings home the central, underlying values embedded in such a manual. Others may find the inclusion of values embarrassing and unscientific; it need be neither. If we acknowledge and identify those embedded values, instead of denying their existence, our diagnostic testimony may be of significant import.

I would argue that some of those embedded values are not just "psychiatric values" but represent, as the law represents in another way, the shared, common values of society. Instead of maintaining a value-neutral, scientific diagnosis, let us admit that we are making moral, value judgments regarding the behavior of another; and although our terms may be foreign and technicalized, our judgments and values do make significant contact with those of the law and the community-at-large. Instead of coming into court from a perspective that eschews values, let us acknowledge and air them. As for the legal concept of "personal responsibility," we need not regard it as a psychological anathema. There is no reason why this concept could not be studied in much the same way that psychologists investigate attitudes, beliefs, and expectations. Thus, we not only may have something of value to say in court, but the value of what we do say may be enhanced by our study, knowledge, and special training.

The second point and problematic area of diagnosis involves inferences to be drawn. Forensic experts go "over the line" when they infer "nonresponsibility" from a "psychotic" diagnosis or the reverse from a "nonpsychotic" diagnosis; neither logic or empirics support such claims. Here we must recognize the limits of our inferences. With DSM-III-R and DSM-III being far more descriptive, less theoretical and less etiological than DSM-II or DSM-I, we are more "data bound" than we might like. But crossing lines to causative factors and responsibility conclusions is in most cases unsupportable. These limitations need not reduce our testimony to slience or inconsequence. Alan Stone, who has adovcated for putting morality back into psychiatry, recognizes a common ground and seeks to cultivate it.

> Psychiatry belongs to a family of disciplines which combine the sciences and the humanities. It is a discipline, therefore that need not be at odds with the law. Law itself a member of our family. Both law and psychiatry must begin a basic rebuilding process, and moral responsibility . . . must be part of both blueprints for the future. (Stone, 1984, p. 53)

Paternalism vs. Autonomy

To set this conflict of values in extreme, I will begin with the "right to refuse treatment" issue and two quotes from two adversaries. The first quote is from Robert Plotkin (1977), a lawyer and patients' rights advocate, who sets the tone in his title, "Limiting the Therapeutic Orgy: Mental Patients' Right to Refuse Treatment." He closes his paper with the following quote:

> Psychiatry has long resisted attempts to diminish its vast powers over invol-
> untarily committed mental patients. However, the most recent professional task
> force to consider the right to refuse treatment has finally conceded that law, and
> not medicine, is the ultimate arbiter. . . . This admission was too long overdue.
> If psychiatry is to survive as a medical science and is to advance our knowledge
> of human behavior, it must learn to accept and welcome criticism—both internal
> and external. Most importantly, if it learns nothing else from the burgeoning
> "patients rights" movement, the lesson must be that the party is over. (p. 503)

The counterpoint to Plotkin is Thomas Gutheil (1980), a psychiatrist,
who also sets a tone in his editorial's title, "In Search of True Freedom:
Drug Refusal, Involuntary Medication, and 'Rotting with Your Rights
On.'" Gutheil minces no words when he calls the freedom or autonomy
that lawyers like Plotkin advocate "a sham freedom," a "freedom of psychosis" that is "a greater slavery." He takes the judicial, legal, autonomy
perspective to task when he states that the point of view

> clearly illustrates the failure of the legal mind to grasp clinical realities. . . The
> physician seeks to liberate the patient from the chains of illness; the judge, from
> the chains of treatment. The way is paved for patients to "rot with their rights
> on." (p. 327)

In closing his editorial with a quote from Solzhenitsyn (1978), he leaves
little doubt about where he sees the law's limited perspective leading to, or
about which side of the debate—law or psychiatry—represents the nobler
cause: "whenever the tissue of life is woven of legalistic relations, there is
an atmosphere of moral mediocrity, paralyzing man's noblest impulses."

These extremist positions, along with their exaggerated interpretations of the other's perspective, lead to an uncompromising stalemate. One
side claims that "Docter knows best" while the other side claims that "the
customer is always right." One side casts patients, their lawyers, and even
judges as incompetent, meddlesome fools who know nothing of clinical
reality. The other side casts healers as coercive jailers, ready at a moment's
notice or at a therapeutic whim to override the constitutional rights of
patients. End of debate. End of dialogue.

As with many conflicts cast in extreme, there is a kernel of truth here;
but the rancorous rhetoric distorts in a simplistic way what is a much more
complicated picture; and it masks the tougher issues that healers, legal
advocates, the courts, and the community need to grapple with. What are
the issues these groups must grapple with? We turn first to the healers.

One of the healers' dilemmas begins with the *Hippocratic Corpus* (Reiser, 1980, p. 329), wherein the healer is given an ethical dialectic consisting
of two apparently contradictory injunctions: the healer is to do all in his or
her power to do away with the patient's suffering, but first of all he or she
is to do no harm. There is a recognition in the *Corpus* that there are cases
where medicine is powerless, cases that demand no action; to intervene in
such cases diminishes medicine for it displays a "self-damaging pride"; it

is arrogance and folly to assert in these instances "that the power of man 'exceeds' the power of nature." In the last two decades, therapists have also had to come to terms with a greater number of ethical, moral, and legal limitations: that in addition to Nature's limits, there are the asserted wishes and rights of others that do not *necessarily* yield to the healer's injunction and power. Nature, Ethics, and Law set certain stops on the therapist's power, autonomy, and practices. Thus "doing good" must also acknowledge "the limits of benevolence" (Gaylin et al., 1978).

From the vantage point of some within the helping professions, and from others within the law, mental health professionals have been slow in grasping and responding to these limitations. The professionals, however, have quickly grasped and responded to what they see as legal encroachments on their turf. The courts, in a series of right-to-refuse-treatment cases, have drawn limits under certain conditions around what treatments are permissible. In addition, the courts and legislatures have radically altered involuntary civil commitment (and release) standards and procedures. As a result, the *parens patriae* rationale (i.e., a therapeutic reason for commitment based upon perceived need for treatment) for commitment has all but given way to the police powers rationale (i.e., the dangerousness standard), and with those changes the mental health professional's control has diminished. And the courts have also drawn limits around the formerly insular world of therapy, finding that therapists have a duty to protect others, which may necessitate their breaking confidentiality.

These three areas—treatment refusal, involuntary commitment, and confidentiality in therapy cases—when taken together represent to many therapists not only curtailments on their discretionary power, expertise, and functioning, but an entrapment in roles they neither relish nor want. Therapists do not want to be mere custodians of the committed and the insane; they want to treat, yet some fear that the judicial binds on treatments prevent therapists from doing all they can. Unlike their earlier predecessors, therapists today do not want to be policemen and claim they cannot be the "guarantors" of the public stafety (Appelbaum, 1985, p. 127); yet many therapists feel that the courts are expecting them to do just that (e.g., in involuntary commitment and in the duty to protect), to live up to standards (e.g., predicting violence) that do not exist, and to pay (i.e., through negligence and malpractice judgments) for their inabilities. Are we to be reduced to hapless civil servants, ancillary policemen, wary lawyers, or defensive psychotherapists (Kraft, 1985, p. 229)?

The question is no doubt overstated, as is the fear. It also masks some problems we would rather not admit or face, choosing instead to focus on the perceived errors of the courts. One such masked problem is our inadequacy in treating the severely disturbed and violent patient. Our success rates are low, recidivism is high, and many "have placed all their bets on medications . . . . all the while knowing that medications are not enough. . ." (Kraft, 1985, p. 233). We also mask the incredibly difficult problem of where to draw the therapeutic line when we perceive patients in *need* but they (and their lawyers and the courts) see *rights,* including the right to be different or to be left alone (Kittrie, 1971). We overlook a problem, endemic to disciplines such as psychology and psychiatry that focus on and treat the individual, "of how to balance the particular good of the identified patient against the general good of the unidentified masses" (Stone, 1984, p. 71). And if we push the therapeutic perspective above all others, as when we testify in court, hoping to turn an insanity defendant into a patient in order to get him or her help instead of punishment, we may be undermining our legal and community standards of what is morally right and wrong.

We, in the helping professions, must come to see much more clearly than we have in the past, that we have different roles and missions to play and reconcile. In part, we are ancillary policemen, predictors of violence, and lawyers. So, I submit, is everyone who adopts "the belief that human beings in an organized society face a moral imperative to come to the assistance of their fellow human beings whose safety is endangered" (Appelbaum, 1985, p. 117). This moral obligation does not arise from *Tarasoff* or our specialty, but from our common link as citizens to our fellow human beings. Yet, as clinicians, we have a specialty and limited expertise that is scientifically grounded and morally bound. Within the bounds of what we cannot do on moral grounds, and within the bounds of what we cannot yet do well because our science and art have not progressed that far, we can still be good clinicians. We can keep a patient's right to refuse drug treatment in mind and still treat "situational," "stereotypic," and "symptomatic," drug refusers in a clinically and therapeutically sound way (Appelbaum & Gutheil, 1980). And we can keep the public peril in mind and still treat our potentially violent patients in therapeutically sound ways (Beck, 1985). There are limitations on the therapist's freedom in taking patients' rights and the public's right to safety into account, but these limits need not clinically straightjacket the therapist as the dire predictors foretell.

These same limitations can serve the mental health professions in positive ways: the limitations force us to reconsider our mission and our moral and ethical principles that support our therapeutic endeavors in clearer, deeper ways (Fitch, Petrella, & Wallace, 1987; Rogers, 1987b; Slovenko, 1987); in realizing that we cannot predict, treat, and control all, and should not, we can focus on what we can do well, opt out of what we cannot, and be willing, in the gray areas, to share responsibility, power, and control.

Tough issues also face the legal advocates, civil libertarians, legislatures, the courts, and the public. For legal advocates and civil libertarians who place autonomy first and foremost among rights and needs, they need to acknowledge that sometimes patients do rot with their rights on. When winter comes to our cities, we see seasonal pictures of former mental patients sleeping outdoors, on subway grates or wherever, perhaps warmed by the rights but freezing and dying in their disordered worlds. As the cover of *Newsweek* (January 6, 1986) announces, they are the "Abandoned, . . . America's castoffs—turned away from mental institutions and into the streets." *Newsweek* asks "Who will care for them?" The question itself is simplistic, for "to care" means, in many cases, a paternalistic imposition of care that overrides autonomy-based rights.

The courts and state legislatures have helped send patients from hospitals back to communities by restricting involuntary commitment to the potentially dangerous, by making it harder to keep patients in hospitals, and by leaving the needy adrift; as we witness the revolving-door cycle of patients going from hospitals to streets and back again, as we see patients being released to communities that do not have the services to treat them adequately, and may not want them, the courts and legislatures must take a hard look at the results of their legal–legislative policy decisions (Mulvey, Geller, & Roth, 1987).

The community is not exempt from tough hard choices. The public may blanch at the images of state hospitals as snake pits, but it has yet to extend a welcoming hand back to released patients. In attitudes, services, and dollars, communities have been unwilling hosts, in the main, to patients in their midst. Where there is a need for halfway houses and group apartments, some neighborhoods, through zoning regulations, have said "not here." So the "here" becomes the streets, the overcrowded shelters and soup kitchens, and the "patient ghettos" in poorer, high crime sections of our cities. Patients may be "dumped" by hospitals back into the community, but the public has yet to resolve its value dilemmas: to care or ignore, to promote integration back into mainstream society or to decide that "out of sight, out of mind" is really what we want. Do we want a society that promotes health and welcomes pluralism or one that protects the public and preserves the general tranquility by excluding those who are "disturbing"? Once again society faces an old "debate": Is it to be the *Ship of Fools* that Sebastian Brant (Zeydel, 1944) wrote about, where a psychological and societal dissociation between folly and reason takes place, or is it to be Erasmus's *Praise of Folly* (1735), where the understanding and incorporation of folly makes us wiser? A clear answer has yet to be given.

UNVEILING THE LAW

When psychologists and psychiatrists come in contact with the courts, be it from a distance, just court watching, or up close, testifying, our training and expertise as therapists come into play in another way. We are trained to look beneath the surface, behind the manifest, and to see through fictions, illusions, and self-deceptions. One such *legal fiction* is that judges and courts do not make policy, but merely interpret the law or the legislative intent (Horowitz & Willging, 1984, p. 364). This is a sham. Courts and judges are deeply involved in policy and political matters, yet their manifest statements and written opinions generally deny this reality. On occasion there is candor, as when Justice Potter Stewart wrote that

> issues concerning mental illness are among the most difficult the courts have to face involving as they often do serious problems of policy disguised as questions of constitutional law. (*Parham v. J.R.*, 1979)

Social scientists have long recognized that politics and policy making occur beneath the sea of legal precedents cited to support a particular court decision. It doesn't take a trained expert to see the major policy and political reverberations of *Brown v. Board of Education* (1954, 1955) for school desegregation or *Roe v. Wade* (1973) for abortion. In the mental-health-related areas, the names and cases of *Jackson v. Indiana* (1972), *Wyatt v. Stickney* (1974), *O'Conner v. Donaldson* (1975), *Tarasoff, Addington* (1979), *Rogers* (1975), *Pennhurst* (1981), *Barefoot* (1983), and many more have significant policy implications. It has long been known by those social scientists and legal advocates who want to affect and change policy that it is to the courts they must turn, not the legislatures.

The aforementioned fiction frustrates social scientists, for these disingenous decisions lead to haphazard policy making at best or inconsistent, contradictory policies at worse. The medico-scientific community points to inconsistencies among court decisions where predicting future dangerousness is the substantive issue. In involuntary civil commitment cases, lower courts seem to have acknowledged the evidence that "no tests or psychiatric examinations can dependably predict a probability of dangerous behavior in the absence of an actual history of a severely violent assault on another person" (Kozol, Boucher, & Garofalo, 1972). The conclusions of the scientists, based on their evidence, is that mental health professions as predictors of dangerousness are not accurate enough (Rappaport, 1977). As the legal advocates state, professionals have not demonstrated any special expertise in the prediction of future violence area (Scott & Ennis. 1975), and presuming such an expertise amounts to "flipping coins in the courtroom" (Ennis & Litwack, 1974). The Supreme Court, in *Addington*, at least recognizes that the profession cannot produce predictive evidence at or beyond "the reasonable doubt" level.

Now for the contradictory decisions. We have the same Supreme Court—in *Barefoot* (1983) a capital punishment case where psychiatric evaluation and predictions of recidivism and future violence were used to determine whether a death sentence would be given (over the objections of the American Psychiatric Association's testimony that professionals could not make such future predictions accurately)—nevertheless sanctioning such testimony, choosing, in this case, not to "disinvent the wheel." The medico-scientific community sees a flagrant contradiction: "You mean to say we can't predict accurately enough for civil commitment, where someone faces *only* the loss of liberty, but where someone faces the loss of life, we can?"

And if we cannot accurately predict future violence, if there is neither test nor standard for doing so, how are we to understand *Tarasoff* (1974, 1976) where the court expects us to accurately predict and live up to "professional standards" that do not exist and holds us accountable for our negligence?

To the medico-scientific community, there is lack of consistency here. Another inconsistency that has long been noted is between civil and criminal law treatment of the mentally ill (see Chapter 9). Lord Erskine remarked on this "wide distinction between civil and criminal cases" in his defense of Hadfield in 1800. In the civil arena, upon evidence of mental illness, the law avoids the acts of the mentally ill who are judged incapable of managing their own property; when it comes to criminal acts, however, such an individual is "considered as possessing all the elements of responsibility," a view that Isaac Ray (1838/1983) called "the height of absurdity" (p. 20). The inconsistency continues today in the differential treatment of insanity acquittees and the civilly committed, as the 1983 case *Jones v. United States* illustrates.

Jones, who was charged with petty larceny for attempted shoplifting, which is a misdemeanor punishable by no more than 1 year in prison, successfully raised the insanity defense. After being kept in a hospital for more than a year, "longer than the maximum term for which he could have been imprisoned had he been convicted—he demanded on due process grounds to be released or at least recommitted pursuant to the applicable civil commitment statue" (Wexler, 1984, p. 145). The Supreme Court rejected Jones's argument. Justice Powell wrote that

> when a criminal defendant establishes by a preponderance of the evidence that he is not guilty of a crime by reason of insanity, the Constitution permits the Government, on the basis of the insanity judgment, to confine him to a mental institution until such time as he has regained his sanity or is no longer a danger to himself or society.

Furthermore, the opinion went on to state that

> there simply is no necessary correlation between severity of the offense and length of time necessary for recovery. The length of the acquittee's hypothetical criminal sentence therefore is irrelevant to the purpose of his commitment.

The Court's 5-to-4 decision is "very disturbing" (Weiner, 1984, p. 34), short-sighted on policy and political grounds, and inconsistent with the other legal rulings. Civilly, confinement is typically based on an assessment that the individual is *now* mentally ill and dangerous, and many states require a recent overt dangerous act or a judgment that the potential violence is imminent for the dangerousness criterion to be established; at a minimum, mental illness and dangerousness must be established at the relevant, present moment. But Jones had no such present assessment done. The Supreme Court ruled that the verdict, which was based on past history, was "sufficiently probative of mental illness and dangerousness to justify commitment and to support an influence of continuing mental illness." This kind of reasoning and justification would be thrown out in the civil arena, but somehow the criminal case is treated differently. Furthermore, the Court used Jones's past shoplifting attempt, a nonviolent crime against property, to establish present dangerousness. And on policy grounds, a decision that permits indefinite hospitalization, long beyond what the criminal prison sentence would be, would certainly dissuade individuals from raising the insanity defense for minor crimes.

If the Supreme Court justices, as a policy plan, hope that their decision will lead to treatment and cure of such individuals, they are mistaken; those individuals will opt for prison, the shorter time, rather than treatment that could go on indefinitely. Is the high court really pursuing a "fading dream of rehabilitation" (Carroll & Lurigio, 1984, p. 312) policy, or is it a disguised policy of retribution or unlimited preventive detention? There is a policy here, but we are unclear what that policy is and in doubt about its soundness.

Mental health professionals recognize that the civil and criminal commitment systems are connected "in theory and in practice" (Wexler, 1984, p. 153). As scientists, we strive for internal consistency within our theories, models, and practices and between our theories and their applications. To the scientist, consistency appears absent from substantively related legal cases that yield disparate decisions. And valuing the value of consistency seems not to be a high priority of the law. The "logic" of the law baffles and escapes us.

Some social scientists either fail to understand or refuse to accept the ways of the law. Deciding cases on the narrowest of grounds seems to guarantee a lack of consistency. So, too, does disguising policy questions as issues of constitutional law. Ideological factions and politically expedient compromises seem to determine decisions that ought to be decided on more conceptually and empirically sound grounds. How, then, do we interact and affect such a system? To answer this question and to close this work, I return to our topic, "insanity," and to those remaining matters.

FINAL RECOMMENDATIONS

There are four matters that still remain: (1) expert testimony, (2) being an advocate in the adversarial process, (3) providing treatment, and (4) deciding the release question. As for mental health professionals and social scientist being granted "expert" status and providing expert testimony, I begin by rejecting the extremes: on one end, professionals should not be answering the "ultimate issue" question of responsibility; on the other end, I reject the views of Szasz, Stone, and Robinson that would eliminate or silence all psychological, psychiatric testimony.

The "ultimate issue" of responsibility in our legal system is for the jury to decide. Whatever doubts and regrets we have about the wisdom of ordinary citizens deciding this matter, our system reflects not only tradition, but a central value of a jury of peers rather than of professionals. For the professionals, then, one prohibition against usurping the jury's prerogative is a value-based prohibition. The second prohibition arises from empirics, the nature of our science at its present state of development: put simply, we cannot make inferences from behavior or diagnosis to *responsibility* that do not leave gaping and reasonable doubts. Even if we put aside the metaphysical question of whether we can ever speak with certainty on this matter, it is clear that we cannot do so now. And as empirical evidence reveals (Homant & Kennedy, 1987), clinicians' judgments of insanity are not solely based on the evidence; subjective factors (e.g., the values and attitudes of clinicians about the insanity defense itself) are highly correlated with clinicians' judgments of insanity.

Forensic experts must get more comfortable with the "scientist's comforts with uncertainty," for we know more than most about the limits of correlational data; to forget our science by dressing up our conclusions leaves us posing in an illegitimate mantle, and the revelation of our nakedness is sure to embarrass and discredit the profession. I would rather see the experts reveal their own shortcomings, as Bazelon and Grisso also suggest.

A second prohibition that we ought to be more mindful of when we testify is our ethical obligation to admit uncertainty, to clearly state what is speculative and beyond the consensually accepted. Our own integrity, and the integrity of our valued legal process, depend in part on our keeping these two prohibitions in mind.

We can offer the courts, as Bazelon (1982) suggests, "a wealth of intermediate observations and conceptual insights that are adequately explained" (p. 116). Regarding an insanity defendant that a professional has interviewed and tested, we have observations, verbal, affective, and motor responses to questions that we can report and which may enlighten the jury. From these responses, we can make low-level inferences as to the mental state and functioning of the defendant. Here, I disagree with where Robinson (1980) would draw the line. He would treat "all statements regarding the mental state of the accused . . . as statements of belief or opinion . . . not to be accorded the status of evidence . . ." (p. 206). This is far too shallow a line. If Robinson's recommendation was rigidly followed, experimental psychologists would not be able to present "evidence" on attention, awareness, perception, memory, and a host of psychological constructs we routinely infer about from the responses of subjects in our laboratories. Since such inferences are allowable within our field and in our journals, excluding them as evidence in court is inconsistent and unnecessarily restrictive.

On another of Robinson's proposals, that which restricts "disease" to a "discernible pathological process in the tissues or organs of the body" and casts "mental disease" as "a metaphor, not as a diagnostic specification," I again disagree, although more reservedly. The problems, misuses, and criticisms of diagnostic labels are well known, and the diagnostic manual of 1980, DSM-III, has not gone unscathed; in the 1987 manual, DSM-III-R, where revision was undertaken "for consistency, clarity, and conceptual accuracy" (p. xvii), the descriptive approach and "consistency with data from research studies bearing on the validity of diagnostic categories" (p. xx) were accentuated points. Since it is more descriptive, less etiological than its earlier versions, it is even more suspect when Robinson's "disease" criterion is used. However, be it both descriptive and metaphorical, it still serves as the diagnostic reference for most psychiatrists and psychologists; and with greater attention paid to descriptive criteria of disorders and differential distinctions between disorders, it is perceived as more reliable.

How useful is such a diagnostic label to the jury? It may inform the jury, if a number of experts give the same diagnosis, that there is some agreement among professionals that the particular array of behaviors (symptoms) the defendant exhibits is so labeled as a "mental disorder." This, by itself, is not greatly informative, but it does say something. The label does not say that an underlying disease exists; nor is a label an explanation. And a label does not allow for syllogistic reasoning to "responsibility" conclusions. If professionals were more careful not to overreach, then a diagnosis of mental disorders may have some limited value to the jury. It is up to the profession to demonstrate reliability for its diagnostic categories and to be ethically and scientifically guided to ensure that "the probative value of the evidence" outweighs "its prejudicial effect"; if we can meet the requirements for the admissibility of expert testimony (*United States v. Amaral*, 1973), then our testimony should not be barred by more restrictive criteria.

On the topic of being an advocate in an adversarial process, I take a far more critical view. The spectre of "guns for hire," so-called defense experts or prosecution experts (Greene, Schooler, & Loftus, 1985) willing to supply testimony for a price, is unseemly. It also presents a serious conflict between taking an oath to tell the truth, the whole truth, and being paid as a partisan to present the best case, or the partisan truth (Stone, 1984, p. 72). Advocates of the adversarial process assume that the truth, the whole truth, will emerge through the questioning and cross-examining of witnesses on both sides. But the lawyers on both sides select or "shop" (Sperlich, 1985, p. 341) for the experts who testify. Jurors may hear, for example, two or three experts testify for the defense that the defendant was schizophrenic at the time of the act, but jurors will not know how many experts interviewed the defendant or how many reached the opinion that the defendant had no mental disorder; those experts will be paid, dismissed, and certainly not called to testify. The prosecution typically has a close working association with the doctors at the hospital defendants are sent to for psychiatric examination; there are questions on that adversarial side too about the "impartiality" of their witnesses and whether such witnesses truly represent the opinions of the profession-at-large.

Are there alternative ways of presenting expert testimony without being a paid partisan? There are. Through Brandeis briefs and *amicus curiae* briefs (Horowitz & Willging, 1984) social scientists can bring relevant empirical findings before the courts, although these methods may be less suited to an individual case involving insanity than they are for addressing a broad issue or a general topic of legal concern. Other alternatives that have been suggested include using "impartial" educators, special masters, *ad hoc* panels of experts, and a science court (Greene et al., 1985; Sperlich, 1985). Proponents of these suggested alternatives seek to bring impartial expertise to bear on the matter before the court. However, the last alternative, the science court, particularly if such a court has the final authority to decide the matter, would take the matter out of the hands of jurors and out of the adversarial system entirely. This bold step, which was the ardent wish of the alienists, does remove the keys and control from the judge and the jury and places both in the hands of this new court of experts. In effect, the jury's decision is usurped. Justice might be able to survive this social science court, but it would not be the adversarial form of justice we know. For this reason, the science court has been criticized and rejected by some. The dilemma, then, is how do we bring impartial expertise before the court without usurping the jurors' decision?

While the litigation model in the United States is *adversarial*, in continental Europe the *inquisitorial* model is used extensively (Horowitz & Willging, 1984, p. 166). In the latter model, judges can appoint witnesses and make their own investigation of the facts. Could aspects of this model be incorporated in our own system? Could judges call their own expert witnesses to testify on the defendant's insanity, for example? I think there is precedent for this. In a 1985 case decided by the Supreme Court, *Ake v. Oklahoma*, the Court ruled that an indigent defendant who raised the insanity defense but could not afford his own expert witness was, on Fourteenth Amendment due process grounds, deprived of his guarantee of fundamental fairness. What is interesting to note is that the Court explicitly states that "this is not to say, of course, that the indigent defendant has a constitutional right to choose a psychiatrist of his personal liking or to receive funds to hire his own." In his concurring opinion, Chief Justice Burger states that he would "make clear that the entitlement is to an independent psychiatric evaluation, not to a defense consultant." I suggest that the *Ake* decision provides a rationale for a "court witness," since the ruling explicitly states that fairness can be achieved without giving the defendant funds to hire his own witness. If the independent witness is not the defense's witness, then the expert called in to ensure fairness is the court's witness.

I suggest we consider extending *Ake* to all insanity cases, indigent or not. The court could call its own witness or witnesses in addition to those that the defense and prosecution may call. This does not stop the adversarial sides from "shopping" for experts or presenting their best case; rather, it gives the court and the jury access to independent, impartial expertise, and it still retains the feature that this court has control and the jury has the ultimate decision.

On the third of our final matters, that of providing treatment, the courts and the professionals must come to realize the issues, limitations, and limits of treatment. In my schema, the questions involving treatment arise in two ways: first, there are those defendants who were judged to have a nonculpable total DOM and who, at a separate hearing, were involuntarily committed to a psychiatric hospital; second, there are those defendants who were judged culpable to some degree and incarcerated. The courts and the professionals both may believe that all of them need treatment. But let us be clear about the *principal* reason for confining. In the second group of cases, we incarcerate (punish) because we believe they are culpable; punishment follows principally on retributive grounds. We may also cite deterrent reasons and desire that they receive treatment, but those reasons are not, and should not be, foremost. The first group is confined not on retributive grounds, since there is no culpability, but principally on deterrent grounds because we judge them to be potentially dangerous: we judge that their liberty interests do not outweigh the safety interests of the public. We may desire that they receive treatment, but we cannot guarantee that treatment will be accepted or effective.

The courts and the treating professionals must clearly keep in mind the principal reason for confinement in each case, and I agree with Alan Stone that they have not. These cases involved moral questions and moral conflicts—the individual's right to liberty vs. society's right of safety and the state's right to punish those judged morally culpable for breaking the law. Too often in the past, "treatment" has been used by the courts and by the professionals to finesse tough decisions. By redefining "the toughest cases" as simply "treatment cases," we create "confusion" and "moral ambiguity," and we "avoid paying the full price of our principles" (Stone, 1984, pp. 242–243).

The availability of professionals expert at treatment must not blind Justice to the principles on the balancing scale. Those principles, the moral question, must be seen clearly, and weighed. Professionals must resist intruding, subverting, or obfuscating this moral decision, even though others, including judges, may be tempted to evade the tough moral question because "it is socially and politically convenient" (Stone, 1984, p. 243) to do so. Professionals must also resist their own temptation to treat the defendant and to treat this matter as one of treatment; it is only partly a matter of treatment, and the lesser part at that. The Hippocratic Corpus reminds us that the desire to treat must be checked by first doing no harm; to treat, first and foremost, harms Justice, our sense and system of justice, and it harms the community's moral sense by evading those tough moral questions. Here, then, are the limits of treatment.

The limitations of treatment (see Chapter 5) are also troubling. Our psychological and medical treatments are currently unable to heal all cases, and they particularly fall short in cases of insanity, potential dangerousness, and in dealing with violent individuals. This is an area where improvements and advances in treatment would be welcomed. However, current and improved treatments are limited also by the receptivity of clients, some of whom may reject our offers of help. How, then, can we treat, or what should we do, when a defendant-turned-patient refuses?

First, I would acknowledge that these defendants-turned-patients have a right to refuse treatment. Since they have gone through a trial and had to be legally competent to do so, a *prima facie* presumption of competence exists. I therefore begin by recognizing their treatment refusal is presumptively a competent refusal. Under these circumstances, when a therapist believes such a "patient" would benefit nonetheless from treatment, the therapist should first try to persuade the individual. If persuasion fails, yet the therapist believes that the patient's refusal is not a competent refusal, a competency hearing is an option, although I would suggest it be the last, not the first, option. The Supreme Court, in *Youngberg v. Romeo* (1982), gives treaters greater discretionary latitude than *Rogers vs. Okin* (1975). Judicial latitude, however, even when coupled with therapeutic best intentions, does not guarantee that legally sanctioned coercive treatment will work.

I do believe that some lessons on how to deal effectively with potentially dangerous patients and medication refusers are now apparent. One lesson is not to turn the matter into a legal contest by attempting to override their rights (i.e., trying to get them declared incompetent) as a first step. The use of good clinical skills and interventions seems to be a therapeutically more effective first step. Even with good clinical approaches and good faith, we will not succeed in all cases. Even with legal support for coercive treatment, we will not succeed in all cases. The limitations of therapy must be acknowledged by therapists and the courts, for grandiosity and illusion lead to double trouble: the courts can maintain the belief that the problem is solved by placing the patient in our care, and the professionals can support that illusion only to face problems they cannot manage and responsibilities they do not want.

We now come to the release question. In my schema, for the five DOM cases that involve culpability and punishment, the maximum sentence, and hence the release date, is already set. Parole boards and judges may consider an earlier, conditional release, and professionals may have something to contribute, but the decision is one that criminal justice must make. As for the former NGRI case who, under this schema, is a nonculpable DOM involuntarily committed, I would recommend that civilly and criminally committed cases be treated in like fashion. This is the opposite of what the American Psychiatric Association in its Statement on the Insanity Defense (1982) recommends:

> The usual civil committee has not, however, committed nor will he commit in the future a major crime. . . By contrast, the "dangerousness" of insanity acquittees who have perpetuated violence has already been demonstrated. Their future dangerousness need not be inferred; it may be assumed, at least for a reasonable period of time. (p. 15)

I disagree with this recommendation for a number of reasons. First, while the American Psychiatric Association is most worried about insanity acquittees who were charged with violent crimes, according to Steadman's data (1980), less serious crimes, minor crimes, and less serious assaults constitute a sizable portion of acquittals in many jurisdictions. For some of these less serious offenses, it may be a matter of the prosecutor's discretion, the family's involvement, or the mental health professional's recommendation that determines whether the case is handled civilly or criminally. In short, the differences between the civil and criminal committees may not be nearly as great as the APA perceives; furthermore, if the differences are not that great, then due process and equal protection (see Chapter 9) should apply.

My second reason for disagreeing with the APA's recommendation is that it infers greater predictive certitude for future dangerousness from the insanity acquittees than for civil committees; I do not think this greater certitude is warranted, given the error rate for dangerous predictions overall. I do adopt the APA's position that "the decision to release an insanity acquittee should not be made *solely* by psychiatrists . . ." and that "such decisions should be made instead by a group similar in composition to a parole board" (p. 16). However, I would extend this recommendation to civil committees as well.

A "committee" has become such through a legal determination, be it civil or criminal. It is thus a legal decision, not a psychiatric decision, that confines that individual. I argue that it should be a legal decision to release such individuals. Mental health professionals may be the experts at judging whether mental illness is present, absent, florid, or in remission, but we are not experts as to dangerousness, the primary reason for confinement and the primary criterion regarding release. We readily admit that we are not expert at predicting future dangerousness in *Tarasoff*-like cases. By acknowledging the same for release decisions and by relinquishing our preeminent claims to determine release, we can place the responsibility where it belongs—with the courts—not on our shoulders. By releasing the release decision to a parole board that is under the aegis of the courts, we may relieve ourselves and our profession of a responsibility that has become painfully burdensome and increasingly litigious.

A Concluding Moral

There is a moral to this story. When the mental health professionals' reach exceeds their expertise, they oftentimes run afoul; they are also likely to be disrobed and derided, if not sued. They may find themselves in charge and responsible for charges who do not want their help, thereby being reduced to hapless custodians or ineffective policemen when neither role is desired. As partisan experts on the witness stand they stand accused of undermining "conventional social morality and traditional moral authority"; with their overdetermined, deterministic explanations they reduced "our fundamental conception of free moral agents" (Stone, 1984, p. 224) to myth and matter, both of which ultimately do not matter; and having turned the bad into the mad, giving up the ghost in the machine in favor of medications and talk (But to whom are they talking?), they seek to treat, cure, and control the patient's release, only to find frequent failure and harsh accusations that they have become the enforcers of "conventional social morality and authority" (Stone, p. 224). In seeking to illuminate insanity and enlighten the Law, mental health professionals are accused of having clouded and obfuscated certain central moral issues and of foisting their own benightedness on the courts and the public. We began our courtship of Law with a battle cry of "let there be light," and we may have pushed back and illuminated the dark waters of insanity to some degree, but new forms of darkness and chaos follow in our wake. Our navigational wisdom, our vision, and our moral ballast are mired in doubt.

There is a moral here for the Law as well. Blind Justice, the marblized embodiment of the Law, is not a victim in this courtship; neither is she blind. At times, though, she feels victimized and feigns blindness. Blind Justice cannot have it both ways: she cannot duck tough issues, divest herself of certain moral obligations, and anoint Psychology to take responsibility and control, and then cry foul, and charge that she's been had. There is something about Judge Bazelon's "disappointed lover" lament that does not ring true and does not convey the whole story, from all sides.

I do think there is a certain "blindness" here. Some degree of blindness results no doubt from a lack of expertise: psychology, mental disorders, treatment, and rehabilitation are not Justice's strong suits. But there is also a degree of blindness that looks like the naïvete of an ingenue, but it comes from the mouth of a well-seasoned *grande dame*. The likely retort is either "You should have known better" or "cut the act!" When psychologists and psychiatrists examine and uncover Justice's blindness, which they have both penchant and training to do, they are apt to discover certain pretenses and self-deceptions. Regarding politics, policies, legal inconsistencies, moral ambiguities, and abdications of responsibility, blind Justice has much to see.

Neither Psychology nor Law wears the mantles of "villain" or "victim." There are no usurpers without abdicators here. What is clear is that both must come to see themselves and each other more clearly, and that includes seeing the limits and limitations of what each can and cannot do. It also requires that we see more clearly and face more squarely our moral questions, our ethical obligations, and the shortcomings of our knowledge and wisdom.

Justice can survive the social sciences and survive without them. But Justice can also be enhanced and improved by social science findings and applications. The methods, critical assumptions, and outcomes of Justice warrant continual scrutiny. If Justice's methods, assumptions, and outcomes are perceived to be unfair, or unfounded, disrespect for the law, *de facto* law, and wild justice are likely to increase; and if the laws are changed, but the changes result from either emotionalism or conceptions unsupported by empirical facts (Rogers, 1987a), then we are likely to repeat our past failures or create new ones. In this regard, the social sciences can play a constructive role. Likewise, the social sciences bear watching and challenging, particularly when their methods, assumptions, and results raise legal, ethical, and moral concerns. Both sides can enhance and criticize the other, with the outcome of this wary check and balance relationship being a net plus for both.

There is more on trial than just insanity, and there is no final verdict. There cannot be one. The "common morality" and "natural law" are two interrelated aspects of our psychological–moral makeup. "Insanity," in both individuals and society, in its virulent and vexing forms, truly takes root when the common nexus is severed, when the dialogue lapses into silence and dissociation.

References

Addington v. Texas, 441 U.S. 418 (1979).

Ake v. Oklahoma, 105 S. Ct. 1087 (1985).

Allard v. Helgemoe, 527 F. 2d 1 (1st Cir. 1978).

Allison, R. B. (1984). Difficulties diagnosing the multiple personality syndrome in a death penalty case. *The International Journal of Clinical and Experimental Hypnosis, 32*(2), 102–117.

Alloy, L. B., & Abramson, L. Y. (1979). Judgment of contingency in depressed and non-depressed students: Sadder but wiser? *Journal of Experimental Psychology: General, 108,* 441–85.

American Law Institute. (1962). *Model penal code,* Proposed Official Draft, S 4.01.

American Psychiatric Association. (1952). *Diagnostic and statistical manual: Mental disorders.* Washington, DC: Author.

American Psychiatric Association. (1968). *Diagnostic and statistical manual: Mental Disorders.* Washington, DC: Author.

American Psychiatric Association. (1980). *Diagnostic and statistical manual of mental disorders* (3rd ed.). Washington, DC: Author.

American Psychiatric Association. (1982, December). *Statement on the insanity defense.* Washington, DC: Author.

American Psychiatric Association. (1987). *Diagnostic and statistical manual of mental disorders* (3rd ed., Rev.). Washington, DC: American Psychiatric Association.

American Psychological Association. (1977). *Standards for providers of psychological services.* Washington, DC: Author.

American Psychological Association. (1979). *Ethical standards of psychologists* (rev. ed.). Washington, DC: Author.

American Psychological Association's Task Force on the Role of Psychology in the Criminal Justice System. (1980). Report of the task force on the role of psychology in the criminal justice system. In J. Monahan (Ed.), *Who is the client? The ethics of psychological intervention in the criminal justice system.* Washington, DC: American Psychological Association.

351

Amicus Curiae Brief for the American Psychological Association. (1987). In the Supreme Court of the United States: *Lockhart v. McCree. American Psychologist, 42*(1), 59–68.

Appelbaum, P. S. (1985). Rethinking the duty to protect. In J. C. Beck (Ed.), *The potentially violent patient and the Tarasoff decision in psychiatric practice* (pp. 109–130). Washington, DC: American Psychiatric Press.

Appelbaum, P. S., & Gutheil, T. G. (1980). Drug refusal: A study of psychiatric inpatients. *American Journal of Psychiatry, 137*(3), 340–346.

Applebaum, P. S., Mirkin, S. A., & Bateman, A. L. (1981). Empirical assessment of competency to consent to psychiatric hospitalization. *American Journal of Psychiatry, 138*, 1170–1176.

Applebaum, S. A. (1982). Challenge to traditional psychotherapy from the "new therapies." *American Psychologist, 37*, 1002–1008.

Arenella, P. (1977). The diminished capacity and diminished responsibility defenses: Two children of a doomed marriage. *Columbia Law Review, 77*(6), 827–865.

Arenella, P. (1983). Reflections on current proposals to abolish or reform the insanity defense. *American Journal of Law & Medicine, 8*(3), 271–284.

Ault, R., & Resse, J. T. (1980). A psychological assessment of crime profiling. *F.B.I. Law Enforcement Bulletin, 49*, 3, 22–25.

Austin, J. (1885). *Lectures on jurisprudence or the philosophy of positive law* (5th ed., revised by Robert Campbell). London: John Murray.

Austin, J. L. (1956–1957). A plea for excuses. *Proceedings of the Aristotelian Society, 57*, 1.

Bailey, F. L., & Aronson, H. (1971). *The defense never rests.* New York: Stein & Day.

Baird, K. A., & Rupert, P. A. (1987). Clinical management of confidentiality: A survey of psychologists in seven states. *Professional Psychology: Research and Practice, 18*(4), 347–352.

Banta, H. D., & Saxe, L. (1983). Reimbursement for psychotherapy: Linking efficacy research and public policymaking. *American Psychologist, 38*, 918–923.

Barefoot v. Estelle, 103. S. Ct. 3383 (1983).

Bartol, C. R. (1983). *Psychology and American law.* Belmont, CA.: Wadsworth.

Baxtrom v. Herold. 383 U.S. 107 (1966).

Bazelon, D. L. (1982). Veils, values, and social responsibility. *American Psychologist 37*(2), 115–121.

Beauchamp, T. L. (1977). Paternalism and biobehavioral control. *The Monist, 60*, 62–80.

Beck, A. T. (1972). *Depression.* Philadelphia: University of Pennsylvania Press.

Beck, J. C. (1985). A clinical survey of *Tarasoff* experience. In J. C. Beck (Ed.), *The potentially violent patient and the Tarasoff decision in psychiatric practice* (pp. 59–81). Washington, DC: American Psychiatric Press.

Beers, C. W. (1935). *A mind that found itself.* Garden City, NY: Doubleday, Doran.

Bergin, A. E. (1971). The evaluation of therapeutic outcomes. In A. E. Bergin & S. L. Garfield (Eds.), *Handbook of psychotherapy and behavior change.* New York: Wiley.

Bergin, A. E., & Suinn, R. M. (1975). Individual psychotherapy and behavior therapy. In M. R. Rosenzweig & L. W. Porter (Eds.), *Annual Review of Psychology* (Vol. 26). Palo Alto, CA: Annual Reviews.

Bermant, G. (1985). Issues in trial management: Conducting the voir dire examination. In S. M. Kassin & L. S. Wrightsman (Eds.), *The psychology of evidence and trial procedure* (pp. 298–322). Beverly Hills, CA: Sage.

Bersoff, D. N. (1987). Social science data and the Supreme Court: *Lockhart* as a case in point. *American Psychologist, 42*(1), 52–58.

Birnbaum, M. (1960). The right to treatment. *American Bar Association Journal, 46*, 499.

Bittner, E. (1973). Police discretion in emergency apprehension of mentally ill persons. In R. H. Price & B. Denner (Eds.), *The making of a mental patient* (pp. 46–69). New York: Holt, Rinehart & Winston.

Blackwood's Edinburgh Magazine. (1850, November). Modern state trials. *68*, 320, pt. 2, p. 570.

Bleuler, E. (1950). *Dementia praecox, or the group of schizophrenias.* New York: International Universities Press.

Bockoven, J. S. (1956). Moral treatment in American psychiatry. *Journal of Nervous and Mental Disease, 124,* 167–183.

Bolton v. Harris, 395 F. 2d 642 (D.C. Cir. 1968).

Bonnie, R. J. (1982). Statement. Hearings before the Committee on the Judiciary, United States Senate. *The insanity defense.* Serial No. J-97-126. Washington, DC: U. S. Government Printing Office, 255–282.

Bonnie, R. J. (1983). The moral basis of the insanity defense. *American Bar Association Journal, 69,* 194–197.

Bracton, H. D. (1915). *De legibus et consuetudinibus Angliae* [On the Laws and Customs of England]. (Woodbine, Ed.). New Haven: Yale University Press.

Brakel, S. J. (1974). Presumption, bias, and incompetency in the criminal process. *Wisconsin Law Review,* 1105–1130.

Bramwell, B. (1874). *Special Report from the Select Committee on Homicide Law Amendment Bill,* P.P. 1874, IX. 27.

Brown v. Board of Education, 347 U.S. 483 (1954).

Bruner, J. S. (1965). *On knowing: Essay for the left hand.* New York: Atheneum.

Buckhout, R. (1979). Discretion in jury selection. In L. E. Abt & I. R. Stuart (Eds.), *Social psychology and discretionary law* (pp. 176–195). New York: Van Nostrand Reinhold.

Bukataman, B. A., Foy, J. L., & de Grazia, E. (1971). What is competency to stand trial? *American Journal of Psychiatry, 127,* 1225–1229.

Burt, R. A., & Morris, N. (1972). A proposal for the abolition of the incompetency plea. *University of Chicago Law Review, 40,* 66–95.

Butterfield, L. H. (Ed.). (1951). *Letters of Benjamin Rush* (Vols. I, II). Princeton, NJ: Princeton University Press.

Cahalan, W. L. (1982). Statement. Hearings before the Committee on the Judiciary, United States Senate. *The insanity defense.* Serial No. J-97-126. Washington, DC: U. S. Government Printing Office, 99–115.

Cahn, E. (1955). Jurisprudence. *New York University Law Review, 30,* 150–169.

Caplan, L. (1984). *The insanity defense and the trial of John W. Hinckley, Jr.* Boston: Godine.

Carroll, J. S., & Lurigio, A. J. (1984). Conditional release on probation and parole: Implications for provision of mental health services. In L. A. Teplin (Ed.), *Mental health and criminal justice* (Vol. 20, pp. 297–315). Beverly Hills, CA: Sage.

Carroll, L. (1970). *The annotated Alice.* With an Introduction and Notes by M. Gardner. New York: Bramhall House.

Cavanaugh, J. L., & Rogers, R. (Eds.). (1984). Presidential assassination. *Behavioral Science and the Law, 2,* 2.

Chingempeel, W. G., Mulvey, E., & Reppucci, N. D. (1980). A national study of ethical dilemmas of psychologists in the criminal justice system. In J. Monahan (Ed.), *Who is the client? The ethics of psychological intervention in the criminal justice system.* Washington, DC: American Psychological Association.

Chu, F. D., & Trotter, S. (1972). *The mental health complex part I: Community mental health center.* Washington, DC: Center for Study of Responsive Law.

Clark, W. L., & Marshall, W. L. (1952). *A treatise on the law of crimes* (5th ed., J. J. Kearney, Ed.). Chicago: Callaghan.

Cocozza, J., & Steadman, H. J. (1976). The failure of psychiatric predictions of dangerousness: Clear and convincing evidence. *Rutgers Law Review, 29,* 1084–1101.

Cohen, R. J. (1979). *Malpractice: A guide for mental health professionals.* New York: Free Press.

Cohn, A., & Udolf, R. (1979). *The criminal justice system and its psychology.* New York: Van Nostrand Reinhold.

Coleman, J. C., Butcher, J. N., & Carson, R. C. (1980). *Abnormal psychology and modern life* (6th ed.). Glenview, IL: Scott, Foresman.

Comrie, J. E. (Ed.). (1922). *Selected works of Thomas Sydenham, M.D.* London: John Bale, Sons & Danielson.

Corballis, M. (1980). Laterality and myth. *American Psychologist, 35*(3), 284–295.

Corballis, M. C., & Morgan, M. J. (1978). On the biological basis of human laterality: I. Evidence for a maturational left–right gradient. *The Behavioral and Brain Sciences, 1,* 261–269.

Corner, G. W. (Ed.). (1948). *The autobiography of Benjamin Rush.* Princeton, NJ: Princeton University Press.

Coyne, J. C., & Widiger, T. A. (1978). Toward a participatory model of psychotherapy. *Professional Psychology, 9,* 700–710.

Daniel M'Naghten's Case, 10 Cl. & Fin. 200, 8 Eng. Rep. 718, (1843).

Davis, J. H., Bray, R. M., & Holt, R. W. (1977). The empirical study of decision processes in juries: A critical review. In J. L. Tapp & F. J. Levine (Eds.), *Law, justice, and the individual in society: Psychological and legal issues* (pp. 326–361). New York: Holt, Rinehart & Winston.

Davis v. Lhim, Mich. Wayne County Circuit Court, No. 77-726989 NM (June 11, 1981).

Davis v. United States, 165 U.S. 373 (1897).

Declaration of Helsinki. (1964). Reprinted in W. T. Reich (Ed.), *Encyclopedia of bioethics* (p. 1770). New York: Free Press.

Declaration of Helsinki. (1975). Reprinted in W. T. Reich (Ed.), *Encyclopedia of bioethics* (pp. 1771–1773). New York: Free Press.

DeLeon, P. H., & Borreliz, M. (1978). Malpractice: Professional liability and the law. *Professional Psychology, 9,* 467–477.

Dershowitz, A. (1970). The law of dangerousness: Some fictions about predictions. *Journal of Legal Education, 24,* 24–47.

Dershowitz, A. (1982). *The best defense.* New York: Random House.

Deutsch, A. (1949). *The mentally ill in America: A history of their care and treatment from colonial times* (2nd ed.). New York: Columbia University Press.

di Beccaria, C. B. (1880). *On crimes and punishments.* (J. A. Paoluci, Trans.). London: Chatto & Windus.

Dix, G. E. (1971). Psychological abnormality as a factor in grading criminal liability: Diminished capacity, diminished responsibility, and the like. *Journal of Criminal Law and Criminology, 62,* 332.

Dixon v. Attorney General, 325 F. Supp. 966, 969 (M.D. Pa. 1971).

Driver v. Hinnant, 356 F.2d 761 (4th Cir. 1966).

Drope v. Missouri, 420 U.S. 162 (1975).

Dukay et al. (1965). *Final Report of the Ionia State Hospital Medical Audit Committee 17.* Unpublished Report.

Duncan v. State of Louisiana, Sup. Ct. Rep. 88, 1444 (1968).

Durant, W. (1954). *The story of philosophy.* New York: Pockets Books.

Durham v. United States, 214 F.2d 862 (1954).

Dusky v. United States, 363 U.S. 402 (1960).

Dworkin, G. (1972). Paternalism. *The Monist, 56,* 65.

Easter v. District of Columbia, 261 F.2d 50 (D.C. Cir. 1966).

Eccles, Sir J. (1980, May 17). *Language, thought, and brain.* Paper presented at Georgetown University, Washington, DC.

Editorial. (1855). The case of Luigi Buranelli. *Lancet,* i, 565.

Eliade, M. (1964). *Shamanism: Archaic techniques of ecstasy* (W. R. Trask, Trans.). Princeton, NJ: Princeton University Press.

Ellison, K. W., & Buckhout, R. (1981). *Psychology and criminal justice.* New York: Harper & Row.

Ellsworth, P. C., Bukatay, R. M., Cowan, C. L., & Thompson, W. C. (1984). The death-qualified jury and the defense of insanity. *Law and Human Behavior, 8*(1/2), 45–54.

Elwork, A., & Sales, B. D. (1985). Jury instructions. In S. M. Kassin & L. S. Wrightsman (Eds.), *The psychology of evidence and trial procedure* (pp. 280–297). Beverly Hills, CA: Sage.

Ennis, B. J., & Emery, R. D. (1978). *The rights of mental patients.* (ACLU Handbook Series.) New York: Avon.

Ennis, B. J., & Litwack, T. (1974). Psychiatry and the presumption of expertise: Flipping coins in the courtroom. *California Law Review, 62,* 693–752.

Ennis, B. J., & Siegel, L. (1973). *The rights of mental patients.* (ACLU Handbook Series.) New York: Avon.

Erasmus, D. (1735/1958). *Moriae encomium: Or, the praise of folly* (W. Kennet, Trans.). London: J. Wilford.

Ewing, C. P. (Ed.). (1985). *Psychology, psychiatry, and the law: A clinical and forensic handbook.* Sarasota, FL: Professional Resource Exchange.

Ewing, C. P. (1987). Diagnosing and treating "insanity" on death row: Legal and ethical perspectives. *Behavioral Sciences & the Law, 5*(2), 175–185.

Eysenck, H. J. (1952). The effects of psychotherapy: An evaluation. *Journal of Consulting Psychology, 16,* 319–324.

Fain v. Commonwealth, 78 Ky. 183 (1879).

Fancher, R. E. (1973). *Psychoanalytic psychology: The development of Freud's thought.* New York: Norton.

Fancher, R. E. (1979). *Pioneers of psychology.* New York: Norton.

Feguer v. United States, 302 F. 2nd 214 (8th Cir.), *cert. denied,* 391 U.S. 871 (1962).

Feild, H. S., & Barnett, N. J. (1978). Simulated jury trials: Students vs. "real" people as jurors. *The Journal of Social Psychology, 104,* 287–293.

Feinberg, J. (1973). *Social philosophy.* New York: Prentice-Hall.

Fenwick, P. (1987). Somnambulism and the law: A review. *Behavioral Sciences & the Law, 5*(3), 343–357.

Fersch, Jr., E. A. (1980). Ethical issues for psychologists in court settings. In J. Monahan (Ed.), *Who is the client? The ethics of psychological intervention in the criminal justice system.* Washington, DC: American Psychological Association.

Fingarette, H. (1963). *The self in transformation: Psychoanalysis, philosophy and the life of the spirit.* New York: Harper & Row.

Fingarette, H. (1972). *The meaning of criminal insanity.* Berkeley: University of California Press.

Fingarette, H. (1974). Self-deception and the "splitting of the ego." In R. Wollheim (Ed.), *Freud: A collection of critical essays* (pp. 80–96). Garden City, NY: Anchor Books.

Fingarette, H., & Hasse, A. F. (1979). *Mental disabilities and criminal responsibility.* Berkeley: University of California Press.

Finkel, N. J. (1976a). From cathartics to catharsis: Psychology's emergence from medicine. *Connecticut Medicine, 40,* 269–271.

Finkel, N. J. (1976b). *Mental illness and health: Its legacy, tensions, and changes.* New York: Macmillan.

Finkel, N. J. (1980). *Therapy and ethics: The courtship of law and psychology.* New York: Grune & Stratton.

Finkel, N. J. (1982, August). *Insanity defenses: Juror's assessments of mental disease, responsibility, and culpability.* Paper presented at the meeting of the American Psychological Association, Washington, DC.

Finkel, N. J. (1984a). Psychology and the courts. In R. Corsini (Ed.), *Encyclopedia of Psychology* (pp. 122–124). New York: Wiley.

Finkel, N. J. (1984b). Right to refuse treatment. In R. J. Corsini (Ed.), *Encyclopedia of psychology* (Vol. 3, pp. 243–244). New York: Wiley.

Finkel, N. J. (1984c). Right to treatment. In R. J. Corsini (Ed.), *Encyclopedia of psychology* (Vol. 3, p. 244). New York: Wiley.

Finkel, N. J. (1988, August). *De jure and de facto insanity tests.* Paper presented at the meeting of the American Psychological Association, Atlanta, Georgia.

Finkel, N. J. (1988). Maligning and misconstruing jurors' insanity verdicts: A rebuttal. *Forensic Reports, 1,* 97–124.

Finkel, N. J., & Handel, S. F. (1988). Jurors and insanity: Do test instructions instruct? *Forensic Reports, 1,* 65–79.

Finkel, N. J., & Handel, S. F. (in press). How jurors construe "insanity." *Law and Human Behavior.*

Finkel, N. J., & Sabat, S. R. (1985). Split-brain madness: An insanity defense waiting to happen. *Law and Human Behavior, 8,* 225–252.

Finkel, N. J., Shaw, R., Bercaw, S., & Koch, J. (1985). Insanity defenses: From the jurors' perspective. *Law and Psychology Review, 9,* 77–92.

Fisher, K. (1987, April). Appeal will consider N. C. "duty-to-commit." *The APA Monitor, 18*(4), 34.

Fisher v. U.S., 328 U.S. 463 (1946).

Fitch, W. L., Petrella, R. C., & Wallace, J. (1987). Legal ethics and the use of mental health experts in criminal cases. *Behavioral Sciences & the Law, 5*(2), 105–117.

Fleischman, P. R. (1973). Report on Rosenhan. *Science, 180,* 356.

Follingstad, D. R. (1985). Systematic jury selection: The quest for a scientific approach. In C. P. Ewing (Ed.), *Psychology, psychiatry, and the law: A clinical and forensic handbook* (pp. 467–505). Sarasota, FL: Professional Resource Exchange.

Foucault, M. (1973). *Madness and civilization: A history of insanity in the age of reason.* New York: Vintage Books.

Frank, J. D. (1961). *Persuasion and healing.* Baltimore, MD: The Johns Hopkins University Press.

Frazer, Sir J. G. (1963). *The golden bough.* New York: Macmillan.

Freud, S. (1963). On psychotherapy (1904). In P. Rieff (Ed.), *Sigmund Freud: Therapy and technique.* New York: Collier Books.

Freud, S. (1974a). Project for a scientific psychology (1895). In J. Strachey (Ed.), *The standard edition of the complete psychological work of Sigmund Freud* (Vol. I). London: Hogarth Press.

Freud, S. (1974b). Splitting of the ego in the process of defence (1940). In J. Strachey (Ed.), *The standard edition of the complete psychological works of Sigmund Freud* (Vol. XXIII). London: Hogarth Press.

Gallatin, J. (1982). *Abnormal psychology: Concepts, issues, trends.* New York: Macmillan.

Garmezy, N. Vulnerability research and the issue of primary prevention. (1971). *American Journal of Orthopsychiatry, 41,* 101–116.

Gaylin, W. (1978). In the beginning: Helpless and dependent. In W. Gaylin, I. Glasser, S. Marcus, & D. Rothman (Eds.), *Doing good: The limits of benevolence.* New York: Pantheon.

Gaylin, W. (1982). *The killing of Bonnie Garland.* New York: Simon & Schuster.

Gaylin, W., Glasser, I., Marcus, S., & Rothman, D. (Eds.). (1978). *Doing good: The limits of benevolence.* New York: Pantheon.

Gaylin, W., Meister, J. S., & Neville, R. C. (Eds.). (1975). *Operating on the mind: The psychosurgery conflict.* New York: Basic Books.

Gazzaniga, M. S. (1985). *The social brain: Discovering the networks of the mind.* New York: Basic Books.

Gazzaniga, M. S., Bogen, J. E., & Sperry, R. W. (1967). Dyspraxia following division of the cerebral commissures. *Archives of Neurology, 16,* 606–612.

Gazzaniga, M. S., & Hillyard, S. A. (1971). Language and speech capacity of the right hemisphere. *Neuropsychologia, 9,* 273–280.

Gazzaniga, M. S., & Le Doux, J. E. (1978). *The integrated mind.* New York: Plenum Press.

Gerber, R. J. (1984). *The insanity defense.* Port Washington, NY: Associated Faculty Press.

Gibson, W. S. (1973). *Hieronymus Bosch.* New York: Praeger.

Gillis, J. S. (1979). *Social influence in psychotherapy.* Jonesboro, TN: Pilgrimmage Press.

Gilman, S. L. (1982). *Seeing the insane.* New York: Wiley.

Giuliani, R. W. (1982). Statement. Hearings before the Committee on the Judiciary, United States Senate. *The insanity defense.* Serial No. J-97-126. Washington, DC: U. S. Government Printing Office, 31–47.

Gobert, J. J. (1973). Competency to stand trial: A pre- and post-*Jackson* analysis. *Tennessee Law Review, 40*(4), 661.

Goffman, E. (1961). *Asylums.* Garden City, NY: Anchor.

Goffman, E. (1969). *Strategic interaction.* Philadelphia: University of Pennsylvania Press.

Goldberg, C. (1977). *Therapeutic partnership.* New York: Springer.

Goldstein, A. S. (1967). *The insanity defense.* New Haven: Yale University Press.

Goldstein, A. P., Heller, K., & Sechrest, L. (1968). *Psychotherapy and the psychology of behavior change.* New York: Wiley.

Gomes-Schwartz, B., Hadley, S., & Strupp, H. H. (1978). Individual psychotherapy and behavior therapy. In M. R. Rosenzweig & L. W. Porter (Eds.), *Annual Review of Psychology* (Vol. 29). Palo Alto, CA: Annual Reviews.

Gottesman, I. I., & Shields, J. (1966). Contributions of twin studies to perspectives on schizophrenia. In B. A. Maher (Ed.), *Progress in experimental personality research.* New York: Academic Press.

Gowers, Sir Ernest (Chairman). (1953). *Report of the Royal Commission on capital punishment 1949-53.* Cmd. 8932, London: HMSO.

Greene, E., Schooler, J. W., & Loftus, E. F. (1985). Expert psychological testimony. In S. M. Kassin & L. S. Wrightsman (Eds.), *The psychology of evidence and trial procedure* (pp. 201–226). Beverly Hills, CA: Sage.

Grisso, T. (1987). The economic and scientific future of forensic psychological assessment. *American Psychologist, 42*(9), 831–839.

Group for Advancement of Psychiatry. (1954). Criminal responsibility and psychological expert testimony, 5.

Group for the Advancement of Psychiatry. (1974). Misuse of psychiatry in criminal courts: Competency to stand trial, *8,* Report 89, 905.

Gutheil, T. G. (1980). Editorial. In search of true freedom: Drug refusal, involuntary medication, and "rotting with your rights." *American Journal of Psychiatry, 137,* 327–328.

Guttmacher, M., & Weihofen, H. (1952). The psychiatrist on the witness stand. *Boston University Law Rev., 32,* 287, 294–295.

Hadfield, 27 State Trials (1800).

Halderman v. Pennhurst State School and Hospital, 446 F. Supp. 1295 (E.D. Pa. 1972), *modified* 612 F. 2d 84 (3rd Cir. 1979), *reversed* 101 S. Ct. 1531 (1981).

Hale, Sir M. (1736). *Historia plasitorum coronae* [The Pleas of the Crown]. London: E.R. Nutt

Haley, J. (1973). *Uncommon therapy: The psychiatric techniques of Milton Erickson, M.D..* New York: Ballantine Books.

Haley, J. (1978). *Problem-solving therapy.* San Francisco: Jossey-Bass.

Hall, J. (1956). Psychiatry and criminal responsibility. *Yale Law Journal, 65,* 761.

Hall, J. (1960). *General principles of criminal law* (2nd ed.). Indianapolis: Bobbs-Merrill.

Hall v. United States, 410 F. 2d 653 (4th Cir.), *cert. denied,* 396 U.S. 970 (1969).

Halleck, S. L. (1971). *The politics of therapy.* New York: Science House.

Hare-Mustin, R. T., Marecek, J., Kaplan, A. G., & Liss-Levinson, N. (1979). Rights of clients, responsibilities of therapists. *American Psychologist, 34,* 3–16.

Harry, B., & Balcer, C. M. (1987). Menstruation and crime: A critical review of the literature from the clinical criminology perspective. *Behavioral Sciences & the Law, 5*(3), 307–321.

Hart, H. L. A. (1963). *Law, liberty and morality.* Palo Alto, CA: Stanford University Press.

Hart, H. L. A. (1964). The morality of the criminal law. Lionel Cohen lectures. Hebrew University, Jerusalem: Magnes Press.

Hart, H. L. A. (1968). *Punishment and responsibility: Essays in the philosophy of law.* New York: Oxford University Press.

Hatch, O. G. (1982). Psychology, society, and politics. *American Psychologist, 37,* 1031–1037.

Hearings before the Committee on the Judiciary, United States Senate, Ninety-Seventh Congress, Second Session. (1982). *The insanity defense.* Washington, DC: U.S. Government Printing Office, Serial No. J-97-126.

Hearings before the Subcommittee on Criminal Law of the Committee on the Judiciary, United States Senate, Ninety-Seventh Congress, Second Session. (1983). *Limiting the insanity defense.* Washington, DC: U.S. Government Printing Office, Serial No. J-97-122.

Hegel, G. W. F. (1952). *Philosophy of right* (T. M. Knox, Trans.). Oxford: Clarendon Press.

Herbsleb, J. D. (1979). When psychologists aid in the voir dire: Legal and ethical considerations. In L. E. Abt & I. R. Stuart (Eds.), *Social psychology and discretionary law* (pp. 169–218). New York: Van Nostrand Reinhold.

Hermann, D. H. J. (1983). *The insanity defense: Philosophical, historical and legal perspectives.* Springfield, IL: Charles C Thomas.

Hiday, V. A., & Suval, E. M. (1984). Dangerousness of the mentally ill and inebriates in civil commitment. In L. A. Teplin (Ed.), *Mental health and criminal justice* (Vol. 20, pp. 227–250). Beverly Hills, CA: Sage.

Hilgard, E. R. (Special Guest Editor). (1984). [Special Monograph Issue]. *The International Journal of Clinical and Experimental Hypnosis, 32,* 2.

Hobbs, N. (1964). Mental health's third revolution. *American Journal of Orthopsychiatry, 34,* 822–833.

Hobbs, N. (1965). Ethics in clinical psychology. In B. B. Wolman (Ed.), *Handbook of clinical psychology* (p. 1508). New York: McGraw-Hill.

Hobson, J., & Rosenfeld, A. (1984, August). PMS: Puzzling monthly symptoms. *Psychology Today,* 30–35.

Hoffer, P. C., & Hull, N. E. H. (1984). *Murdering mothers: Infanticide in England and New England 1558–1803.* New York: New York University Press.

Holmes, O. W., Jr. (1881). *The common law.* Boston: Little, Brown.

Holstein, J. A. (1985). Jurors' interpretations and jury decision making. *Law and Human Behavior, 9*(1), 83–100.

Homant, R. J., & Kennedy, D. B. (1987). Subjective factors in clinicians' judgments of insanity: Comparison of a hypothetical case and an actual case. *Professional Psychology: Research and Practice, 18*(5), 439–446.

Horney, K. (1948). The value of vindictiveness. *American Journal of Psychoanalysis, 8,* 3.

Horowitz, I. A. (1977). *The courts and social policy.* Washington, DC: Brookings Institution.

Horowitz, I. A. (1985). The effect of jury nullification instruction on verdicts and jury functioning in criminal trials. *Law and Human Behavior, 9*(1), 25–36.

Horowitz, I. A., & Willging, T. E. (1984). *The psychology of law: Integrations and applications.* Boston: Little, Brown.

Howard, J. (1784). *The state of the prisons in England and Wales* (3rd ed.). Warrington, England: William Eyres.

Humphrey v. Cady, 405 U.S. 504 (1972).

Inouye, D. K. (1983). Mental health care: Access, stigma, and effectiveness. *American Psychologist, 38,* 912–917.

In re Banks, 88 Cal. App. 3d 864, 152 Cal. Rptr. 111 (1979).

In re Mental Commitment of M. P., 500 N. E. 2d 216 (1986).

In re Rose, 109 Misc. 2d 960, 441 N.Y.S. 2d 161, 163 (Sup. Ct., Kings Co. 1981).

In re Winship, 397, U.S. 358 (1970).

Insanity Defense Reform Act of 1984. Public Law 98-473, Sec. 401, 402 20 (1984).

Jackson v. Indiana, 406 U.S. 715 (1972).

Jacoby, S. (1983). *Wild justice: The evolution of revenge.* New York: Harper & Row.

James, R. M. (1959a). Jurors' assessment of criminal responsibility. *Social Problems, 7,* 58–67.

James, R. M. (1959b). Status and competence of jurors. *The American Journal of Sociology, 64,* 563–570.

Joint Commission on Mental Illness and Health. (1961). *Action for mental health.* New York: Basic Books.

Jones, E. E., & Davis, K. E. (1965). From acts to dispositions. In L. Berkowitz (Ed.), *Advances in experimental social psychology* (Vol. 2). New York: Academic Press.

Jones v. United States, 103 S. Ct. 3043 (1983).

Jung, C. G. (1966). *The collected works of C. G. Jung.* Bollingen Series XX, Vol. 16. Princeton, NJ: Princeton University Press.

Jung, C. G. (1970). *Mysterium conjunctionis.* Translated by R. F. C. Hull. Bollingen Series XX.

From *The collected works of C. G. Jung*, Vol. 14 (2nd ed.). Princeton, NJ: Princeton University Press.

Kadish, M. R., & Kadish, S. H. (1977). The institutionalization of conflict: Jury acquittals. In J. L. Tapp & F. J. Levine (Eds.), *Law, justice, and the individual in society: Psychological and legal issues*, (pp. 308–318). New York: Holt, Rinehart & Winston.

Kaimowitz v. Michigan Department of Mental Health, Civil No. 73-19434-AW 42 U.S.L.W. 2063 (Mich. Cir. Ct. 1973).

Kalven, H., Jr., & Zeisel, H. (1971). *The American jury*. Boston: Little, Brown.

Kant, I. (1953). *The critique of pure reason* (N. K. Smith, Trans.). New York: Macmillan.

Kant, I. (1978). *Anthropology from a pragmatic point of view* (V. L. Dowdell, Trans.). Carbondale, IL: Southern Illinois University Press.

Kaplan, M. F., & Schersching, C. (1980). Reducing juror bias: An experimental approach. In P. D. Lipsitt & B. D. Sales (Eds.), *New directions in psycholegal research* (pp. 149–170). New York: Van Nostrand Reinhold.

Karasu, T. (1980). The ethics of psychotherapy. *American Journal of Psychiatry, 137*, 1502–1512.

Kassin, S. M., & Wrightsman, L. S. (1985). Confession evidence. In S. M. Kassin & L. S. Wrightsman (Eds.), *The psychology of evidence and trial procedure* (pp. 67–94). Beverly Hills, CA: Sage.

Kelley, H. H. (1973). The processes of causal attribution. *American Psychologist, 28*, 107–128.

Kelly, G. A. (1963). *A theory of personality: The psychology of personal constructs*. New York: Norton.

Kenefick, D. P. (1968). Problems of public consultation in medicolegal matters: A symposium. *American Journal of psychiatry, 125*, 42–59.

Kiesler, C. A. (1982). Public and professional myths about mental hospitalization: An empirical reassessment of policy-related beliefs. *American Psychologist, 37*(12), 1323–1339.

Kirschner, B. (1978). Constitutional standards for release of the civilly committed and not guilty by reason of insanity: A strict scrutiny analysis. *Arizona Law Review, 20*, 233.

Kittrie, N. N. (1971). *The right to be different: Deviance and enforced therapy*. Baltimore: Johns Hopkins University Press.

Kluger, R. (1979). *Simple justice: The history of Brown v. Board of Education and black America's struggle for equality*. New York: Knopf.

Knecht v. Gillman, 488 F.2d 1136 (8th Cir. 1973).

Kopelman, M. D. (1987). Crime and amnesia: A review. *Behavioral Sciences & the Law, 5*(3), 323–342.

Kozol, H. L., Boucher, R. J., & Garofalo, R. F. (1972). The diagnosis and treatment of dangerousness. *Crime and Delinquency, 18*, 371–394.

Kraft, P. B. (1985). The right to refuse psychiatric treatment: Professional self-esteem and hopelessness. In C. P. Ewing (Ed.), *Psychology, psychiatry, and the law: A clinical and forensic handbook* (p. 229). Sarasota, FL: Professional Resource Exchange.

Krauthammer, C. (1987, May 8). Let Hinckley go. *The Washington Post*, p. A23.

Lamiell, J. T. (1981). Toward an idiothetic psychology of personality. *American Psychologist, 36*, 276–289.

Lamiell, J. T., & Trierweiler, S. J. (1986). Personality measurement and intuitive personality judgments from an idiothetic point of view. *Clinical Psychology Review, 6*, 471–491.

Lasky, R. (1982). *Evaluation of criminal responsibility in multiple personality and the related dissociative disorders: A psychoanalytic consideration*. Springfield, IL: Charles C Thomas.

Lebensohn, Z. M. (1970). Defensive psychiatry or how to treat the mentally ill without being a lawyer. In W. E. Barton & C. J. Sanborn (Eds.), *Law and the mental health professionals*. New York: International Universities Press.

Leifer, R. (1964). The psychiatrist and tests of criminal responsibility. *American Psychologist, 19*, 825–830.

Lipari v. Sear, Roebuck & Co., 497 F. Supp. 185 (D. Neb. 1980).

Lipsitt, P. D. (1984). Foreword. In D. L. Shapiro, *Psychological evaluation and expert testimony: A practical guide to forensic work* (p. vi). New York: Van Nostrand Reinhold.

Lipsitt, P. D., Lelos, D., & McGarry, A. L. (1971). Competency for trial: A screening instrument. *American Journal of Psychiatry, 128,* 105–109.

Lipsitt, P. D., & Sales, B. D. (Eds.). (1980). *New directions in psycholegal research.* New York: Van Nostrand Reinhold.

Lochner, P. (1973). Some limits on the application of social science research in the legal process. *Law and the Social Order,* 815–848.

Lockhart v. McCree, 106 S. Ct. 1758 (1986).

Loftus, E. (1979). *Eyewitness testimony.* Cambridge: Harvard University Press.

Loftus, E., & Monahan, J. (1980). Trial by data: Psychological research as legal evidence. *American Psychologist, 35*(3), 270–283.

Loh, W. D. (1985). The evidence and trial procedure: The law, social policy, and psychological research. In S. M. Kassin & L. S. Wrightsman (Eds.), *The psychology of evidence and trial procedure* (pp. 13–39). Beverly Hills, CA: Sage.

London, P. (1964). *The modes and morals of psychotherapy.* New York: Holt, Rinehart & Winston.

Lynch v. Overholser, 369 U.S. 705 (1962).

Mackenzie, Sir G. (1678). *The laws and customs of Scotland in matters criminal.* Edinburgh: pt. I, tit. I, section 8.

Maeder, T. (1985). *Crime and madness: The origins and evolution of the insanity defense.* New York: Harper & Row.

Maher, W. B., & Maher, B. (1982). The ship of fools: *Stultifera navis* or *ignis fatuus? American Psychologist, 37,* 756–761.

Malinouskos v. United States, 505 F. 2d 649 (5th Cir. 1974).

Margolin, G. (1982). Ethical and legal considerations in marital and family therapy. *American Psychologist, 37,* 788–801.

Matthaeus, A. (1644). *De criminibus ad lib.* XLVII et XLVIII *Dig. Commentarious.* Amsterdam: Prolegonena, Cap. II, 6.

Maudsley, H. (1863). Homicidal insanity. *Journal of Mental Science, 9,* 327–43.

Maudsley, H. (1876). *Responsibility in mental disease.* New York: Appleton.

McCarthy, C. (1983, December 17). Crime, punishment and victims. *The Washington Post,* p. A19.

McDonald v. United States, 312 F.2d 847, 851 (D.C. Cir. 1962).

McGarry, A. L. (1973). *Competency to stand trial and mental illness.* Washington, DC: U.S. Government Printing Office.

McGarry, A. L., & Bendt, R. H. (1969). Criminal vs. civil commitment of psychotic offenders: A seven year follow-up. *American Journal of Psychiatry, 125,* 93–100.

McIntosh v. Milano, 403 A. 2d 500 (N. J. Supr. Ct. 1979).

McNulty, F. (1980). *The burning bed.* New York: Harcourt Brace Jovanovich.

Mechanic, D. (1962). Some factors in identifying and defining mental illness. *Mental Hygiene, 46,* 66–74.

Mednick, S. A. (1970). Breakdown in individuals at high risk for schizophrenia: Possible predispositional perinatal factors. *Mental Hygiene, 54,* 50–63.

Meehl, P. E. (1962). Schizotaxia, schizotypy, schizophrenia. *American Psychologist, 17,* 827–838.

Meisel, A., Roth, L. R., & Lidz, C. W. (1977). Toward a model of the legal doctrine of informed consent. *American Journal of Psychiatry, 134,* 286.

Menninger, K. (1958). *Theory of psychoanalytic technique.* New York: Harper & Row.

Menninger, K. (1966). *The crime of punishment.* New York: Viking Press.

Mill, J. S. (1930). *On liberty.* London: Watts (Thinker's Library).

Miller, D. (1967). Retrospective analysis of posthospital mental patients' worlds. *Journal of Health and Social Behavior, 8,* 136–140.

Mills, M. J., & Beck, J. C. (1985). The *Tarasoff* case. In J. C. Beck (Ed.), *The potentially violent patient and the Tarasoff decision in psychiatric practice.* Washington, DC: American Psychiatric Press.

Mills v. Rogers, 457 U. S. 291 (1982).

Monahan, J. (1980). Foreword. In R. Roesch & S. L. Golding, *Competency to stand trial*. Urbana, IL: University of Illinois Press.

Monahan, J. (1981). *The clinical prediction of violent behavior*. Washington, DC: U.S. Government Printing Office.

Monahan, J. (1982). The case for prediction in the modified desert model of criminal sentencing. *International Journal of Law and Psychiatry, 5,* 103–113.

Monahan, J., & Monahan, L. C. (1977). Prediction research and the role of psychologists in correctional institutions. *San Diego Law Review, 14,* 1028–1038.

Monahan, J., & Steadman, H. J. (1983). Crime and mental disorder: An epidemiological approach. In M. Tonry & N. Morris (Eds.), *Crime and justice: An annual review of research* (Vol. 4, pp. 145–189). Chicago: The University of Chicago Press.

Moore, M. S. (1984). *Law and psychiatry: Rethinking the relationship*. Cambridge: Cambridge University Press.

Moore, R. A. (1978). Ethics in the practice of psychiatry—Origins, functions, models and enforcement. *American Journal of Psychiatry, 135,* 157–163.

Moran, R. (1981). *Knowing right from wrong: The insanity defense of Daniel McNaughtan*. New York: Free Press.

Moran, R. (1983). Statement. Hearings before the Subcommittee on Criminal Justice of the Committee on the Judiciary, House of Representatives, *Insanity defense in federal courts*. Washington, DC: U.S. Government Printing Office, Serial No. 134, 432–439.

Morris, G. (1983). Acquittal by reason of insanity: Developments in the law. In J. Monahan and H. J. Steadman (Eds.), *Mentally disordered offenders: Perspectives from law and social science* (p. 137). New York: Plenum Press.

Morris, N. (1982). *Madness and the criminal law*. Chicago: The University of Chicago Press.

Morrison, J. K. (1979). A consumer-oriented approach to psychotherapy. *Psychotherapy: Theory, research, and practice, 16,* 381–384.

Morse, S. J. (1978). Crazy behavior, morals, and science: An analysis of mental health law. *Southern California Law Review, 51,* 527–654.

Morse, S. J. (1984). Statement on behalf of the Association for the Advancement of Psychology and the American Psychological Association. Hearings before the Subcommittee on Criminal Justice of the Committee on the Judiciary, House of Representatives. *Reform of the federal insanity defense*. Washington, DC: U.S. Government Printing Office, Serial No. 21, 311–402.

Morse, S. J. (1985). Excusing the crazy: The insanity defense reconsidered. *Southern California Law Review, 58,* 780–836.

Mowrer, O. H. (1960). "Sin," the lesser of two evils. *American Psychologist, 15,* 301–304.

Mulvey, E. P., Geller, J. L., & Roth, L. H. (1987). The promise and peril of involuntary outpatient commitment. *American Psychologist, 42,* 6, 571–584.

Munsterberg, H. (1908). *On the witness stand: Essays on psychology and crime*. New York: Doubleday, Page.

Nagel, T. (1974). Freud's anthropomorphism. In R. Wollheim (Ed.), *Freud: A collection of critical essays* (pp. 11–24). Garden City, NY: Anchor Books.

Nemeth, C. J. (1979). Group dynamics and legal decision-making. In L. E. Abt & I. R. Stuart (Eds.), *Social psychology and discretionary law* (pp. 271–285). New York: Van Nostrand Reinhold.

Newman v. Missouri, 394 F. Supp. 83 (W.D. Mo. 1974).

O'Connor v. Donaldson, 422 U.S. 563 (1975).

Olin, G. B., & Olin, H. S. (1975). Informed consent in voluntary mental hospital admissions. *American Journal of Psychiatry, 132,* 938–941.

Orland, L. (Ed.). (1973). *Justice, punishment, treatment: The correctional process*. New York: Free Press.

Orne, M. T., Dinges, D. F., & Orne, E. C. (1984). On the differential diagnosis of multiple personality in the forensic context. *The International Journal of Clinical and Experimental Hypnosis, 32*(2), 118–169.

Ornstein, R. E. (1972). *The psychology of consciousness.* San Francisco: Freeman.

Osgood, C. E., Luria, Z., Jeans, R. F., & Smith, S. W. (1976). The three faces of Evelyn: A case report. *Journal of Abnormal Psychology, 85,* 249–270.

Overholser v. Lynch, 109 U.S. App. D.C. 404 (1959).

Overholser v. Lynch, 288 F. 2d 388 (1961).

Packer, I. K. (1987). Homicide and the insanity defense: A comparison of sane and insane murderers. *Behavioral Sciences & the Law, 5*(1), 25–35.

Parham v. J.R., 442 U.S. 5844, 624–625 (1979).

Parker, K. (1976). Comment: On a contractual model of treatment. *American Psychologist, 31,* 257–258.

Parsons v. State, 2 So. 854 (Ala. 1887).

Pate v. Robinson, 383 U.S. 375 (1966).

People ex rel. Myers v. Briggs (1970), 46 Ill. 2d 281, 288, 263 N.E. 2d 109, 113.

People v. Crosswell, Johnson's Cases, 3, 336–413 (1804).

People v. Gorshen, 51 Cal. 2d 716, 7200-21, 336 P. 2d 492, 494–95 (1959).

People v. Grant, 71 Ill. 2d 551, 377 N.E. 2d. 4 (1978).

People v. Heral, 62 Ill. 2d 329, 342 N.E. 2d 34 (1976).

People v. Lang, 391 NE 2nd 350 (1979).

People v. Lang, (1967), 37 Ill. 2d 75, 19 Ill. Dec. 231, 62 Ill. App. 3d 688.

People v. Ray, 14 Cal. 3d 29, 533 p. 2d 1017, 120 Cal. Rptr. 377 (1975).

People v. Wolff, 61 Cal. 2d 795, 394 p. 2d 959, 40 Cal. Rptr. 271 (1964).

Perlman, D. (1980). Attributions in the criminal justice process: Concepts and empirical illustrations. In P. D. Lipsitt & B. D. Sales (Eds.), *New directions in psycholegal research.* New York: Van Nostrand Reinhold.

Petersen v. Washington, 671 P. 2d 230 (Wash. 1983).

Pinizzotto, A. J. (1984). Forensic psychology: Criminal personality profiling. *Journal of Police Science and Administration, 12*(1), 32–40.

Plotkin, R. (1977). Limiting the therapeutic orgy: Mental patients' right to refuse treatment. *Northwestern University Law Review, 72*(4), 461.

Porter, B. (1983). Mind hunters. *Psychology Today, 17*(4), 44–52.

Pribram, K. (1962). The neuropsychology of Sigmund Freud. In A. J. Bachrach (Ed.), *Experimental foundations of clinical psychology* (p. 443). New York: Basic Books.

Proprietary Articles Trade Assn. v. Att. Gen. for Canada, 1931 A.C. 324 (1931).

Puccetti, R. (1973). Brain bisection and personal identity. *British Journal for the Philosophy of Science, 24,* 339–355.

R. v. Davis, 14 Cox C. C. 563 (1881).

R. v. Dwerryhouse, 3 Cox (Criminal Law Cases) 291 & 446 (1847).

R. v. Ferrers, 19 St. Tr. 885 (1760).

R. v. Frith, 22 St. Tr. 307 (1790).

R. v. True, Cr. App. R. 164 (1922).

Rabkin, R. (1977). *Strategic psychotherapy.* New York: Basic Books.

Rappaport, J. (1977). *Community psychology: Values, research and action.* New York: Holt, Rinehart & Winston.

Ray, I. (1838/1983). *A treatise on the medical jurisprudence of insanity.* New York: Da Capo Press.

Read, R. A. (1982). Statement. Hearings before the Committee on the Judiciary, United States Senate, *The insanity defense.* Washington, DC: U.S. Government Printing Office, Serial No. J-97-126, 61-71.

Redlich, F., & Mollica, R. F. (1976). Overview: Ethical issues in contemporary psychiatry. *American Journal of Psychiatry, 133,* 125–136.

Regina v. Tolson, 23, Q.B.D. 168, 187 (1889).

Reich, W. T. (Ed.). (1978). *Encyclopedia of bioethics* (p. 1764). New York: Free Press.

Reiser, S. J. (1980). Refusing treatment for mental illness: Historical and ethical dimensions. *American Journal of Psychiatry, 137*(3), 329.

Rennie v. Klein, 476 F. Supp. 1294 (D. N.J. 1979), *modified*, Nos. 79-2576 and 79-2577 (3rd Cir., 1981).

Restak, R. (1987, May 17). The fiction of the "Reasonable Man." *The Washington Post*, p. C3.

Rex v. Arnold, 16 How. St. Tr. 684, 764 (1723).

Roberts, C. F., Golding, S. L., & Fincham, F. D. (1987). Implicit theories of criminal responsibility: Decision making and the insanity defense. *Law and Human Behavior*, 2(3), 207–232.

Robey, A. (1965). Criteria for competency to stand trial: A checklist for psychiatrists. *American Journal of Psychiatry*, 122, 616–622.

Robinson, D. N. (1973). Therapies: A clear and present danger. *American Psychologist*, 28, 129–133.

Robinson, D. N. (1974). Harm, offense and nuisance: Some first steps in the establishment of an ethics of treatment. *American Psychologist*, 29, 233–238.

Robinson, D. N. (1976). What sort of persons are hemispheres? Another look at "split-brain" man. *The British Journal for the Philosophy of Science*, 27, 73–78.

Robinson, D. N. (1980). *Psychology and law: Can justice survive the social sciences?* New York: Oxford University Press.

Robinson, D. N. (1982a). Cerebral plurality and the unity of the self. *American Psychologist*, 37, 904–910.

Robinson, D. N. (1982b, June 23). The Hinckley decision: Psychiatry in court. *The Wall Street Journal*, p. 26.

Robinson, E. (1935). *Law and the lawyers*. New York: Macmillan.

Robinson v. California, 370 U.S. 660 (1962).

Roe v. Wade, 410 U.S. 113 (1973).

Roesch, R., & Golding, S. L. (1977). *A systems analysis of competency to stand trial procedures: Implications for forensic services in North Carolina*. Urbana, Il: University of Illinois Press.

Roesch, R., & Golding, S. (1979). Treatment and disposition of defendants found incompetent to stand trial: A review and a proposal. *International Journal of Law and Psychiatry*, 2, 357.

Roesch, R., & Golding, S. (1980). *Competency to stand trial*. Urbana, IL: University of Illinois Press.

Rogers, C. R. (1951). *Client-centered therapy*. Cambridge, MA: The Riverside Press.

Rogers, R. (1987a). APA's position on the insanity defense: Empiricism versus emotionalism. *American Psychologist*, 42(9), 840–848.

Rogers, R. (1987b). Ethical dilemmas in forensic evaluations. *Behavioral Sciences & the Law*, 5(2), 149–160.

Rogers v. Okin, Civil Action 75-1610 (D. Mass. 1975).

Rogers v. Okin, 478 F. Supp. 1342 (D. Mass. 1979), *aff'd in part, rev'd in part*, 634 F.2d 650 (1st Cir. 1980), *cert. granted*, 49 U.S.L.W. 3779 (1981).

Rokeach, M. (1960). *The open and closed mind: Investigations into the nature of belief systems and personality systems*. New York: Basic Books.

Rosenberg, A. H., & McGarry, A. L. (1972). Competency for trial: The making of an expert. *American Journal of Psychiatry*, 128, 82–86.

Rosenhan, D. L. (1973). On being sane in insane places. *Science*, 179, 250–258.

Rosenhan, D. L., & Seligman, M. E. P. (1984). *Abnormal psychology*. New York: Norton.

Rosenthal, D., Wender, P. H., Kety, S. S., Schulsinger, F., Welner, J., & Ostergaard, L. (1968). Schizophrenics' offspring reared in adoptive homes. In D. Rosenthal and S. S. Kety (Eds.), *The transmission of schizophrenia* (pp. 377–391). Oxford: Pergamon Press.

Rothman, D. J. (1971). *The discovery of the asylum: Social order and disorder in the new republic*. Boston: Little, Brown.

Rouse v. Cameron, 387 F.2d 241 (D. C. Cir. 1967).

Roy v. Hartogs, 381 N.Y.S.2d 587 (1975).

Rubin, B. (1972). Predictions of dangerousness in mentally ill criminals. *Archives of General Psychiatry*, 27, 397–407.

Runes, D. D. (Ed.). (1947). *The selected writings of Benjamin Rush*. New York: Philosophical Library.

Ryle, G. (1949). *The concept of mind*. New York: University Paperbacks.

Sadoff, R. L. (1982). Statement. Hearings before the Committee on the Judiciary, United States Senate. *The insanity defense*. Serial No. J-97-126. Washington, DC: U. S. Government Printing Office, 460–469.

Saks, M. J., & Hastie, R. (1978). *Social psychology in court*. New York: Van Nostrand Reinhold.

Sales, B., & Hafemeister, T. (1984). Empiricism and legal policy on the insanity defense. In L. A. Teplin (Ed.), *Mental health and criminal justice* (Vol. 20, pp. 253–278). Beverly Hills, CA: Sage.

Sales, B., Rich, R. F., & Reich, J. (1987). Victimization policy research. *Professional Psychology: Research and Practice, 18*(4), 326–337.

Samenow, S. E. (1984). *Inside the criminal mind*. New York: Time Books.

Sartre, J. P. (1974). *Mauvaise foi* and the unconscious. In R. Wollheim (Ed.), *Freud: A collection of critical essays* (pp. 70–79). Garden City, NY: Anchor Books.

Schacter, D. L. (1986). Amnesia and crime: How much do we really know? *American Psychologist, 41*(3), 286–295.

Scheff, T. J. (1973). The societal reaction to deviance: Ascriptive elements in the psychiatric screening of mental patients in a midwestern state. In R. H. Price & B. Denner (Eds.), *The making of a mental patient*. New York: Holt, Rinehart & Winston.

Schmidt v. Goddin, 297 S.E. 2d 701 (1982).

Schofield, W. (1964). *Psychotherapy: The purchase of friendship*. Englewood Cliffs, NJ: Prentice-Hall.

Schwitzgebel, R. K. (1975). A contractual model for the protection of the rights of institutionalized patients. *American Psychologist, 30*. 815–820.

Scott, E. P., & Ennis, B. J. (1975). *Motion for leave to file amicus curiae*. Washington, DC: Mental Health Law Project.

Scotte v. Plante, 641 F 2d 117, 129 (3d Cir. 1981), *appeal pending*.

Seligman, M. E. P. (1975). *Helplessness: On depression, development and death*. San Francisco: Freeman.

Shah, S. (1977, February). Editorial. *APA Monitor*, 2.

Shakespeare, W. (1959). *The tragedy of Macbeth*. New York: Washington Square Press.

Shapiro, M. H. (1974). Legislating the control of behavior control: Autonomy and the coercive use of organic therapies. *Southern California Law Review, 47*, 300, n. 215.

Shaw v. Glickman, Md. App., 415 A.2d 625 (1980).

Siegel, M. (1977, February). Editorial. APA Monitor, 5.

Sieling v. Eyman, 478 F. 2d 388 (1961).

Sieling v. Eyman, 478 F. 2d 211 (9th Cir. 1973).

Simon, R. J. (1967). *The jury and the defense of insanity*. Boston: Little, Brown.

Sinclair v. State, 161 Miss. 142, 132 So. 581 (1931).

Skinner, B. F. (1971). *Beyond freedom and dignity*. New York: Bantam.

Slobogin, C. (1985). The guilty but mentally ill verdict: An idea whose time should not have come. *The George Washington Law Review, 53*, 494–527.

Slovenko, R. (1978). Psychotherapy and informed consent: A search in judicial regulation. In W. E. Bartin & C. J. Sanborn (Eds.), *Law and the mental health professions*. New York: International Universities Press.

Slovenko, R. (1987). The lawyer and the forensic expert: Boundaries of ethical practice. *Behavioral Sciences & the Law, 5*(2), 119–147.

Smith, A. (1969). Nondominant hemispherectomy. *Neurology, 19*, 442–445.

Smith, M. B. (1961). Mental health reconsidered: A special case of the problems of values in psychology. *American Psychologist, 16*, 299–306.

Smith, R. (1981). *Trial by medicine: Insanity and responsibility in Victorian trials*. Edinburgh: Edinburgh University Press.

Smith, W. F. (1982). Statement. In *The insanity defense.* Hearings Before the Committee on the Judiciary, United States Senate. Washington, DC: U.S. Government Printing Office, Serial No. J-97-126.

Smith, M. L., & Glass, G. V. (1977). Meta-analysis of psychotherapy outcome studies. *American Psychologist, 32,* 752.

Smith, D., & Kraft, W. A. (1983). DSM-III: Do psychologists really want an alternative? *American Psychologist, 38,* 777–785.

Smith, K., Pumphrey, M. W., & Hall, J. C. (1973). The "last straw": The decisive incident resulting in the request for hospitalization in 100 schizophrenic patients. In R. H. Price & B. Denner (Eds.), *The making of a mental patient.* New York: Holt, Rinehart & Winston.

Solomon, R. C. (1974). Freud's neurological theory of mind. In R. Wollheim (Ed.), *Freud: A collection of critical essays* (pp. 25–52). Garden City, NY: Anchor Books.

Solzhenitsyn, A. (1978, June 8). Harvard commencement address. *Harvard University Gazette,* 1–3.

Sommer, B. (1984, August). PMS in the courts: Are all women on trial? *Psychology Today,* pp. 36–38.

Sparf v. U.S., 156 U.S. 52 (1895).

Sparks, R. F. (1964). Diminished responsibility in theory and practice. *Modern Law Review, 27,* 9–34.

Specht v. Patterson, 386 U.S. 605 (1967).

Sperlich, P. W. (1985). The evidence on evidence: Science and law in conflict and cooperation. In S. M. Kassin and L. S. Wrightsman (Eds.). *The psychology of evidence and trial procedure* (pp. 325–361). Beverly Hills, CA: Sage.

Sperry, R. W. (1966). Brain bisection and consciousness. In J. Eccles (Ed.), *Brain and conscious experience.* New York: Springer-Verlag.

Sperry, R. W., Gazzaniga, M., & Bogen, J. E. (1969). Interhemispheric relationships: The neocortical commissures: Symptoms of hemispheric deconnection. In P. J. Vinken and G. W. Bruyn (Eds.), *Handbook of clinical neurology, 4,* 273–290.

Sperry, R. W., Zaidel, E., & Zaidel, D. (1979). Self-recognition and social awareness in the disconnected minor hemisphere. *Neuropsychologia, 17,* 153–166.

Springer, S. P., & Deutsch, G. (1981). *Left brain, right brain.* San Francisco: Freeman.

Staff. (1983, July 18). Arguing life and death. *Newsweek,* p. 57.

Staff. (1986, January 6). Abandoned: The chronic mentally ill. *Newsweek,* p. 14.

Stanford Law Review (Note). (1969). A study of the California penalty jury in first-degree murder cases. *Stanford Law Review, 21,* 1296–1497.

State v. Bianchi, No. 79-10116 (Wash. Super. Ct. October 19, 1979).

State v. Pike, 49 N.H. 399 (1869).

State v. Strasburg, 60 Wash. 106, 110 (1910).

Steadman, H. J. (1975). Violence, mental illness, and preventive detention: We can't predict who is dangerous. *Psychology Today,* pp. 32–33.

Steadman, H. J. (1979). *Beating a rap? Defendants found incompetent to stand trial.* Chicago: The University of Chicago Press.

Steadman, H. J. (1980). Insanity acquittals in New York State, 1965–1978. *American Journal of Psychiatry, 137,* 321–326.

Steadman, H. J. (1983). Statement. Hearings before the Subcommittee on Criminal Law of the Committee on the Judiciary, United States Senate. *Limiting the insanity defense.* Serial No. J-97-122. Washington, DC: U. S. Government Printing Office, 367–373.

Steadman, H. J., & Braff, J. (1983). Defendants not guilty by reason of insanity. In J. Monahan & H. J. Steadman (Eds.), *Mentally disordered offenders: Perspectives from law and social science* (pp. 109–129). New York: Plenum Press.

Steadman, H. J., & Cocozza, J. J. (1978). Selective reporting and the public's misconceptions of the criminally insane. *Public Opinion Quarterly, 41,* 523–532.

Steadman, H. J., & Hartstone, E. (1983). Defendants incompetent to stand trial. In J. Monahan and H. J. Steadman (Eds.), *Mentally disordered offenders: Perspectives from law and social sciences* (pp. 39–62). New York: Plenum Press.

Stephen, J. F. (1877). *A digest of the criminal law (crimes and punishments)*. London: Macmillan.

Stephen, Sir J. F. (1883). *History of the criminal law of England*. London: Macmillan.

Stevenson, R. L. (1937). *The strange case of Dr. Jekyll and Mr. Hyde*. New York: The Spencer Press.

Stone, A. A. (1984). *Law, psychiatry, and morality: Essays and analysis*. Washington, DC: American Psychiatric Press.

Stuart, R. B. (1975). *Guide to client–therapist treatment contracts*. Champaign, IL: Research Press.

Sydenham, T. (1695). *Compleat method of curing almost all diseases* (7th ed.). London: printed for Hugh Newman at the Grafshopper in the Poultry.

Szasz, T. S. (1961). *The myth of mental illness: Foundations of a theory of personal conduct*. New York: Harper & Row.

Szasz, T. S. (1963). *Law, liberty and psychiatry*. New York: Macmillan.

Szasz, T. S. (1965). *The ethics of psychoanalysis*. New York: Basic Books.

Szasz, T. S. (1970a). *Ideology and insanity: Essays on the psychiatric dehumanization of man*. Garden City, NY: Anchor Books.

Szasz, T. S. (1970b). *The manufacture of madness*. New York: Dell.

Szasz, T. S. (Ed.). (1973). *The age of madness*. Garden City, NY: Anchor Books.

Szasz, T. S. (1976). *Schizophrenia: The sacred symbol of psychiatry*. New York: Basic Books.

Szasz, T. S. (1977). *Psychiatric slavery*. New York: Free Press.

Szasz, T. S. (1978). *The myth of psychotherapy: Mental healing as religion, rhetoric, and repression*. Garden City, NY: Anchor Press.

Szasz, T. S. (1982). The psychiatric will: A new mechanism for protecting persons against "psychosis" and psychiatry. *American Psychologist, 37*, 762–770.

Szasz, T. S. (1984). *The therapeutic state: Psychiatry in the mirror of current events*. Buffalo, NY: Prometheus Books.

Szasz, T. S. (1987). *Insanity: The idea and its consequences*. New York: Wiley.

Tarasoff v. Regents of the University of California, 118 Cal. Rptr. 129, 529 P.2d 553 (1974).

Tarasoff v. Regents of the University of California, 17 Cal. 3d 425, 131 Cal. Rptr. 14, 551 F.2d 334 (1976).

Teplin, L. A. (Ed.). (1984). *Mental health and criminal justice* (Vol. 20). Beverly Hills, CA: Sage.

Terman, L. M. (1931). Psychology and the law. *The Los Angeles Bar Association Bulletin, 6*, 142–153.

Thibaut, J., & Walker, L. (1975). *Procedural justice: A psychological analysis*. Hillsdale, NJ: Erlbaum.

Thigpen, C. H., & Cleckley, H. M. (1957). *The three faces of Eve*. New York: McGraw-Hill.

Thigpen, C. H., & Cleckley, H. M. (1984). On the incidence of multiple personality disorder: A brief communication. *The International Journal of Clinical and Experimental Hypnosis, 32*,(2), 63–66.

Tidyman, E. (1974). *Dummy*. Boston: Little, Brown.

Toulmin, S. (1960). *The philosophy of science*. New York: Harper & Row.

Tuke, S. (1813/1964). *Description of the retreat: An institution near York for insane persons of the Society of Friends*. London: Dawsons of Pall Mall.

United States ex rel. Konigsberg v. Vincent, 526 F. 2d 131 (2d Cir. 1975), *cert. denied*, 426 U.S. 937 (1976).

United States v. Adams, 297 F. Supp. 596 (S.D.N.Y. 1969).

United States v. Amaral, 448 F. 2d 1148 (1973).

United States v. Currens, 290 F.2d 751 (1961).

United States v. Ecker, 543 F 2d (D.C. Cir. 1976), *cert. denied*, 429 U.S. 1063 (1977).

United States v. Guiteau, 12 D.C. 498, 546 (D.C. Sup. Ct. 1882).

United States v. Hinckley, 525 F. Supp. 1342 (D.C. 1981).

United States v. Horowitz, 360 F. Supp. 772 (E.D. Pa. 1973).

United States v. Lancaster,408 F. Supp. 225 (D.D.C. 1976).

United States v. Spock, 416 Fed. Reptr. 2d 165 (1969).

Vidmar, N. (1972). Effects of decision alternatives on the verdicts and social perceptions of simulated jurors. *Journal of Personality and Social Psychology, 22,* 211–218.

Virginia Law Review (Note). (1982). Competence to plead guilty and to stand trial: A new standard when a criminal defendant waives counsel. *Virginia Law Review, 68*(5), 1139–1155.

Visher, C. A. (1987). Juror decision making: The importance of evidence. *Law and Human Behavior, 11*(1), 1–17.

von Hirsch, A. (1978). Proportionality and desert: A reply to Bedau. *Journal of Philosophy, 75,* 623.

von Hirsch, A., & Hanrahan, K. (1979). *The question of parole: Reform, retention, or abolition?* Cambridge, MA: Bollinger.

Wada, J. A., Clarke, R., & Hamm, A. (1975). Cerebral hemispheric asymmetry in humans. *Archives of Neurology, 32,* 239–246.

Wald, P. M., & Friedman, P. R. (1978). The politics of mental health advocacy in the United States. *International Journal of Law and Psychiatry, 1,* 137–152.

Walker, N. (1968). *Crime and insanity in England: Vol. I. The historical perspective.* Edinburgh: Edinburgh University Press.

Walters, H. A. (1981). Dangerousness. In R. H. Woody (Ed.), *The encyclopedia of clinical assessment.* San Francisco: Jossey-Bass.

Wasserstrom, R. A. (1967). H. L. A. Hart and the doctrines of *mens rea* and criminal responsibility. *The University of Chicago Law Review, 35,* 95–96.

Watkins, J. G. (1984). The Bianchi (L. A. hillside strangler) case: Sociopath or multiple personality? *The International Journal of Clinical and Experimental Hypnosis, 32*(2), 67–101.

Wear v. United States, 218 F. 2d 24 (D.C. Cir. 1954).

Weihofen, H. (1979). *The urge to punish: New approaches to the problem of mental irresponsibility for crime.* Westport, CN: Greenwood Press.

Weiner, B. A. (1983). Not guilty by reason of insanity: A sane approach. In Hearings before the Subcommittee on Criminal Law of the Committee on the Judiciary, United States Senate, *Limiting the insanity defense.* Washington, DC: U.S. Government Printing Office, Serial No. J-97-122, 331-359. (Reprinted from *Chicago-Kent Law Review,* 1980, *56,* 4, 1057–1085).

Weiner, B. A. (1984). Interfaces between the mental health and criminal justice system: The legal perspective. In L. A. Teplin (Ed.), *Mental health and criminal justice* (Vol. 20, pp. 21–41. Beverly Hills, CA: Sage.

Wells, G. L. (1985). The eyewitness. In S. M. Kassin & L. S. Wrightsman (Eds.), *The psychology of evidence and trial procedure* (pp. 43–66). Beverly Hills, CA: Sage.

Wenk, E. A., Robinson, J. O., & Smith, G. W. (1972). Can violence be predicted? *Criminal Delinquency, 18,* 393–402.

Westbrook v. Arizona, 384 U.S. 150 (1966).

Wexler, D. B. (1981). *Mental health law: Major issues.* New York: Plenum Press.

Wexler, D. B. (1984). Incompetency, insanity, and involuntary civil commitment. In L. A. Teplin (Ed.), *Mental health and criminal justice* (Vol. 20, pp. 139–154). Beverly Hills, CA: Sage.

Wexler, D. B. (1985). Redefining the insanity problem. *The George Washington Law Review, 53,* 528–561.

White, L. T. (1987). Juror decision making in the capital penalty trial: An analysis of crimes and defense strategies. *Law and Human Behavior, 11*(2), 113–130.

White, M. D., & White, C. A. (1981). Involuntarily committed patients' constitutional right to refuse treatment: A challenge to psychology. *American Psychologist, 36,* 953–962.

REFERENCES

Whytt, R. (1767). *Observations on the nature, causes, and cure of those disorders which have been commonly called nervous, hypochondriac, or hysteric* (3rd ed.). Edinburgh: Becket and DeHondt.

Widiger, T. A., & Rorer, L. G. (1984). The responsible psychotherapist. *American Psychologist, 39,* 503–515.

Wigmore, J. H. (1909). Professor Muensterberg and the psychology of testimony: Being a report of the case of Cokestone v. Muensterberg. *Illinois Law Review, 3,* 399–445.

Will, G. (1983, December 11). Shocking crimes, astounding sentences. *The Washington Post,* p. C7.

Williams, G. (1961). *Criminal law: The general part* (2nd ed.). London: Stevens & Sons.

Williams v. New York, 337 U.S. 241, 248 (1949).

Willis, T. (1679). *Pharmaceutice partionalis: Or, an exercitation of the operations of medicines in human bodies.* London: Harrow.

Wilson, J. Q., & Herrnstein, R. J. (1985). *Crime and human nature.* New York: Simon & Schuster.

Winick, B. J. (1983). Incompetency to stand trial: Developments in law. In J. Monahan and H. J. Steadman (Eds.), *Mentally disordered offenders: Perspectives from law and social sciences.* New York: Plenum Press.

Winslow, F. (1843/1983). *The plea of insanity in criminal cases.* New York: Da Capo Press.

Winslow, F. (1854). The psychological vocation of the physician. In *Lettsomian lectures on insanity* (p. 39). London: Churchill.

Witelson, S. F. (1977). Developmental dyslexia: Two right hemispheres and none left. *Science, 195,* 309–311.

Wojtowicz v. United States, 550 F. 2d 786 (2nd Cir. 1977).

Wootton, B. (1959). *Social science and social pathology.* London: George Allen & Unwin.

Wootton, B. (1960). Diminished responsibility: A layman's view. *Law Quarterly Review, 76.*

Wootton, B. (1963). *Crime and criminal law.* London: Stevens and Sons.

Wyatt v. Stickney, 325 F. Supp. 781, 784 (M.D. Ala. 1971), 334 F. Supp. 1341 (M.D. Ala. 1971), 344 F. Supp. 373 and 387 (M.D. Ala. 1972), aff'd *sub nom Wyatt v. Aderholt,* 503 F.2d 1305 (5th Cir. 1974).

Yarmey, A. D. (1979). *The psychology of eyewitness testimony.* New York: Free Press.

Yochelson, S., & Samenow, S. E. (1976). *The criminal personality.* New York: Jason Aronson.

Youngberg v. Romeo, 457 U.S. 307 (1982).

Youtsey v. United States, 97 F. 937 (6th Cir. 1899).

Zangwill, O. L. (1976). Thought and the brain. *British Journal of Psychology, 67,* 301–314.

Zeydel, E. H. (1944). *The ship of fools by Sebastian Brant.* New York: Columbia University Press.

Zilbergeld, B. (1983). *The shrinking of America: Myths of psychological change.* Boston: Little, Brown.

Zilboorg, G. (1943). *Mind, medicine, And man.* New York: Harcourt, Brace.

Zilboorg. G. (1949). The reciprocal responsibilities of law and psychiatry. *Shingle, 12,* 79–96.

Zilboorg, G., & Henry, G. W. (1941). *A history medical psychology.* New York: Norton.

Zimbardo, P. G. (1967). The psychology of police confessions. *Psychology Today, 1*(2), 25–27.

Index